"**A solid, balanced, and very useful guide** for the investor who is interested not only in a healthy return but a healthy future for our children and our planet."

BOB DUNN
President and CEO, Business for Social Responsibility

"**Both visionary and practical, *Investing with Your Values* fuels the growing urge to unite in the creation of a new, more sustainable economy**. As investors and consumers, everyone has the ability to influence the course of events in a meaningful way; for every dollar we invest or spend is a vote for the type of future we want to manifest."

STEVE SCHUETH
Chair and President, Social Investment Forum

"The authors have made a complex set of issues surprisingly simple! **With this book in hand, it is easy, profitable, and yes—natural, to invest in harmony with your values**."

WINSTON FRANKLIN
President, Institute of Noetic Sciences

"**An up-to-date and very instructive primer on the basics of socially responsible investing**, from shareholder advocacy to using one's investments for community economic development."

TIM SMITH
Executive Director, Interfaith Center on Corporate Responsibility

"**A great book!** *Investing with Your Values: Making Money and Making a Difference* is concise, well-written, and an important guide for those who want to make money—and make it count."

JOHN W. ROGERS, JR.
President, Ariel Mutual Funds

"Ancient wisdom holds that where a person's treasure is, there shall his heart be also. *Investing with Your Values* makes the powerfully appealing case that the converse can be true, too, and highly rewarding—**a must read for those who yearn for guidance in how to do the right thing and the smart thing with their treasure.**"

RAY C. ANDERSON
Chairman and CEO, Interface, Inc.

"***Investing with Your Values* is a succinct, informative guide** providing practical advice on social investing. The book provides easy-to-understand answers to the financial basics and presents a thought-provoking view of the social issues."

JANET PRINDLE
Principle, Neuberger Berman, LLC, and Fund Manager,
Neuberger Berman Socially Responsible Fund

"***Investing with Your Values* is a comprehensive and inspiring handbook for individual investors. It belongs on the bookshelf of every person who owns a mutual fund, opens a bank account, or invests in a retirement plan.** As we prepare to enter the 21st century, we will see the authors' 'heart ratings' added to the short list of preferred benchmarks for mutual fund comparisons."

BARBARA KRUMSIEK
President and CEO, Calvert Group

"For all those who seek and work toward a gentler, kinder, fairer and healthier economy. **If enough of us—including consumers, employees and voters, join the investors and business people described in this book, we can all help build a saner, safer, greener world for everyone.**"

HAZEL HENDERSON
Author of *Building a Win-Win World: Life Beyond Global Economic Warfare*

"Investing with values is not a contradiction in terms. It is a trillion dollar, growing industry. ***Investing with Your Values* offers a rare combination: the pragmatic tools of disciplined investing with a thoughtful methodology for melding difficult financial decisions with fundamental and cherished personal values.**"

JOAN SHAPIRO
Former Executive Vice President, South Shore Bank and Consultant, Corporate Social Responsibility

"I have always believed that we are allowed to make money so we can make a difference. **Reading this book shows how we can direct our investments to increase good in the world, and prosper.**"

LAURIE BETH JONES
Author of *The Path: Creating Your Mission Statement for Work and for Life* and *Jesus, CEO: Using Ancient Wisdom for Visionary Leadership*

Investing WITH YOUR Values

Also available from
Bloomberg Press

Smart Questions to Ask Your Financial Advisers
by Lynn Brenner

The Latino Guide to Personal Money Management
by Laura Castañeda and Laura Castellanos

The Winning Portfolio:
Choosing Your 10 Best Mutual Funds
by Paul B. Farrell

Don't Die Broke:
How to Turn Your Retirement Savings into Lasting Income
by Margaret A. Malaspina
(June 1999)

Investing in Latin America:
Best Stocks, Best Funds
by Michael Molinski
(July 1999)

The Inheritor's Handbook:
A Definitive Guide for Beneficiaries
by Dan Rottenberg

A Commonsense Guide to Your 401(k)
by Mary Rowland

The New Commonsense Guide to Mutual Funds
by Mary Rowland

Investing WITH YOUR Values

Making Money & Making a Difference

HAL BRILL, JACK A. BRILL,
& CLIFF FEIGENBAUM

Foreword by
AMY DOMINI

BLOOMBERG PRESS
PRINCETON

Books are available for bulk purchases at special discounts. Special editions or book excerpts can also be created to specifications. For information, please write: Special Markets Department, Bloomberg Press.

BLOOMBERG, BLOOMBERG NEWS, BLOOMBERG FINANCIAL MARKETS, OPEN BLOOMBERG, BLOOMBERG PERSONAL FINANCE, THE BLOOMBERG FORUM, COMPANY CONNECTION, COMPANY CONNEX, BLOOMBERG PRESS, BLOOMBERG PROFESSIONAL LIBRARY, BLOOMBERG PERSONAL BOOKSHELF, and BLOOMBERG SMALL BUSINESS are trademarks and service marks of Bloomberg L.P. All rights reserved.

This publication contains the author's opinions and is designed to provide accurate and authoritative information. It is sold with the understanding that the author, publisher, and Bloomberg L.P. are not engaged in rendering legal, accounting, investment-planning, or other professional advice. The reader should seek the services of a qualified professional for such advice; the author, publisher, and Bloomberg L.P. cannot be held responsible for any loss incurred as a result of specific investments or planning decisions made by the reader.

First edition published 1999
1 3 5 7 9 10 8 6 4 2

Library of Congress Cataloging-in-Publication Data
Brill, Hal, 1956–
Investing with your values: making money and making a difference /
Hal Brill, Jack A. Brill, and Cliff Feigenbaum.
p.   cm.
Includes bibliographical references and index.
ISBN 1-57660-026-2
1. Investments—Moral and ethical aspects.   I. Brill, Jack A.
II. Feigenbaum, Cliff, 1961–   .   III. Title.
HG4515.13.B75   1999
332.6—dc21   99-17947
                                                                  CIP

Printed on recycled paper

Acquired and edited by JACQUELINE R. MURPHY

Book Design by LAURIE LOHNE / Design It Communications

We believe that most people want to be helpful and kind, and that most want to leave the world a better place for their children and future generations.

We believe that these qualities are "natural," and that it is natural to include these basic human tendencies in all important decisions.

We define a "Natural Investor" as someone who actively seeks to balance their need for financial return with their yearning to make life a little better for others and the Earth.

—HAL BRILL, JACK A. BRILL, AND CLIFF FEIGENBAUM

Contents

The Four Spokes of the Natural Investing Wheel

S e c t i o n   T h r e e

The Natural Portfolio Guidebook

.

Section Four

The Sustainability Revolution:
Designing a Greenprint for the Future

Foreword
by
Amy Domini

L ET YOUR CONSCIENCE be your guide. It's advice as ancient as civilization, and yet it has never been investment advice—until now. Investing with a conscience springs from the finest of human desires: the desire to live one's life in accordance with one's own code of ethics and the desire to leave the world a better place than one found it. By integrating personal ethics and social goals into their investments, individuals and institutions are able to maintain consistency with their mission in life while simultaneously making a real difference.

It isn't often that a person feels empowered to make a difference. We are assaulted daily by the obvious signs of a disintegrating social fabric. A disheveled body on a sidewalk evokes no pity. Forced labor provides us with cheap goods that we buy on impulse and discard on a whim. Our schools are armed camps. Our weather patterns are deteriorating; our wildlife is vanishing. Our governments give up sacred lands to be stripped of their natural resources and left an oozing scar on the landscape.

Most of us, if given a chance to aid in the creation of a better world, would grab it. But the problems seem so overwhelming, so global in nature, that we shy away from the very thought. But by shying away, we commit ourselves to using up the planet until it is gone. It hardly matters whether this result is caused by greed or by blindness; it will inevitably be the result unless a global commitment to creating a just and sustainable economic system emerges.

To comfort and nurture humankind is a noble goal, but through the generations we have allowed our economic systems to lose sight of that much-sought-after result. Today most of us believe that corporate managements' purpose should be to maximize shareholder return—full stop. It is a dangerous belief. When shareholders send this message, management teams are pressured into decisions with lasting and disastrous results. They feel their mandate is to strip resources today with no regard for the damage done in the process or the welfare of future generations. They will close domestic plants and purchase from factories characterized by horrific working conditions, even slave labor. They will scrimp on safety, knowing that the cost of a few harmed individuals is cheaper than retooling the line.

Yet it isn't corporate management alone that has accelerated the race to the bottom. Shareholders have historically demanded financial returns and the future be damned. But a new set of shareholders has begun to emerge. Many individuals and institutions now recognize the disastrous long-range results of an unchecked incentive to look only at this quarter's results. These shareholders recognize that corporations represent the strongest possibility of bringing about a better world for our grandchildren. They realize that by investing their dollars in a socially responsible way they can both be a force for positive social impact on the planet and be far more consistent with their own goals and value systems.

Two goals—personal consistency and advancing corporate social responsibility—work together to shape the ways in which we invest with values. But generally it is the first goal that creates awareness of the underlying issues.

Some years ago, when I was a stockbroker working in Harvard Square, a client of mine called me in some distress. She was a gentle woman who relied somewhat on an investment portfolio for the extra things in life. One of her largest holdings was stock in a paper company that had been purchased for her by her father. He had done business with the company and liked its management.

My client was an avid bird-watcher and through this activity had become alarmed at the effects of spraying dioxin, a practice then in widespread use by paper companies. In one of her bird-watching journals she had discovered that the company least willing to speak with conservationists about the devastating effect of dioxin on birds was in fact the very company that she owned and had felt quite fond of. For her this created a terrible dilemma. Giving the stock away or selling it felt in some way like disavowing her father, but she could not bear the idea that she was benefiting from the casual poisoning of songbirds. Over time, she did sell some of the stock and gave the rest of it to nonprofit organizations working on the issue. When we invested the proceeds from her sales, my instructions from her were to look for companies that demonstrated a higher regard for the interests of all God's creatures, not just shareholders.

Neither my client nor I, at that point, realized that this sort of dilemma was constantly being faced and resolved in this way by many others. In some instances it is a doctor refusing to benefit from tobacco products; in others it is an endowment program for a women's shelter refusing to benefit from the manufacture of alcohol. It might be a Quaker meeting that avoids investments in weapons manufacturers. The simple avoidance of profiting from a practice you abhor helps bring you closer to a consistency or a holistic sense of purpose.

But investing with values brings more than consistency; it has led directly to the dramatic growth of systematic research into corporate social impact. Today, corporate management teams hear from firm after firm, representing an ever larger shareholder base. They are asked about diversity programs, employment benefits, community giving and support, product safety, standards for purchasing from overseas vendors, environmental impact, and even their own pay levels. Corporations themselves now collect data on how they accomplish their social goals. Furthermore, while this research is developed for investors, it is also used by shareholder activists and community groups as the basis for selecting the dialogues and campaigns they wish to undertake.

Investing in the better companies is a long-term strategy; immediate needs can be addressed in other ways. Caring shareholders enter into direct dialogue with corporations through the annual general meeting and the shareholder proxy process that surrounds it. Shareholders raise issues ranging from doing business in Nigeria or Burma to plant closings, environmental reporting, Equal Employment Opportunity disclosure, and smoke-free environments. Each year corporations and their owners (shareholders) together find solutions to some of the toughest issues facing society.

And yet there are disenfranchised people that traditional capital movements have been unable to help. Here, too, the investing public can play an important role. By placing our savings dollars into community development financial institutions, investors are directing capital to those who could never qualify for traditional loans. This in turn helps economically disadvantaged people lift themselves out of the cycle of poverty.

Investing with Your Values: Making Money and Making a Difference is such a tremendously exciting contribution to the field of socially responsible investing precisely because it takes these complex and intertwined concepts and gently guides the reader to personal solutions.

The authors have added a new dimension to the field by describing a four-spoked wheel that they call the wheel of Natural Investing. Each spoke represents one of the key strategies used by values-based investors: Avoidance Screening, Affirmative Screening, Community Investing, and Shareholder Activism. These are the spokes that lend strength to the rim and allow Natural Investors to travel down the path of creating a better world.

With examples and anecdotes packed into every page, this book serves everyone from the novice to the most sophisticated investor. It intertwines the concepts of maximizing returns and avoiding trade-offs between financial and spiritual or societal gain. It guides us through a process that presents difficult issues but also offers answers. Through these answers, the reader gains recognition that one individual *can* make a difference.

In the face of challenging circumstances as we enter the third millennium, *Investing with Your Values* offers a helping hand. The first spoke of the Natural Investing Wheel is Avoidance Screening, and the authors guide us through the philosophy and methodology for avoiding investments that are inconsistent with our own sense of purpose. They provide a concise overview of each social issue and show us how to pinpoint the socially screened mutual funds and individual investments that are most appropriate to meeting our particular concerns. All the tools needed to follow an avoidance path are here.

This wonderful book also teaches the reader how to prospect for companies that are more consistent with a sustainable future, perhaps even models in some aspects of their business. Coverage of emerging fields such as alternative energy and natural foods as well as the latest developments in industrial ecology represent rich veins of opportunity. Newsletters, Web sites, and other sources of research are identified. No matter what your particular interests or investment objectives might be, the opportunity to meet them through Affirmative Screening can be found here.

Investing with Your Values provides the most comprehensive introduction to Community Investing of any book in its field. Inspirational stories from around the world illustrate the power and effectiveness of this tool. Readers who want to use even their cash reserves or savings accounts to help make the world a little safer for an at-risk family will find myriad opportunities. By presenting options—such as community banking, credit unions, and loan funds—the authors show how each of us can be more deliberate and conscientious in even such simple decisions as where to do one's banking.

Through anecdotes and examples, the somewhat arcane field of Shareholder Activism also becomes clear. A shareholder's opportunity to participate in the process would be an eye-opener for many readers. We are shown ways to participate in this important work, with sources of information and simple steps anyone can take to be a more active investor.

What can one person do? Quite a lot. Perhaps that is the most uplifting message in this book. *Investing with Your Values* is a powerful tool that enables each of us to become a part of building a just and sustainable world. One person at a time, the introduction of values into investments is taking place. As these values take hold in the corporate soul, the means to clean our rivers, to heal our communities, to bring peace and stability to emerging nations, and to look forward with courage to the next century will be created.

AMY DOMINI, CFA, is one of the foremost voices in socially responsible investing. She is a coauthor of *Investing for Good* and president of the Domini Social Equity Fund.

Acknowledgments

O N A CHILLY Montana afternoon in October 1997, the three of us met to map out the writing of this book. We had just spent several days in those majestic mountains, energized by the talents and perspectives that hundreds of participants brought to the annual SRI in the Rockies conference. Remaining in the silence of the mountains, our path became clear: to bring the good works of this diverse community to a wider audience. Our acknowledgments begin with a dedication to our deepest source of inspiration, this beautiful earth, and to the caring hearts of the many people who have devoted their efforts to creating a sustainable economy.

We want to introduce you to the fourth member of our team, Jim Cummings. Jim, a longtime friend of Hal's, was our editor. But this title does not begin to cover his central role. Jim's friendly voice speaks throughout this book, weaving together the distinct styles of three co-authors into a flowing whole. His quick mastery of complex themes, along with a solid connection to the overall vision, transformed the writing process into an exciting journey of discovery. Thanks, Jim!

Special thanks also to Steve Lyons, who spearheaded work on Shareholder Activism and Avoidance Screening. His thorough research and strong communications skills brought power and clarity to these crucial topics.

There is no way to thank all the innovators whose ideas and projects grace these pages, but several gave freely of their time and expertise. We are grateful to Hazel Henderson, who saw the need and potential for this book even more than we did; Tim Smith, for clear guidance on Shareholder Activism issues; Steve Scheuth, for his skill in expressing the subtleties of values-based investing; Susan Davis, for her leading-edge perspectives on social investing; and Joan Shapiro, Tim Freundlich, Kirstin Moy, and Mark Pinsky, for helping to make Community Investing come alive. Of course, we're enormously grateful to Amy Domini, a woman of true dignity and vision. Many other social investment activists and business leaders gave invaluable advice, including Peter Kinder, Patricia Aburdene, Lloyd Kurtz, Simon Billeness, Frank Coleman, Jon Lickerman, James Berry, George Gay, Ken Birch, Stephen Morris, David Goldbeck, and Alis Valencia.

We each thank some of the people who supported us personally:

From Hal: Thanks to my extended circle of support, in Paonia, in Santa Fe, and around the country (and beyond!). To Sherry Cox, for her dedication to building sustainable local economies rooted in the heart. To my clients, who inspire me to keep growing professionally. To the many who looked over my shoulder and gave encouragement and advice, including Winston Franklin, Elisabet Sahtouris, Michael Kramer, Donal Kinney, Bob Jones, Marsea Marcus, and Beth Richman. To Ora, Rahaman, Terri, Kristin, Ildi, Narayan, Bernie, Judy, and many others for spiritual nourishment. Finally, thanks to my friends in Tribal Revival; playing music with you has kept my spirit dancing.

From Jack: The job of compiling data on socially screened mutual funds and investment choices was made possible because of the support I received from Steve Lydenberg and Tom Kuh of KLD, Patrick McVeigh of Franklin Research & Development, all of the mutual fund managers, and so many more whose names I can't possibly mention. Jay Benjamin and Hy Sou researched and summarized information with enthusiasm and skill. Bob Dreizler provided insightful comments on the manuscript. Their invaluable assistance has helped us develop and extend the art of Natural Investing.

From Hal and Jack: Thanks to Sandra Brill (Jack's wife; Hal's mom), for her unswerving love and support, many hours of digging into research, sharing her expertise as an enrolled agent, making suggestions that helped us get unstuck at just the right moments, and, especially, for making business trips a lot more fun! To Ilene Brill, Blanche Klein, Anne Picarsky, and all our relatives for their love and support. And to the dedicated professionals of First Affirmative Financial Network—this book would not exist without the support we receive from being part of the most extraordinary organization in the financial industry.

From Cliff: My sincerest thanks go to each of the following people: Ted Ketcham, my friend and mentor and a great editor; Doree Desmond, who was there when it all started; Tom Kliewer, who helped bring a vision to reality back in 1992. To William McDonough, Paul Hawken, Ray Anderson, Bob Dunn, and Vicki Robin, for showing me what is possible; Marianne Williamson, for writing what I needed to read; and Sharon Drew Morgen, for being you. To the crew at Co-op America and the Social Investment Forum: Steve, Alisa, Denise, Elizabeth, and Russ (keep it going!). To all my friends in the SRI industry (you are part of my family) and the numerous people who have advised and supported me through this amazing journey. Most of all, my thanks go to Hal, Jack, and Jim, with whom I shared many months of work and an evolving vision of what came to be this volume. This book is for my daughter, Candice, and her future.

Finally we thank Jacqueline Murphy and her talented, hard-working team at Bloomberg Press. Jacque had the clear vision of bringing together the prestigious reputation and resources of Bloomberg with the cutting edge of responsible investing. We salute her foresight, her willingness to accommodate our quirky demands, and her determination to bring this message to the world.

Building a Bridge Between Money and Values

W ELCOME TO *Investing with Your Values.* You are about to journey into a surprisingly vast and rapidly changing landscape, a place where personal values and personal finance dwell together in mutually supportive symbiosis. Be prepared to open your mind, and your heart, to an exciting new reality: you *can* achieve your financial goals *and* help make this world a better place in which to live.

Natural Investors—our term for those who bring along their values—are shunning conventional wisdom that says we must abandon ethics when making financial decisions. Like the Berlin Wall, this "unnatural" partition is being torn down piece by piece. In its place we find the bridge of Natural Investing, providing a path that links who we are inside to what we do with our money in the world. Growing numbers of Natural Investors are crossing this bridge, attracting worldwide attention as they prosper and put down roots smack dab in the middle of an incredulous Wall Street.

Investing with Your Values helps you identify *your* priorities and guides you through the process of creating a values-inclusive portfolio that works for you. People of all income levels, from across the entire political spectrum, can use the tools and resources in this book to find profitable investments. Nearly every mainstream investment option now has a values-based equivalent. You don't need a lot of money—several screened mutual funds and community banking options welcome small investors who can start with as little as $50. All that's really needed is the willingness to identify and consider your personal values—not someone else's agenda—when making decisions about your money.

This does, of course, entail a bit more work than simply ignoring the ethical consequences of your financial decisions. Bringing your heart into the investment process requires both earnest soul-searching and unglamorous research. We will do our best to keep you encouraged and inspired, and we promise that your efforts will bring many deeply satisfying rewards. The quest to bring humane values back into our economic system is the most urgent task of our times:

➤ There are many critical situations on our planet desperate for healing—*Natural Investing can provide the financial medicine.*

➤ There is much dis-ease among good-hearted people, disturbed by the knowledge that their money is being used contrary to their beliefs—*Natural Investing offers a path toward wholeness and integration.*

Natural Desires:
Our Common Humanity

IN OUR WORK with investors, we develop relationships that go beyond superficial discussions of stocks and bonds. Our real job is to help people identify their hopes for themselves and the world and to co-create a financial plan that balances all of their concerns. Everyone is unique and has their own financial goals. Most wish for enough money to feel secure and happy, to support them in fulfilling life dreams, to take care of loved ones, and maybe to have a little left over just for fun. Many are interested in finding ways to become less financially encumbered; they seek to keep debt low or to minimize unnecessary consumption. Natural Investing fills these needs by helping people develop a healthy relationship to their money. Living expenses, investments, and charity are combined in a balance that works for each person's individual situation.

But money alone does not feed the soul. And no amount of money can guarantee security in a world facing its ecological and social moment of truth. When we delve deeper with our clients, exploring their true aspirations, two cardinal, nonmaterial desires nearly always come up. We began calling these desires "natural" because they transcend all class or cultural groupings. They seem to call each of us in a different way—speaking for the human spirit, reminding us of our highest qualities. Although they are difficult to express with words, we've synthesized these yearnings-of-the-heart in this way:

➤ The natural desire to be of service, to "make a difference" and help improve life on Earth, for ourselves, our children, and children yet unborn.

➤ The natural desire for integrity, to "walk our talk" and live in ways that are consistent with our values.

The goal of Natural Investing is to provide a framework that enables people to bring these natural desires into their financial decisions. We recognize that our choices regarding money have strong consequences in the world and make a powerful statement about our values. Many consumers have begun to bring this awareness into their daily purchasing decisions by, for example, seeking out locally made or natural products. Yet most investors feel completely disconnected from the ethical component of their investments. We allow anonymous bank or fund managers to direct our capital without following any social guidelines. Although this money appears to be out of our hands, it is actually doing our bidding in the global economy, working hard around the clock, often for decades. The question we all must face is: *how* do I want my money to represent me in the world?

A New Voice for Your Money

MOST OF THE money zipping around the planet today says only one thing: "my person/owner wants me to earn the highest possible return, without concern for anything, anyone, or the planet." This is hardly surprising. Our economic system is built on a deeply ingrained but questionable idea: if each of us pursues our own self-interest, then the "invisible hand" of the market will assure that the highest good for all is simultaneously achieved. As this idea has come to be enshrined in our society, the distorted result has been that the quest for individual or corporate profit nearly always takes precedence over community, environmental, and spiritual concerns.

The world today reflects our society's priorities. The United States is the richest country ever, and material progress has brought immea-

> **"** *Although I have made a fortune in the financial markets,*
> *I now fear that the untrammeled intensification of*
> *laissez-faire capitalism and the spread of market values into all*
> *areas of life is endangering our open and democratic*
> *society. The main enemy of the open society, I believe, is*
> *no longer the communist but the capitalist threat.* **"**
>
> —GEORGE SOROS[1]

surable benefits to the world. But the pursuit of wealth-at-any-cost is also responsible for human suffering, gross inequities in the distribution of this wealth, and environmental devastation. Our current trajectory cannot be sustained indefinitely. In 1992, over 1,600 scientists, including most of the living Nobel laureates, released their *Warning to Humanity.* In direct and simple terms, their letter warns that "human beings and the natural world are on a collision course . . . that may so alter the world that it will be unable to sustain life in the manner that we know."[2]

Today outdated economic prerogatives that give financial concerns dominion over our lives and the Earth are being reconsidered . . . and found lacking. Yet even as we question the idea that our best decisions are made by purely "market-driven" forces, we recognize that our global economy is *the central nexus* of human activity on the planet; its influence radiates into every sphere of human endeavor. Citizens and activists of every persuasion are realizing that our planetary challenges can be solved only by infusing the economic system with a new sense of social responsibility.

Two doorways are open to anyone wishing to play a constructive role in realigning the economy with his or her values: the political and the financial. Political action is crucial, and we strongly encourage participatory democracy. This book will touch on policy issues; however, our primary focus is on money because it is here, through our spending and investing, that we *directly* affect even the most powerful multinational corporations and institutions. Natural Investors are taking their places within the economic system, using their financial clout as leverage to catalyze social and ecological progress.

While giving complete coverage to personal investing, we will also venture beyond the confines of an ordinary investment guide. This book touches on all aspects of our financial lives and explores the deeper currents of thought that underlie today's changing economic realities. There are many ways other than investing to "make a difference" with our money. Therefore we'll examine working, spending, and giving in the context of integrating our values and our actions.

We'll look at promising strategies for transforming our communities and the economic system. There will be excursions into history, philosophy, spirituality, and trend analysis that supply integral pieces of the picture. Ultimately we'll see how Natural Investing is rooted in a changing worldview based on both new and ancient understandings of the natural world.

Spokes of the Natural Investing Wheel

FOR EVERY INVESTOR who has already started down the path of Natural Investing, there are many more who have yet to take their first steps. One reason often given by those who are reluctant is a feeling of being overwhelmed by the enormous complexity of social and moral evaluations. Indeed, the world does not divide people, or companies, into neat categories of "good" and "bad." But Natural Investing is not about perfection; we know that every investment raises at least a few questions. Efforts to link our money and our values force us to consider all sides of an issue, frequently resulting in the need to make difficult tradeoffs. This can be frustrating; yet the only other alternative is to ignore the ethical implications of our financial choices. We encourage you to start out gently on this path, taking small steps with one or two issues that speak most directly to your values.

For those of you new to this field, we've got some great news to share: you don't have to reinvent the wheel. The tools in this book will help you set a direction for your financial life that includes both monetary and social goals, then to steer a course using strategies already pioneered by values-motivated investors. The "Four Spokes of the Natural Investing Wheel" will be our road map.

Each of these four spokes addresses an aspect of bringing values into the marketplace. The most familiar of the four is **Avoidance Screening.** This is the well-known approach of choosing *not* to invest in industries by which you do not wish to profit; tobacco and weapons are two of the most common such screens. Its complement is **Affirmative Screening,** in which you actively seek out investments in activities in which you *do* want to be involved. This often focuses on small leading-edge companies, but it can also include investments in large companies with good records in areas important to you, such as minority hiring, and in government programs you support, such as low-income housing. The third spoke is **Community Investing**. This rapidly emerging branch of Natural Investing is especially useful for getting your money into the hands of grass-roots programs and economically marginalized people, locally or globally. And finally, **Shareholder Activism** provides a means for changing companies from the inside, using various means to get the attention of management. Section 2 offers in-depth looks at each of these spokes and helps you to decide which ones you want to work with.

For beginner and veteran investors, *Investing with Your Values* serves up hundreds of specific, values-inclusive investment opportunities and resources. Never before have so many choices been available to investors of every philosophical ilk and income level. With this road map, virtually anyone can take decisive steps down the road to financial wellness.

The Straw Men Come Alive: Answering the Skeptics of Natural Investing

IF YOU'RE READING this book, it's likely that you are at least curious to learn more about the interface of money and morals. But we should

warn you that if you go spouting off on this topic to friends and neighbors, you're likely to run smack into the same wall of misconceptions
that we face in our encounters with the public. It takes courage to
examine honestly the ethical component of one's investments. The
process is often uncomfortable, especially for those who haven't yet
given it much thought. So it is understandable that many people try to
avoid the issue by leaning on one or both of the following myths. The
fact is, these common claims are nothing but empty straw men, set
up as easy targets but bearing no relation to the reality of Natural
Investing.

> ➤ *Myth One:* Limiting one's investment choices by using social,
> environmental, or ethical criteria results in lower financial returns.
> ➤ *The Facts:* It is true that Natural Investors voluntarily limit their
> choices, *but this has not led to any systematic underperformance* in
> the universe of stocks typically chosen by Natural Investors.[3] In
> fact, solid statistical evidence shows that investments chosen with
> social, environmental, or ethical criteria perform *as well as or bet-*
> *ter than* those chosen with financial criteria alone. In 1990, the
> Domini 400 Social Index was launched; it includes socially

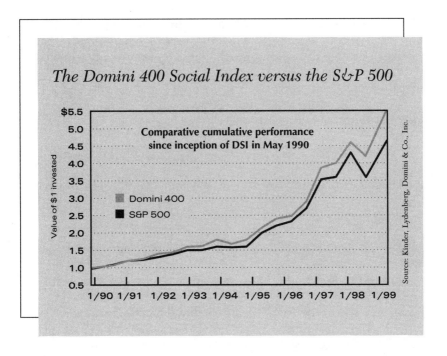

The Domini 400 Social Index versus the S&P 500

Comparative cumulative performance since inception of DSI in May 1990

Domini 400
S&P 500

Value of $1 invested

Source: Kinder, Lydenberg, Domini & Co., Inc.

screened companies in a similar range of sizes and industries as the unscreened Standard and Poor's 500. From its inception in 1990 through December 31, 1998, the Domini 400 has outpaced the S&P 500 with a total return of 442 percent compared with the S&P's 366 percent. This is a truly remarkable feat, but as we'll see in our chapter on Natural Performance, it is only one of many studies that show a *positive* correlation between corporate responsibility and corporate profitability. So much for the myth that "good guys finish last."

It's also worth noting that although Natural Investors select from a smaller universe of banking, stock, bond, and mutual fund choices, it's still a pretty big universe. You'll run out of money to invest long before you run out of investment choices.

➤ *Myth Two:* Natural Investing is only for tree-hugging radicals and aging hippies.

➤ *The Facts:* Natural Investing in the United States traces its origins to Quakers and other Christians who could not live with the inconsistencies between their beliefs and their investments. Today a diverse range of strategies are available to support investors with wide-ranging values, from conservative Christians to farm-belt traditionalists to environmental visionaries. Most screened mutual funds aim at a broad cross section of common interests. Natural Investors are not antibusiness, nor are they dabbling in collections of fringe companies. For example, the Domini 400 includes many household names, including Home Depot, Xerox, Johnson & Johnson, Coca-Cola, and BankAmerica. Although none of these companies is free of controversy, each has particular strengths that led to its inclusion in the index.

Investing with Your Values is designed to help you bring your particular social, environmental, or ethical concerns to the money table. Although most Natural Investors grapple with mainstream issues like corporate responsibility and workplace conditions, we will show you how your investments can be customized to focus on a nearly unlimited array of activities. Community Investing allows you to support, for example, women in the villages of India who are escaping poverty by starting their own microenterprises. Affirmative Screening enables you to choose to finance small companies involved in environmental cleanup. There are even a few narrowly screened mutual funds that emphasize specific issues like gay rights or abortion. So go ahead and bring your creativity into your portfolio—there's something here for everyone.

The Road Ahead

WHEN PRESENTED WITH a choice, surveys show that mainstream investors are eager to include their values in the financial decision-making process. A 1996 survey of investors in mutual funds found that 83 percent want their financial advisers to understand their concern for social and environmental issues before making an investment recommendation.[4] In addition, 81 percent said they would be more likely to invest in a mutual fund if they knew it did not invest in companies that harm the environment; 73 percent favored investing in companies that have a good record of hiring and promoting women. But the same study showed that most do not realize that they have a choice; only 30 percent of these investors were even aware that socially screened mutual funds already exist.

Although Natural Investing is still undiscovered territory for many investors, the flow of capital being directed into ethically chosen investments is rapidly growing. Many of the biggest names on Wall Street are beginning to smell the roses. Salomon Smith Barney, the huge brokerage firm, manages over a billion dollars in screened investments. Industry leaders such as Merrill Lynch and Prudential are also getting into the act. A 1997 study by the Social Investment Forum estimated that well over $1 trillion is invested using some social criteria. One money manager summed up future potential this way: "Once the research on the correlation between social investing and long-term performance becomes widely known, I believe the vast majority of Americans will want their investments not only to make money, but also to work for what they believe."[5]

Choose Your Handle: Socially Responsible, Values-Based, Ethical, . . . or Natural

PEOPLE HAVE BEEN grappling with the thorny interface between money and values for a long, long time. One irate social-change advocate reportedly kicked some money changers out of a sacred temple! Arguments have been common ever since. One contentious point has been what to call it. In the United States, Socially Responsible Investing is the best-known label, partly because of the pleasing way its acronym—SRI—rolls off the tongue. ("Ethical Investing" gets the nod in Great Britain and Canada.) But the term *social responsibility* sometimes opens a can of worms. Who defines what it means to be responsible? Every person has their own definition, but by calling your own actions responsible you may make others feel they are being labeled irresponsible.

There are a lot of names out there; nonetheless, we're going to add to the melee by coining one more: *Natural Investing*. Our hope is that a new term, with its own cogent, *inclusive* philosophy, will help more people embrace the general concept of bringing values into financial decisions. One day soon, we expect that investing with one's values will indeed be seen as natural, whereas the current practice of separating financial choices from one's beliefs will end up in history's dustbin.

A Guide to This Guidebook

THIS BOOK IS arranged in four sections. The first, "Values in the World of Finance," charts the emergence of values-based investing, from the earliest coins and corporations to the most recent performance results. Chapter 1 provides a history of Natural Investing, with a look at how it has grown into a trillion-dollar industry. Chapter 2 looks to the future, exploring major trends that point toward Natural Investing's coming of age as a key player in our economic future. Chapter 3 gets into the nitty-gritty of performance, presenting studies that show stunning financial results. We end this section with a look at the spiritual dimensions of Natural Investing and a worksheet that helps you integrate your social and financial objectives.

In Section 2, you'll be designing your Natural Investment strategy, learning about the tools you can use to bring your finances into line with your values. Chapter 4 introduces the Four Spokes of the Natural Investing Wheel, each of which is fleshed out in the chapters that follow. Chapter 5 introduces Avoidance Screening, taking us into real-world issues organized as single-issue snapshots. Chapter 6 features one of the more exciting elements of the process, as we explore Affirmative Screening, wherein we go prospecting for proactive companies forging a sustainable future. Chapter 7 highlights the people-to-people power of Community Investing, which lets anyone with a checking account begin to make a real difference in their local community. In Chapter 8, we take a look at how Shareholder Activism is shaking up the system from the inside, and how you can join in. At the end of this section, you'll be guided through a series of worksheets that will help you choose your strategies, prioritize your issues, and clarify how much of a "gray area" you are comfortable with as you bring your values onto the financial field.

The next section is called "The Natural Portfolio Guidebook"; it is dedicated to steering you through the myriad of responsible mutual funds, community investment options, stocks, bonds, and much more. We've packed in dozens of user-friendly charts, stories, tools, and anything else we could find or dream up to help you make specific investment choices. Chapter 9 is a primer on the nuts and bolts of investing, especially useful for beginning investors. Chapter 10 contains a directory and profiles of socially screened mutual funds, including financial data and our NIS Social Rating^{SM} to evaluate the social strength of these funds. Chapter 11 breaks new ground by presenting hundreds of special-interest mutual funds that are worthy of consideration by the Natural Investor. Chapter 12 brings us to the world of stocks, bonds, and beyond, providing resources needed to access the rest of Wall Street in a responsible way.

The book's fourth section, "The Sustainability Revolution," considers possibilities for change at the personal, community, national, and global levels. Chapter 13 examines how individuals are changing their relationship with money, with a focus on the noninvesting side of life. We'll explore the growing interest in simple living that we call "Voluntary Abundance" (because it results in having more time!). We'll also look at various issues centering around work, socially conscious consumption, philanthropy, and community building. Chapter 14, "The Healing of Wall Street," looks at innovative efforts to reform our economic system, including tax code proposals, new economic indicators that reflect "genuine progress," and other leading-edge ideas for creating a healthier economy. In Chapter 15, we take a philosophical look at the profound transition we're making from a mechanical view of the world to an emerging natural worldview. We close with a vision of how a new "natural economy" can help us create a healthy, sustainable world.

Some Final Notes

OUR PRIMARY PURPOSE in writing this book is to inspire, support, and encourage you to take tangible steps, large or small, that help align your money with your convictions. Our motivations are partly selfish: we want to live in a happier, healthier, more peaceful, equitable, and sustainable world. This book beckons for a new sort of economic populism; it's a call to action for all caring people, regardless of their particular central issues. The cumulative effect of millions of people bringing values into the investment process offers one of our greatest hopes for the future.

We also know that some visitors are here simply to hunt for the golden goose of high returns. You are very welcome—we've got absolutely nothing against making money. In fact, we're all for it! Natural Investing is not for martyrs, and it will only gain widespread acceptance if it provides both financial and social rewards. As Woody Allen put it, "Money is better than poverty, if only for financial reasons."

Most of all, we hope that this book will be an easily accessible guidebook that offers concrete benefits for both beginners and professionals. You'll find here the information you need to invest wisely, tools that will help you determine which of your values you most want your money to carry into the world. By the book's end, you will revel in the excitement of taking control of your finances in this era of economic gigantism.

On the meeting ground between your values and those of your neighbors is a core place of human decency that has been sorely lacking in our financial systems. Given the choice, we know that very few of us will choose greed and destruction of community or the environment. Rather, most of us will be excited to find ways to direct our savings to nurture life and be a part of whatever social values we hold dear. As a new century dawns, we have the opportunity to enter a new era of economic responsibility. *Investing with Your Values* is a bridge that invites you to become an active part of this promise.

Section One

Values in
the World of
Finance

Chapter One

Natural Investing's Coming of Age

O
F ALL THE opportunities that life presents, raising or teaching children can be the most challenging, and the most rewarding. We must both nurture and inspire, keeping kids safe while encouraging them to explore their own unique potentials. Taking responsibility for a child entails a dual role: supporting his or her physical health and growth, and providing guidance based on our personal values. In many ways, responsible money management is no different.

Natural Investing is first and foremost a responsible approach to personal finance. Through comprehensive planning and consciously directing money into the world, Natural Investors both care for their savings and pass along their most cherished values. If we could be as carefree as children, investing would be a snap. Romping on the playground of finance, we could skip from playing ball to climbing monkey bars to rolling on the grass. Most investors are well aware that financial matters are not a game; dangerous investments or lack of follow-through could result in a large loss. In general, we assume the first responsibility of "parenting" our money pretty well: we do our best to protect it from harm and nurture its growth by balancing the risks and rewards of various investments.

Where most investors fall short is the second responsibility. By concentrating entirely on our first duty—protecting and nurturing growth—we've completely ignored the opportunities to impart our values to our money. As we said in the Introduction, most people naturally desire to make a difference and live consistently with their beliefs. But the social, environmental, and ethical components of most portfolios are completely random. They might as well have been determined by children throwing darts. We commonly meet health practitioners invested in tobacco, environmentalists owning stocks in the dirtiest polluters, and evangelical Christians holding a "sinful" portfolio of gambling halls and liquor. Most of the time, people aren't even aware of these contradictions!

In a perfect world, we could be more like children, trusting the good nature of all. Unfortunately, that is not always the way it is. Imagine it's 1940, and you are a shareholder of Texaco, pleased at the booming market for oil and at your company's central role in the industry. As the horrors of World War II begin arousing the American people, you learn the following:

> In June 1940, the president of Texaco hosted a party at New York's Waldorf-Astoria to celebrate Nazi Germany's victory over France. Even after the start of World War II, Texaco ignored sanctions by supplying oil to the Germans. In 1940 Texaco harbored a German intelligence agent in its New York offices. The *New York Herald Tribune* disclosed that this agent provided Berlin with a detailed picture of the American aircraft industry—a report prepared by Texaco economists.[1]

How would you have felt if you had been a Texaco stockholder? What would have been your response? Could you have shrugged it off and said "business is business"? Would you have felt responsible to take some action? When these facts came to light, public outrage ensued and shareholders forced Texaco's president to resign.

Today Natural Investors grapple with dozens of issues facing our world. Repressive regimes did not end with the fall of Berlin; social injustice and ecological degradation are still prevalent; community-based projects are still in need of financing. Investors have only two choices: close their eyes to the world and blindly send their money off to pursue the highest profit, or explore win-win options that produce both financial and social returns. For the first time in history, a substantial number of investors, collectively controlling over $1 trillion in the United States, are taking the second path.

We begin our exploration of Natural Investing by going back in time, taking a brief look at the origins of money and corporations. As human economies have grown more complex, the ethical questions surrounding business and wealth have posed ever greater challenges to societies. Natural Investing builds on an ancient legacy—a story of people seeking ways to align their economic and social interests.

Money Goes Global

THEY SAY THAT "money makes the world go 'round," but for most of humanity's existence we somehow got along without it. Trade and barter were the only ways to make exchanges, and all economic activity was closely tied to tribal and family bonds. Eventually certain commodities came to represent value. Shells, beads, camels, seeds—and in modern times cigarettes—all have been used like cash. Our favorite is chocolate money, used by the Aztecs of what is now Mexico. In *The History of Money,* Jack Weatherford points out that the Aztecs' use of the cacao bean had one great advantage over our cold currency: if they got a sweet tooth, they could "grind their cacao money into chocolate paste . . . to make a delicious drink that they greatly prized."[2]

In ancient Mesopotamia, silver rings were used as money; written languages were created not to write poetry but to keep accounts. The first jingle of coins was heard 2,600 years ago in a place called Lydia, an obscure Turkish kingdom. Coinage enabled the creation of the world's first recorded retail marketplace (as well as two other currency-related Lydian innovations: dice for gambling and the first known brothels). Later the Greeks utilized this revolutionary mercantile system to create a great flowering of architecture, philosophy, science, and the arts. Money allowed the Greeks to structure life in complex ways that had not been available before the invention of money.[3]

Through the commercial market, ordinary people could create an interdependent web of relationships, leading to greater autonomy from rulers. But along with social progress, money created new ethical dilemmas. Aristotle grappled with the rules of the marketplace, feeling that the wealthy should be charged a higher price for goods than poor people. Plato argued for severe restrictions on personal wealth, believing that only dishonest, immoral men could obtain riches.[4] Christianity and Islam both have strong tenets against usury, the charging of excessive interest. Roman civilization crumbled under a glut of lavish consumption, repressive taxes, ecological devastation, and a massive trade imbalance with Asia. (Does this sound familiar?)

Despite its moral conundrums, money proved invaluable at lubricating the flow of material progress. From its emergence in the city-states, the use of currency spread gradually into surrounding regions. Banking first appeared in the Italian Renaissance, taking its name from the *bancos* or benches that early money merchants set up at fairs.[5] But well into this century, much of the world (including much of rural America) utilized a "mixed economy" that blended community self-sufficiency, some structured bartering, and limited cash exchanges, usually for a few specific items required from afar.

From these humble beginnings, money today is leaping into cyber-space. The vast majority of money is now represented not by hard cash but as electronic blips. Credit cards, ATMs, and Internet commerce have revolutionized our daily transactions. Meanwhile, an unfathomable $2 trillion changes hands *every day* on foreign exchange markets, mostly traded by currency speculators in what has been called the "global casino." Money permeates every aspect of our lives and the world economy, and still the ethical questions raised by Aristotle and Plato remain unresolved. Natural Investing reopens the door to addressing these timeless dilemmas.

Corporations on the Rise

CORPORATIONS ARE ONE of the most successful innovations of all time. Not only have they produced the abundance of goods and services that flows through our society, they have also worked their way up to the highest positions of power. Throughout their long history, society has struggled to find a balance that takes advantage of corporate efficiencies but maintains oversight over corporate activities.

The roots of the modern corporation stretch back to the Romans and Anglo-Saxons. In those times, corporations were established primarily to serve the public good, funding projects such as guilds and universities. But in the sixteenth century, as European powers prowled the globe in a fierce search for riches, corporations began to be organized for the express purpose of making money.[6] The English took the lead, chartering corporations like the East India Company to undertake high-risk trade ventures that could benefit the Crown. These companies operated with monopoly power over the colonies, and they were often responsible for ruthless economic repression, such as that made famous by the Boston Tea Party. For example, colonists could not produce their own hats; they had to ship the raw materials to England and import the finished product.[7] The American Revolution was a rebellion against the tyranny of both monarchs and corporations. Upon victory, the founders designed a constitutional framework that deliberately omitted any mention of corporations, leaving their regulation to the individual states.

Early America was dominated by family farms and businesses, cooperatives, and worker-owned enterprises. Companies tended to be notably democratic and reflected a community's sense of itself.[8] Corporations were only chartered for specific, socially useful purposes by individual states, and were kept on a very tight leash. States could, and frequently did, put a company out of business simply by revoking its charter. In New York, the corporation authorized to construct and operate turnpikes was warned that it would have its "turnpike gates thrown open . . . if the road is not kept easy and safe for public use." Charters limited the number of years over which a corporation could operate; Maryland, for example, restricted manufacturing companies to a life span of forty years.[9] Even the rates corporations could charge were often specified by legislators.

The nineteenth century marked a pivotal transformation of the U.S. economy. David Korten, in *When Corporations Rule the World*, documents the "continuing pressure by corporate interests to expand corporate rights and to limit corporate obligations." During the first half of the century it was fairly common for state legislators to amend, revoke, or simply fail to renew the charters of corporations that exceeded their boundaries. But after the Civil War, corporations took advantage of governmental disarray, eventually managing virtually to rewrite the laws governing their own creation. In 1886, the Supreme Court declared that a private corporation is a "natural person," entitled to protection for such things as privacy and free speech under the Bill of Rights. This extension of individual freedoms to financial entities baffled even future Supreme Court Justice William O. Douglas, who commented that "there was no history, logic, or reason given to support that view."[10] (Today, as we'll see in Chapter 8, there are new rumblings from citizens petitioning state governments to pull the plug on errant corporations.)

Corporations eagerly embraced their new position. Subsequent court rulings explicitly directed corporations to pursue maximum

The Giving Heart of Capitalism

IN OUR WORLD today, it is common to hear attacks on our capitalist economic system. Many feel that businesses are predators and investors care only for their own selfish interests. Although the abuses and excesses of capitalism are serious (and indeed they are the focus of much of this book), Natural Investing recognizes that, at its core, business arose as a means for people to contribute their talents to the world.

"Capitalism begins not with taking but with giving," says George Gilder in *Forbes ASAP*. "Tribal capitalists were not warriors or predators; they were the feast givers, and the potlatchers." These leaders "transcended the constraints of barter simply by making offerings to their neighbors." It is here with our tribal ancestors, says Gilder, a conservative advocate of capitalism, that we find the giving heart of free enterprise:

> The most successful givers are the most altruistic, the most responsive to the desires of others. In the most rewarding and catalytic gifts, the giver fulfills an unknown, unexpressed, or even unconscious need in a surprising way. The recipient, startled and gratified by the inspired and unexpected sympathy of the giver, is thus eager to repay.[11]

These same talents are needed to succeed in business; the desire to serve one's community (and improve one's status by doing so) is strikingly similar to the visionary dreams of today's entrepreneurs. Producers struggle against great odds, sacrificing their sweat and resources in the hope that their efforts will be appreciated by others. This transformative quality of the entrepreneurial spirit offers humanity its best hope of solving the ecological and social challenges of our times.

production, without consideration of human, social, or environmental effects. Over the course of twenty years, from 1888 to 1908, over 700,000 workers were killed in industrial accidents.[12] America was thrust into great social instability. Labor organized to oppose inhumane working conditions, child labor, and poverty wages. Corporations fought back with both private and governmental militia; blood was spilled on many occasions. Most of the violence subsided by the 1940s, due to both some pragmatic compromise on the part of corporations and the patriotic tone of the times.

The Gradual Awakening of Natural Investing

NATURAL INVESTING IS the latest chapter in an age-old story. The Quakers are often credited as history's first socially responsible investors. These devout worshippers believed that their lives needed to demonstrate their convictions. Quakers began applying moral criteria to their investments in the sixteenth century. As one example, they refused to invest in slaves because it clashed with their belief in the equality of humankind before God.[13]

Of course, many indigenous peoples have long histories of social responsibility, centering on the common practice of thinking past the short term in decision making. One well-known form of this idea is the Iroquois principle of considering the effects of one's actions on seven generations to follow. Benjamin Franklin was strongly influenced by these teachings; the Iroquois system of confederated democracies served as a model for Franklin's Albany Plan of Union in 1754, a document that in turn became the basis for the U.S. Articles of Confederation and our present-day Constitution.[14]

Not until the 1920s do we find the architects of the first formalized socially responsible investment policy—religious Christians. In *The Thoughtful Christian's Guide to Investing*, Gary Moore points out that "many Christians would never even consider operating a casino, owning a liquor store, manufacturing weapons, using near-slave labor, or operating a lending business charging usury rates." These same individuals, says Moore, should therefore "pay attention to the ultimate destination of their investments through stocks, bonds, and bank deposits."[15] In 1928, in order to serve church groups who wanted to avoid investing in "sins," the Pioneer Fund was formed. Today it stands as the longest-

The Inspiring Legacy of South Africa

IT'S HARD TO imagine, but as we entered the 1990s Nelson Mandela was serving his twenty-seventh year in prison, racially mixed marriages were banned, citizens of South Africa were required to register by racial groups, and residential districts were assigned to individual racial groups—with blacks assigned to "homelands." These and other measures constituted the repressive system known as "apartheid," keeping races apart but giving control to the white minority.

South Africa was the catalyst that propelled SRI into the national spotlight. For the first time, a large, influential group of Americans applied their economic power to demand positive change: the creation of a democracy in South Africa. In the late 1960s, students had begun pressuring universities to divest from companies that had South African operations. In 1971, General Motors was petitioned by the presiding bishop of the Episcopal Church to leave South Africa. Five years later, beginning in Madison, Wisconsin, cities and states began passing laws that prohibited governments from doing business with companies who operated in South Africa.

By the 1980s, the anti-apartheid movement was in full stride. Hundreds of billions of dollars were divested from South Africa–related companies. A majority of U.S. companies in South Africa—including Mobil, Goodyear, RJR Nabisco, and Johnson & Johnson—either sold their operations or just pulled up stakes and left.[16] The U.S. government enacted statutes, such as the Comprehensive Anti-Apartheid Act of 1986, banning new investments. The South African economy reeled under economic sanctions, and finally, in 1989, Prime Minister F. W. de Klerk started the reform process.

running screened fund, having avoided investments in alcohol, tobacco, gambling, and firearms for more than seven decades. Its founder, Philip Carret, was actively involved in the fund until his death at 102 years of age in 1998. Remarkably strong, consistent performance helped earn it the title of "best fund ever" from *Mutual Fund Magazine*.

In 1993 a victorious Nelson Mandela expressed deep gratitude to Americans for using their economic clout to help black Africans win the difficult but remarkably nonviolent struggle against their oppressors. Mandela called for the international community to lift economic sanctions and resume foreign investment. Socially screened mutual fund companies—including Parnassus, Domini, Calvert, Working Assets, Pax World, and Dreyfus Third Century—dropped their restrictions on South African investments. Today South Africa has gone from an avoidance screen to an affirmative screen, as many Natural Investors direct capital toward strengthening the South African economy.

What can we learn from the story of efforts in the United States to aid the anti-apartheid movement in South Africa? In *Loosing the Bonds: The United States and South Africa in the Apartheid Years,* Robert Massie provides a moving summation of the message:

➢ Acts of protest and conscience, so often dismissed as pointless, can gradually accumulate into an irresistible force for change. It suggests, in an era when people feel overwhelmed by the power of elites, that social transformation can take place "from below." It outlines the circumstances under which economic calculations about institutional self-interest can give way to a broader concern for human well-being. It counters our sense of futility by reminding us that amazing changes can and do take place in history—and that they depend not only on the evolution of impersonal forces but also on human imagination and commitment. We have control over our ideas, our ideas have material consequences, and, in the end, as a people, we become what we believe.[17]

Natural Investing remained in this embryonic stage for the next four decades. Wars came and went, the boob tube and suburbia prospered, and anything evil had the color red. Then the 1960s brought paradigm-shaking rebellions, movements, and leaders to the forefront. Vietnam, Kent State, Martin Luther King, the Kennedys, and Rachel Carson's

Silent Spring stunned America with a rousing wake-up call. Government panicked at the prospect of losing control over society, while business fretted as an entire generation questioned middle-class consumerism.

This wrenching period helped bring issues like civil rights, the environment, nuclear power, and the arms race out of the shadows. But just as important, a new strategy was born that addressed the underlying causes of our social strains. After centuries of wearing blinders to the connections, ordinary people began to see that economic power, even more than political power, held the key to solving social problems and moving society toward a positive future. Governor Ronald Reagan succeeded in putting down Berkeley's street riots, but this same revolutionary energy gradually migrated from Telegraph Avenue to Wall Street, challenging time-honored, sacrosanct investment principles.

The 1970s and 1980s saw SRI—Socially Responsible Investing— launched as a movement. During the height of the Vietnam protests in 1971, peace-oriented Pax World became the first mutual fund to offer screened investments on a broad range of social issues. Soon Dreyfus Third Century, Calvert, Working Assets, New Alternatives, and Parnassus joined the pack. South Shore Bank in Chicago pioneered community banking, while the Institute for Community Economics and the E. F. Schumacher Society developed tools for job creation and affordable housing using community loan funds and land trusts. Franklin Research & Development was founded by Joan Bavaria in 1982 to stimulate shareholder activism as a part of social money management. The Social Investment Forum, a trade association for SRI professionals, was incorporated in 1985. Several research organizations, including the Council on Economic Priorities, took up the critical task of monitoring corporate behavior. Investment firms like First Affirmative Financial Network and Progressive Asset Management discovered a large, untapped market of investors eager to include their values. Co-op America brought attention to consumer boycotts and developed a network of socially conscious businesses.

The 1990s have seen the practice of Natural Investing gain acceptance in the mainstream. Much of its growth is now client-driven. Simply put, an ever-growing number of investment houses are managing socially responsible portfolios because investors, both individuals and institutions, are demanding it. Doubts about performance are being put

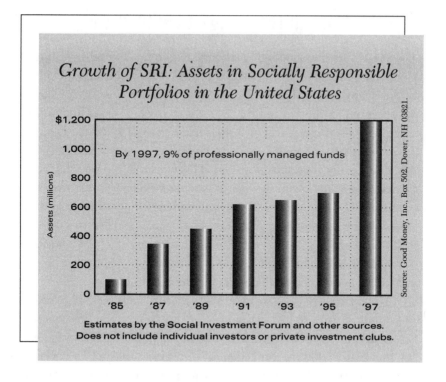

Growth of SRI: Assets in Socially Responsible Portfolios in the United States

By 1997, 9% of professionally managed funds

Assets (millions)

Source: Good Money, Inc., Box 502, Dover, NH 03821.

Estimates by the Social Investment Forum and other sources.
Does not include individual investors or private investment clubs.

to rest, and a new awareness is dawning that companies managed with an eye toward environmental and social health might actually make *better* investments. As Peter Kinder puts it, "We knew something was up when the phone started ringing off the hook. Mainstream investors, who had no real interest in social issues, were calling us for social research because they knew we were on to something. They felt that our methods could help identify better performing stocks."[18]

In 1992, *Investing From the Heart,* by Jack Brill and Alan Reder, became the best-selling SRI book in history. That same year, Cliff Feigenbaum launched the quarterly *GreenMoney Journal.* Both quickly became trusted resources both within the SRI community and among investors. The mid-1990s have seen the debut of a flurry of screened mutual funds. Community investing has gained widespread acknowledgment, even from the World Bank, as a leading tool in the fight against poverty. Internet sites such as socialinvest.org and greenmoney.com now offer Web surfers easy access to information and news.

Natural Investing's First Trillion

LIKE BLADES OF grass emerging through concrete, Natural Investing is penetrating the fortresses of Wall Street. A 1997 study conducted by the Social Investment Forum found that $1.2 *trillion* in assets are under management in the United States in "socially and environmentally responsible portfolios"—an increase of 227 percent since the Forum's 1995 study. Nearly *one out of every ten dollars* invested in America is part of a socially conscious portfolio. This considerable wealth is allocated according to each of the main strategies used by Natural Investors:

➤ $529 billion is invested using Avoidance and/or Affirmative Screening.
➤ $736 billion is in assets controlled by investors who play an active role in shareholder advocacy.
➤ $4 billion is dedicated to community investments.

Natural Investing has grown into a mature industry. The Social Investment Forum serves as the hub for investment practitioners and institutional investors who are dedicated to promoting SRI. Its membership includes a wide range of financial professionals, such as advisers, analysts, portfolio managers, and community development organizations. (See Appendix A for key Natural Investing resources.)

Two annual events serve as a meeting place for people working in SRI. The Forum and Colorado Springs–based First Affirmative Financial Network cosponsor a conference every fall called SRI in the Rockies. Started in 1990 with fifty attendees at a remote dude ranch, this event has become the primary SRI networking event, at which hundreds of SRI professionals come to exchange ideas.

Every June another social investment conference, called Making a Profit While Making a Difference, is held in New York City. Created by Capital Missions Company of St. Charles, Illinois, this event is designed especially for institutional investors. It showcases large and small companies that demonstrate high market returns and high social dividends. Educational sessions for wealthy families, foundation and religious-group treasurers, investment managers, analysts, and venture capitalists are led by social investment experts.

Worldwide, Natural Investing has landed on many foreign shores. The United Kingdom, Canada, Australia, New Zealand, and many European countries are developing their own unique forms of Natural Investing.

In developing countries, microenterprise banks and loan funds are prov-ing to be highly effective tools in alleviating poverty. Natural Investing stands as a modern-day example of the trail-blazing role that Americans can play when we use our freedoms in service of the common good.

It's been a long journey from chocolate money to the Social Invest-ment Forum. The emergence of currencies and corporations unleashed a vast wave of change that altered our social relationships without giv-ing much consideration to values. Gradually, humanity is coming to terms with the resulting imbalances in our society; we are in the early stages of reintegrating economics with core human values. People are learning to work *within* the walls of power by paying attention to the ways in which money is directed. Natural Investors today are playing a historic role—bringing life-enhancing human values back into the cen-ter of our economic lives.

Chapter Two

The Millennial Convergence: Four Roads to Natural Investing

O NE QUALITY THAT puts savvy investors ahead of those who simply follow the herd is an awareness of significant trends, both on Wall Street and in society at large. Natural Investing is flourishing within the context of several supporting social trends. As you begin to wield the tools presented in this book in a truly personal and profitable way, you become an active player in these dynamic social forces. As John Naisbitt and Patricia Aburdene say in *Megatrends 2000*, "The individual can influence reality by identifying the directions in which society is headed."[1]

Our world is in the midst of profound transformations. Social scientist Duane Elgin is not alone when he opines that the changes we are living through are as "momentous as that which occurred in the transition from the agricultural era to the industrial era."[2] Natural Investing has emerged in sync with the pace of change—its growth accelerating as the challenges facing society have grown more evident. Four main drivers point convincingly to further expansion in the field of values-based investing: the popularization of investing, changing values, the expanding role of corporations, and ecological unraveling. Each of these trends is a roadway funneling more and more investors into the Natural Investing hub.

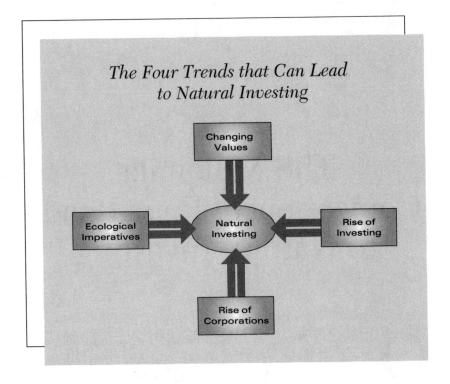

The Four Trends that Can Lead to Natural Investing

Changing Values

Ecological Imperatives

Natural Investing

Rise of Investing

Rise of Corporations

Flocking to Stocks

DO YOU EVER get tired of hearing about the rise and fall of the Dow Jones Average on every hourly newscast? We sure do—and we work in this field! It's as if we are monitoring the vital functions of a critical patient. When did stock market shenanigans become such a national obsession?

Once upon a time, ordinary people didn't think much about investing. Most households would try to keep some money in the bank or buy U.S. Savings Bonds. Social Security and company pension plans offered long-term security. The stock market was a game played by a small, elite slice of society. But today we have become a nation of investors. Your auto mechanic may offer recommendations on his favorite spark plug . . . and his favorite mutual fund. Social gatherings can turn into heated debates between bulls and bears. An entire planet hangs on every utterance of Federal Reserve Chairman Alan Greenspan.

There are many reasons for this shift, including greater prosperity. But financial uncertainty—people's fears about their future well-being—is certainly a factor. Americans can no longer rely on the promise of lifetime employment and a generous pension. In this age of downsizing and outsourcing, many people live in fear of an unexpected summons to the personnel office; in 1998, over 500,000 workers received pink slips.

Furthermore, the demographics of the Baby Boomers' looming retirement makes the promise of Social Security look more like quicksand to younger workers—it takes but won't give anything back. Our society is aging, and 76 million Boomers will start reaching retirement age in 2008. A poll reported in the *Atlantic Monthly* found that "Americans under thirty-five are much more likely to believe in UFOs than to believe that they'll ever receive Social Security benefits."[3]

But wait, don't fret! Wall Street has come to the rescue! The financial industry has seized the day, enticing Americans into the wild world of stocks and bonds. Books like *Personal Finance for Dummies,* the CNN Financial Network, and slick mutual fund ads bring investing to the masses. The Internet provides enormous amounts of financial data and news, while numerous on-line discount brokerage firms offer pajama-clad Web surfers twenty-four-hour stock trading. And the record-breaking bull market of the 1990s, which saw the Dow quadruple in less than eight years, lured cautious savers off the sidelines.

As a result, we are now much more likely to own some stocks or mutual funds than our parents were a generation ago. According to an article entitled "United Shareholders of America" in the *New York Times Magazine,* more than half of all Americans are now investors in the stock market. For the first time in world history, we have a mass culture of investing; an aging population and greater availability of information assure that this trend will continue. If proposals to save Social Security by investing our funds in the stock market are enacted, nearly every American will be hitched to Wall Street. As the sheer numbers of investors increase, and as new investors grow more sophisticated about investing for profit and change, Natural Investing is certain to garner its share of the growth.

" *Every few hundred years in Western history there occurs a sharp transformation. Within a few short decades, society—its world view, its basic values, its social and political structures, its arts, its key institutions—rearranges itself. . . . We are currently living through such a transformation.* **"**

—PETER DRUCKER, management consultant[4]

Changing Values: The Sudden Rise of Cultural Creatives

TREND WATCHERS PLACE a strong emphasis on studying people's values. A major shift in value systems like the one Drucker describes ripples through every aspect of our society. In 1995, sociologist Paul Ray of the San Francisco–based research firm American LIVES published the results of an exhaustive, ten-year study that categorized Americans' value systems. He identified a "new and distinctive social force" that is committed to what he calls "post-material" values. Surprisingly, this large, growing population now includes one-fourth of all American adults.

Ray dubbed this group the "Cultural Creatives" because "they are the ones coming up with most of the new ideas in American culture, operating on the leading edge of cultural change." Creatives share five distinctive values: a commitment to building an ecologically sustainable culture, a respect for global cultural diversity, an emphasis on relationships of all kinds (family, community, bioregional), a desire to integrate their daily lives with their emotional and spiritual cores, and a strong sense of social awareness combined with an optimistic belief that change is possible.[5]

Before 1960, only a few "odd ducks" would have qualified as bona fide Cultural Creatives. But in 1995 Ray estimated that roughly 24 percent of the U.S. adult population, or 44 million people, would identify most strongly as Creatives. The other two groups are the Modernists (47 percent), the still dominant group who place a higher value on materialism, success, and technology, and the Heartlanders (29 percent), who prioritize tradition and conservative values. This sudden emergence from obscurity to near-parity with Heartlanders portends great change.

Cultural Creatives tend to be well educated and relatively affluent;

the group is largely (60 percent) female. Their growing economic clout has not been lost on the business world. Among the indicators of this influence are a burgeoning natural food industry; the rise of alternative health care (such as herbal medicine and homeopathy); the proliferation of self-help and spiritual books on the best-seller lists; growing support for alternative energy and recycling; increased interest in living simply; and rising sales of environmentally sound products.

Business is doing much more than simply responding to the market demands of Cultural Creatives—it is being profoundly changed from within. In the early 1980s, astute observers like Willis Harman in *Global Mind Change* noted the growing acceptance in management circles of terms like *intuition* and *creativity*. As we'll see in Chapter 13, many companies are turning away from the old command-and-control model and are beginning to treat employees as whole human beings who desire opportunities for personal growth and fulfillment in the workplace.

The accelerating growth of values-inclusive investing owes much to Cultural Creatives, who have always been well represented in the SRI movement. This is bound to continue for several reasons. It is only during the last few years that SRI has had both the wide range of investment opportunities and the proof of solid performance needed to entice cautious investors. In addition, more Creatives are beginning to receive inheritances, transferring a vast reservoir of wealth from Heartlanders and Modernists to people more likely to invest with their values.

Of course, Natural Investing is not for Cultural Creatives alone. Its promise is ripe for discovery by Heartlanders, whose devotion to community and caring human values is undermined by many conventional investments. Many Modernists as well will find that Natural Investing is a great outlet for their desire for personal expression, as well as their profit-seeking sensibilities. Whereas Creatives may have driven much of the recent growth in Natural Investing, we suspect that the next few years will see a broader range of our population turning to these proven and rewarding methods of managing their money.

Globalization: Citizens Demand a Seat at the Table

LEAVING THE "SOFT" world of values and ideals, let's visit the halls of power, where most important decisions are made. Did you think we meant Congress or the White House? Guess again. We're off to Corporate America.

An enormous power shift has occurred in the last few decades. As David Korten puts it, "Corporations are the real governance system of this country, and in fact the world." Money and power are being concentrated (through mergers and acquisitions) "into fewer and fewer multinational corporations, which are increasingly becoming more detached from local communities and all human responsibilities."[6] Just as the Middle Ages were dominated by the Church, and powerful governments ruled the Industrial Age, in the blink of an eye we have been ushered into the "Corporate Age."

Today many corporations exert economic impacts larger than those of even good-sized countries. For example, Wal-Mart's annual sales now roughly equal the entire gross domestic product of Finland. Ford's revenues are larger than the economies of Ireland, New Zealand, and Hungary combined!

Politically the debate around corporate issues is scrambling the old left-right dichotomies. The fierce controversy over NAFTA was an early indication that we were entering a new era in politics. Ralph Nader, the tireless crusader for corporate accountability; perennial presidential dark horse Ross Perot; and Pat Buchanan, darling of the Christian Coalition—an unlikely trio!—all opposed the pact. By 1997, this alliance had gained significantly more clout. President Clinton's Fast Track legislation, intended to speed passage of future international trade agreements, was defeated by a broad coalition that included environmentalists, organized labor, and religious, minority, family farm, and small business groups.

Consumers are showing increasing concern about how and where products are made. "Proudly Made in America" campaigns bring patriotism into the economic arena; this has been perhaps the strongest expression of economic values to emerge from the Heartlanders. Grassroots organizations like Co-op America monitor consumer boycotts while their National Green Pages directory lists hundreds of socially and environmentally responsible businesses. Children flooded Nike with stacks of letters asking them to take better care of foreign workers.

Even daytime talk radio has dived into the fray. A passage by syndicated radio talk show host Jim Hightower, former Texas commissioner of agriculture, illustrates the growing populist sentiments emerging from America's Heartland:

As most ordinary folks have learned, the corporation has gotten way too big for its britches, intruding into every aspect of our lives and forcing changes in how we live. . . . Less than a decade ago, your medical needs rested in the hands of a doctor whom you got to choose. But quicker than a hog eats supper, America's health care system—including your personal doc—got swallowed damn-near whole by a handful of corporate mutants called HMOs. . . . When did we vote on this? Did I miss the national referendum in which we decided that remote corporate executives with an army of bean counters would displace my handpicked doctor, and would decide which (if any) hospital I can enter, how long I can stay?[7]

Once people understand that corporations are making most decisions of consequence in our society, they will look for ways to have influence. A company can be influenced in several ways: by its customers, its workforce, community pressure, governmental action, or its investors. Of these, investment is the only strategy to offer ordinary Americans the right to sit at the table, to be an insider and work for change. Socially conscious investors have known this for decades, scoring significant victories through dialogue with corporate management. When these talks fail, shareholder activists can pull out potent tools like divestment and shareholder resolutions to push for improvements in corporate behavior.

The centrality of corporate issues means that Natural Investors—with their commitment to integrating values and money—will continue to find their ranks swelling. Shareholders have a great opportunity—and a great responsibility—to help strengthen the expression of humane values in the corporate world. The future will see an increasingly powerful alliance of large institutional investors, such as labor pension funds and religious and foundation endowments, combined with concerned individual investors, all exercising their voice within the financial system.

Eco-cide: A Planet Approaching Its Moment of Truth Brings Environmental Issues to the Forefront

IF THE EARTH went for a checkup, what would the doctor say? Many of us are all too familiar with the litany of horrors about which environmentalists get worked up. So let's hear instead from a less-likely messenger—Ray Anderson, CEO of Interface Carpet, a billion-dollar, energy- and chemical-intensive corporation that manufactures carpet tiles: "Every life support system, every living system that comprises the biosphere where we and all the other creatures live, that thin shell of life, is stressed and in decline."

As Anderson says, "this is not good news for our species, let us not kid ourselves. We cannot live without those life support systems any more than the other species can. It is the crisis of our times."[8] In Chapter 6 we'll see how Anderson is addressing this crisis by launching initiatives aimed at turning Interface into a model, sustainable corporation.

People throughout the world recognize the importance of environmental issues. In 1993, Gallup International conducted a poll involving twenty-four nations, both rich and poor, to query attitudes toward the global environment. It found that people worldwide are aware "that our planet is indeed in poor health, and that they have great concern for its future well-being."[9] Despite economic problems, majorities in half of the developing nations and all the industrialized countries indicated a willingness to pay higher prices to protect the environment.

What does all this have to do with investing? Plenty. Already, socially conscious investors have said that the environment is one of their top concerns. Many enlightened corporations have voluntarily made substantial environmental progress. Environmental offenders are being excluded from portfolios and pressed hard by consumers and shareholders to clean up their act. Liabilities for toxic sites and other violations can severely affect the bottom line. Meanwhile, innovative companies that come up with solutions to these problems are in an excellent position to prosper. As ecological issues—concerning our very survival as a species—come to the forefront, Natural Investing is bound to gain substantial clout thanks to investors wanting to stop the destruction and create a sustainable future.

And the Beat Goes On. . . .

TAKEN TOGETHER, THE combination of cultural, social, financial, and environmental trends highlighted in this chapter is propelling the growth of Natural Investing. When we add (in the next chapter) evidence that shows that values-inclusive portfolios earn as much of a return (or more!) as mainstream investing, the door should be wide open. Once we enter that door, we find an ever-increasing array of investment opportunities—such as screened mutual funds and community banks—that offer expression for an ever-wider range of values.

The Natural Investing ship is just beginning to sail into prominent view before the world at large. As the movement grows, investors voting with their dollars will have an increasingly strong influence on the direction of our society. One thing is certain: our economic system will continue gyrating in unpredictable ways. Yet Natural Investors who keep these long-term, overarching trends in mind will be among those best able to profitably navigate the shifting tides. A little knowledge can go a long way, providing stability during sudden storms of change. The voyage is bound to be exciting . . . and people from all walks of life are climbing on board!

Chapter Three

Natural Performance: Money and Soul

T HE YEAR 1984—better known for Orwell's eerie Big Brother premonitions—marked the beginning of a sea change from values-blind investing to values-inclusive investing. At that time, only a half-dozen or so SRI mutual funds existed; Wall Street could basically ignore Natural Investors as quirky, harmless eccentrics. All that changed when Amy Domini and Peter Kinder wrote *Ethical Investing*, with the tag line "How to make profitable investments without sacrificing your principles."

The book proved to be extremely influential and succeeded in getting SRI onto the radar screen of the financial press. *Ethical Investing* opened with three bold assumptions that sailed against the prevailing winds, raising controversies still unsettled. Their continued relevance bears repeating here:

➤ Every investment—whether in stocks or savings accounts or savings bonds—has an ethical dimension.

➤ Investors can and should apply their ethical standards to potential investments.

The authors immediately acknowledged that these assertions are philosophical and moral. People can agree or disagree with them, but they are not subject to rational "proof." However, their final assumption hit Wall Street right in the wallet, and it has raised a firestorm that is far from being quelled:

➤ Investors who apply their ethical criteria to investments *are more successful* than those who do not (our italics).[1]

Hold it! Stop right there! Can you imagine the indignation of mainstream investment professionals upon hearing that the inclusion of values could improve investment performance? It defies logic! "Limiting your choice of investments invariably reduces returns!" cried the statisticians.

At first glance, it does seem that Domini and Kinder might not have been playing with a full deck. But in the fifteen years since they took that bold posture, the burden of proof has shifted from SRI's proponents to its critics. As we're about to see, a wide range of studies now confirm that Natural Investing does not, by design or default, result in low returns. Indeed, Natural Investors today are commonly achieving the higher levels of success—both financially and socially—presaged in their book.

Beating the Market

WRITING *ETHICAL INVESTING* was not the end of the road for Domini and Kinder, but the beginning of an ambitious new project. They realized that SRI needed a statistically rigorous method that could track the performance of socially screened investments and compare it to that of the market as a whole. So they designed a socially responsible stock index: the Domini 400 Social Index. This is not as simple as it might sound. What is this "market as a whole"? And how does one select a subset of socially screened stocks that will offer a meaningful comparison?

Investors use various stock indexes to get a picture of how the market is doing. The famous Dow Jones Industrial Average takes the stock price of thirty of America's largest corporations and comes up with a single number that is now reported on every evening newscast. But another index, the Standard and Poor's (S&P) 500, gives a somewhat better indication of the market as a whole. The 500 companies on the S&P represent the lion's share of corporate wealth while giving a bigger, more complete picture than the Dow.

The S&P was chosen as a benchmark for the Domini 400 partly to gain credibility with institutional investors. Institutions (such as pension funds) control most of the investment capital in the stock market. As Kinder put it, "If the index wasn't accepted by the institutions, we'd be marginalized forever. Therefore, we made the Domini primarily an index of the large corporations that institutions favor. We started with the S&P 500 and ended up with about 250 of these companies that passed our screens. Then we screened the next-largest companies until we had added another hundred. Finally we included 50 smaller companies with notably strong social performance."[2] Overall, every effort was made to create a mix of companies that closely reflected the range of industries represented in the S&P. (See Appendix B for lists of companies in the Domini 400 and the other Natural Stock Indexes mentioned in this chapter.)

Selecting social screens for the Domini 400 proved to be a delicate process. The authors surveyed social investors and found many diverse interests; some only cared about a single issue while others had numerous, strict screens. The index needed to forge a consensus—to find a common ground that would identify a constructive social agenda without being perceived as being too extreme. Several key screens emerged that represented the then-current state of SRI:

➤ *Exclusionary Screens:* alcohol, tobacco, gambling, military weapons, nuclear power (investment in South Africa was an original screen, but it was dropped in late 1993)

➤ *Qualitative Screens:* product quality and consumer relations, environmental performance, corporate citizenship, employee relations

On May 1, 1990, the Domini 400 was ready to fly. With bated breath, the SRI community watched as Domini figures started rolling in. Now, after more than eight years, we know that Natural Investors can indeed toss out half the S&P, replace it with more responsible companies, and come out ahead!

The performance of the Domini 400 has been truly remarkable. During much of its existence, large-company stocks have been the market's best performers. Yet the Domini had to eliminate many of these

Domini 400 versus S&P Total Return

	ONE-YEAR	THREE-YEAR*	FIVE-YEAR*
Domini 400	34.55%	32.02%	26.08%
S&P 500	28.75%	28.29%	24.07%

*Annualized returns as of 12/31/98.   Source: Kinder, Lydenberg, Domini & Co., Inc.

behemoths for social reasons, replacing them with somewhat smaller companies. Outperforming the S&P under these circumstances is especially noteworthy.

Kinder is careful to point out that these numbers "indicate, but do not prove, that we may well be on to something. Social screens may lead investors to better-performing companies." The reason for the qualifying tone is that we have not experienced a significant bear market—a prolonged period of negative returns—for the life of the Domini 400. There is some chance that the Domini could underperform in those circumstances. However, during the market decline in the summer of 1998, the Domini lost less than the S&P.

For those of you brave enough to talk about Natural Investing to curious friends or skeptical in-laws, you might want to keep a copy of the Domini 400 graph on hand. Or perhaps you'd prefer a catchy bumper sticker, like "Don't Be Standard and Poor—Dominate with Domini." It can be surprisingly hard to get people to absorb this information; the preconception that "doing good" has to cost something is deeply ingrained in the modern psyche.

More Natural Stock Indexes

ALTHOUGH KINDER AND DOMINI raised the performance debate to high-profile stature, they were not the first to claim a positive correlation between values and performance. SRI pioneer Milton Moskowitz made the suggestion in an article in 1972, and Professor Ritchie Lowry, creator of the Good Money Web site, designed a rival to the Dow back in 1976. The Good Money Industrial Average (see Appendix B, p. 310) is composed of "thirty socially acceptable industrial companies." As with the Domini, no changes are ever made to try to get better performance. If a company is dropped for social or other reasons, Good Money seeks to replace it with another from the same industry. As the graph on the next page shows, the Good Money Average has far outpaced the world-famous Dow for over twenty-two years!

Lowry notes that during the October 1987 crash, the Good Money Average held up significantly better than its Dow counterpart. "Far from being a liberal, dreamy-eyed approach to investing . . . SRI encourages precisely the opposite. Social investors eschew short-term

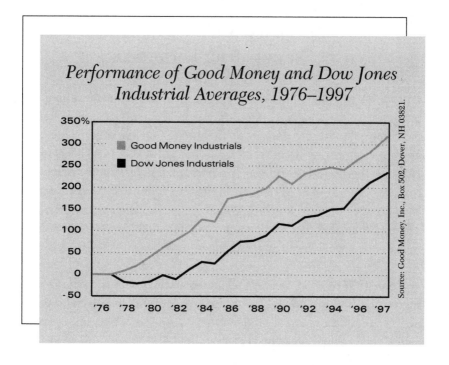

Performance of Good Money and Dow Jones Industrial Averages, 1976–1997

Good Money Industrials
Dow Jones Industrials

Source: Good Money, Inc., Box 502, Dover, NH 03821.

profits and look for the long-term gains in stable, growing companies that provide badly needed goods and services. It is this economically conservative aspect of SRI that the traditional investment community and business press have yet to recognize."[3]

Finally, one more SRI index deserves mention—the Citizens Index. Started by Citizens Funds, a family of SRI mutual funds, the Citizens Index has also shown strong market-beating performance. From its inception on December 31, 1994, through December 31, 1998, the Citizens has a commanding lead of 260 percent total return versus 189 percent for the S&P 500.

The Citizens is similar to the Domini in that it is designed to be compared to the S&P 500; however, it only contains 300 companies, of which 200 are also on the S&P. The Citizens differs from the Domini in its social policies, using a more comprehensive set of social screens. For example, the Citizens screens out companies that test personal care products on animals. It completely avoids investments in the oil industry, whereas the Domini seeks out oil companies with the strongest environmental records. To make up the difference, the Citizens holds more technology stocks than either the Domini or the S&P.

Screened Mutual Funds
Get Serious about Performance

THE THREE NATURAL indexes prove that investors can achieve market-beating results while screening for a wide range of social issues. But most mutual funds are not closely tied to any specific index. There are now dozens of screened funds that have various financial objectives. How are these funds performing? Comparisons with their unscreened counterparts should give a good indication of how Natural Investors have fared in the real world. Because of significant changes and many new additions that took place among the universe of screened funds in recent years, we'll break our assessment into two time periods.

➢ *From 1971 to 1995,* there were only a handful of funds, so the sample was not really large enough to give a meaningful comparison between SRI funds and the mutual fund world at large. Pax World showed consistent good performance for a balanced fund. In 1988, two of the top-ten growth funds in America were SRI funds: Parnassus and Ariel Growth. The Domini Social Equity fund, which debuted in 1991, also showed high returns. But the Calvert Group had several years of struggle with its Social Equity fund, and some small funds floundered and were closed. *Performance assessment:* Slightly below average. Some moments of greatness, but also some laggards.

➢ *Starting in 1995,* however, the SRI fund industry made a powerful commitment to investment performance. Funds that lagged, such as Dreyfus Third Century and Calvert Social Equity, fired their managers; established Wall Street pros like Eddie Brown joined the movement and teamed up with SRI social screening experts. As demand increased and performance improved, more funds were launched, some by traditional investment powerhouses. *Performance assessment:* On a par with unscreened funds. Competition and growth bring higher-quality management to SRI, resulting in strong, consistent returns.

We appear to be in a new era for socially screened funds; these funds now are producing highly competitive returns. As a result, mutual fund investors are pouring more money into screened funds, and new fund entrants are keeping researchers like ourselves hopping.

The latest Morningstar rankings are a real eye-opener. Morningstar is the industry's leading mutual fund rating service. They release annual rankings of mutual fund returns, divided into four quartiles. By definition, the top quartile consists of the 25 percent of all mutual funds that post the best annual returns. In recent years, screened funds have been more favorably represented in the top-two performance quartiles.

Percent of Forty-Seven Screened Funds Placing in
Top Quartile of Their Respective Investment Categories
(e.g., Large-Cap, Balanced)[4]

One year ending September 1998	**49** percent
Three years ending September 1998	**34** percent
Five years ending September 1998	**32** percent

OK, so a third to a half of screened funds are showing up in the top quarter of the total funds universe; that shows that a disproportionate number of these funds are posting exceptional performance. But what of the rest?

Morningstar "star ratings" are given to all funds with at least a three-year track record and are designed to reflect the risk-adjusted performance of a fund. In this case, a third of all funds are rated with one or two stars (these are the poorest performers), a third are given three stars, and the top third are given four or five stars. Once again, screened funds show up in significantly higher proportions in the top group and, reassuringly, significantly lower proportions in the lowest group. (This time, by definition, 33 percent of all funds should be in each group.)

Morningstar data provide further evidence that screened funds as a group are outperforming their nonscreened peers. Those new managers are really doing the trick! In Chapter 10, our Natural Investing Mutual Fund Honor Roll will point you toward the cream of the crop.

Percent of Thirty-Seven Screened Funds with Star Ratings as of November 1998[5]

Four or five stars	51 percent
Three stars	41 percent
One or two stars	24 percent

The Frontiers of Research: Finding the Link Between Profits and Corporate Behavior

DO SOCIAL SCREENS lead investors to companies that are more profitable? Studies are now examining specific corporate behaviors to see exactly which attitudes and policies can give a company the financial edge. Curtis Verschoor, Ledger & Quill Research Professor in the School of Accountancy at DePaul University, undertook a thorough study of the link between corporate ethics and profits. Verschoor found that "companies making a public commitment to follow ethical business practices are more profitable than companies which do not make ethics a key component of their overall management."[6]

The prestigious *Journal of Investing* devoted its entire winter 1997 issue to SRI, with several quantitative studies aimed at performance factors. One study, conducted by ICF Kaiser, found a stock price benefit of up to 5 percent for companies that have strong environmental management practices. Three benefits of such corporate care can translate into bottom-line benefits. First is a reduction of the costs associated with environmental disasters or fines. Second is the benefit that accrues at the retail level from being perceived as a caring company. Third, and perhaps most important, is the suggestion that the very act of designing management practices that address deeper and less traditional issues strengthens the organization. Companies that develop cross-team, multidisciplinary approaches to dealing with environmental or other social issues reap the benefits of that holistic corporate intelligence in solving other business issues. The result is often increased performance and more timely responses to all sorts of marketplace challenges.

Jack Brill Takes on the Experts

 IN 1993, THE *New York Times* asked five of the nation's leading investment advisers to design model portfolios for a hypothetical retirement fund. The participants were all well-known, highly regarded investment professionals. On the heels of his first book, *Investing From the Heart,* Jack Brill was invited to try his luck against this formidable lineup using only socially screened mutual funds.

This competition, which appears in the *Times* quarterly mutual fund review, has become a high-profile opportunity to watch the evolution of Natural Investing's success. Keep in mind that the other participants could choose from thousands of funds, while Jack was limited to a few dozen. At first, Jack's portfolio lagged behind those of the others, due in part to the underperformance of an environmental sector fund and a short-lived market-timing fund that misgauged the strength of the bull market.

Since January 1, 1997, however, Jack's portfolio has been far and away the best performer. For the two years ending December 31, 1998, his portfolio was up 54 percent, while the others posted gains of from 15 to 31 percent. In 1998, he gained 22 percent while his competitors gained between 4 and 8 percent. After more than five years Jack is in second place with a cumulative 124 percent return. The returns for his competitors range from 76 to 130 percent.

The *Times* series shows that Natural Investors face the same challenges and have the same opportunities as other investors. The combination of building a conservative portfolio and responding to market realities (such as the lagging environmental sector) has allowed Jack to prove that a socially screened portfolio can give the experts a run for their money. While "past performance is no guarantee of future results," the current situation certainly stands traditional Wall Street logic on its head!

In 1996 the Social Investment Forum began awarding the Moskowitz Prize for excellence in social investment research. Named after socially responsible investment pioneer Milt Moskowitz, the award supports academic research in diverse fields such as social screening, competitive performance, and community investment. The 1998 Moskowitz Prize was awarded to the University of Oregon's Michael Russo and Golden State University's Paul Fouts for their examination of the economic and environmental performance of 243 Fortune 500 companies. Their work corroborated the work done by ICF Kaiser, showing that companies with superior environmental performance have higher returns on investment compared with their competitors.[7]

To many Natural Investors, it is just common sense that companies who treat their employees, communities, and the environment well would make better investments. But now we have three methods of quantifying the impact of investing with values: academic research, socially screened stock indexes, and mutual fund performance. Each offers compelling evidence that Natural Investing can tackle Wall Street's heavyweights on their own turf and emerge victorious. By addressing the performance question head on, these pioneering efforts are putting to rest the myth that doing the right thing extracts a financial cost. With this obstacle out of the way, Natural Investing is exceedingly well positioned to become a major force in our economic future.

Is Natural Investing Good for the Soul?

NOW LET'S MAKE a little shift. Breathe in. Breathe out. . . . Good! All this talk of money can get pretty heady. Let's get to the heart of the matter and explore the spiritual dimensions of Natural Investing. We know that you can "make money and make a difference" with Natural Investing. But what about the personal side of life? Are there spiritual returns for all your hard work?

This discussion brings us full circle to the beginning of the chapter, when Domini and Kinder argued that every investment has an ethical dimension and that investors should apply their ethical standards to investments. Unlike studies of financial returns, the realm of the soul

Fortune's *Most Admired*

FOR ANY TRUE-BLUE Wall Street types out there who remain skeptical of all these studies, we invite you to consult one of the elite vanguards of capitalism, *Fortune* magazine. Every year *Fortune* surveys top business leaders to compile their prestigious list of America's Most Admired Companies. In 1998, three of the criteria used to judge corporate fitness were financial. The rest look suspiciously like . . . social, ethical, and quality screens! Among *Fortune*'s "key attributes of reputation" are quality of management, the ability to attract and keep employees, quality of products and services, and corporate and environmental responsibility.

Of the five companies *Fortune* admires most, four are also among Domini's top-five holdings (Microsoft, Intel, Coca-Cola, and Hewlett-Packard). This may be the strongest indication yet that Natural Investing has reached the mainstream, changing the way analysts examine a company's profit potential and pushing companies to treat people and the environment with a little more kindness.

In a separate study, *Fortune* selected the fifty companies that have the best records on minority issues. Among their benchmarks were racial composition of management, hiring and promotion, and use of minority-owned suppliers. As an afterthought, they examined the performance of these companies relative to the S&P 500. Surprise! Making extra efforts to be racially inclusive *increased* the return to investors, by 11 percent over three years and 16 percent over five years.

offers no statistics to prove anything. But we will start you out with one tidbit from a 1998 *USA Weekend* poll: spirituality was cited as the single most important factor in personal happiness, after health. "Spiritual and emotional well-being are overriding factors for the happiness of Americans," said Amy Eisman, *USA Weekend* executive editor.[8] We figure that happiness is a pretty universal goal for investors (are any of you investing with the goal of being *un*happy?), so it seems wise to see how the spiritual perspective ties in with investing.

Let's look first at how Wall Street (used here as a metaphor for traditional investment theory) responds to questions about its spiritual side. "I'd invest in the devil himself if it made money," says one tobacco analyst. "Given a choice between investing for social good or their own greed," says a mutual fund consultant, investors should "opt for their own self-interest and use more conventional charitable routes to pursue causes."[9] This is about as far as the discussion usually goes—make as much money as you can using any legal means; then, if you want, do something good with a portion of your gains.

The performance studies in this chapter have pretty much taken the wind out of *that* sail—you can do just as well by doing good. But this doesn't really address the philosophical differences between Wall Street and Natural Investing. Wall Street says: split yourself off from your values and invest strictly for profit. Natural Investing says: invest with as much integrity as possible by striving to be consistent with your values. Which approach is right for you?

One likely place to look for answers would be the world's great religious teachings. Through the ages, it is to them that most people have gone for guidance on how to live a moral life. And if there is one universal starting point, it would have to be the Golden Rule. All the world's spiritual traditions affirm the biblical ground rule for appropriate conduct: treat others as you would want yourself to be treated. Despite our many differences, every major civilization has arrived at this same ethic for describing appropriate conduct:[10]

> **"***As you wish that men would do to you,
> do so unto them.***"**
>
> —CHRISTIANITY (Luke 6:31)

> **"***No one of you is a believer until he desires for
> his brother that which he desires for himself.***"**
>
> —ISLAM (Sunan)

> **"** *Hurt not others in ways that
> you yourself would find hurtful.* **"**
>
> —BUDDHISM (Undanavarga)

> **"** *What is hateful to you, do not do to your
> neighbor: that is the whole Torah; the rest
> is commentary; go, study.* **"**
>
> —JUDAISM (Hillel, Babylonian Talmud)

> **"** *Do naught unto others which would
> cause you pain if done to you.* **"**
>
> —HINDUISM (Mahabharata 5:1517)

It is worthwhile to read over each of these teachings and contemplate how they relate to investing. Imagine there is a company that is doing something that you find particularly offensive, conducting activities you wouldn't want done unto you. Now imagine buying stock in that company with the hope that it will make a big profit. How does this make you feel?

Many people have a strong emotional response when they find themselves in such a situation. An uncomfortable state of dissonance occurs when our actions are out of alignment with our hearts. It is only possible to live with such inconsistencies by putting on blinders—by maintaining that an investor has no responsibility for the actions of the companies (or governments, for that matter) in which his or her money is invested. But such conflicts are real, and no amount of denial can make them disappear.

Popular author Marianne Williamson, in *The Healing of America*, calls on us to reverse this dissonance through the "coherence of ends and means." History through the ages has given us leaders who, despite great adversity, relied on nonviolence to achieve justice. Violence of any kind will not bring forth peace. Martin Luther King said, "The first principle of this movement is that the means must be as pure as the end . . . for in the long run of history, immoral destructive means cannot bring about moral and constructive ends." Gandhi said simply, "My life is my message."[11] In a humble way, Natural Investors seek to embody this kind of integrity by choosing investments that are coherent with their values.

Moral guidelines are not the only fruit of spirituality. "The great religions share a common core in that they all advocate a personal inner awakening," says Peter Russell, author of *Waking Up in Time*. "Such a change of consciousness has, I believe, now become an imperative."[12] Many people, both within and outside organized religion, are engaged in a wide variety of contemplative practices that bring such tangible benefits as peace of mind and better health. Nearly one-fifth of Americans have meditated and over half pray every day.

How does this more inward side of spirituality connect with investing? To begin with, most practices emphasize awareness—getting in touch with what is happening in one's mind or body. Natural Investing also teaches awareness—getting in touch with what is happening with one's money.

Second, contemplative practices help dissolve the boundaries between ourselves and the rest of Creation. Many people report having mystical experiences that bring about a heightened sense of interconnection with both the physical and nonphysical worlds. A direct realization of being connected to "all that is" can be a life-changing event. For investors, these experiences can serve as a tangible reminder that our actions do not occur in a vacuum. As the Native American leader Chief Seattle put it, "Whatever man does to the web of life, he does to himself."

Our field has sometimes been lightly referred to as "good karma investing." *Karma* is a concept from the East that basically holds that every action has its consequences. This idea is also found in the Bible— "As you sow, so shall you reap." These teachings promise future rewards for good deeds and punishment for bad, either in this lifetime or in some sort of afterlife or reincarnation. We'll leave you to your own beliefs on this—although some people might want to accumulate "good karma points" just in case! We prefer to focus on the present; there are plenty of immediate benefits for being in integrity and including your values, whereas dissonance carries an immediate cost.

Performance: How Much Is Enough?

EVERY NATURAL INVESTOR must come to terms with the very personal subject of investment performance. We've seen that ethical values can be included in a portfolio without sacrificing return. This is great news, and we hope all of our readers will do their part to let the uninitiated know the facts.

Although the Domini 400 and other studies make a powerful case for Natural Investing, numbers can blind us to even deeper questions. What if you want to invest in something that really moves your soul, something you believe can make a positive difference? And what if this investment has less profit potential than other opportunities? Would you be willing to sacrifice some financial return for the satisfaction that making your heartfelt choice could bring?

You see, Wall Street is not entirely wrong when it says that limiting your investment opportunities can limit your returns. It's a matter of degree. At some point, if your screens are extremely restrictive or you are committed to a specific social agenda, it becomes more difficult to find investments that meet your criteria. Those that do may fail to keep up with the market. For example, if you invest only in worker-owned recycling companies (which may be great long-term investments), you could suffer financially when the market for scrap metals takes a dive. There is nothing wrong with being a purist, but it should be done with open eyes.

Natural Investors align themselves along a purity spectrum that runs from "I won't give up a dime in order to include my values" to "I don't care at all about return; I want to do good." This is one of the most important questions to clarify right at the start, as it influences virtually every aspect of building a portfolio.

Now It's Your Turn

THIS CHAPTER HAS taken us smack into two of the most fundamental yet most contentious issues that Natural Investors face: financial returns and ethical implications. In the next section, we take these discussions of money and soul into the real world. We go into greater depth about the strategies you'll be using and the social issues you want reflected in your portfolio.

You are entering uncharted territory; the landscape is full of bewildering nooks and enticing peaks. You will need to create your own map to get where you want to go. We close this chapter, and this introductory section, with our first worksheet. It is designed to help you clarify the approach you want to see reflected in your investment decisions. We hope that you will take the time to really let yourself sit with these questions, and that you will return to them often.

Worksheet #1: Values and Money

Creating your own values-based portfolio begins with defining your general approach to investing. The studies in Chapter 3 demonstrate that a portfolio may be screened for a variety of social issues without sacrificing return. But for the moment, let's put that information aside and consider the following question:

Which of the following best describes your priorities for your investments?
A. _____ Achieving my financial goals is primary. I would not be willing to give up any financial return in order to include my values.
B. _____ Achieving my financial goals *and* including my values are both important. I assign the following relative importance to each goal (1 = low; 5 = high):
Financial return: 1 2 3 4 5
Social return: 1 2 3 4 5
C. _____ My investments must fully represent my social, environmental, and ethical values. If necessary, I would be willing to accept somewhat lower financial returns to achieve this.

This information will be particularly useful as you consider engaging in Community Investing, Shareholder Activism, and Affirmative Screening.

Section Two

The Four Spokes of the Natural Investing Wheel

C h a p t e r 4 *F o u r*

Natural Investing
Strategies

I F THERE IS one overarching message that Natural Investing brings
to the world of business it is this: *change is possible!* Natural
Investors know that courageous stick-to-it-iveness can bring positive results, even in the face of seemingly intractable problems or
unmovable institutions. This optimistic outlook is seen in the actions of
a seventy-five-year-old nun challenging the chairman of General Electric to clean up pollution, in the entrepreneurial spirit of a young Mexican mother using a "microloan" to start her own business, and in countless ordinary investors deciding to shun profiting from activities they
find distasteful.

In this section, you'll begin your journey into the world of Natural
Investing, learning how to put your beliefs into action. This chapter
will acquaint you with the four strategies, or spokes, of the Natural
Investing Wheel: Avoidance Screening, Affirmative Screening, Community Investing, and Shareholder Activism. Next, the two screening
chapters take you on a "tour of the issues"—a look at the major
predicaments and opportunities facing society—so that you can evaluate prospective investments according to their alignment with your values. In the following chapters, you'll learn about ways to use community investing and shareholder activism as tools for acting on your
concerns and desires. Finally, at the end of the section, a series of
worksheets will guide you through the process of defining the partic-

ular strategies and issues that you'll be using to accomplish your financial and social objectives.

Natural Strategies:
The Four Spokes of the Wheel

CHOOSING YOUR STRATEGIES is one of the fun parts of Natural Investing. This important step is the one in which you map out a game plan for bringing your values into the financial world. The "spokes" may be mixed and matched in any way that suits you. No need to limit yourself to one when others look enticing; many Natural Investors happily engage in all four!

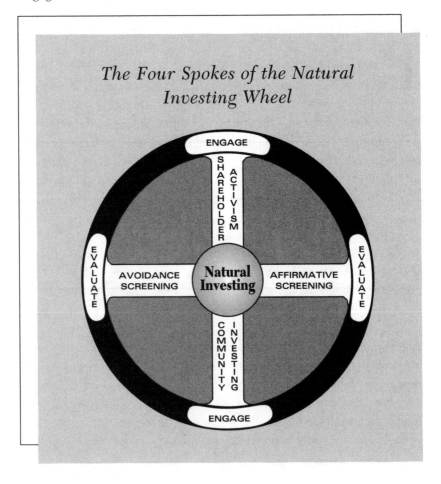

The Four Spokes of the Natural Investing Wheel

Evaluation = Making Choices

USING OUR WHEEL as a compass, let's look first at the axis that runs from West to East. Here lie the strategies of evaluation, through which we decide who we will or will not allow into our portfolios. In the West, the place of sunsets and quiet reflection, we find Avoidance Screening, the most familiar Natural Investment Strategy. Here we focus on the *exclusion* of investments that violate an investor's social or environmental criteria. For example, Philip Morris wouldn't get through the avoidance screens of an investor who has a "no tobacco products" screen.

In the East, where the sun rises on new ideas, we find the strategy of Affirmative Screening, which we also refer to as "prospecting." Affirmative Screeners conduct an active search for investments that show financial promise *and* support activities in which these investors believe. For example, prospectors may buy stock in companies that demonstrate a high level of commitment to their workers, their communities, or the environment. In its highest expression, Affirmative Screening allows Natural Investors to seek out investments that are bringing their vision of a positive future into the world.

In between Avoidance and Affirmative Screening lie the "quality screens"—a vast middle ground that is not so black-and-white. Here we weigh both strengths and weaknesses, seeking investments that lean toward the positive side of the scale. We'll find that many of the quality screens considered by Natural Investors—such as product quality and management issues—overlap with the concerns of mainstream analysts.

Engagement = Direct Participation

RUNNING VERTICALLY IS the axis of engagement, encompassing the more active methods of Natural Investing. Down at the Southern end, where the sun shines the brightest, is Community Investing. It is through such investing that the "grass roots" are nourished, for example by community financial institutions that channel money to people who may not qualify for loans from more mainstream sources. Community Investing initiatives include affordable housing, small business lending, targeted investment in both urban and rural areas of the country, and microenterprise development throughout the world.

As we head North, we move up in scale toward larger corporations. Shareholder Activism is for those investors who refuse to sit on the sidelines when they object to some behavior of a company they own. Shareholder activists have a wide range of tools available to them, including:

➤ Dialogue with companies on issues of concern
➤ Sponsorship of shareholder resolutions when companies refuse to talk or when the dialogue breaks down
➤ Voting proxies in support of shareholder resolutions on social issues

Choosing Your Natural Strategies

ONE SHORTCUT FOR narrowing your choices is to look at your financial situation. For example, if you are in debt or have only a small bank account, then you may be limited to Community Investing. Or, if you own stock in a company you don't like but can't sell your shares right now (perhaps because of tax considerations), you can still become a Shareholder Activist. The following chart paints in broad strokes the types of investments that can be made with each strategy:

NATURAL INVESTING STRATEGY	INVESTMENT TYPE(S)*	SOCIAL CHARACTERISTICS
AVOIDANCE SCREENING	Stocks and bonds: Any, but generally those of medium to large companies and government issues	Avoids "negative" activities
AFFIRMATIVE SCREENING	Stocks: Often focuses on smaller companies, but can include larger company stocks and government bonds; venture capital	Seeks "positive" activities
COMMUNITY INVESTING	Banks, credit unions, and community loan funds	Funds community lending programs, e.g., for jobs and housing
SHAREHOLDER ACTIVISM	Stocks: Any, but usually those of medium to large companies	Influences corporate policies

*Note: Mutual funds that utilize these strategies are also available (see Chapter 10).

As you work through this book, you'll see how your personal financial situation and social priorities can best be expressed on the Natural Investing Wheel. Now let's take a peek at four very different investors to see how they play the game:

MS. CARING is a retired teacher whose only investments are in her IRA. When questioned, she says her main desire is to not hurt anyone. Her husband died of lung cancer, and her granddaughter loves birds.
Natural Strategy:
➤ *Avoidance Screening.* Ms. Caring decides to screen out investments in tobacco and environmental polluters.

GEORGE AND KATHY FASTRACK are in their late forties. They met in the 1960s at a peace march but have since taken corporate jobs and are accumulating significant investments.
Natural Strategies:
➤ *Avoidance Screening.* The Fastracks retain their '60s idealism and decide to screen their investments for a wide range of social and environmental issues.
➤ *Affirmative Screening.* They also decide to allocate a small amount of their portfolio to small companies that produce natural foods.
➤ *Community Investing.* For the conservative side of their portfolio, the Fastracks have a money-market fund and a CD with a local community bank.

THE SISTERS OF THE IMMACULATE HEART PENSION FUND has placed its funds with an investment manager specializing in religious institutions.
Natural Strategies:
➤ *Avoidance Screening.* The pension fund forbids investments in such "sin" issues as alcohol, tobacco, weapons, and gambling stocks.
➤ *Shareholder Activism.* The order initiates shareholder resolutions and votes proxies on such issues as child labor, discrimination, and nuclear weapons.
➤ *Community Investing.* A sizable amount of the portfolio is directed into community loan funds that help poor people around the world create jobs and housing for themselves.

BILLY EXER is a thirty-year-old activist who has inherited some stocks. He is passionately committed to local economic control and solar energy.
Natural Strategies:
➤ *Community Investing.* People-to-people economics fits in best with Billy's philosophy, and he doesn't mind giving up some financial return to engage in it.

➤ *Affirmative Screening.* Although he abhors the stock market, Billy did buy shares in an alternative energy company.

➤ *Shareholder Activism.* Billy has kept the stock he inherited in the local electric company; he joins with other shareholders to vote in favor of shutting down a nearby nuclear power plant.

To Screen or Not to Screen?

BEFORE WE MOVE on, let's tackle one of the biggest controversies swirling around Socially Responsible Investing. Most of the criticism leveled at SRI concerns just one of Natural Investing's four strategies— Avoidance Screening. Some complain that screening doesn't get at the heart of corporate responsibility; others say that current methods used to rate companies are inadequate. We agree that by itself Avoidance Screening cannot bring about all the changes that are needed in our economic system. This is why we place such strong emphasis on the other three spokes of the wheel *and* the systemic and lifestyle issues covered in Section 4.

Nevertheless, Avoidance Screening has an appropriate place in the life of nearly every investor. Indeed it is the most common entry point for investors wanting to include their values. Who couldn't find at least one corporate practice from which they would be unwilling to profit?

Much of the screening debate is healthy, leading to improvements in methodology. However, there are times when Natural Investors find themselves confronted with snide cynicism, as when the *Wall Street Journal* calls SRI funds "touchy-feely portfolios that profess ideological purity."[1] It's important to understand the rational reasoning behind screening. So let's eavesdrop on a hypothetical conversation between Annie and Bob as they get into the thick of it:

Bob: What's the use of screening investments, Annie?

Annie: Everyone has their own reasons, but it usually comes down to this. People value integrity; they don't want to profit from activities with which they disagree. In addition, many want to change the way business operates in the world.

Bob: I don't think screening does either of those things. Let's look at that first point. When people buy stocks, they are usually just trading through the stock markets. The company doesn't even see their money—why should they care what we think?

Annie: That's true, but it's not the whole picture. When you own stock, say in a retail store at which you shop, don't you like to see people loading up their shopping carts and spending lots of money?

Bob: Sure I do.

Annie: You become a cheerleader for the company when you buy shares. But what if that company is doing things that you find reprehensible? What if they pollute the river on which you go fishing, or promote products that killed someone you love? You'd have to split yourself in half, alternating between cheering on the profits and cringing in disgust.

Bob: I see what you mean. But I'm just a small investor. I'm not responsible for what those companies do. That's up to their managers.

Annie: Buying stock means more than just watching the price go up and down. Many people have forgotten this, but stock represents a fractional ownership position in the company. You're an *owner,* Bob! And that means you have both rights and responsibilities. Screeners are saying that owners should *act* like owners. And that starts with *not owning* companies whose actions would keep you up at night if you were doing those things yourself.

Bob: OK, Annie, if I screen out companies whose policies I disagree with, I might *feel* better about myself. But I still don't think I make a whit of difference to some mega-corporation, certainly not enough to make them change!

Annie: If it was just you against Goliath, you'd probably be right. But don't forget that Natural Investing is growing . . . fast! Every day, countless investors are dumping stocks in companies they dislike. This exerts a downward force on those shares. It's hard to know how much influence this has on stock prices—it may be quite negligible. Nevertheless, corporate CEOs and their boards of directors are *hypersensitive* to anything that *might* drag their stock prices down. In the last few years, social researchers have gained the ear of upper management; companies want those good grades for corporate responsibility and are making real reforms in order to earn them.

Bob: I can't imagine a company changing just because a few kooks threaten to sell their stock!

Annie: The real power of screening comes when it's combined with a variety of actions from all stakeholders. Companies hate negative publicity. Remember the anti-apartheid movement? Companies that were adamant about staying in South Africa suddenly picked up and left. Why? Because college students protested, consumers boycotted, and investors put forth shareholder resolutions *and* divested! Activists work at changing a company through dialogue, but if that fails, the screeners say "we're outta here!"

Bob: You're pretty convincing, Annie. But to tell you the truth, the reason I haven't done it is that it seems so overwhelming. There are so many issues, so many complications, and whatever I avoid, someone else might support!

Annie: You're right about that, Bob—the world today *is* a big moral conundrum. But you don't stop voting just because someone else votes for the other candidate, do you? You can start with just one issue about which you feel passionately. Learn about it; find out what others who care about the same thing are doing with their investments. If you want help, do what many Natural Investors do: find screened mutual funds that best fit your values and priorities. Hire those fund's managers to do the nitty-gritty work of screening for you.

On the Road

WITH THIS ORIENTATION, you're ready to start down the road of Natural Investing. Our first stop will bring us to the realm of avoidance and quality screening. Here you'll need to decide if you agree with Annie and want to screen investments for issues that concern you. From there we'll continue on our tour to the other three spokes.

This journey is a very personal exploration of how you wish to bring your values into your financial life. You will travel with your own unique mix of financial vehicles and social directions. We'll provide the road map, but *your* hands are on the wheel. Have a great trip!

C h a p t e r **5** *F i v e*

Avoidance Screening:
A Tour of the Issues

BRACE YOURSELF! The first stops on our tour through the world of Natural Investing run through some of the more sobering aspects of modern life. Faced with the constant bombardment of bad news from the media, it is easy to fall into an ostrich-like pose, ignoring, denying, or simply resigning oneself to hopelessness. Conversely, fear-based overreactions can lead to obsessions, in which life is seen as a holy crusade against evildoers.

Natural Investing offers a middle path. It starts with awareness—an open-minded inquiry that examines all sides of a question. We encourage you to chew on these issues and facts for a while to see where you stand on the question of making money from each of these business activities and practices. Some of the questions may prompt you to an immediate *yes* or *no*, whereas others might require further thought or research.

In this chapter, we'll begin to work our way along the "evaluation" axis. We're going to start by screening out negative behaviors—putting our feet down and tossing the dregs out of our house. From there we move to more qualitative evaluations—looking at the pluses and minuses of what a company does and how they do it—to decide who gets in and who doesn't. Then, in the next chapter, we go out prospecting—searching for companies we'd really like to invite in for dinner.

The following eleven "snapshots" cover the most common avoidance screens being used by Natural Investors today. They provide a quick overview of each issue, including the most poignant facts we could unearth. Obviously each topic could fill a book in its own right—this is not the place to engage in a full-scale debate. We're simply looking at why some investors choose these screens. Appendix C lists companies involved in many of these areas, and Appendix E directs you to resources that enable you to delve more deeply into any that pique your interest.

All right, put on your seat belts and join us for a tour of the issues. You're not the first to take this journey, nor will you be the last. Even if you feel you already know about these issues and have firmly held beliefs on them, we encourage you to read through the profiles. Reviewing these issues again in the context of working with this book will help you complete your next task: integrating your social positions and your financial choices. Take your time, pause when you need to, and remember that, when you've completed this tour, you'll be ready to free yourself of ties to any objectionable holdings you choose to target in your investment plan. Ready? Here we go. . . .

Alcohol

The Question: Do you want to avoid investments in the alcohol industry? This includes companies that produce, market, or promote the use of alcoholic beverages.

The Issue: The avoidance of alcohol-related investments was first advocated by church groups, who attributed signs of moral decay to activities like drinking. Although most adults consume alcohol on occasion, many investors are concerned with its addictive quality, health-damaging effects, and negative social consequences. Critics charge that alcohol advertising, by making drinking socially acceptable, is actually intended to increase consumption among "problem drinkers."

The Case for Screening Alcohol-Related Investments:

➤ Heavy and chronic drinking can harm virtually every organ and system in the body, causing illness and death from liver and cardiovascular diseases. It depresses the immune system and results in a predisposition to infectious diseases, including respiratory infections, pneumonia, and tuberculosis.[1]

➤ Alcohol contributes to 100,000 deaths annually, making it the third leading cause of preventable mortality in the United States.[2] Nearly one-fourth of all persons admitted to general hospitals have alcohol problems or are undiagnosed alcoholics being treated for the consequences of their drinking.[3]

➤ Of all traffic fatalities (the leading cause of accidental death), 41 percent are alcohol related.[4] Alcohol is involved in about half of all homicides and serious assaults, as well as a high percentage of sex-related crimes, robberies, and incidents of domestic violence.[5]

➤ Two-thirds of the population drinks, but 10 percent of all drinkers drink half of all the alcohol consumed.[6] An estimated 6.6 million children under the age of eighteen live in households with at least one alcoholic parent.[7]

Animal Rights

The Question: Do you wish to avoid investing in companies that treat animals inhumanely? This could include any of the following activities: killing or injuring animals in the course of medical or product testing, raising animals for food under cruel living conditions, sport hunting and trapping, containing them in unnatural environments (zoos, circuses), or abusing animals in the entertainment industry or for the sake of any other business activity.

The Issue: No longer a fringe issue, the animal rights movement has brought to mainstream attention the magnitude of abuses animals suffer at the hands of humans each year. Proponents claim that nonhuman animals have the basic right to live without threat of being arbitrarily tortured or killed to gratify human needs and pleasures, particularly when there are other nonharmful alternatives.

The issue of animal rights is not a simple one. Many people strongly oppose Department of Defense military experiments that kill or torture animals to test new weapons or the effects of chemical warfare or radiation exposure. Many others object to products made of fur and leather. But the questions get thornier when addressing medical research. Is animal testing acceptable if it is done for the purpose of saving human lives? Are there alternatives to animal testing that could achieve the same purpose?

Factory farming is another controversial area. Many people are concerned about the conditions to which animals are subjected in the pursuit of profit. Much of the livestock industry today is based on an industrial model that is highly mechanized to achieve assembly-line efficiencies. Animals are simply considered another food product.

The Case for Screening Animal Testing–Related Investments:

➤ It is estimated that 50 million animals are killed annually in U.S. laboratories.[8] Yet the Physicians Committee for Responsible Medicine reports that sophisticated nonanimal research methods are more accurate, less expensive, and less time consuming than animal-based methods.[9] By combining data from human volunteers, case studies, autopsy reports, mathematical and computer models, and tests that use vegetable proteins to mimic human tissue reactions, the use of animals can be drastically reduced or eliminated.

The Case for Screening Factory Farming–Related Investments:

➤ Livestock are not subject to protection under the federal Animal Welfare Act. Animals may be crammed into the smallest possible space, deprived of natural light, exercise, and fresh air. They may be fed unnatural diets that include growth hormones, appetite stimulants, and sometimes recycled dead animals. Stress-induced cannibalism is not uncommon, and compromised autoimmune system functioning requires almost continual use of antibiotics. A citizen keeping a cat or dog under these conditions could be charged with animal cruelty.[10]

➤ Some 15 million pounds of antibiotics, or 50 percent of all antibiotics manufactured in the United States, are fed to animals each year. Studies by the U.S. Centers for Disease Control and the Food and Drug Administration warn that high levels of antibiotics and other contaminants in commercially raised meat pose a serious danger to human health.[11]

Environment: Global Warming

The Question: Do you want to avoid investments in companies that are major contributors to global warming? This may include producers of coal and oil, some utility and transportation companies, forestry and energy-intensive industries.

The Issue: Our high-octane civilization depends on fossil fuels to keep us warm, transport ourselves and our goods, and grow our food. Although we have all partaken of the benefits of this once-in-a-billion-year blowout sale on fossil fuels, attention is now focusing on its hidden costs. Burning oil and coal releases copious amounts of carbon dioxide (CO_2) and other "greenhouse" gases, changing the composition of the Earth's atmosphere. A vast majority of scientists believe this human-generated alteration of the atmosphere is causing global warming. In recent years, we have seen alarming evidence of a warming trend, including record-breaking heat, extreme weather, melting glaciers, rising sea levels, unusual animal and plant species migrations, and the augmented spread of infectious diseases. Industry groups like the Western Fuels Association contend that human activity is insignificant, that rising temperatures are due to natural causes, and that increasing CO_2 levels are beneficial to humanity.[12]

The Case for Screening Global Warming–Related Investments:

➤ CO_2 concentrations in the atmosphere have increased 30 percent since oil was discovered in the 1800s. At no time in the last 160,000 years have atmospheric CO_2 concentrations been anywhere near as high as they are today.

➤ Every day we burn an amount of oil, coal, and gas that took the planet twenty-seven years to create.[13] Americans, who make up only 4 percent of the world's population, are the heaviest users of its fuels: our fuel consumption produces over five tons of CO_2 annually, or 23 percent of the world total. Of the roughly 6 billion tons of carbon emitted each year from the burning of fossil fuels, only about 3 billion is reabsorbed by oceans and forests.[14] The remainder is building up in our atmosphere.

➤ The year 1998 was the warmest recorded in the over 100 years that consistent weather records have been kept. Worldwide, 1998's average temperature was a full degree Fahrenheit above the historic average.[15] Scientists in Antarctica are warning that massive ice sheets may melt within the next generation, causing sea levels to rise by as much as 20 feet.[16]

➤ Before 1987 only one weather-related catastrophic event had caused more than $1 billion in damage. Since then there have been eighteen such events.[17] As a result, the insurance industry has begun lobbying for curbs on CO_2 emissions. More than fifty insurance companies have signed on to the United Nations Environment Program's Insurance Industry Initiative, which calls for "early, substantial reductions in greenhouse gas emissions."

➤ By conserving energy and developing renewable resources, such as solar, wind, and hydrogen power, we could phase out our dependence on fossil fuels. BP Amoco, one of the world's largest oil companies, plans to invest $1 billion in solar energy development by 2007. BP Amoco's forecasts indicate that the global market for solar power will grow twentyfold by 2010.

➢ In 1997 the historic Kyoto Summit resulted in an international pact that binds industrial countries to cut greenhouse gas emissions by an average of 5 percent below 1990 levels by the year 2010.

Environment: Pollution and Toxic Products

The Question: Do you want to avoid investments in businesses that cause significant damage to the environment? This may include companies whose industrial processes result in hazardous waste, water or air pollution, and destruction of the natural environment. It can also include producers of toxic products, such as pesticides, ozone-depleting and other dangerous chemicals, and certain plastics (like plastic toys made of PVC).

The Issue: We are all aware that our environment is becoming increasingly degraded. Pesticides and herbicides, used by agribusiness in increasing quantities to kill insects and weeds, have infiltrated many of our nation's water supplies; the incidence of respiratory disease is rising as a result of air pollution. The destruction of rain forests is contributing to global warming and climatic changes. Plant and animal species are becoming extinct at an alarming rate. The ozone layer is being depleted. Many manufacturing processes, and often the manufactured products themselves, release significant amounts of chemicals and other pollutants into the environment. All of these toxins can wind up in our communities, our homes, our offices . . . and our bodies.

The Case for Environmental Screens:

➢ *Human Health.* We are losing the war against cancer. Over recent decades, the incidence of cancer in the United States and other industrialized nations has escalated to epidemic proportions. From 1950 to 1998, the overall incidence of cancer rose about 54 percent, with lifetime cancer risks reaching one in two for men and one in three for women. Evidence suggests that much of this increase is due to exposure to an increasing amount of carcinogenic chemicals found in the nation's air, water, food, and consumer products.[18]

➢ Every day, 1 million American children age five and under consume unsafe levels of a class of organophosphate pesticides that can harm the developing brain and nervous system. Nonorganically grown peaches, apples, pears, and grapes are the most common sources of exposure.[19] During the course of one day, the typical American ingests more than twenty different pesticides.[20]

➤ Many scientists are alarmed by the discovery that many synthetic chemicals are acting as "endocrine disruptors," interfering with the actions of hormones in humans and wildlife. Some of the documented impacts include impaired ability to reproduce, diminished intelligence, alteration in behavior, and reduced ability to resist disease.[21]

➤ In 1993 and 1994, more than 53 million Americans drank water that did not meet Safe Drinking Water Act standards owing to chemical and biological contamination. Millions of people are made sick from drinking unhealthy tap water. The EPA estimates that nearly 10,000 community wells contain pesticides, which are linked to cancer as well as liver, kidney, and nervous system damage.[22]

➤ Of the United States' 263 million residents, 100 million face health problems from breathing dirty air; 64,000 Americans die prematurely each year from respiratory illness and heart attacks linked to air pollution.[23] Indoor air pollution, including radon gas, kills 20,000 to 30,000 people every year. In addition, as many as 30 percent of new and remodeled buildings cause health problems due in part to chemical contaminants.[24]

➤ *Biological Health.* Rain forests, home to some 50 percent of all life forms on earth, are being destroyed at a rate of approximately 78 million acres per year—an area larger than Poland. Every year 50,000 species of life forms are driven into extinction.[25]

➤ Worldwide, species are disappearing into extinction at a rate unknown on the Earth since the mass extinction of the dinosaurs. A recent study conducted by the University of Tennessee estimates that 50 percent of the world's forest-bird species will be doomed to extinction because of deforestation over the next half-century. If current trends continue, humans may cause between one-third and two-thirds of *all* plant and animal species on the planet to disappear.[26]

Gambling

The Question: Would you invest in the gambling industry? This might include operators of casinos and suppliers of equipment used for lotteries and legal gambling.

The Issue: Many of us, enticed by the prospect of easy riches, have bought a lottery ticket or visited a casino. (Studies show that almost half the adult population of the United States has placed a wager at a casino at some point in their lives, and two-thirds or more have purchased a state lottery ticket.) The amount of money legally wagered in America rose from $17 billion in 1974 to over $500 billion in 1995; casinos reported over 150 million visits. Three-fourths of all Americans now live within 300 miles of a casino.[27] Thirty-seven states run lotteries, spending millions on advertising that encourages people to take up potentially addictive behavior that can devastate families.

The Case for Screening Gambling-Related Investments:

➤ About 10 million Americans have gambling addiction problems.[28] Ten percent of all lottery players contribute 50 percent of all dollars wagered.[29] Lotteries are a form of regressive tax, for the poor buy six times more lottery tickets than the middle and upper classes.[30]

➤ Crime rates—including those of assault, robbery, and counterfeiting—increase dramatically in states that have legalized gambling.[31] It is estimated that for every dollar a state receives from gambling revenues, it spends three dollars on social service and criminal justice agencies.[32] Conservative estimates in Minnesota put the social costs of problem gambling at more than $200 million per year in taxes, lost income, bad debts, and crime.[33]

Labor: Discrimination

The Question: Do you want to avoid investing in businesses that deny workers equal opportunities based on race, gender, national origin, religion, or sexual preference?

The Issue: Title VII of the Civil Rights Act was enacted in 1964 to protect individuals against employment discrimination on the basis of race as well as national origin, gender, or religion. It was a giant step forward in the attempt to create equal employment opportunities for everyone, and it has done much to break the barriers of bigotry and prejudice. However, discrimination against women and minorities in the workplace continues. In some cases the discrimination is blatant and easily recognized; in other situations it is more subtle—as when capable, talented employees find that despite their qualifications they cannot advance beyond the "glass ceiling."

The Case for Discrimination Screening:

➤ The U.S. Department of Labor's Glass Ceiling Commission study concluded that equally qualified and similarly situated citizens are being denied equal access to advancement into senior-level management on the basis of gender, race, or ethnicity. Fully 95 percent of senior managers at Fortune 500 companies are white males.[34]

➤ A significant wage gap still remains between women and men with comparable education and work experience doing similar jobs. Women earn around $.74 for every $1 earned by men. Jobs traditionally held by women remain clustered at the lower end of the pay scale, while traditional men's jobs—even those having similar requirements as to education and time and effort on the job—pay more. Thus secretaries are routinely paid less than truck drivers even if both jobs are of equal importance to a company.[35]

➤ The average income for Hispanic women with college degrees is less than the average for white men with high school diplomas.[36] The Civil Rights Act does not provide protection against discrimination on the basis of sexual orientation. Competent, qualified people are routinely—and, in most of the country, legally—denied protection from harassment and equal opportunities based on sexual orientation.

Labor: Exploitation (Sweatshops and Child Labor)

The Question: Do you wish to avoid investing in businesses that exploit poor people here and abroad through low wages and oppressive working conditions?

The Issue: All businesses want to reduce costs and increase profits. To do this, some companies are eliminating jobs in places where workers earn higher wages and belong to unions to protect their rights. These companies are moving factories to countries in which they can find cheap labor and lax environmental and social standards. Some "sweatshop" factories pose health hazards such as a lack of sanitation, exposure to toxic chemicals and dangerous equipment, and long workdays with inadequate breaks. Children are often exploited, and workers' wages are so low they have no chance to escape poverty. Attempts to organize unions are actively and forcefully suppressed by the companies. In countries with repressive regimes, government troops have been used to attack labor organizers (indeed, this pattern of violence is reminiscent of the early years of the U.S. labor movement).

The Case for Labor Exploitation Screening:

➤ Haitian workers earn about $.28 an hour, or only $.07 for every pair of Disney *Pocahontas* pajamas that are sold for $12. These wages amount to one-half of 1 percent of the sale price. Workers live in abject poverty, unable even to afford milk for their children.[37]

➤ In 1995 Mattel paid then-CEO John Amerman over $22 million in salary and stock options—more than the combined annual salary of the 11,000 Mattel workers making Barbie dolls in China. A fourteen-year-old child working in Mattel's Indonesian factory would have to work 152 years to earn what Amerman earned in a single day.[38]

➤ Throughout the world, 250 million five- to fourteen-year-olds are employed; half of these work full time. Many children work in industries in which they are exposed to harmful chemicals or other dangerous conditions. In Sri Lanka, more children die of pesticide poisoning from their farm labor jobs than from a combination of childhood diseases including malaria, tetanus, and whooping cough.[39]

Maquiladoras: Maquiladoras are assembly plants along the U.S.-Mexican border that produce finished goods for the U.S. market. Approximately 4,000 maquiladoras produce electronic goods, auto parts, chemicals, furniture, machinery, and other goods, employing nearly a million people. Ninety percent of the plants are American-owned, many by some of our largest corporations (e.g., AT&T, Ford, DaimlerChrysler, General Electric, Kodak, and PepsiCo). Maquiladora workers are paid around $50 to $60 per week, but the cost of living is approximately the same as in the United States. There are widespread reports of abuses, including sexual harassment (most workers are young women), twelve-hour days, inadequate safety provisions, and exposure to toxic chemicals.[40]

Nuclear Power

The Question: Do you want to avoid investments in nuclear power? This may include companies that operate nuclear power plants, as well as manufacturers of nuclear reactors and related equipment.

The Issue: The production of electricity from nuclear fission has been controversial since the first plants were constructed in the late 1950s.

Concerns focus on accidents and near misses, the lack of long-term storage solutions for radioactive waste, security issues, and high financial costs. Nuclear power in the United States is on the decline. Back in 1974 the country had 236 nuclear reactors operating, under construction, or on the drawing board. Defects, accidents, cost overruns, and antinuclear protests have led many to be closed or canceled. Today there are only 109 reactors still operating, and analysts predict 25 or more plant closures by 2002. Outside the United States, however, the promise of cheap, unlimited power is alive and well. South Korea, Taiwan, France, and Japan rely heavily on nuclear power. Energy-hungry, developing countries like China and India (with thirteen reactors between them) have plans to build more.

The Case for Nuclear Power Screening:

➤ Each 1,000-megawatt nuclear power plant produces 500 pounds of plutonium a year. One pound of plutonium could cause cancer in millions of people.

➤ It is estimated that there will be 400,000 tons of nuclear waste in the United States by the year 2000. Such radioactive waste must be allowed to decay in isolation for 10,000 years or more before it is considered safe.

➤ Deaths from radiation poisoning from the 1986 Chernobyl reactor meltdown in the Ukraine are estimated to be as high as 125,000 people so far. The rate of thyroid cancer in some parts of Russia, Belarus, and Ukraine is 100 times the normal rate. During the next century, some scientists believe as many as 500,000 more people, over a much wider region, will die from various types of cancer because of the persistence of low-level radiation.[41]

Repressive Regimes

Question: Do you want to invest in companies whose businesses support undemocratic regimes that violate the human rights of their citizens?

The Issue: What constitutes a repressive regime? Heavy censorship of the media, human rights violations, brutal military law, a ban on labor unions and strikes, restrictions on the freedom to assemble, and environmental destruction are common attributes. The ruling elite practices a form of internal colonialism, often with the complicity of foreign companies. Rulers become increasingly entrenched, and wealthy, multinational corporations gain access to cheap labor and natural resources (including oil, gas, timber, and minerals), and the common citizens suffer. Corporation activities are often carried out under the protection of the elite-controlled military; labor unions are banned or broken; environmental protesters are jailed or worse. Compulsory relocations and forced labor are not uncommon.

The Case for Screening Investments Linked to Repressive Regimes:

➤ Following are several countries that have been targeted for avoidance by some investors because of their repressive governments. Natural Investors for whom this is an important concern should remain alert to changing political situations and adjust their portfolios accordingly. Human rights organizations, government agencies, Web sites, and the media can be useful sources of information on these topics.

➤ *Burma (also known as Myanmar).* Burma has been ruled by a military dictatorship since 1962. Nobel Peace Prize Laureate Aung San Suu Kyi won Burma's national elections in 1990, but she and the National League for Democracy were denied power by the military junta. She subsequently spent six years under house arrest. Prodemocracy supporters are being imprisoned. Widespread torture, rape, and murder committed by government troops are reported throughout southern Burma. Many native inhabitants are virtually enslaved, forced to build military camps and roads to serve oil pipelines.[42]

➤ The principal investors in Burma are oil companies, including Unocal and Total. Texaco withdrew from Burma in 1997, Atlantic Richfield in 1998. Both succumbed to investor and consumer pressure. Oil and gas companies account for two-thirds of foreign investment in Burma. To transport gas, Unocal and Total are building a pipeline from their offshore concession across southern Burma to Thailand. In preparation for the construction, the military has been forcefully evicting entire villages of Mon, Karen, and Tavoy people from their homelands.[43]

➤ *China.* Thousands of political prisoners are being held in China, many without charge or trial; torture is common; thousands of people are sentenced to death and many of them executed each year. The authorities instigate constant crackdowns against prodemocracy activists, human rights defenders, labor organizers, and members of minority ethnic and religious groups.[44]

➤ In formerly independent Tibet, thousands have been arbitrarily detained and many tortured for demonstrating in favor of Tibetan independence. Demonstrators have been shot or imprisoned. The ancient Tibetan culture has been devastated, with most Buddhist monasteries looted and destroyed. Tibet's spiritual leader, the Dalai Lama, lives in exile.[45]

➤ *Other Hot Spots.* In Indonesia, concern centers on resource extraction industries, which have decimated the homelands of millions of indigenous people. The United States–based mining giant Freeport McMoRan was sued by the Amangme tribe for its role during twenty-five years of cultural abuse, including poisoning of ancestral lands and such human rights abuses as abduction, torture, and executions intended to intimidate and eliminate local opposition to its activities. Indonesia is also under pressure from international human rights activists because of its twenty-three-year occupation of East Timor, where violence has claimed the lives of a third of the island's population.

➤ Nigeria has been the site of intense conflict, including the annulment of free elections by the military, mass arrests, and the execution of the leader of a nonviolent campaign to press Royal Dutch/Shell Oil to carry out environmental reclamation and pay fair compensation to the Ogoni tribe for use of their land. Recent political developments offer hope that this situation will be improving.

➤ Unfortunately, the situation in Afghanistan is dismal. The U.S. State Department reports a state of civil war and massive human rights abuses, such as political killings, torture, and kidnappings. In some areas, women are beaten if they are not fully covered and are not allowed to work outside the home. Unocal had planned to build a trans-Afghanistan pipeline that would have supported the ultraconservative ruling Talibans. But in December 1998, citing pressure from feminist groups, Unocal withdrew its support for those plans.

Tobacco

The Question: Would you consider investing in the tobacco industry?
The Issue: "Tobacco is still the biggest killer we've got," says Richard Peto, a professor of medical statistics and epidemiology at Oxford University, adding that 100 million people will die from smoking

worldwide over the next twenty years.[46] Not only is tobacco deadly, it is expensive. Our country spends over $50 billion each year treating smoking-related illnesses.[47] To this must be added damage caused by fires, increased insurance premiums, illness from secondhand smoke, and lost productivity.

Many concerned investors have weeded tobacco out of their portfolios. Mainstream groups such as the American Medical Association have joined with social investment firms, urging investors to divest themselves of tobacco holdings. Indeed, tobacco screening is now a common denominator for practically all SRI investments. Over 97 percent of managers running screened portfolios and 84 percent of all socially screened assets now avoid investing in tobacco companies.

The Case for Screening Tobacco-Related Investments:

➤ Smoking is by far the most significant cause of preventable, premature death in the United States. Over 400,000 Americans die each year of tobacco-related diseases. This toll exceeds the number of deaths from AIDS, homicide, suicide, alcohol use, illegal drug use, fires, and auto accidents combined. Recent estimates suggest that 25 million Americans will die prematurely from a smoking-related disease.[48]

➤ Smoking during pregnancy is more dangerous than using crack. Smoking is blamed for causing 141,000 spontaneous abortions, 61,000 low-birth-weight deliveries, 1,200 to 2,200 sudden infant deaths, and 4,800 perinatal deaths every year.[49]

➤ Only 5 percent of smokers who quit cold turkey are able to refrain from smoking for more than a year. Nicotine can be more addictive and harder to quit than heroin for many users.[50]

➤ Tobacco companies spent millions of dollars over the last thirty years to find ways to "manipulate" and "augment" nicotine, according to tobacco industry documents. Scientists at Philip Morris reported on human experiments that showed they could produce "enhanced" nicotine effects on a smoker's nervous system. The report was written by company scientists two months after tobacco executives testified that they did not "manipulate or independently control" nicotine levels.[51]

➤ Each year the tobacco industry loses about 1.3 million smokers who manage to quit and another 420,000 who die. Critics charge that the tobacco industry tries to replace them by enticing children to start smoking. Numerous tobacco industry documents make clear that the industry has perceived children as young as thirteen years of age as a key market, studied the smoking habits of children, and developed products and marketing campaigns aimed at them. Every day 3,000 teenagers become smokers.[52]

Weapons and the Military

The Question: Are you opposed to profiting from investments in weapons manufacturers and suppliers? This can include weapons employed in the national defense, those intended for personal use, or both.

The Issue: Having a strong military is still necessary in today's world. However, some investors do not want to profit from the defense industry. They argue that developing and deploying ever more sophisticated weaponry and selling weapons to politically unstable, nondemocratic countries escalates armed conflict and the potential for nuclear or chemical war. Many are also concerned with the inherent dangers of nuclear weapons and the enormous outlay on defense systems of tax dollars that could be used for life-enhancing purposes.

The weapons issue is also controversial on the domestic level. Weapons are designed to hurt or kill—a fact that troubles investors who want their money to do no harm. Cities and other government entities are beginning to sue gun manufacturers and sellers to reclaim some of the costs of gun-related violence. Efforts to pass gun control legislation are highly charged political issues.

The Case for Screening Weapons-Related Investments:

➤ Although the cold war is over, current military spending still approximates 85 percent of the 1976–90 annual average. At $270 billion, it makes up half the government's discretionary spending. The Pentagon says we need to defend ourselves against "rogue states"; however, North Korea spends only $5 billion per year on its military and Iraq, $1 billion.[53]

➤ The United States is arming the world, controlling 63 percent of worldwide arms sales. Millions of taxpayer dollars are spent annually on promoting commercial weaponry sales.[54] The U.S. arms industry sells $10 billion of weapons per year to antidemocratic governments that abuse the human rights of their citizens, engage in armed aggression against their neighbors, and are of questionable stability. The last five times U.S. troops were sent into conflict, including the Gulf War, they faced an enemy equipped with American-supplied weapons, technology, or training.[55]

➤ The presence of a gun in the house triples the risk of homicide in the home and increases fivefold the chance of a suicide.[56] Firearms kill more people between the ages of fifteen and twenty-four than all natural causes combined.[57]

➤ In 1996 handguns were used to murder 2 people in New Zealand, 213 in Germany, 15 in Japan, 106 in Canada, 30 in Great Britain— and 9,390 in the United States.[58] Including suicides and accidents, 37,502 Americans were killed that year with firearms. In comparison, 33,651 Americans were killed in the Korean War and 47,364 Americans were killed in the Vietnam War.[59]

Other Screening Issues

Religious Issues: Abortion, Birth Control, and "Family Values": Many institutional and individual investors do not wish their monies to support abortion or birth control. Thanks to church endowments that are screened on these issues (avoiding companies that make donations to groups such as Planned Parenthood), this is one of the top-five social screens in terms of monies affected. However, unlike the screens used more widely by SRI mutual funds and the Domini 400 Social Index, there are no performance studies to indicate what effect these screens have on the investors' bottom line.

Media and Products That Promote Violence: Some investors avoid segments of the entertainment industry whose movies, television programs, video games, and toys promote violence. These investors are concerned about the possible links between the casual or glorified violence in these products and the increasingly violent tendencies of our children and our society in general.

The U.S. Treasury: Some Natural Investors screen out U.S. Treasury bonds because the proceeds from their sale finance all aspects of government operations, which are sure to include some programs considered wasteful or wrong by virtually anyone.

Executive Pay: Many investors are outraged by multimillion-dollar CEO salaries and benefits, especially when a company is laying off workers and shifting jobs overseas. The CEO of a Fortune 500 company in 1998 made 326 times the average factory worker's pay, compared with only 44 times the average factory pay in 1965.[60] "There is no greater symbol of betrayal by Corporate America," says Chuck Collins, director of United for a Fair Economy, a nonprofit group addressing issues of economic justice. Activists are stepping up their pressure on corporations by introducing shareholder resolutions aimed at reining in excessive compensation.

Biotechnology: Many investors are concerned about the unforeseen consequences of genetic manipulation of plants and animals, and the patenting of life forms. Others, including many indigenous peoples, are upset at the "mining" of DNA from remote tribal peoples, which is viewed as the most profound cultural exploitation yet attempted; of concern are both cultural integrity and the lack of compensation when companies patent genetic traits culled from other cultures. In addition, many investors do not support the objectives of current research, such as the creation of herbicide-resistant plants that would enable agribusiness to apply massive doses of farm chemicals to the land.

The Medical Industry: There are several distinct rationales for avoiding the medical industry. Some people, such as alternative health advocates and Christian Scientists, feel that pharmaceuticals and Western medicine in general are disrupting our natural abilities to fight disease or intervening in a matter that is not ours to control. Others do not wish to profit from the operation of the HMO-based delivery system, which is seen as excluding the poor, valuing profits over good medicine, or both.

Resource Extraction: Many investors are uneasy with the environmental impacts of logging, mining, fossil fuel extraction, and overfishing. Those concerned about long-term sustainability may either avoid these industries or seek out innovative, often small-scale, companies that are supplying our demand for such products with minimal environmental impact and maximum responsibility.

Congratulations! You've made it through the issues that get Natural Investors riled up. But before we leave the avoidance screening spoke, we wish to note that there are many investors who screen for issues other than the ones we've covered. You, of course, are free to screen for any issue, product, or service that offends your common sensibilities. It's your house, so screen out anything you don't want to live with.

Screening for Quality: A Traditional Approach with a Twist of Social Conscience

NOW WE MOVE to the center of the evaluation axis. We've booted the most intolerable offenders out of our portfolio and we are ready to meet the rest of the investment universe. Here we find a world of companies that—no surprise—have their good points and their weaknesses. Our goal is to find profitable investments that lean toward the positive.

Some of these "quality issues" bring Natural Investors into realms that are very familiar to Wall Street. Financial analysts typically examine a company's products and services to see if they have qualitative advantages over those of the competition. Similarly, it is widely recognized that good management is a prime indicator of financial success.

Other issues on which Natural Investors focus are considered tangential by mainstream analysts. For example, having a strong record of charitable contributions and encouraging employees to volunteer in the community doesn't count for much on Wall Street. Yet initiatives like these frequently do translate to the bottom line through, for example, increased customer loyalty and improved employee morale.

Quality Issues

THIS SECTION IS modeled on the screening methodology developed by Kinder, Lydenberg, Domini & Co. to operate the Domini 400 Social Index. We have modified and added to some of their criteria in order to formulate this overview of quality screening.

Quality of Products and Services
Most of us have experienced the dismay of buying something that looked good but turned out to be a lemon. This is not so terrible if it's a blender, but what if you needed a heart pacemaker? One basic ethical tenet that makes good financial sense is to invest the way you shop—avoid companies that make junk and seek out those that emphasize quality products and services.
Strengths: A strong, companywide quality program and a recognition as a leader in the field. Active research and development of new, improved products and innovative services.

Concerns: A history of prosecution or involvement in controversies over product safety, consumer fraud, government contracting, or advertising and marketing practices.

Quality of Workplace

A company is made up of people. How people are treated has a major bearing on the bottom line. Some companies cling to the old "command-and-control" model, whereas others are constantly innovating as they seek ways to create satisfying, challenging workplaces.

Strengths: Employee involvement in decision making and innovative teamwork. Strong union representation. Profit sharing and good retirement benefits. Healthy and safe workplace conditions.

Concerns: Mass layoffs. Safety violations. Lack of retirement benefits. Poor union relations. Poor internal communications.

Quality of Diversity

In addition to screening out flagrant examples of discrimination, investors will want to determine whether the company encourages participation from a broad constituency among its management, workforce, and contractors.

Strengths: Board of directors and top management that include women and minorities. Family-friendly programs like child care and flex-time that support working parents. Innovative hiring programs for the disabled. Contracts with a significant number of women- and/or minority-owned businesses. Progressive policies toward gays and lesbians, such as provision for same-sex domestic partner benefits.

Concerns: Lack of woman and minority representation among senior managers and the board.

Quality of Community Participation

Corporations receive many benefits from our economic system; they should also give something back to the world and the communities in which they operate.

Strengths: Generous charitable giving, especially to programs that promote self-sufficiency among the poor. Support for housing and education programs. Programs that encourage volunteerism among employees.

Concerns: Adverse effects on the community. Controversies such as plant closings, environmental damage, and disruption of community life through corporate actions.

Quality of Environmental Practices

How do a company's operations affect the community and the Earth? Is it making messes or cleaning them up? Environmental issues are of vital importance to all of us. Companies that act responsibly often show improved profits, whereas those that pollute and waste resources may suffer unwanted financial consequences.

Strengths: A strong commitment to pollution prevention and reduction of resource consumption (including recycling programs). Honest public communication about the company's environmental impact. Prospectors (see the next chapter) may choose companies whose products or services directly contribute to a cleaner environment, such as those involved with remediation projects, recycling, and the promotion of energy efficiency or the use of renewable energy.

Concerns: Regulatory problems, liabilities for hazardous waste sites, pollution of various forms, and production of dangerous chemicals.

Quality of Corporate Disclosure

All efforts to screen and evaluate companies would be futile if they operated in complete secrecy—there would be little information to go on. Fortunately, U.S. securities laws require corporations to provide audited details of their financial operations. Investors and the public are now asking corporations to be more "transparent" regarding their social and environmental practices by providing objective, verifiable data and reports.

Strengths: Open communication about corporate activities, such as environmental impacts (including resource consumption and waste and pollution generation); employment practices (such as salary differentials between the best- and worst-paid employees); relations with subcontractors (especially in developing countries); and campaign contributions and lobbying activities. Look for signatories to voluntary codes of conduct (see Chapter 8) that require independent auditing of corporate social or environmental performance.

Concerns: Closed-door policies that limit access to anything other than corporate propaganda. Unwillingness to meet or engage in constructive dialogue with shareholders, customers, and citizen watchdog groups.

Shades of Gray: Life on the Road of Evaluation

AS YOU REFLECT on what you've learned on your tour of the issues, please keep one crucial tip in mind: Don't drive yourself crazy trying to find the perfect investment—it doesn't exist! Likewise, beware of the tendency to demonize companies that don't pass your screens. Our colorful world doesn't divide up neatly into black and white. Like people, companies are complex and changeable. Evaluating investments for their ethical suitability is an ongoing process of self-reflection and education. This is the "earnest soul-searching and unglamorous research" we cautioned you about in the Introduction. Here are just two examples of ethical quandaries cited in *Investing From the Heart* that are not unlike the dilemmas every conscientious investor must face:

> Amalgamated Automobile (fictitious) has an excellent record of hiring minorities (yea!). On the other hand, it has no female executives (boo!). It makes one of the highest-quality automobiles on the road, its cars giving consumers great value for their money and superb fuel economy (yea!). It has lobbied against stricter federal air pollution standards (boo!).
>
> The developers of trash-to-energy plants champion their process as a viable solution to both our nation's landfill shortage and our overdependence on fossil fuels. Of course, "trash-to-energy" sounds, on first blush anyway, like the essence of good environmentalism. However, in many communities where these projects have been proposed, citizens and environmental groups have resisted them, charging that the burning process released dangerous pollutants into the atmosphere.[61]

Avoidance Screening is a little like a parent taking the baseball bat away from a child after a window has been broken with it for the second time. The child is not evil—but he or she has crossed over a boundary and must suffer the consequences. With investing, you will need to think carefully about where you draw the line. Let's say you are opposed to investing in companies that make weapons. Would you invest in a consumer electronics company that derives 5 percent of its revenue from a military contract for a missile guidance system? What if it were only 1 percent? How about a telephone company that services a nuclear weapons installation?

We never guaranteed purity—it doesn't exist in our imperfect world. As you review your positions on each issue, be thinking about how much wiggle room you are comfortable with. Some issues may hit you very strongly, and you will decide that zero tolerance is essential. Moving down a notch, you could decide on a strong avoidance policy but include a slight margin of flexibility so that an otherwise suitable investment isn't eliminated.

Furthermore, even within an industry you dislike, you may decide to buy the stock of a company that is forging socially responsive practices. For instance, over a third of the Canadian economy is involved in resource extraction industries. Rather than avoiding these activities, many Canadian ethical investors make a conscious choice to invest in logging or mining companies that adhere to the highest environmental standards. This best-of-the-industry strategy is designed to reward companies that demonstrate the most sustainable practices. It also sends a message to major polluters that if they clean up their act they will be eligible for future investments.

Getting in Touch with Your Values

YOU HAVE NOW begun the nitty-gritty work of bringing your values into the world of investing. It requires courage, strength, and compassion to navigate through this maze of social issues. We hope you feel empowered by the process, knowing that you may choose to avoid investing in any of these areas. In the next chapter you'll find the skies a good bit sunnier, as we turn our attention to seeking out investments that speak to your positive aspirations!

Chapter 6 *Six*

Affirmative Screening: Prospecting for a Sustainable Future

N OW IT'S TIME to move beyond the confines of Avoidance Screening. We're about to venture into the wilderness, prospecting for treasures that excite our minds and ignite our passions. Like an old-time miner, prospectors sift through the corporate world, seeking flecks of gold that reflect their own sense of values. You may find this to be the highlight of your journey, a place where your unique interests and perspectives help you discover leading-edge companies doing something you especially want to support.

Searching for emerging, innovative companies is certainly not unique to Natural Investing. Wall Street is full of small-cap funds and newsletters trying to find the next Microsoft or Coca-Cola. But Natural Investors go one step beyond—not only must a company show great financial promise, it must also offer services or products that make a positive contribution to our world.

As with all Natural Investing strategies, we encourage you to bring your values into Affirmative Screening. For example, you moms (and dads) might want to peruse the list of "The 100 Best Companies for Working Mothers" (see Appendix B) for investment prospects. Some people focus on mainstream sectors such as medical research or agricultural productivity. Others have a connection with a particular company; maybe your daughter got a great job at Starbucks, or you love your Macintosh computer. Buying stock allows you to participate in the fortunes of companies that you frequent and respect.

Conservative or income-oriented investors can use bonds for Affirmative Screening. For example, municipal bonds can be purchased that
generate revenue for community projects like schools and hospitals (as
discussed in Chapter 11).

Sustainability: The Natural
Investor's Mother Lode

WE'RE ABOUT TO head into relatively undiscovered territory for
investors—business sectors leading the transition to a *sustainable economy*. Paul Hawken, in his landmark book *The Ecology of Commerce*,
defines sustainability as living in ways that do not reduce the capacity of
the environment to provide for future generations.[1] This is certainly the
defining issue of our times. As Norman Meyers of Oxford University
puts it, "The global economy is a wholly owned subsidiary of the planetary ecosystem."[2]

How will we go about changing humanity's unsustainable relationship with the Earth? Hawken declares that *business* is the only institution powerful enough to reverse global environmental and social degradation.[3] Interface Carpet CEO Ray Anderson fully embraces this
challenge, reminding fellow executives that business "is responsible for
most of the damage, but we can also be part of the solution. . . . We
must *take the lead* in directing the Earth away from collapse, and
toward sustainability and restoration."[4] When business sets its mind to
producing material goods it can rarely be stopped—imagine what could
happen if business turned this same power toward assuring the long-
term survival of our species!

This chapter covers several emerging trends within basic sectors of
the economy—including energy, food, forests, and transportation—that
are helping us move toward a sustainable economy in the twenty-first
century. Following this, we explore some big-picture initiatives that are
moving larger corporations away from Industrial Era plundering
(Anderson's term) of the Earth's resources. Corporations like Interface
and Xerox are leaders in a Second Industrial Revolution, redesigning
industrial processes with the goal of becoming sustainable.

To get you started on your prospecting quest, we've compiled in
Appendix B lists of companies that are involved in the sectors we're

about to explore. Appendix E contains various resources that will help you learn more about these topics and monitor late-breaking developments. Please note that the fact that a company is mentioned in this book does *not* imply that we are recommending purchase of their stock—situations change too rapidly to provide current tips in a book of this type. In addition, many of the leaders in the sustainable business arena are small companies; at the end of this chapter we'll take a look at both the great opportunities *and* the significant risks that small-company investing entails. But now, let's see if we can find some choice nuggets to add to your portfolio.

Warm Prospects for Renewable Energy and Conservation

FOSSIL FUELS PROVIDE 85 percent of the electricity and fuel we use in the United States. The twin dilemmas of limited supply and unwanted side effects have sparked a global search for solutions that depend on clean, noncarbon, "renewable" (inexhaustible) resources. Every possible avenue is being explored—even moon power: the moon's gravitational pull is responsible for tides, and in some coastal areas the amount of water flowing in and out is sufficient to run a turbine.[5] On the consumption side of the equation, conservation strategies are helping us reduce the need for new power plants.

Two methods of generating renewable energy, hydroelectric and geothermal, are already well established. Large hydropower dams produce inexpensive electricity but are controversial for various reasons, including disruption of fish habitat, flooding of scenic waterways, and siltation problems. Some dams are even being torn down. However, smaller hydropower systems that use existing flow are finding increasing applications in rural areas. Geothermal power (which heats the country of Iceland) is limited to areas where the Earth's crust is thin enough to get at the heat stored in magma below the surface.

If renewables are going to become the primary provider of power in the new century, then emerging technologies must be perfected and accepted in the marketplace. Corporate players—including BP Amoco, Enron, and Shell Oil—are making substantial investments in research. Government initiatives like the Million Solar Roofs Program are helping

to lower costs. Natural Investors who keep up with the latest developments have the opportunity to help capitalize promising technologies and
reap healthy profits. Here we focus on three technologies—two ancient
and one futuristic—that are ripe for Affirmative Screening investors.

Solar Power

The energy in the sunlight that hits the Earth every thirty minutes is
equivalent to humanity's annual energy consumption.[6] This energy can
be converted to electricity through various technologies. Photovoltaic
(PV; *photo-* = light, *-voltaic* = electricity) cells, the most common
device, were developed in the 1950s by Bell Laboratories.[7] One-quarter
of our nation's electricity needs could be met by covering 5,000 square
kilometers of roof space with such cells.[8]

Until now, the story has been one of incredible potential but frus-
tratingly slow implementation. The reason is simple: cost. The price per
watt generated has not been competitive with that of cheap "grid" electricity. But costs are coming down, from $60 per kilowatt-hour in 1970
to $1 in 1980 to $.20 to $.30 today (although even at this level they still
average three to four times the cost of electricity from fossil fuel
sources). And usage is climbing rapidly—over 120 megawatts of PV
cells were produced in 1997, a quadrupling of the production of a
decade ago. American manufacturers remain the world leaders but
are increasingly worried about competition from Japan and Germany,
both of which spend more than the United States to support solar
power programs.

PV cells are most commonly used in remote areas away from power
lines. Roughly half the usage is nonresidential, to power such facilities
as water pumps, portable highway signals, and telecommunications
repeater stations. Other uses for PV cells are in small consumer devices
such as calculators and watches. But residential demand is powering
the current boom. Some 500,000 homeowners are now generating their
own electricity. In the developing world, PV cells could provide nearly
2 billion people with essential electric services—such as lighting, communications, and refrigeration—for far less than the cost of adding
power lines to the main grid.[9]

Other promising uses of the sun's rays include solar thermal power
stations. Using concentrating mirrors, these desert-based systems produce temperatures as high as 3,000 degrees Celsius. Water is turned
into steam and run through turbines to make electricity. Solar power is

also used directly to heat buildings and water. Over a million solar water heaters have been sold in America, to be used in homes, factories, laundries, and swimming pools.[10] Buildings can utilize both passive systems, in which the building is designed to take advantage of winter sunlight, and active systems, which move and store heat. And, of course, providing natural, healthy lighting is simple—just install skylights!

Many companies, large and small, are jockeying for position in the growing solar power industry. As just one example, United Solar Systems offers thin-film "solar shingles" that turn an ordinary roof into a household power supply. Prospectors wishing to target solar electricity specifically may want to look at the stock offered by several domestic PV cell manufacturers and distributors (see Appendix B for listings and resources).

Wind Power

Wind power is now the fastest-growing energy source in the world. Installed wind electric generating capacity reached an estimated 9,600 megawatts in 1998, double what was in place in 1995. Worldwide, there is now enough capacity to generate about 21 billion kilowatt-hours of electricity—enough to meet the power needs of 3.5 million suburban homes.[11] Most of America's wind turbines are in California. However, three wind-rich states alone—North Dakota, South Dakota, and Texas—have enough wind potential to satisfy our nation's entire electrical appetite. Currently we know of no publicly traded stocks for companies specifically focused on wind power, but prospectors interested in this technology should keep an eye out for initial public offerings.

Fuel Cells and the Age of Hydrogen

Now we move into a realm that until recently was the secret province of spaceship designers. A cluster of companies and government researchers are feverishly working to rush fuel cells out of the lab and into our lives. Fuel cells are being primed to replace internal combustion engines, batteries, and power lines with a safe, clean fuel whose only exhaust is water vapor. This revolutionary technology is already here. Welcome to the age of hydrogen!

Hydrogen is the lightest and most abundant element in the universe. It constitutes about 93 percent of all atoms, or three-quarters of the mass of the universe—so we're not going to run out of it any time soon!

It is found in water (H_2O), fossil fuels (basically compounds of hydrogen and carbon), and all plants and animals.[12] However, hydrogen is not a primary fuel in the same sense as natural gas, oil, and coal. No wells pump it out of the Earth. Rather, hydrogen is a secondary form of energy that must be produced from other raw materials.

The race is on to develop cost-effective ways for making hydrogen gas. Several methods are being used—including ones that rely on the use of electricity, conversion of natural gas or coal, gasification of biomass (plant materials or sewage), direct use of sunlight, or even photoactive microbes. Ultimately it should be possible to produce hydrogen using completely renewable, nonpolluting sources.

What are fuel cells? From the outside, a small fuel cell could look like a battery that has a fuel tank hooked up to it. It just sits there and produces electricity without burning anything or making a peep. Inside, a chemical reaction is going on that splits the hydrogen molecules and combines them with oxygen (right out of the air). The result? Water vapor and electricity—nothing else!

The fuel cell was invented in 1839, but it wasn't until 1950 that the first practical, working fuel cell was demonstrated. Work accelerated in the 1960s as fuel cells were found to be the best choice for use in the Gemini and Apollo space missions. Today fuel cells provide the space shuttle with all its needs for electric power, and as a bonus supply pure drinking water.

General Electric is hot on fuel cells; in a joint venture with Plug Power, a fuel cell manufacturer, they aim to introduce home fuel cells in the year 2000. During 1999 test units will be in place in some homes; these lucky pioneers will be among the first to be able to unplug from the grid and make their own electricity with 40 percent efficiency (growing to 85 percent when heat is cogenerated in the process). The goal is to market units that produce electricity for less than $.10 a kilowatt.

There are a few companies working on hydrogen and fuel cell research whose stock can be purchased. One of these pioneers may one day become an industry titan in this new field. But prospectors be warned: speculative Wall Street investors have already jumped on board, causing some share prices to soar. You will want to learn all you can about the field and get to know the players before leaping in.

Green Power Comes Home

Recently changes in the utility industry have created a new lode for prospectors to explore—"green power." As utilities are deregulated, consumers are gaining the opportunity to choose among different power providers. Many customers have said they would be willing to pay a premium for electricity generated through renewable resources such as wind and solar. Now they are getting their chance.

Buying green power does not mean the actual electrons running your lights were produced by alternative means—all power still goes through the grid. It does mean that your utility payments will be supporting the producers who promise to add green power to the grid. Certification programs are coming on board so consumers can be certain that their money is being directed toward building and operating green power plants.

In 1998 privately held Sun Power Electric in Boston became the first all-PV solar utility company; they plan to mount solar panels on the flat roofs of retail stores. Patagonia, a California outdoor clothing manufacturer, has contracted to run all fourteen of its facilities on wind energy purchased from Enron Energy; to supply them, Enron is building a 16-megawatt wind farm near Palm Springs. In Minnesota, Northern States Power Company, which already had 265 megawatts of wind capacity installed as of 1998, has been ordered to construct an additional 400 megawatts by the Public Utility Commission; citizens' testimony on the issue was nearly unanimous in favor of moving forward with wind development, even if it costs a little bit more on their monthly bills.[13] If green power catches on in the marketplace, prospectors may soon have the opportunity to invest in a 100 percent renewable utility company.

Energy Conservation

Though lacking the glamour of fancy new power sources, energy conservation offers immediate, cost-saving solutions. The key is to identify where energy is wasted, so that the same work can get done more efficiently. This strategy runs the gamut from low-tech (like insulating the water heater) to ultra-high-tech, as in new computer chips that can run on less electricity. Amory Lovins, cofounder and director of research for the Rocky Mountain Institute, estimates that by using the most efficient technologies that already exist, we could save from one-half to three-quarters of our national energy tab.[14]

America has already started down the road to improved energy efficiency. Utility companies have discovered that it is cheaper and more profitable to help consumers plug air leaks and distribute compact fluorescent light bulbs (Southern California Edison has given away more than a million of these bulbs) than to build new power plants. Homeowners are choosing more efficient appliances and discovering that insulation can save money in the long run. Industry, subject to intense price competition, is investing in efficiency to improve the bottom line.

Prospectors will want to keep their eyes open for new technologies that get the job done using less juice. Manufacturers of better windows and lights, more efficient motors for industry, and advanced air conditioners and appliances are examples of companies that should prosper, especially when energy costs rise. Specialty retailers offer another promising avenue for investors. Real Goods Trading Company sells both renewable energy and conservation supplies via mail order and retail outlets. Their unique Solar Living Center in Hopland, California, demonstrates these technologies and has become a tourist destination.

Clean Transportation

A NEW GENERATION OF cleaner, greener vehicles are cruising off the drawing boards and onto the highways. Electric vehicles, using the latest nickel metal-hydride batteries, can now go over 260 miles on a charge, easily enough to drive from Boston to New York. General Motors was first to commercialize an electric car, the EV1. Toyota is having great success in Japan with a hybrid (gas and electric) car, the Prius, which gets 66 miles per gallon. Toyota plans to bring the Prius to North America in the year 2000. Virtually every major auto manufacturer is pouring R&D money into the race to create marketable alternative vehicles.

Two automotive giants, Ford and DaimlerChrysler, have joined with fuel cell pioneer Ballard Power Systems to commercialize fuel-cell-powered vehicles, with plans to have cars on the market by 2004. Other auto makers—including General Motors, Nissan, Honda, Volkswagen, and Volvo—are also developing cars around Ballard's "proton exchange membrane" fuel cell. With so many heavy hitters behind the technology, you know something will come of it. Keep your eyes peeled.

The Hypercar Center at the Rocky Mountain Institute, spearheaded by Amory Lovins, is pushing the envelope of vehicle design. A "hypercar" is ultra-light, with a carbon-fiber body that is safer than steel because it absorbs crash energy better; ultra-slick, due to its low wind resistance; and ultra-efficient, getting between 100 and 200 miles per gallon (even more once fuel cells have been incorporated). It runs on a small motor-scooter-sized engine and reversible electric motors that can recapture braking energy. And Lovins always emphasizes that these are not golf carts—hypercars will be fun, sporty, and fast! Of course the hypercar may idle auto mechanics, because it has one-tenth the moving parts of today's car. Dozens of companies are working on various aspects of hypercar design.

Hybrids and hypercars are exciting, but they will not solve all our transportation-related problems. Mass transit alternatives are being developed slowly in the United States—much of the rest of the world is way ahead of us. Meanwhile, bicycle sales have soared to over 100 million per year, with China in the lead. U.S. transportation planners are now required to incorporate bicycle use into new master plans. Electric bikes are also coming on fast both here and abroad, led by visionary companies like ZAP Power Systems. Natural Investors are wise to gaze down the road and seek out transportation solutions that minimize harm to the Earth and human communities.

Tree Savers

THROUGH THE AGES, people have delighted in both the beauty and the tangible gifts bestowed by the world's forests. Trees provide nearly everything a person needs to live: food, firewood, lumber, paper, medicine, and much more. Forests hold the soil, provide habitat for diverse creatures, and serve as the lungs of the planet, purifying and oxygenating the air. But as our population and rates of resource consumption have soared, human impact on forests has reached the danger point. Nearly half the forests that once covered the Earth are gone, and the scope and pace of deforestation are expanding and accelerating. The health and quality of our remaining forests are declining.[15]

Both consumers and industry must find ways to reduce consumption of virgin wood. Entrepreneurial opportunities await businesses that can satisfy our need for pulp and lumber without cutting down trees. Efforts have focused on two readily available sources: recycled materials and nonwood fibers. The extent of paper recycling has increased substantially, but there is still plenty of room for improvement. Companies like Seventh Generation make high-quality paper towels and bath tissue out of recycled paper. Many paper mills are increasing the proportion of recycled materials used in their products.

In the building trades, Kafus Environmental has developed an exciting tree-saving technology. Medium-density fiberboard (MDF) is a high-quality product used to make items like doors and cabinets. MDF is normally made by grinding up trees and gluing the particles into panels. But Kafus has a patented process that allows them to use landfill debris (which costs little, if anything) to make MDF. Their process also eliminates toxic outgassing of formaldehyde from the finished product. The first plant will go on line in Riverside, California, in 1999; Kafus has already presold the output to a furniture company that is building their plant next door.

The use of agricultural fibers also shows great promise. In the United States, over 300 million tons of economically and environmentally recoverable agricultural residues like rice, wheat and grass straw, and corn stalks are beginning to be utilized for building construction, paper, and other products. In addition, high-grade fiber could be grown on idle agricultural land, helping support rural farmers. Kenaf is a new crop that grows 14 feet tall in seven months and produces two to three times more fiber per acre per year than southern pine forests. Kenaf is drought-resistant, requires little fertilizer and no pesticides or herbicides, and can be recycled more effectively than paper from trees. Kafus Environmental is also a leader in this field; they are in the process of obtaining permits for the world's first kenaf paper mill, to be built in Texas. Mill effluent will be used to irrigate surrounding fields, and the paper will supply Texas publishers. Kenaf will also be used to make recyclable, biocomposite materials for automobile interiors.

Prospectors should keep a close eye out for new technologies and ongoing developments. For example, it is quite likely that industrial hemp (a nonpsychoactive relative of marijuana that was banned from cultivation early in this century) will make a comeback in America. Canada has already lifted its prohibition on the crop, and rural American farmers in several states are pressuring legislators to reopen the door to this incredibly useful plant. Certainly many other changes are in store as we learn how to take the burden off our precious forests.

Natural Food and Healthy Living Products

A GENERATION AGO, "health food" was the province of a small counterculture. Granola and tofu were still relatively unknown to the world at large; white bread was king. Today the natural foods market is growing at a phenomenal pace, working its way into America's heartland. Natural health care, including herbal medicines, nutritional supplements, and body care products, is gaining wide acceptance in the mainstream.

Several factors are contributing to this growth. People are learning that good nutrition is a major contributor to health. Many are concerned about ingesting chemicals used to grow and process food. Interest in natural healing methods is on the rise. Environmental concerns also weigh in; modern agriculture is plagued by excessive soil erosion, pesticide poisoning of workers and water aquifers, and dependence on heavy energy and water inputs. The family farm has all but disappeared in the face of corporate agribusiness. While bountiful harvests have fed a growing world, ecologists warn that these practices are unsustainable for the long haul. In 1997 U.S. spending on natural products reached $15 billion, with recent annual growth rates of 20 percent showing no signs of slowing. The success of natural supermarket chains such as Whole Foods and Wild Oats has led conventional grocery stores to increase their natural foods offerings, making it difficult to find a grocery store today that does not contain at least some natural food options. Wall Street is also taking notice, with a flurry of new conferences, newsletters, and Web sites keeping investors informed on this growing industry. Over $1 billion in capital was raised in public markets in 1997, with a record number of healthy living companies conducting initial public stock offerings (IPOs).

Blistering financial growth has spurred the creation of natural business stock indexes that track performance. (See Appendix B for lists of companies in these indexes.) The Natural Business Composite Index (NBCI) is composed of sixty-one natural food and consumer companies broken down into four categories—Botanicals and Supplements, Food and Beverage, Consumer Products, and Retail and Distribution.

The NBCI gained 44 percent in 1997, exceeding both the Dow and the Standard & Poor's 500 by a wide margin.

Healthy prospectors should follow their appetites and keep their eyes out for tasty stocks. Watch especially for IPOs from established names in the natural products industry. Despite all the recent growth, natural foods still account for only 2.4 percent of the total dollars spent on food. There is a great possibility that the industry's 20 percent annual growth rate could continue for years to come. Internet sites, such as www.naturalinvestor.com and www.naturalbiz.com, are a great way to keep up with the latest news in this field.

Recycling

EVEN THOUGH MORE and more cities and towns are offering recycling at the curbside or at landfills, the recycling industry is still in its adolescence. Industrial and construction recycling is a relatively new idea, and some companies are beginning to design their products for more complete reuse and recycling. Affirmative Screeners will want to keep abreast of the leading edges of this field, where they will find candidates for revolutionizing our attitudes toward industrial and residential waste. Magazines like *In Business* and *Biocycle,* as well as on-line research, are especially helpful in this area.

Environmental Cleanup

WHAT A MESS! Our industrial society has created a vast assortment of toxic substances that are not easily disposed of. Polluted surface water and groundwater, leaking storage tanks, radioactive waste, toxic lagoons, and oil spills all spell trouble for human and environmental health. But for concerned entrepreneurs, these trouble spots represent promising business opportunities.

Prospectors interested in cleaning up the planet must look carefully at the methods being used. Some so-called solutions, such as incineration, can create a whole new set of problems. But in the last decade exciting research has been performed on a more environmentally friendly approach known as bioremediation. Microbes and plants, nature's own cleanup crew, are capable of digesting some of our nastiest industrial by-products. Natural wetlands can convert raw sewage into drinking-quality water. We can expect to see increasing attention focused on these sorts of partnerships between technology and nature.

Green Real Estate

THROUGHOUT THE TWENTIETH century, two innovations have marched hand-in-hand across the American landscape: the automobile and suburbia. Increased mobility allowed us to gobble up inexpensive open space and agricultural land for tract housing. Although suburban living does offer material comforts, its inefficient use of resources, expensive infrastructure, and loss of neighborly interactions are causing many to rethink this model. People in both urban and rural areas are developing new forms of community that feature clustered housing, mixed-use (commercial and residential) zoning, and increased open space.

In Tucson, Arizona, Civano is the first large, mainstream real estate development to make sustainability a major design component. This showcase of what is known as the "new urbanism" will feature 2,800 solar homes, many of which will be built with alternative methods such as rammed earth and straw bales. Narrow, shaded streets will encourage walking and discourage speeding cars, while shops and community facilities will be designed to foster social interaction.

On a smaller scale, dozens of "cohousing" neighborhoods are springing up around the country. These clustered residential communities are designed to be family- and senior-friendly. Cars are kept to the periphery, and the "community house" features a dining hall and recreation facilities.

Investors will have to do a little digging to find green real estate opportunities. Developers in need of capital often turn to private investors, so you may want to contact developers of projects that interest you. As new forms of community spread, it's only a matter of time before we see the first green real estate investment trust (REIT).

The Next Industrial Revolution

AT THE CONFLUENCE of a number of themes of this book—sustainability, investing in leading-edge companies, and modeling our systems after nature's ways—a far-sighted group of industrial designers, executives, scientists, and environmental thinkers are busy plotting the next

Industrial Revolution. Natural Investors would be well advised to keep their radar tuned for signals from this direction, as companies restructure their production methods to improve both their financial and their ecological bottom lines.

The simple machines and systems at the heart of the first Industrial Revolution were based on the belief—reasonable at the time—that there was an inexhaustible reservoir of raw materials from which to draw and an infinite capacity for disposing of our wastes. As we now know, these assumptions were untenable over the long term. "What we thought was boundless has limits," acknowledges Monsanto CEO Robert Shapiro, speaking for many industrial leaders, "and we're beginning to hit them." He enthusiastically predicts that there's "a huge opportunity for reinvention . . . businesses grounded in the old models will become obsolete and die."[16]

New Industrial Design

A central tenet of the "new industrial design" movement is that we should generate *no* waste. Or, more to the point, recognize that one facility's waste can become another facility's raw material. William McDonough, visionary architect, points out that nature is not especially *efficient* (note the thousands of blossoms on a fruit tree, aimed at generating one or at best a few more trees); it is, however, highly *effective*. One measure of this effectiveness is that all the blossoms and fruits that never spawn trees eventually break down into nutrients for other trees and plants.

Unlike nature, in which everything is a nutrient for something else, McDonough calls attention to the fact that our industrial systems produce three distinct classes of products. *Consumable* products can be broken down by nature and become soil; he feels we should maximize our use of such products. *Industrial* products do not biodegrade; in his view, we must design closed-loop systems that allow us to reuse these products continually. *Toxic* products are harmful to life and should not be produced at all. The simple, key point made by McDonough is that these three processes must be kept separate.[17]

Obviously, to achieve these goals we must engage in extensive redesign of our production, building, and community systems. Paul Hawken highlights a consortium of industrial facilities in Kalundborg, Denmark, as an example of how groups of companies can step back and think big together. The Asnaes power plant recycles its waste heat in the form of steam, which it sends directly to the Statoil refinery and the Novo Nordisk pharmaceutical company. Surplus heat is used to warm greenhouses and residents of the local town. Meanwhile, the refinery produces surplus gas that it sells to a sheetrock factory; the sulfur that Statoil removes from the gas is sold to a chemical company. Waste heat from the refinery is used to warm the waters of a fish farm, and its fish sludge goes to local farmers as fertilizers . . . and the list goes on. Working together, these companies have created a very effective local exchange of nutrients, selectively feeding both biological cycles (fish and plant farms) and technical cycles (heat, gas, wastes, minerals).[18]

Closer to home, Interface, the world's leading commercial carpet company, has become the poster child of the new design revolution. Their "Evergreen Lease" transforms carpet tiles from a product (which produces waste) into a service (which maximizes employment). Rather than purchasing and installing carpet, customers pay a monthly lease fee assuring them of a constant supply of fresh-looking carpeting. As carpet tiles wear out and are replaced, the old ones are recycled and made into new tiles. Over time, the amount of virgin material use will drop but employment will rise—all while saving the customer money and providing a superior product. Meanwhile, Interface has streamlined its production processes, cutting pollution and energy consumption. CEO Ray Anderson proudly points to the fact that in 1997 waste reduction programs allowed the company to increase sales by 20 percent without taking any more materials from the Earth.[19]

Xerox, too, has devoted significant attention to new industrial design. Their "Green Machine" document center product line is part of the Xerox Zero Landfill initiative. All parts are earmarked for reuse or reconstruction into other useful products. These sorts of retoolings and rethinking of basic design priorities take significant amounts of time and money; yet more companies are making these deep and transformative commitments. They believe that the benefits, both financial and social, will far outweigh the costs.

> **"** *Our thinking is backwards: We shouldn't use more of what we have less of (natural capital) to use less of what we have more of (people).* **"**
>
> —PAUL HAWKEN

The Natural Step

In 1989 Swedish physician Karl-Henrik Robèrt's Natural Step process emerged out of an extensive consensus process among fifty leading scientists whose goal was to develop a concrete, scientific foundation for designing sustainable systems. Since then, The Natural Step (TNS) has found a foothold in government and business circles in both Europe and North America. By avoiding the tendency to point fingers, and relying instead on seeking the wisdom of the business world in resolving pressing imbalances in our systems, TNS is fast becoming the new design movement's most important training process. Says Robèrt, "I think most people in business understand that we are running into a funnel of declining resources globally. . . . Those who direct their investments more skillfully towards the opening of the funnel will do better in business than their competitors."

The core of TNS training and design revolves around four "system conditions" that underlie a sustainable society. First, substances from the Earth's crust must not systematically increase in nature. Second, substances produced by society must not systematically increase in nature. Third, the productivity and diversity of nature must not be systematically diminished. And fourth, we must be fair and efficient in meeting basic human needs. As you can see, these principles are simple and direct; they are concepts that businesses can get their hands around, and use as levers for making concrete changes in their own internal systems. As applied to society as a whole (many local and regional governments have begun applying TNS in their planning), the approaches include community education, more efficient cycling of resources, and an emphasis on being equitable with the resources that are available.

Small Is Beautiful, Powerful, . . .
and a Little Scary!

SUSTAINABLE PRINCIPLES ARE now being embraced by businesses ranging from a horse-drawn recycling company in Vermont to multinational energy-and-chemical-intensive giants. Although large-company initiatives are essential to the health of our planet, many Affirmative Screeners turn to small companies for more of a "pure play." Often founded by visionary, committed entrepreneurs, these companies are nimble enough to capitalize on niches overlooked by the big guys. With skill and a little luck, they can efficiently target emerging market opportunities and grow them into a successful business. Since smaller companies operate under the radar screen of most institutional investors, Affirmative Screeners may discover unappreciated seedlings that could produce profitable fruits.

Every company needs capital to take root and grow; prospectors can play a crucial role. By investing in smaller start-up companies, you help provide the financial fertilizer needed to make their good ideas flourish. It is also possible to help plant these seeds of sustainability even before a company offers stock to the public. This is the realm of venture capital, in which far-sighted (and very risk-tolerant) investors provide funds for the earliest stages of a new company's operations. We cover venture capital more fully at the end of Chapter 12, but we mention it here because it is an important financial tool for creating a new sustainable economy.

Before jumping into the world of small companies, here's one big cautionary note: Keep your eyes open at all times! Just because an idea sounds good or resonates with your ideals doesn't mean it will succeed in the competitive marketplace. As one prospector put it, "These companies are trying to do something that has never been done before, with people who have never done it before."

In addition, structural imbalances in our economy can work against young upstarts. Running an environmentally conscious business has been likened to driving with the brakes on. Our economic system frequently allows the price of environmental damage (e.g., the health consequences of pollution) to be "externalized," meaning that the cost is picked up by the public instead of the producer. This has the effect of penalizing responsible companies who take extra precautions to protect the environment or otherwise operate in a more sustainable manner. Government policies can also skew the field. For example, massive subsidies that support the nuclear and fossil fuel industries (including a sizable chunk of the Defense Department budget) dwarf the limited funding for renewable energy research.

In short, these stocks can take you on a roller coaster ride. If you don't have the stomach for unpredictable volatility then, please, just say "no, thank you." If you *do* go small-company prospecting, use only a small portion of your overall portfolio—one that allows you to remain within your financial comfort zone. Of course, careful research is also crucial, so do your homework!

Following the Leaders

ALBERT EINSTEIN ONCE observed, "The world will not evolve past its current state of crisis by using the same thinking that created the situation." Look for more companies to adopt the cyclical thinking of new industrial design in the years to come. These companies are building on a deep understanding of the way natural processes unfold in the world around us. As science and industry begin to understand the vastly more subtle, cyclical, and connective processes of nature, the next Industrial Revolution will no doubt yield a transformative array of products and social designs. The companies that lead the way may well become the economic giants of tomorrow; by investing in them you can participate in what is sure to be an exciting period for humanity.

Chapter Seven

Community Investing

L INDA KRUHMIN-FRIEDMAN probably wouldn't call herself rich, but she has been building her savings and investments for a while now. Wishing her money could have a more direct impact on the world, she also looked for a human return. Though she didn't make enough to donate large amounts to charitable groups, she still wanted to make a difference.

Through a friend, Linda learned of the Calvert Foundation, through which individuals could safely invest in low-income communities and families. Linda decided she could commit some resources to an investment that preserved her capital while creating opportunity for those less fortunate. She purchased a one-year $3,000 Calvert Community Investment Note, with a 3 percent interest return. With this investment, Linda had safely sent her money to work in dozens of different programs throughout this country and abroad.

Meanwhile, not far from Linda, in Chicago's mostly Latino Little Village, Justina Santa Maria was supporting herself with day jobs, rising daily at 5:00 A.M. to pack goods or clean a factory. Wages were low, the take-home pay minimal after taking out the agency's fee. Justina, however, began to make traditional Mexican relish: *jalapeños en escabeche.* With her husband Fernando, she prepared 500 two-pound containers each week, cooking one small pot at a time. Gradually, she built up a list of clients, including fruit markets and grocery stores. But the process was so time consuming they could not increase their production. Then

Justina discovered Accion Chicago, one of the organizations funded by Linda's Calvert Community Investment Note.

With the help of an Accion Chicago microloan, Justina and Fernando rented a small commercial space with a restaurant-quality stove and increased production with tamperproof glass jars and labels. They have since grown to serve more than 135 stores in greater Chicago— and have even hired an employee. Though Linda and Justina have never met, and perhaps never will, their lives are connected. Community investing has created a bond between them.

Hundreds of Lindas can grow to thousands; and those thousands, willing to invest in communities around the world, can make a difference—one microloan, one renovated housing unit, one Justina Santa Maria at a time.

COMMUNITY INVESTING IS a powerful local form of putting your money to work in the service of your values. By providing hardworking individuals and organizations with the financing they need to help themselves, Community Investing offers solutions to many twenty-first-century challenges, from inner-city decay to the decline of the rain forests. Anyone who remembers banker George Bailey's service to his own hometown in the movie *It's a Wonderful Life* realizes that community banking is hardly a new idea. It boils down to investing money in the people who are making the community a better place to live.

Unlike screened stock purchases or even shareholder activism, both of which keep the investor at some distance from the action, community development financial institutions (CDFIs) let you put your money directly into the hands of people operating at the grass-roots level of social change. These organizations catalyze a lasting sort of self-help that is built on individuals working together to solve their own problems. Your CDFI investment can help revitalize a community, alleviate poverty, empower individuals and families, and provide access to capital for those traditionally confined to the economic sidelines. Not a bad social return to any Natural Investor's portfolio.

This chapter features profiles of a representative sampling of CDFIs, located both at home and abroad. We share some success stories to illustrate the growing enthusiasm of savers and borrowers. These institutions are not "the best"; they are simply a sampler of the sorts of programs of which you can seek to be a part through Community Investing.

You may want to support a local bank, while also investing in a certificate of deposit (CD) or loan fund at another institution that supports a type of social impact that is especially important to you. Appendix D includes contact information that can help you locate local, regional, and international options.

Our definition of CDFIs includes community banks and credit unions, as well as community loan funds and international microcredit programs. **Community banking** offers a way for virtually all of us to bring values into our financial lives. Even if you only have a checking account, you can find a bank or credit union that reflects your sense of community while it holds your hard-earned paychecks. Savings accounts and small beginning investments such as CDs and Individual Retirement Accounts (IRAs), also available through community banks and credit unions, are exciting ways for many to take the first steps toward investing without sacrificing, or ignoring, their principles. Most of these vehicles pay standard market rates and provide comparable deposit insurance.

Most community banks are committed to specific, targeted needs in their own areas. Some focus on low-income housing, others on women- or minority-owned businesses; many become active in the nonprofit sector by making initial loans to programs such as homeless shelters or health care organizations. In many cases, the beneficiaries of community banks would not ordinarily be served by mainstream banks; these loans often support the crucial first steps to entering the economic mainstream.

For socially conscious investors seeking to improve their own hometowns with immediate and even participatory social results, community banking constitutes an important investment option. George Bailey would be happy to know that in this era of global corporate banks with few ties to local settings, some banks remain committed to recycling their financial resources within the communities in which they operate.

Community loan funds take the principle of getting capital to the underserved a step further. In some areas, loan funds fill gaps in the availability of community banking; in others, they serve borrowers who cannot afford or qualify for bank loans. Loan funds get their capital from investors who support their specific areas of focus.

Moving to the international arena, one of the most dramatic developments in recent years is the global recognition of the power of

microcredit to introduce economic development on a scale that works for, rather than against, the interests of individuals and communities. By providing small, low-interest loans to poor but aspiring entrepreneurs with little or no collateral, microcredit pioneers have paved the way for a revolution in local economies throughout developing countries.

Bob Hope once quipped that "a bank is a place that will lend you money if you can prove that you don't need it." Indeed, traditional financial institutions like to make big loans to people who already have a lot of money. It seems safer to them, since the customer has a proven track record and can put up collateral. In contrast, CDFIs tend to make small loans to people with very little money. At first glance this would seem to be a risky proposition. But borrowers from CDFIs have an excellent track record of repaying loans; most institutions report loan repayment rates of 96 to 99 percent. Not only is this well above traditional bank repayment rates, but when there are defaults, internal loss reserves protect investors.

Why are these "risky" borrowers so successful? There are two key reasons, both of which offer powerful nonfinancial collateral—securing the loans in ways traditional banks may not recognize. First, these customers are hardworking and highly motivated, knowing that this may be their only chance to begin climbing the ladder of financial freedom. Second, potential borrowers are thoroughly screened for creditworthiness; those who are lacking in some area (perhaps accounting or marketing skills) are coached until they are deemed ready to utilize a loan profitably. Most CDFIs offer technical assistance—training and support in managing small enterprises. The power and usefulness of this service cannot be overestimated.

The Financial Advantages

NOT ONLY IS Community Investing an effective way to get money into the grass roots, it's also a wise outlay in a diversified portfolio. As you make your asset allocation decisions, any monies that you choose to keep in cash or in low-risk investments might be considered as potential Community Investment assets. The parts of your portfolio that offer moderate, consistent returns, such as savings accounts and money-market checking accounts, could be replaced with proactive community-oriented vehicles.

For those willing to consider sacrificing some return on a portion of their portfolio, many loan funds and microcredit institutions accept investments only at below-market interest rates, ranging from 0 to 4 percent. These funds serve programs and individuals at the margins of the economy, offering footholds on the climb to more traditional economic participation. Those with special concern for social justice may be very happy to put a substantial portion of their assets into such programs. Their principal is safe from stock market volatility, moral dilemmas, or both, and they will be putting their money directly into the hands of those who can make the most socially powerful use of it. A small reduction in annual interest payments translates into putting a large amount of money to work throughout the life of the loan; it's an unusually abundant form of easy philanthropy.

Although the amount and proportion of the portfolio devoted to community banking will depend on the investment style and priorities of each individual, a good number to consider is 10 percent. Ten percent offers a solid—often FDIC-insured—safety net to any Natural Investing portfolio. You can choose to focus on your own community, or to put some monies to work in extremely disadvantaged areas of America or the world.

Community Development Banks and Credit Unions

COMMUNITY BANKS AND credit unions rank among the safest CDFI investment opportunities; accounts are FDIC-insured up to $100,000. Typically these institutions offer checking, savings, and money-market accounts, CDs, and IRAs.

Community banks base their loan-making decisions on community needs as much as on profitability. They do not forgo profitability, but their primary business goal may not be profit maximization. Community development credit unions operate as member-owned nonprofit financial institutions, offering all the services available at conventional credit unions. If your area has no community banks or credit unions, you can establish savings or checking accounts at a distant institution, so long as you don't mind mailing your deposits and making electronic withdrawals from an ATM or a local bank you use for this purpose.

Albina Community Bank (Portland, Oregon): Sustaining a Minority Neighborhood

It was a story often repeated. The E & M Community Market, the last major grocery store to serve the largely African-American neighborhoods of northeast Portland, Oregon, was to close its doors after years of steady decline in an area beset by the typical big-city problems of unemployment, poverty, and crime. For an elderly population to whom a trip across town to shop for groceries was an extreme hardship, the closing made an already difficult life even harder.

A group of community lenders, inspired by a local pastor, joined together to save the store. They recognized that preserving and improving the community store could be a way to revitalize the entire neighborhood. Albina Community Bank led the $800,000 financing effort; their initial funding brought Key Bank and the Portland Development Commission into the project, which has also garnered the support of the religious community, local schools, and the police department. Today not only do these residents still have the E & M, they've also had the community-rebuilding experience of having worked together to solve a common problem.

Albina's story is a good example of how community banking can be a serious, politically dynamic force in local cultures, changing living conditions in ways that build directly on the goals and gains of the civil rights movement. Leon Smith, founding CEO of Albina, has boldly declared, "Economic development is critical to the health and welfare of the African-American community, indeed, of all minority groups. Progress towards creating a whole and healthy African-American community will come only when we treat economic achievement with the same urgency, conviction, and organization as when we occupied the moral high ground to achieve unfettered civil rights. We can achieve it through collective economic effort."[1]

Shorebank Pacific (Ilwaco, Washington): An Eco-Bank Looks to the Future

Created through the combined efforts of Chicago's South Shore Bank and Ecotrust, a Portland-based environmental organization, Shorebank Pacific is a bit of a hybrid in the community banking field. Instead of trying to be a financial force for the poor, Shorebank functions as a voice for the environment, again seeking to meet the investor's needs for profit through enterprise that is consistent with ecological goals.

By helping safeguard the environment, create jobs, and improve the economy, the bank and its depositors aim to be a force for rebuilding healthy rural communities. Shorebank Pacific's goal is conservation-based development, working with companies that meet a number of key requirements. Their standards are chock full of hard-core sustainability benchmarks, including reducing and using waste, utilizing the most energy-efficient methods, and improving industry standards for restorative fishing, farming, and forestry.

The type of local partnership they advocate is taking shape in the Columbia River and Willapa Bay region. One of the last clean estuaries in the United States, this area was ripe for proactive vision. Ecotrust staffers rallied local residents to recognize the opportunity they had to maintain their vibrant ecosystem and to safeguard the long-term stability of their harvests. Business owners involved in this program earn a good living while ensuring that the oysters, salmon, timber, cranberries, and other resources on which the region's economy depends will continue to be harvested for generations.

Vermont National Bank's Socially Responsible Banking Fund (Brattleboro, Vermont): A Bank within a Bank as a New Model for Change

Enid Wonnacott, director of the Northeast Organic Farming Association of Vermont (NOFA), kept hearing a familiar tale from small organic farmers: their banking needs were not being met. Most farmers described the same set of financing problems. First, loans to farmers (especially small loans used for farm equipment and working capital) often have high interest rates. Second, the seasonality of a farmer's monthly income makes conventional loan payment schedules difficult to meet. And finally, many banks are simply unfamiliar with farming, especially organic farming.

A $90,000 low-interest loan from Vermont National's Socially Responsible Banking Fund, along with an anonymous $30,000 gift from a Fund supporter, have allowed NOFA to set up a revolving loan fund to address these needs. Applications are reviewed by an advisory board that includes farmers, extension agents, and technical assistance providers. As loans are repaid, funds become available for future borrowers.

Vermont National's Socially Responsible Banking Fund represents a growing trend in community banking: the establishment of a small, community-oriented fund within a larger, traditional bank. These dedicated deposit programs are often catalyzed by grass-roots activists, who work with bank management to set up an independent management team and board of advisers. When you open an account at Vermont National, you can choose to dedicate your deposits to the Socially Responsible Banking Fund. This model is beginning to be replicated around the country; examples include BankBoston's First Community Bank and First National Bank of Santa Fe's Community Connections fund.

Social fund deposits support flexible loans for affordable housing, environmental and conservation projects, sustainable agriculture, education, and small and dual-bottom-line (i.e., social and financial) businesses. "The key to every loan is that the borrower must be benefiting the community," says former director David Berge. "It is perceived that it's risky to loan to small borrowers and nonprofit organizations. That's a stereotype that's simply not true. Borrowers from the fund seldom default on loans and they are rarely late in making payments. We try to function as though we live next door to everybody in our community. We're not reinventing banking, we're uninventing it. We make smaller loans, but they have a high community impact; and we're outperforming other banks."[2]

Wainwright Bank & Trust Company (Boston, Massachusetts): Financing Essential Social Services

At Wainwright, Natural Investors have met social justice issues head on. In the Boston area, Wainwright represents one-quarter of a percent of the total banking assets but has financed over 50 percent of the housing for people living with AIDS. The bank's progressive agenda includes a commitment to affordable housing, food banks, legal service for low-income residents, breast cancer research, environmental protection, women's rights, and the gay and lesbian community. The success of such an agenda offers its own best evidence. The 20 percent of Wainwright's loan portfolio that is currently committed to community development lending is the best-performing segment of the portfolio, with a default rate of less than 1 percent.

South Shore Bank (Chicago, Illinois): The Definitive Modern Community Bank

South Shore Bank has the oldest community banking program. In twenty-five years South Shore's Development Deposits has enabled South Shore to lend over $400 million to more than 11,000 businesses and individuals. Since 1973 South Shore has financed the rehabilitation of 17,000 affordable housing units, getting residents and local businesses involved in neighborhood reclamation in the process. By putting the human side of banking first, South Shore has contributed substantial support to the notion that investors can profitably invest their capital in worthwhile social endeavors. Their leadership role has attracted both deposits and emulation from across the country.

Self-Help Credit Union (Durham, North Carolina): Microlending Pioneers

Self-Help Credit Union has taken an active role in many areas typical of community banking: minority-owned business, low-income home ownership, and local social service programs. Beyond this, Self-Help is also at the forefront of the new microlending movement. Tailored banking services address the unique needs of immigrant communities such as Latinos and Vietnamese, who may possess entrepreneurial drive and experience but lack collateral, credit, or established business records in this country. To give these business owners a start, Self-Help has developed the Staged Microloan program, through which owners can borrow and repay successively larger amounts, starting with as little as $500. Once borrowers establish a sound credit history with these loans, they become eligible for larger loans. Many staged microloans are for home-based businesses, providing such services as child care and auto repair.

Community Development Loan Funds

COMMUNITY INVESTING STEPS even closer to marginalized sectors of our economy with community development loan funds (CDLFs). There are over 300 such funds in the United States, most operating in specific geographic areas. Like the community development banks, they vary greatly in size and purpose.

In general, CDLFs pick up where most banks leave off, providing loans to individuals and organizations that find it difficult to get bank loans. In many cases, they serve customers who would find it hard to meet the fairly traditional loan terms of even the community banks. Virtually all receive grants and subsidies to cover some of their operating expenses; these often allow them to make loans at below-market rates. Likewise, they tend to bring their investors into the spirit of cooperation and usually pay less than market rates for funds loaned to them. Most CDLFs are small by banking standards; the capital they gather from investors is pooled into a revolving loan fund from which they make small loans to their clients.

Because the FDIC does not insure them, CDLFs are considered the riskiest form of CDFIs. However, these funds are not charities; they apply due diligence in making loans, and the National Community Capital Association reports that through 1997 its members have loaned $709 million with a cumulative repayment rate of 99 percent.

To illustrate the range of activities being pursued by CDLFs, we profile a few representative examples. Appendix D includes a more complete listing of local loan funds, which you can use to discover the ones that best match your social or geographical investing goals.

Institute for Community Economics (Springfield, Massachusetts): Catalyzing the Formation of Land Trusts

In Gloucester, Massachusetts, a traditionally working-class fishing port and summer resort north of Boston, expensive and scarce housing squeezes lower-income families out of the housing market. Wellspring House, a local grass-roots organization providing shelter for homeless families, learned about community land trusts (CLTs) at an Institute for Community Economics (ICE) conference and saw that a CLT would provide a way to preserve and create affordable homes in Gloucester. With technical assistance from ICE, the Community Land Trust of Cape Ann (CLTCA) was born in 1989.

CLTCA wanted not only to provide housing but also to rebuild neighborhoods in this tightly knit New England community. CLTCA envisioned revitalizing a whole street located on Gloucester's working harbor and plagued by absentee-owned slum housing, crime, drug dealing, and domestic violence. It acquired one "triple-decker" building on Granite Street in 1991, renovated the apartments, and sold them to first-time home buyers. After three years of planning, CLTCA acquired eight buildings in 1996 and renovated nineteen apartments. In 1997 it sold the first home on the newly rechristened Haven Terrace—a name reflecting the new life of the street. As part of ICE's long-term support, site visits from its staffers helped CLTCA to address the thorny issue of creating homeownership without displacing the current tenants of the street and strengthened the residents' ability to raise funds effectively in their community.

ICE was created in 1977 to encourage changes in patterns of land and housing ownership and increase the flow of capital into low-income communities. Through its National Revolving Loan Fund, capitalized by investments from individuals and institutions, ICE has provided over $30 million in short-term loans for a variety of community-strengthening projects. ICE tailors its loan packages to meet the diverse needs of CLTs and other organizations. This customization allows ICE to collaborate creatively with other financial players, including banks, foundations, and government agencies.

Along with Robert Swann of the E. F. Schumacher Society, ICE pioneered the CLT model and today is the nation's leading source of information on CLTs. ICE publishes manuals and offers training programs and consulting services. They have assisted community activists in establishing more than 100 CLTs nationwide, providing more than 4,400 units of permanently affordable housing.

Northern California Community Loan Fund (San Francisco, California): Social Impact through Revolving Loans

Brava! For Women in the Arts, located in San Francisco's largely Latino Mission District, received a loan to acquire and renovate the old York Theater, which had been abandoned for five years. The Brava! Theater Center will include two theater spaces and five storefronts. The Northern California Community Loan Fund (NCCLF) committed a loan of $285,000 and provided the only private funding involved in the acquisition of the theater. Brava! has developed several innovative programs that bring together the arts and community-building in this low-income neighborhood; in one program, youth residing at a nearby public housing project learn basic theater skills, write performance pieces, and study videography.

The Black Coalition on AIDS (BCA) offers innovative programs to San Francisco's African-American communities. Its Rafiki House, a path-breaking transitional residence for people with HIV, is the only city program that accepts people coming directly from detox programs without an extended period of sobriety. The NCCLF extended a $25,000 line of credit at a pivotal time in the organization's development, so that BCA could meet their day-to-day operating needs—an area often overlooked by traditional lenders.

Through these and other similar ventures, the NCCLF has taken a proactive role in meeting the social needs of low-income communities.

In addition to its core activity of lending to nonprofit organizations, NCCLF also finances developers of affordable housing, providers of human services such as health care clinics and employment organizations, and generators of jobs and economic activity for local residents. It operates throughout northern California. During its first decade of operations, NCCLF disbursed $4.8 million in fifty-seven loans.

Cascadia Revolving Fund (Seattle, Washington): Capital for New Business

Cascadia has filled a key niche in the Pacific Northwest, providing start-up capital for small businesses deemed too risky for bank loans. In its first ten years of operation, it lent over $7 million, primarily to lower-income women and minority-owned businesses and to environmentally focused companies. More than 90 percent of the businesses it has supported were still in business in 1997, and they had created or preserved over 7,000 jobs. In all of its years of lending, Cascadia has lost less than 1 percent of its loan dollars and no investor dollars.

Accion U.S. (Somerville, Massachusetts): Microcredit in America's Cities

Accion International is a world leader in microlending, as we'll see in the following section on international microcredit banking. Their U.S. Bridge Fund allows Natural Investors to participate in building the loan portfolios of its six U.S. associate programs, located in Brooklyn, San Antonio, El Paso, Albuquerque, Chicago, and San Diego. Since 1994 the U.S. network has provided over 3,000 loans totaling more than $8 million to microenterprises unable to obtain credit from traditional sources. The results so far are tangible and impressive. Accion San Diego's experience offers typical evidence for the impact of microcredit. More than 28 percent of its loans are made to clients who receive some sort of public assistance. A 1994–95 study of repeat clients shows a 281 percent increase in the dollar value of the owners' equity and a 30 percent increase in average monthly business profits. Most impressively, the number of jobs supported tripled, from under one to nearly three employees per business.

International Microcredit Banking

WE NOW TURN to what is for many the most exciting venue in Community Investing: microcredit banking. Both nationally and internationally, microcredit is enjoying a boom of expectations and attention. On every continent, millions of investment dollars are flowing into vegetable stalls, mini–grocery stores, shoe repair stands, and other businesses conceived and nurtured by the world's poorest entrepreneurs.

Evidence from around the world has demonstrated that with small loans, business training, and peer support, microentrepreneurs can create personal and economic success for themselves, their children, and their communities. With affordable credit have come savings opportunities, the development of leadership skills (especially among women), and many other social benefits. Children tend to stay in school longer, while communities report more balanced gender roles, individual empowerment, and a restored sense of hope.

> **"** *The first Microcredit Summit announces to the world a discovery of enormous power. The seed of sustainable development ·and the road out of poverty, so elusive despite enormous efforts, lie not in massive public handouts but in tapping the wealth found even in the most economically fragile sectors of our societies: the self-initiative of the world's poor men and women.* **"**
>
> —MICHAEL CHU, President of Accion International

The International Microcredit Summits in 1997 and 1998 have launched a global initiative to take credit to half a billion of the poorest people on the planet by the year 2005, and to all of the world's 1.3 billion poor by the year 2025. The goal is to channel $21.6 billion into microcredit loan funds over the next quarter-century. The two summits were attended by representatives of 110 countries. Participants included heads of state, officials of international corporations and financial institutions, microcredit practitioners, and representatives of bilateral donor agencies, nongovernmental organizations, foundations, educational institutions, religious organizations, and United Nations development agencies.

The microcredit movement bodes well for the 1.3 billion individuals who live in what the United Nations calls "absolute poverty." According to the Microcredit Summit, ten new community banking organizations emerge each week, each emulating the Grameen Bank model in important ways. Therefore, we'll center our look at microcredit on the amazing journey of Muhammad Yunus and Grameen Bank.

The Grameen Story: The First Community Bankers

Muhammad Yunus, a Fulbright scholar who earned his Ph.D. at Vanderbilt University, was headed for a career consistent with the comfort and success of the wealthy business family into which he had been born. After earning his degree in 1971, he returned to Bangladesh to teach, rising quickly to become chair of the economics department at Chittagong University.

It was the famine of 1974 and a chance meeting with Sophia Khatoon that changed his life. Sophia, a twenty-two-year-old skilled furniture-maker in a tiny village, worked seven days a week, looked twice her age, and lived in poverty. She made stools and chairs out of bamboo, which she had to sell to a money-lender that provided the credit to buy the raw material. The price she received barely covered her costs. Yunus calculated that Sophia was paying interest at an effective rate of 10 percent a day—more than 3,000 percent a year. Yunus could not reconcile the fact that a hard-working woman who produced such beautiful furniture and created wealth at such a high rate was earning so little.

Yunus loaned her 50 taka, just a few dollars. Within a few months she repaid the loan, increased her income sevenfold, and became officially self-employed. The Grameen Bank Project was born.

Yunus states, "In fact, the poor all over the world are trapped in such exploitation. While they work extremely hard and create enormous wealth, the middle-men, money-lenders, and employers keep the fruits of their labor. The poor have no access to 'institutional credit,' which you and I have, because they cannot provide collateral. The system keeps them firmly trapped in debt, poverty, and exploitation."[3]

Yunus has by now spent a quarter-century building the Grameen Bank, one of the world's most remarkable financial institutions. He is among the leading social innovators of his generation, and perhaps in the history of our economic system—a social entrepreneur who has pioneered microlending. Microlending changed a fundamental rule of world finance: lend big to people with money. Instead, Yunus's rule is to lend a little to people with no money, while providing the training and structure that can help small economies succeed. The lessons of this new business model have fueled the explosion of Community Investing the world over.

Yunus and Grameen (which means *village* in Bangladeshi) focus on making loans as small as $30—just enough to get a microbusiness started. A fundamental Grameen principle is the *less* you have, the *higher* priority you get in receiving loans from the bank. Grameen does not ask for collateral; instead, it requires borrowers to organize into small groups and guarantee one another's loans. The group plays a key role in the Grameen style of banking—it acts as a loan committee and as a monitoring, supervising, and problem-solving body.

The lending is almost exclusively to women, who account for 94 percent of the bank's customers. Loans are paid back in weekly installments; each week Grameen staffers go to all 36,000 villages to do banking with their borrowers on their own doorsteps. The Grameen staff walks borrowers through the basics of business and credit, as well as literacy and human dignity. By combining access to credit with access to information, they change the game for the rural poor.

The results have been stunning. Over the past two decades, Grameen Bank has grown to include nearly 1,100 branches, covering every corner of Bangladesh. It has made more than 2 million loans worth a combined $2 billion, boasting a loan-repayment rate of 97 percent. Borrowers buy everything from tools for mending fishing nets, to seeds for planting, to goods to sell door-to-door or in markets.

Do poor villagers in Bangladesh make good capitalists? Yunus answers, "All human beings are basically entrepreneurs. People want to solve problems, take on challenges, and discover their talents. It's just a matter of opening up the environment and giving them opportunity. Getting people into the market is the best way to let them solve their problems. That's what we do. We get them used to testing their sense of enterprise, their competitive spirit, their productivity."[4]

It would be an oversimplification to say that Grameen borrowers succeed simply through entrepreneurship. Villagers prosper in part by incorporating clearly articulated values that serve not only business but social ends as well. Often illiterate, Grameen borrowers must learn the rules and operations of the bank and the Grameen philosophy. Bank officials conduct an oral examination in which prospective borrowers must repeat the Sixteen Decisions—often referred to as the social development constitution of Grameen Bank, promoting physical, social, and emotional well-being. In the most direct way, Grameen unites the monetary system with a strong set of social values.

From these humble beginnings and core values has emerged a force that could change the face of world poverty. Today more than 168 organizations around the world are operating microcredit programs modeled on Grameen Bank. Through Grameen Investments, a program of Calvert Community Investments, individuals and institutions stateside can become partners in this groundbreaking work.

Accion International: Bringing Microcredit to Latin America

Accion International was founded in 1961 by an idealistic lawyer, Joseph Blatchford, who was haunted by the images of the Latin American urban poor that he witnessed while on a goodwill tennis tour of twenty Latin American cities. After twenty years, Accion has grown into an umbrella organization for a network of microfinance institutions in thirteen Latin American countries and, as we've seen, in six U.S. cities. Accion's BancoSol in Bolivia is the first private, commercial microfinance bank in the world. All told, in the last six years the Accion network has loaned over $1.7 billion to more than 1.4 million microentrepreneurs, bettering the lives of an estimated 5 million people. By providing access to credit and basic business training to the self-employed, Accion encourages the economic self-reliance of impoverished working women and men throughout the Americas.

> **"** *Serving the poor is not a matter of charity. Serving the poor can be managed with the same standards and rigor that people bring to increasing earnings per share—except that you're changing lives. That for me is the real revolution.* **"**
>
> —MICHAEL CHU, President of Accion International

Shared Interest: Economic Justice in the Wake of Apartheid

Since the emergence of democracy, South Africa has struggled for both civil and economic justice. Citizens there have come to rely on Shared Interest in their attempts to work toward greater prosperity in their lives.

Shared Interest is a not-for-profit social investment fund that guarantees South African bank loans to community lending institutions, which in turn use their expertise and community knowledge to make credit available to very small individual and cooperative businesses and communities, building low-cost housing and offering small-business financing.

> **"** *Shared Interest creates the means for U.S. social investors to invest in community-based economic projects that will create not only jobs, but also alternative models of control and ownership.***"**
>
> —NELSON MANDELA, President of South Africa

Ecumenical Development Cooperative Lending Society: Churches Joining to Benefit the World's Poor

The Ecumenical Development Cooperative Society (EDCS) serves rural, poor communities in more than sixty countries in Africa, Asia, and Latin America. Its funds originate from churches, church-related organizations, and individuals of all faiths who subscribe to the promotion of development as a liberating process aimed at economic growth, social justice, popular participation, self-reliance, and respect for creation. It relies on nongovernmental organizations and other agencies to provide capacity-building training. Once local groups have achieved vision, organizational strength, and self-confidence, EDCS provides the financing necessary to help them realize their goals. It has active lending relationships with approximately 250 organizations in sixty-four countries. During 1997, new loans totaling $13 million were approved to thirty-five new partner groups.

How Do I Invest?

THE NATURAL INVESTOR must be willing to work a little to find appropriate opportunities for engaging in Community Investing. Most community banks, credit unions, and loan funds constitute individual investments. That is, they are not generally available through pooled investments like mutual funds. Though there are some new exceptions to this rule, most Natural Investors will want to seek out and establish relationships with particular loan funds or banks that appeal to their sense of social action. In the case of banks it's pretty straightforward, indeed no different from any banking relationship you've had before. Community loan funds, however, are a different matter. Because of regulatory issues, most financial advisers cannot steer you to these funds; you'll need to approach them yourself and determine your own comfort level. You can contact any of the loan funds listed in Appendix D to get more information on individual programs and investment procedures.

Over the past decade, several mutual funds began allocating a small amount (usually around 1 percent) of their portfolios to community investments. Calvert, Parnassus, and others have led the way in this regard (see the matrix in Chapter 10 for details on which mutual funds are involved). This is a step in the right direction; the financial impact of these investments on the funds' overall performance is insignificant, and they provide a modest Community Investing element for mutual fund investors.

The Social Investment Forum has initiated a program to help pave the way for more active involvement in this sector. Its initiative, begun in 1998, aims to help catalyze the creation of more standardized financial reporting by CDFIs. This should ease the way for more mutual funds and individuals to make informed community investment decisions. In addition, the Forum has made Community Investing the focal point of a new campaign aimed at raising public awareness of the rewards of investing in this spoke of the Natural Investing Wheel.

At the same time, the Calvert Social Investment Foundation (a nonprofit offshoot of Calvert Group mutual funds) has begun a similar process, working individually with many CDFIs. They have recently launched several related initiatives, sharing the common aim of making Community Investing a recognized asset class. Calvert Community Investment Notes are the first registered security that allows Natural Investors to put their resources into a pooled investment of community loan funds. This portfolio encompasses microcredit, affordable housing, small business, and community development lenders across the country and around the world, with some seventy-five organizations represented as of late 1998.

The investor chooses the term (one, three, or five years) and the interest rate (0 to 4 percent). Investors can choose to allocate their investments to loan funds in a specific region or worldwide; larger investors may allocate their monies to specific programs. Being a registered security means that Calvert is required to exercise a high level of due diligence, investigating the operations and track record of each institution. Individual investors are buffered from loss by a loss reserve, funded partially by several foundation grants made to support the growth of Community Investing. The bottom line is that your monies are quite safe with these notes—no guarantees, but more security (and diversification) than you would have by making a direct investment in a particular institution.

Calvert has also pursued direct partnerships with key nonprofit lenders. Grameen Investments is the first of many planned "private label" community investment options available under the Foundation's banner. In addition, a partnership with Progressive Asset Management allows investors to purchase fixed-rate Community Investment Notes targeted to the issues most important to them, including low-income housing, microcredit lending, and community development.

By taking the lead in this way, the Calvert Foundation is blazing a trail for the future of Community Investing. Their success at drawing attention and capital to these programs will no doubt inspire other financial players to join in similar initiatives. As these small, local programs begin to find a place at the financial table alongside more familiar investment vehicles, more capital will flow in this direction, opening up unimaginable possibilities.

Spreading Optimism

CDFIS ARE IN the vanguard of today's infusion of social values into the economic system. Many Natural Investors find Community Investing's ability to leverage multiple benefits to be the most rewarding part of their portfolios. Shared Interest has calculated that every dollar they use for loan guarantees in South Africa creates a hundred times as many jobs as the same dollar invested there by a multinational corporation.

The promise of Community Investing is just beginning to be realized. Community Investing advocate David Berge is one of many in the field who speaks to the need for expanded public education about Community Investing: "On the lending side, banks have both direct and indirect impacts on communities. We know that every dollar we lend to a community organization, to an organic farm, or to a school has an immediate positive impact on that borrower. That positive impact is then amplified by all of the work done by those same borrowers that affects others in the community."

However, Berge goes beyond the positive power of money in his vision for an expanded Community Investment future. He suggests that community banks must encourage people to go beyond lending money; time and energy are also needed to heal our communities. Indeed many of the programs that benefit from financing by CDFIs would not be able to operate without the equally important contributions of "sweat equity" by countless volunteers, working week to week, month to month, year to year.

We concur that investors should be careful not to slip into treating our contribution to community as a commodity that we can buy with investments in CDFIs. Community Investing constitutes only one part of what Natural Investors do in the quest for a better community, but that monetary element is powerful and direct. Money is a medium for communication; it can communicate faith, hope, and even love for the people with whom life is shared.

In *It's a Wonderful Life,* George Bailey discovered that through capital from his savings and loan institution he had helped people in his town lead fulfilling and productive lives. This glorious fact existed prior to his awareness of it, but only his eventual realization allowed him to experience its redeeming power.

For the Natural Investor we wish the same empowering awareness that capital—be it money, energy, or time—invested consciously in one's own community can lead to a more fulfilling life for recipients and investors alike.

Faith, hope, and love. A pretty good return for a few well-invested dollars.

Chapter Eight

Shareholder Activism: Politics by Other Means

I F YOU WANT to start a firestorm at the next party you attend, try bringing up the topic of corporate power. On one side of the room will be free-market capitalists who are generally uncritically probusiness, asserting the right—even the duty—of corporations to deliver maximum profits with no ethical strings attached. On the other side will be environmentalists, labor organizers, and other progressive activists who tend to launch into coarse, anticorporate tirades. This book calls for a truce, asking each side to listen to the other.

As we've stated throughout, Natural Investing weaves together the best of each viewpoint. Business can make a profit *and* be an ally of social change and environmental progress; in fact, it's one of the most important players on the team. The role of shareholder activists is to encourage companies to work toward this double bottom line. Although it is sometimes necessary to take an adversarial stance, many companies are discovering that the social and environmental requests of shareholder activists are frequently in the best long-term financial interests of the company.

Among the four spokes of the Natural Investing Wheel, Shareholder Activism offers the most direct path to influencing corporate policies. Like Community Investing, this strategy of engagement is receiving more and more attention from Natural Investors. Led by shareholder advocacy groups like the Interfaith Center for Corporate Responsibility (ICCR), and engaged social money management firms like Franklin

Research & Development, the shareholder resolution process is gaining popularity. Shareholder resolutions on social and corporate responsibility issues more than doubled (from 144 to 303) between 1994 and 1996.[1] New initiatives of the Social Investment Forum are helping more individual investors become involved in Shareholder Activism.

Investors may engage in Shareholder Activism at several levels of commitment. For many shareholders, voting their proxies for policy changes is a simple first step. Those wanting to go further can engage in dialogue with companies, propose shareholder resolutions, and champion codes of corporate conduct. Both investors and the general public can participate in various citizen's campaigns, such as passing selective purchasing laws and promoting consumer boycotts. Taken together, these tools are a direct and potent force for change.

In the early days of corporate history, joint stock companies (the entities from which modern corporations are descended) operated on the premise that shareholders would take direct responsibility for business operations. This may have been the case at first, but two factors eventually eroded the connection between ownership and responsibility. The first was limited liability: stockholders were not financially or legally liable for the actions of their corporations. Second, the easy liquidity of stocks led to a gradual yet dramatic process of diluted ownership. Most companies begin with a small group of committed investors. Over time, as initial investors sell all or part of their holdings, ownership is spread among a much larger, and less involved, group of shareholders. Thus we have the modern corporation, in which ownership and control are separated—with control firmly in the hands of management.

Many in the corporate world believe that's the way it should remain. Thomas Donlan, in the June 9, 1997, issue of *Barron's,* put it this way: "A corporation is not a structure for pleasing stockholders but a structure for gathering capital and protecting passive investors."

The key word here is *passive.* Investors (who own the company!) are expected to sit back and let management make money for them—in any way management sees fit. Shareholders who investigate company practices and voice concern about the moral or ethical implications of a company's behavior are often seen as out of place by those who believe decisions should be based solely on financial judgments. As Donlan expresses in the same article, "Those who buy, sell or vote stock based on sentiment may be wonderful human beings, but they are not

investors. They are public-relations specialists, too often in the service of anti-business politicians."[2] Activist investors are certainly not
dupes of "antibusiness" forces, but they also aren't going to sit around
as passive bystanders. They recognize that the lack of shareholder
responsibility for corporate actions has contributed to many environmental, social, and ethical abuses. And they recognize the power of
corporations to become agents for social change.

A growing number of CEOs and corporate officials are receptive to
bringing a sense of social responsibility into corporate policies. These
managers appreciate, and sometimes need, a bit of a nudge from
investors. They rightfully fear public outrage and reduced sales when
caught discriminating, polluting, or selling shoddy products. And they
know that being attuned to changing public attitudes is crucial to their
long-term success. Indeed, many companies are quite willing to enter
into dialogue and head off problems before they become public relations
nightmares.

Shareholder activists use three related approaches to bring values
into corporate policies: **dialogue** with management, filing **shareholder
resolutions**, and **divestment**.

Dialogue

CONCERNED SHAREHOLDERS WHO discover ethically offensive or fiscally
unsound behavior can use their voice. They can contact management
and establish a dialogue! This may start by simply writing a letter to the
company. Although a company's initial reaction may be defensive, open
dialogue allows each side, management and shareholders alike, to voice
its perceptions of the problem, offer courses of action, and, in the best
scenario, to work for a "win/win" solution. In many cases, dialogue alone
is enough to prompt companies to implement change.

Investors with small holdings have only a slim chance of reaching
the ear of upper management. But organized groups of concerned
investors are listened to. Institutional investors such as large pension
fund managers and mutual fund managers, along with investor coali-
tions such as the ICCR, have an attention-getting voice. If you are
served by an institution such as a church, university (as a student, alum-
nus, or taxpayer), or pension fund, you may want to encourage its
investment managers to become more active. Individuals who invest in

socially screened mutual funds that engage in such dialogue are also helping to strengthen this effort.

Shareholder Resolutions

IF DIALOGUE WITH the company fails to achieve change, activists can turn to the shareholder resolution process. Through the years, many shareholder resolutions have prompted companies to take action on social issues. The issues raised by resolutions are also good for the financial bottom line; when companies fail to address their governance, environmental, and social impact problems, shareholders too often pick up the tab.

For example, when Home Depot's management failed to deal with workplace discrimination, it cost shareholders $104 million to settle discrimination lawsuits. Concerned shareholders proposed a resolution asking the company to provide a report on company initiatives to expand opportunities for women and minorities. The company balked, and even sought and won permission from the Securities and Exchange Commission (SEC) to omit the resolution—but they ended up putting the measure on their proxy statement anyway when pressed by the resolution's proponents. It received a 14.4 percent vote, making it one of the highest-scoring social-issues resolutions of 1998.[3] The whole escapade has led some social screening researchers to question whether Home Depot, long considered a socially responsible company, should remain in mutual funds and indexes that screen for workplace issues.

Any shareholder who owns at least $2,000 of stock in a company for over one year may file a shareholder resolution. Most resolutions are nonbinding requests or recommendations by shareholders to management. Even with a majority vote, a resolution does not become company policy without management approval. Resolutions appear on the company's proxy statement and are voted on by shareholders at the company's annual meeting.

Proxy voting is not like electoral politics. Each shareholder has one vote for every share owned—but if an individual or institution does not vote its proxy, the votes default to management. The proxy statement, a small pamphlet supplied to all shareholders, contains the full text of each shareholder resolution to be voted on. With the proxy statement,

Every Vote Counts

WE URGE ALL shareholders to review and vote their proxies. Make certain to pay close attention to any shareholder resolutions on the ballot; they will often be worthy of your support. Vote in protest against the proposed slate of candidates for the board of directors if you are unhappy with the composition (e.g., a lack of diversity) of the board. It is also worthwhile to send a letter to the company telling them how you have voted and why.

Even though most resolutions garner low percentages of support, all investors should be an active part of the process. Companies really notice when an issue manages to get even modest—and especially more widespread—attention from shareholders. Dripping water in the same spot on a rock over time creates a hole in the rock. Similarly, corporate change is achieved slowly and gradually; it is hardly noticeable with each effort but eventually has dramatic effects.

the shareholder receives a small sheet of paper that looks like a ballot. Actually, it is a power of attorney (a proxy) that authorizes a representative to vote the shares as the shareholder specifies.

Proxy resolutions can be surprisingly effective even when they don't pass. The proponents' goal is not so much the resolution's passage but to encourage a dialogue with management that leads to changes in policies or practices. SEC rules allow shareholder proponents to continue to bring an issue forward as long as repeated votes show increasing shareholder support for the initiative. Over a period of years, this strategy has a way of wearing down corporate resistance and opening doors to a resolution of the issue. When significant numbers of investors support a resolution, such reaction warns the company that it may also have disgruntled customers. To prevent loss of revenues, a company may find that changing a policy as called for makes good business sense.

Most social resolutions fail to gain more than 10 percent of the vote;

A Sample Shareholder Resolution

THE FOLLOWING IS an excerpted and lightly edited example of a corporate governance shareholder resolution. It was submitted to General Electric Corporation by Franklin Research & Development during the 1998 proxy season.

WHEREAS, in 1996, U.S. CEOs earned on average 209 times the average factory worker's pay, a dramatic rise from the 42 times reported in 1980;

WHEREAS, considering executive pay in the global context, U.S. CEOs make on average 2,141 times the wage of Mexican maquiladora workers ($2,700 a year) and 11,562 times the minimum wage of workers in Vietnam ($500);

WHEREAS, General Electric's CEO in 1996 was the 15th highest paid U.S. CEO, making $27.6 million or 4.8 times the pay of the average CEO, 1,003 times the average U.S. factory worker, and 10,276 times the minimum wage for Mexican workers, a nation where General Electric continues to expand;

WHEREAS, growing research on effective organizations stresses the importance of empowering front-line workers, a goal undermined by compen-

but they do bring into focus important issues that companies sometimes do not want called to public attention. The threat of exposure is often enough to motivate companies into taking actions they otherwise would not. Exposure is even more of a concern today, when information travels quickly, is easily available, and is being monitored by social investors, activist groups, the media, and the public at large.

In 1998, the American Medical Association asked investors to avoid owning Sara Lee Corporation stock when they discovered the company had a little-known foreign unit that sold cut tobacco for hand-rolled cigarettes. Concerned shareholders filed a resolution asking the company to sell the division; the resolution received a whopping 10 percent vote. Sara Lee got the message and announced that it would sell the tobacco business, acknowledging that outside pressure had contributed to its decision.[4]

sation policies that reward top executives at the expense of workers closest to the customers and production;

THEREFORE, BE IT RESOLVED that shareholders urge the Board to address the issue of runaway remuneration of CEOs and begin to close the gap between highest-paid and lowest-paid workers by

1. Establishing a cap on CEO compensation expressed as a multiple of pay of the lowest-paid worker at General Electric.
2. Explaining to shareholders in next year's proxy materials the determinations used in order to determine the appropriate cap.

Supporting Statement

In asking General Electric to establish a cap on executive compensation, we have not sought to impose our own arbitrary cap on executive compensation. Instead we have asked our company to wrestle with the issue of the rising wage gap that exists between corporate executives and those they seek to lead. By imposing the financial discipline of a pay cap, we hope our company can help reverse a long-standing trend that is good for neither business nor society.

PLEASE VOTE YES![5]

Divestment

WHEN ATTEMPTS TO influence a company's behavior through dialogue and shareholder resolutions fail, more drastic measures are called for. Divestment, the act of selling off stocks, is a last resort. It sends a powerful message to companies that turn a deaf ear to shareholders' concerns about business practices or that actively suppress attempts by shareholders to influence policy. It also often galvanizes a broader public awareness of corporate responsibility issues.

A growing number of pension fund managers, for example, have expressed their distaste for tobacco by ridding their portfolios of the offensive stocks. State employee retirement funds in several states have divested from tobacco. The Kentucky Teachers Retirement System—in a surprise move, considering that their state is the second-largest tobacco

Shareholders' Rights Defended

MANY CORPORATIONS WOULD like to limit the ability of shareholders to bring forth resolutions. In 1997, the SEC, under pressure from corporate interests, proposed new rules limiting shareholders' rights. According to Steve Scheuth, president of the Social Investment Forum, "these rules would have decimated the rights of shareholders to bring important issues to corporate management."[6]

The Social Investment Forum responded vigorously, applying back-testing to see what effect the new rules would have had on the movement. Looking back, the Forum found that every social resolution addressing South Africa, executive compensation, environmental issues, and race and gender would have faced steep hurdles for resubmission.[7] This would have undermined the ability of shareholders to maintain healthy dialogue and negotiation with corporations. Management could simply refuse to discuss an issue and wait one or two years for the resolution to fail to meet the amplified requirements—after which it would die.

Fortunately, investors took action. In a surprising show of concern that reflects the growing presence of Natural Investors, the SEC received thousands of letters protesting the proposed changes. The SEC responded by withdrawing the proposed increases in resubmission thresholds and even went a step further, reversing a policy barring shareholder proposals on hiring policies.

grower—sold $50 million of tobacco stocks (over half its total holdings) in 1996.[8] More than fifty colleges and universities have also divested themselves of tobacco investments. These actions are part of the reason that tobacco stock prices have been depressed in recent years.

Divestment—and the threat of divestment—has played its most important role by preventing or stopping companies from doing business with countries led by repressive regimes. The U.S. government has been enforcing a policy of divestment against Cuba since the 1960s. However, as we saw in Chapter 1, the greatest example of the power of divestment in international politics is the part it played in bringing an end to apartheid in South Africa.

Today Burma (also known as Mynamar) is in the spotlight. Aung San Suu Kyi, the National League for Democracy leader, won the national elections in 1990 but was barred from taking power by the ruling military regime and put under house arrest. In an interview in *Business Week*, Suu Kyi thanked Americans for divesting from companies doing business with the junta: "We very much appreciate the U.S. sanctions [on investments in Burma] because they have been a tremendous psychological boost for the democracy movement, and they have made businesses think carefully about what is really going on in Burma. . . . We do not think investing [here] at this time really helps the people of Burma. [Investment by Western companies] gives the military regime reason to think that they can continue violating human rights. . . . We want investment to be at the right time—when the benefits will go to the people of Burma, not just to a small, select elite connected to the government."[9]

Citizen Strategies

BECAUSE THEY OWN a part of the business, shareholders can exert influence from within the company. But there are other tactics that can put on the heat from outside the company. Citizens who wish to send a message to corporations based on their position as consumers have several avenues to pursue. These include **boycotts, demonstrations, selective purchasing policies,** and **corporate charter challenges.** Through consumer boycotts and demonstrations outside stores, activists successfully pressured Eddie Bauer, Columbia Sportswear, and Liz Claiborne to stop buying apparel made by factories in Burma. And at Harvard University, students pressured dining services to deny PepsiCo a $1 million-dollar contract because of its investments in that country. Other student unions and universities did the same. As a result, PepsiCo decided to withdraw completely from Burma.

Selective purchasing policies and laws are perhaps the most effective of these tactics. Once a city council or a state enacts a selective purchasing law against a country, the city or state's purchasing managers are effectively barred from buying goods and services from firms doing business in that country. Selective purchasing laws were one of the most important tools of the campaign against apartheid in South Africa. During the anti-apartheid campaign, fifty-two cities, fourteen counties, and five states enacted restrictions on the purchase of goods and services from companies doing business in South Africa.[10] More recently, when the state of Massachusetts passed a selective purchasing law barring state agencies from buying goods and services from companies doing business in Burma, Apple Computer, Eastman Kodak, Hewlett-Packard, and Phillips Electronics withdrew from the country rather than lose the state's business.

In late 1998 the National Foreign Trade Council, an alliance of major U.S. exporters, succeeded in striking down the Massachusetts selective purchasing law in court, classifying it as an "unfair trade practice." In addition, both the European Union and Japan have challenged the state law before the World Trade Organization. Although the case is under appeal, this could be a major blow to citizen activism. Rep. Byron Rushing, who authored the law, responded by pointing out that "if this ruling stands, taxpayers and local governments around the country will lose the right to decide whether to do business with companies that support brutal regimes such as Burma." He also added that "if selective purchasing had been banned ten years ago, Nelson Mandela might still be in prison today."[11] Simon Billenness of Franklin Research & Development has been instrumental in bringing this issue to the attention of investors and activists. (Appendix B contains a list of companies that serve as directors of the National Foreign Trade Council.)

Reclaiming the Corporate Charter

RECENTLY SEVERAL CAMPAIGNS have attempted to shut down corporations that repeatedly and consistently operate in ways that are harmful to society. Citizens are attempting to regain control over the vital seed that enables a corporation to exist—its charter. This is by far the most aggressive approach to challenging corporate behavior, utilizing safeguards against corporate power that were put in place by the framers of the U.S. Constitution. Most states still have laws on the books that provide for revoking the charter of companies that break the law. In recent years, the New York state attorney general used such a law to ask a court to revoke the charters of two tobacco "research" corporations, and a judge in Alabama, acting as a private citizen, petitioned to revoke the charters of the tobacco companies themselves.

The first broadly based citizens campaign to revoke a charter was launched in 1998 against oil giant Union Oil of California (Unocal). Thirty public interest organizations presented a petition to California's attorney general, asking him to initiate proceedings to revoke Unocal's charter. The petition alleges that Unocal has a long history of law-breaking, including environmental devastation (the Santa Barbara oil spill), unethical treatment of workers (hundreds of OSHA violations), and undermining U.S. foreign policy in Burma and Afghanistan (complicity in human rights violations, such as forced labor and destruction of villages).[12]

Unocal will not be dissolved any time soon; the petition was rejected by the attorney general, and the petitioners are appealing this decision. But the publicity surrounding this action caught corporations by surprise, serving notice that the most egregious may one day need to defend their raisons d'être. It also served a valuable educational purpose, reminding Americans that corporations exist only as long as the public wills to grant them life.

Corporate Codes of Conduct

A LESS CONFRONTATIONAL strategy being used by those working to increase corporate responsibility is voluntary codes of conduct, which address issues ranging from environmental impact to employment and labor practices.

As for other Shareholder Activism tactics, South Africa was a proving ground for this approach. The Sullivan Principles, developed by the Reverend Leon H. Sullivan in 1977, promoted racial equality in the employment practices of U.S. corporations that operated in South Africa.[13] More recently, the Maquiladora Standards of Conduct for Mexico and Central America address the exploitation of workers in factories that assemble parts for U.S. corporations.[14]

At first most corporations considered adopting codes only as a result of strong pressure from shareholders; the media; workers-rights, environmental, and consumer groups; or competitors. Today many adopt codes for reasons that blend self-interest, ethics, and good business sense. As the CEO of Levi Strauss & Co. pointed out: "Our company's experience demonstrates that a company cannot sustain success unless it develops ways to anticipate and address ethical issues as they arise. Doing the right thing from day one helps avoid future setbacks and regrets. Addressing ethical dilemmas when they arise may save your business from serious financial or reputational harm."[15]

The value of a good corporate image is a strong motivator. Many companies want to be seen as good corporate citizens who are socially responsible—but often their shortcomings must be pointed out to them. Starbucks Coffee Company, for example, decided to introduce a code of conduct for all its coffee bean suppliers after receiving hundreds of letters from consumers and investors upset about poor working conditions on Guatemalan coffee plantations. A Starbucks executive admitted that the protesters had "prodded" the company into developing the code.[16]

Merely creating codes is no longer a problem. Companies like Nike, Reebok, Gillette, Polaroid, Hallmark, Home Depot, and Honeywell have all created in-house codes to govern their foreign operations. But who's there to verify their actions? Can the public trust that these codes are more than words? To satisfy the need for independent oversight, as well as more unified standards and monitoring, several major initiatives have been launched. Here we look at two of these: one focused on international workplace conditions, the other on environmental responsibility.

Social Accountability 8000

The Social Accountability 8000 (SA8000) initiative is designed to protect workers' rights. It defines a set of global standards and provides for an independent auditing process. SA8000 addresses child labor, compensation, discrimination, forced labor, working hours, health and safety, freedom of association, and disciplinary practices. The standards are based on conventions of the International Labour Organization and related international human rights instruments, including the Universal Declaration of Human Rights and the UN Convention on the Rights of the Child.

The standards were drafted by the Council on Economic Priorities (CEP), with the help of union representatives, human rights and children's rights organizations, retailers, and manufacturers. CEP's advisory board includes representatives from Amnesty International, Avon,

Franklin Research & Development, the National Child Labor Committee, Reebok, and Toys R Us.

SA8000 was launched in 1997. During its first year, several companies have made commitments to adopt it: Toys R Us will require its 5,000 suppliers to adopt SA8000; Avon will be implementing SA8000 in their nineteen factories; Otto Versand (the largest mail-order company in the world and the owner of Eddie Bauer) will implement SA8000 with its key suppliers.[17]

The CERES Principles

In 1989, when the Exxon *Valdez* spewed oily toxins into the Gulf of Alaska, outraged environmentalists and a broad spectrum of socially responsible business and investment professionals, churches, community groups, and labor unions, led by Joan Bavaria of Franklin Research & Development, formed the Coalition of Environmentally Responsible Economies (CERES). Realizing that ecological wisdom had never been spelled out in terms usable for business, the group drafted a ten-point code of environmental policy aimed at guiding corporations toward greater responsibility. Originally dubbed the "Valdez Principles," it now goes by the less provocative "CERES Principles."

Clarifying and drafting the principles was a magnificent first step. But how do you get the corporations to seriously consider them? The strategy of the CERES partners was to use their ownership of approximately $150 billion in investor assets to bring forward shareholder resolutions asking corporations to adopt the CERES principles. This approach has been highly successful. For example, when ICCR members filed a resolution asking General Motors to adopt the CERES principles, GM agreed to negotiate with the ICCR and ultimately decided to endorse the principles.[18]

CERES is the first to point out that signing the principles does not mean that a company is "green." Indeed, the principles are careful to state that signatories are working *toward* "consistent, measurable progress" in the implementation of the principles. GM provides an obvious example: its opposition to higher gas-mileage requirements and zero-emission cars raises the hackles of many environmentalists. Nonetheless, CERES felt that GM's participation would provide a meaningful point of influence to help guide the company toward long-term improvement. CERES focuses on creating an open, nonhostile climate within which to share information, ideas, and creative problem-solving. When conflicts arise, CERES often acts as an intermediary between citizens groups and the companies.

One of the most important features of CERES is the requirement for signatories to report on their environmental performance. The CERES Report is a self-evaluation of progress made toward implementing the principles. Although it is widely recognized as the most comprehensive, standardized format for corporate environmental reports to date, CERES is committed to further refining the reporting system. In 1997 it created the Global Reporting Initiative, whose mission is to bring together the numerous reporting initiatives that have developed independently around the world and shape them into one set of coherent, consistent global standards.[19]

As of this writing, forty-eight companies have signed the principles. The first companies to sign on, like Seventh Generation and Aveda Corporation, were smaller companies who already had "green" reputations. CERES reached the big leagues in 1993 when Sun Oil Company became the first Fortune 500 firm to adopt the principles. Given the origins of CERES, it was a pleasant irony that an oil company would be the first major corporation to make this public endorsement. Recent additions include Coca-Cola, BankAmerica, and ITT.[20]

Ultimately the success of initiatives such as CERES depends on management's realizing that ecological responsibility leads to a more efficient and profitable company. Investors concerned about the environment or labor issues would be wise to track the progress of CERES, SA8000, and other voluntary initiatives.

The Transformation of Business

THROUGH INSTITUTIONAL INVESTORS and groups such as ICCR, Natural Investors are gaining increasing clout within corporate boardrooms. When matched with the increasing social conscience of company management and the cooperative spirit of such efforts as CERES, Shareholder Activism promises to become an accepted avenue of communication between corporations and the public at large. Companies that have the foresight to embrace social responsibility and make the necessary policy adjustments are likely to improve their competitive advantage and avoid publicity nightmares. Rather than fighting the rising tide of ethical standards, these visionary companies are creating new profit opportunities for a changing world.

This section has taken us deep into the belly of capitalism, exposing us to the best and the worst of what business brings to our world. Incidents of corporate malfeasance sometimes incite critics to demonize the entire business community, but this is a serious mistake. As we have pointed out previously, Natural Investing is not antibusiness. Corporations are run by people, most of whom share the same hopes for the world that we all do. Many are acutely aware of the unsustainable trends that endanger our planet, and they are working from within to make essential changes. Organizations such as Business for Social Responsibility are facilitating high-level discussions of ethics and accountability.

Although corporate horror stories make headlines, it's important to note that there are just as many inspiring stories of companies demonstrating outstanding ethical practices. So let's close this section with an inspiring example that has touched the hearts of people around the world:

In 1995, Aaron Feuerstein's Malden Mills, based in Lawrence, Massachusetts, burned to the ground. Malden Mills runs on two cardinal principles: (1) The corporation has a responsibility to its people: to treat them the way we want them to treat us, to extend the loyalty to them that we want. (2) The corporation has a responsibility to the community. After this tragedy, Feuerstein stuck with his principles and, rather than throwing 3,000 employees out on the street and moving the company south of the border, he decided to keep paying his employees while they rebuilt. He was more than a little taken aback by the worldwide acclaim that resulted from simply doing what he knew was right.

Ten days later the superintendent of the one plant (out of four) that had been saved called Aaron to tell him "we're operating!" Says Feuerstein: "It shocked me because I knew that it would take many months to get a plant like that back to operation. But I walked over to the plant, opened the door, and I heard beautiful music and the humming of machinery. And all my workers were standing next to the equipment and all my management from all the other plants that burnt down—they're all standing there with tears in their eyes and with broad smiles on their faces." Just 45 days later, thanks to the ingenuity and dedication of the Malden Mills workforce, the plant was producing 50% more than it ever produced prior to the fire.[21]

You've now completed the "big picture" overview of the landscape of Natural Investing. Section 1 set the stage, with a journey through the historical foundations on which we're building today, along with a look at the forces that are creating the new values-based approach to finance. Section 2 has taken us around the Natural Investing Wheel, learning about the strategies you'll be using to build your own relationship with your investments. In the next section we are going to dive into the nitty-gritty of planning the financial side of your investments.

In preparation, we invite you to spend a few moments deciding how you want to use the tools that have been presented in Section 2. The following worksheets will help you define how you want to work with each of the four spokes of the Natural Investing Wheel, and clarify the issues for which you wish to screen and prospect. This will be the map you will use later to select specific investments that align with your vision for the world.

Worksheet #2: Choosing Your Strategies

Take a moment to review the four spokes of the Natural Investing Wheel and determine your own Natural Strategy. You may refer to Chapter 4 for a quick review or flip through each of the preceding four chapters to refresh your memory as to the choices. Check the box that best represents your level of interest for using that strategy in your portfolio.

	STRONG INTEREST	GENERAL INTEREST	LOW INTEREST
Avoidance Screening			
Affirmative Screening			
Community Investing			
Shareholder Activism			

As you gain more experience with the four spokes you may want to revisit this worksheet. Similarly, if your financial situation changes (for the better, we hope!) then you could explore using some new strategies.

Worksheet #3: Screening Scorecard: Avoidance and Quality Issues

Chapter 5 took us squarely into the world, opening our minds to many situations that are not as we might wish them to be. Now it's time to sort through the "snapshots" we've taken, organize our notes, and see where we stand. In completing the following scorecard, indicate the issues that you want accounted for in your portfolio. You may want to flip through Chapter 5 as you do so to refresh yourself on these issues.

Rate in importance: 1 = low, 5 = high

AVOIDANCE ISSUES

Major screens:

Alcohol	1 2 3 4 5
Animal Rights	1 2 3 4 5
Environment: Global Warming	1 2 3 4 5
Environment: Pollution/Toxic Products	1 2 3 4 5
Gambling	1 2 3 4 5
Labor: Discrimination	1 2 3 4 5
Labor: Sweatshops/Child Labor	1 2 3 4 5
Nuclear Power	1 2 3 4 5
Repressive Regimes:	1 2 3 4 5
Specific Country(ies) _____	
Tobacco	1 2 3 4 5
Weapons and the Military	1 2 3 4 5

Other Screening Issues:

Religious, Ethical, or Moral Issues	1 2 3 4 5
Specify _____	
Violence: Media and Products	1 2 3 4 5
U.S. Treasury	1 2 3 4 5
Executive Pay	1 2 3 4 5

Industries:

Biotechnology	1 2 3 4 5
Medical	1 2 3 4 5
Resource Extraction	1 2 3 4 5
Other _____	1 2 3 4 5

QUALITY ISSUES

Products and Services   1 2 3 4 5

Workplace Issues   1 2 3 4 5

    Check specific issues

       _____Union Representation

       _____Workplace Conditions

       _____Participatory Management

Diversity Issues   1 2 3 4 5

    Check specific issues

       _____Gay/Lesbian

       _____Minorities

       _____Women

Corporate Community Participation   1 2 3 4 5

Environmental Practices   1 2 3 4 5

Corporate Disclosure   1 2 3 4 5

OTHER PERSONAL SCREENING ISSUES:

_____

_____

_____

_____

_____

Worksheet #4: Screening Scorecard:

Affirmative Issues

Here's your chance to compile a list of the industries and initiatives that you'd like to investigate further for proactive investing. In some cases, you may feel ready to begin identifying specific companies in which to invest; for other issues, you may want to engage in some more research on technical and economic details. This scorecard can serve as a handy personal reference and reminder as you begin to devote some time and money to this especially engaging form of Natural Investing.

Issue/Industry	Seek Companies	Learn More
Renewable Energy	☐	☐
Clean Transportation	☐	☐
Tree Savers	☐	☐
Natural Food and		
Healthy Living Products	☐	☐
Energy Conservation	☐	☐
Recycling	☐	☐
Environmental Cleanup	☐	☐
Green Real Estate	☐	☐
New Design Principles	☐	☐

OTHER PROSPECTING ISSUES I WOULD LIKE TO EXPLORE:

_____

_____

_____

_____

_____

_____

Worksheet #5: Community Investment Scorecard

As you consider how to engage in Community Investing, consider the following questions:

➤ What amount in dollars, or proportion of your portfolio, would you like to allocate to community investments? $_____ or _____%

➤ Of that money, what amount or percentage would you be willing to invest in below-market rate loans to community loan funds or micro-credit institutions? $_____ or _____%

➤ Of the funds you devote to Community Investing, what are your key areas of interest?

Topic	Important	Consider
Local Institutions	☐	☐
Developing Country Institutions	☐	☐
Inner-City Areas	☐	☐
Rural Areas	☐	☐
Affordable Housing	☐	☐
Small Business Loans	☐	☐
Environmental Business	☐	☐
Social Services		
Arts	☐	☐
Health	☐	☐
Homeless	☐	☐
Other Issues	☐	☐

Now begin to compile a list of specific community investments that fit the above criteria. You might find all the information you need in Chapter 10, or you may wish to research local or regional options. In addition, you may want to use the resources in the Appendixes to begin gathering information on community investments around the country (and the world!) to find ones that share your interests. Keep adding to this list as you find new options that appeal to you.

SOME SPECIFIC COMMUNITY INVESTMENTS I AM INTERESTED IN:

_____

_____

Section Three

The Natural
Portfolio
Guidebook

C h a p t e r **9** *N i n e*

Nuts and Bolts

N OW IT'S TIME to take some practical steps that will move you toward the fulfillment of your dreams. "Money is more than a commodity to accumulate; it is a resource that provides you with options," says financial consultant Bob Dreizler in *Tending Your Money Garden.*[1] What dreams do you have for your life? Getting in touch with your personal dreams—a new home, an exotic vacation, retiring early, starting a new career, or supporting a favorite cause—will help motivate you to create and carry out a long-term investment strategy. There is no better time to start than right now; if you invest $100 a month for twenty-five years and earn an annual return of 11 percent (the long-term average for the stock market), you will reap over $150,000! So let's get going!

We begin this chapter with a few basic definitions, then move toward developing your investment plan. The first step will be to clarify your investment goals: that is, when and how are you going to spend your investment money? Second, we look at a central and difficult question: with what level of risk (and its attendant possible rewards) are you most comfortable? In the next few chapters, you will choose specific mutual funds and/or individual investments that will give life to all the preliminary decisions you've made along the way. By the end of the section you'll be far more engaged and empowered, and your money will, at long last, be working for you *and* your visions of the world, rather than just for itself!

If you are currently working with or expecting to work with an adviser, this chapter will prepare you to be an informed client, saving you time and confusion. If you are planning to manage your own portfolio, you will probably want to read one or more other books with more thorough discussions of many of these topics. We've listed some of our favorites in Appendixes A (page 300) and E (page 326).

Definitions: Kinds of Stocks and Bonds

WHEN ONE CUTS away all the bells and whistles overlaid on the investment world, there are really only two ways you can invest your money. You can be an "owner" who buys shares of a company, or a "lender" who loans money to a bank, business, or government agency.

Ownership. There are many different ways to own a piece of a company, but buying stock is by far the most popular. Stock ownership ties your fortunes to the success of a company in the marketplace. It's important to know that the value of your shares (and thereby your investment) can rise or fall rather dramatically over time.

Lending money. You may not have realized it, but you became a lender when you opened your first bank account, lending your money to a bank for them to reinvest. Bonds provide investors with higher-yield lending opportunities. The process is simple (though there are many complex variations): you lend your money to a corporation or government agency, and they pay you interest for the life of the bond, then return your principal at the end of the term. Bond prices are usually much more stable than those of stocks. Although it receives less attention than the pulse-quickening stock market, the boring bond market is actually far larger than the stock market in total dollars invested, and it is an important part of our financial system.

Both lending and owning can be done through individual investments, picking one stock or bond at a time. Another popular way to invest is through mutual funds, which are pooled investments in a group of stocks, bonds, or both.

Stocks

Common stocks are certificates of ownership that impart the rights to vote at the annual meeting and to receive dividends if dividends are declared. Stocks are the most popular investment in the world, and corporations love to raise capital by issuing stock. When they need money to build facilities, buy equipment, or conduct research, the sale of stock gives them the cash they need without adding to their debt load. Stocks in a company are first sold through an initial public offering; from then on, the same shares are bought and sold over and over again. The price is determined by the market; if demand for the stock is high, the price will rise, and vice versa.

Preferred stocks carry no voting rights and are issued like bonds. They also act more like bonds, paying fixed dividends and changing relatively little in value.

Bonds

When you buy a bond you are lending your money to a corporation or a government. The bond is a certificate that spells out the terms of the loan, including the interest you will receive, when the interest payments will be made, and when the borrower will repay the debt. The bond interest rate is known as the *coupon*, and interest is usually paid twice a year. The principal is repaid at the bond's maturity, which can range from a few months to forty years from the date of issue. One catch to watch for is the fact that most bonds are *callable;* that is, the issuer has the option of recalling and redeeming the bonds prior to their maturity date.

All bonds are issued with a $1,000 face value, and a minimum purchase of at least five bonds is required. This puts individual bond ownership out of reach for most small investors; however, mutual funds enable small investors to access the bond market with a $1,000 minimum investment.

One variation on the basic bond is the **zero-coupon bond**. This type of bond is one that does not pay periodic interest. Instead the bond is bought at a discount from the face amount. The face value is returned at the bond's maturity or when the bond is called. For example, a twenty-year, 10 percent $1,000 zero-coupon bond will cost $149 at issue. The holder of the bond at maturity collects the $1,000.

Every bond issuer—whether a corporation or a government agency— is rated to determine its creditworthiness. Two rating agencies, Standard & Poor's and Moody's, are the best known. Standard and Poor's uses an all-capital-letter system, with AAA the highest and C the lowest. Moody's uses a capital letter–small letter system. Standard and Poor's BBB or Moody's Baa are the minimum ratings needed to qualify a bond as "investment grade," meaning it carries little risk. Bonds rated below that level are deemed speculative and are commonly referred to as "junk" bonds. To entice investors, junk bonds must pay a higher rate of interest.

Corporate Bonds

Corporations find that issuing bonds is a relatively low-cost way to raise funds for capital improvements and expansion. Corporate bonds are either secured by mortgages on plant and equipment or backed by the general credit standing of the issuing company. Yields on corporate bonds are usually higher than those on comparable government bonds.

U.S. Government Bonds

The U.S. treasury issues bonds to cover government expenditures. They are considered among the safest investments in the world because of the financial stability of the United States. Interest is taxable on your federal income tax return but is exempt from state and local income taxes.

The Treasury issues debt instruments in three classes:

➤ Treasury bills (T-bills): bonds with terms from ninety-one days to one year.
➤ Treasury notes: bonds with maturities from one to five years.
➤ Treasury bonds: bonds with five- to forty-year maturities.

Many Natural Investors feel uncomfortable buying U.S. Treasury issues. They know this money is used to finance the entire gamut of federal programs, and everyone has at least one pet peeve with how the government spends our money: some people object to high military expenditures, others to "corporate welfare" programs such as tobacco subsidies, and so on. As an alternative, many investors turn to government agency bonds.

Government Agency Bonds

Government agencies are private corporations chartered by Congress to provide specific services such as affordable housing or student loans. They are authorized to raise money by issuing bonds. Many Natural Investors prefer government agency bonds to Treasury bonds precisely because the money is used for specific programs. They are only a smidgen less safe than Treasury bonds, backed by "the full faith and credit of the United States Government" rather than being a direct obligation of the Federal Reserve Bank. Government agency bonds typically pay interest somewhat higher than that of comparable Treasury bonds and bank certificates of deposit (CDs). The most popular government agency bonds are described on page 235.

Mortgage-Backed Bonds

Mortgage-backed bonds issued by the Government National Mortgage Association (GNMA) and other agencies are unique. Unlike other bonds, which pay back the investor's principal in one lump sum at maturity, they are "self-liquidating." They pay back a portion of principal and interest monthly. These payments are not consistent because, as homeowners pay off their mortgages, the bondholders receive bond principal payment. This makes for complex bookkeeping. The minimum purchase quantity for new-issue bonds is $25,000, and $10,000 can buy seasoned bonds. Therefore it is best that these bonds be bought through the mutual funds listed on page 218.

Municipal Bonds ("Munis")

Munis are debt obligations of states, cities, and other qualified government entities. They are generally considered socially responsible because they support the local needs of the community. However, it is still important to look at each individual issue; some pay for industrial facilities, prisons, or sports stadiums that you may not wish to support. Mutual funds invested in munis hold a broad array of bonds. If you want a more targeted approach, consider buying individual bonds (but remember that there is a $5,000 minimum) that support schools, hospitals, pollution control, or mass transit.

Munis are one of the last available tax shelters. There are now about $1.1 trillion of munis outstanding, with 75 percent of these held by individuals. Bond interest is exempt from federal income tax; residents of the state of the bond issuer are also exempt from state and local income taxes. Thus munis are commonly known as "tax-free" bonds.

Tax-free bonds pay lower interest than taxable bonds. Before investing, compare the *after-tax* benefit of taxable bonds to the yield paid by the tax-free bonds. If you are in the 28 percent or higher federal tax bracket, chances are that your in-pocket returns from tax-free municipal bonds will be greater than those from the taxable variety. Investors in lower tax brackets may be better off with taxable bonds.

Investment Planning: Four Easy Steps

Setting Goals

One easy-to-understand approach to deciding how to invest your nest egg is to consider the time frame within which you are working. Are

On Your Own, or with a Helper?

AN IMPORTANT DECISION to consider from the outset is whether to seek the help of a financial professional. Do you want help in clarifying your financial goals and understanding the relative risks and tax consequences of various types of investments? Do you feel comfortable going it alone when choosing specific investments?

There are two ways in which financial professionals charge for their services. A registered representative works with a broker and charges a commission on each transaction. A registered investment adviser (RIA) may be independent or may work with a larger firm. RIAs generally charge a quarterly management fee (a small percentage of your total portfolio value) or work on an hourly basis. Don't let the issue of paying commissions or management fees cloud your decision. Paying for professional advice may well be the best investment you ever make.

Choosing a financial adviser is both a practical and a personal decision. Certainly the adviser should have expertise in values-inclusive investing. But remember: you'll be sharing intimate financial details and exploring your social visions with this person. Make sure you feel very comfortable with your adviser, that his or her style fits your own. Seek recommendations from friends, and don't be afraid to interview several candidates. Co-op America and the Social Investment Forum offer resources to help you locate professionals.

With today's plethora of guidebooks (like this one!), magazines, and Internet resources, more investors than ever are managing their own portfolios, finding both financial success and personal satisfaction. But even if you do choose to manage your portfolio yourself, you may want to have periodic meetings with an investment and/or tax professional to help plan and review your investment strategy.

you socking away your savings, not to touch them until a retirement that is still far over the horizon? Are you intending to buy a house or land, or fund a child's college education, in a few years? Or do you want steady income right away from your investments?

Getting clear on whether you are investing for the long term or for shorter-term needs will help you allocate your assets accordingly. In general, the longer your timeline, the more you can focus on principal growth and allow for the inherently volatile nature of stock prices. As your need for available cash gets closer, you're likely to want to shift to a more conservative posture, sacrificing growth potential in order to minimize price fluctuations. If you want immediate, steady income, you are not likely to achieve much principal growth at all.

What if you want to draw from your savings occasionally, say for travel, buying cars, or other big-ticket items? You could simply cash in an investment when the need arises. Another approach would be to keep a portion of your portfolio in more liquid form, such as short-term bonds or a money-market account. This way, the need to spend doesn't force the sale of a long-term investment at a bad time.

Retirement Planning

The U.S. Congress has created a complex maze of plans intended to encourage people to set aside money during their working years. The many variations include Individual Retirement Accounts (IRAs), Self-Employment IRAs (SEP-IRAs), Money Purchase and Profit Sharing ("Keogh") Plans for the self-employed, 401(k) plans for employees of for-profit companies, and 403(b) plans for employees of nonprofits. Recently, Educational IRAs and SIMPLE IRAs were added. And we can't forget the Roth IRA, an entirely different animal (tax-wise) than all the others. How wonderful of our elected leaders to make life so thoroughly confusing! We strongly recommend that you confer with a financial professional (an investment adviser, an estate planner, or both) every few years to be sure your retirement planning is up to date.

Every screened mutual fund has an IRA plan that can be used by individuals. Employees whose companies offer pension plans should request socially screened options. In 1998 the Department of Labor ruled that socially responsible investments are acceptable for pension fund holdings so long as they provide returns equal to those of traditional investments.

Understanding Risk and Reward

Every time you invest you take a financial risk. Even if you stuff your money into a mattress or deposit it in a low-interest bank account, it is not totally safe since inflation may cause you to lose future purchasing power. There are many types of risk: risk of inflation, risk of market volatility (dropping stock values), risk to principal, risk of tax changes, risks connected with liquidity and market conditions when you need to retrieve your money. All of these must be considered, but one plays a primary role in any investment decision: the risk of losing money in the quest for higher returns. As a general rule, investments that offer higher possible rewards carry with them inherently higher risks.

The Wealth Indexes of Investments Chart gives a good overview of the returns on different investments with respect to inflation.

Over the long term, stocks have significantly higher returns than bonds (although there have been exceptional periods when bonds outperformed stocks). This is not surprising, as bonds are designed for a fixed return and stocks are free to follow the trends of the market. But the increased rewards do come at a cost: stocks are much more volatile than bonds. Though bond prices may drop or rise a bit, stock prices can rise or fall by 20 percent or more in a single year (even, occasionally, in a single week or a single day!). The long-term rewards of the stock market have been on the order of 12 percent per year for the last twenty years. By contrast, high-quality bonds today generally pay 5 to 7 percent per year and rarely change much in principal value.

Stock Risks. The strength of the stock market, although impressive over the past sixty years, is tied intimately to the strength of our economy as a whole; there is never a guarantee of future growth. The dizzying rise of the market during the 1990s was far from ordinary: from 1993 to 1998, annual increases averaged 23 percent, approximately twice the historical average. The summer of 1998 cooled those jets somewhat, yet it is likely that the market will return to the 10 to 12 percent annual returns garnered before 1993.

It's also worth keeping in mind the dramatic stock crashes of the past. In 1929 the market fell over 40 percent in one day. The decline continued until 1932. It took many years to recoup that loss. In 1987, there was a one-day drop of 23 percent; it took the market a year and a half to return to its former level.

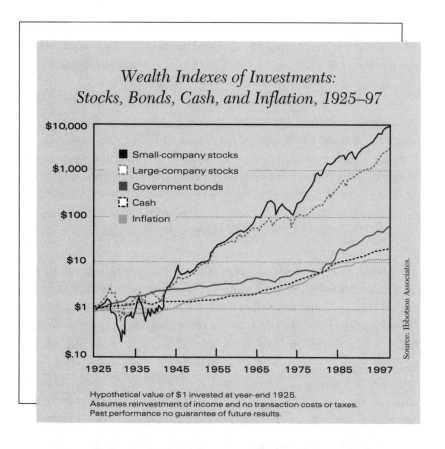

Wealth Indexes of Investments:
Stocks, Bonds, Cash, and Inflation, 1925–97

- ■ Small-company stocks
- ▫ Large-company stocks
- ■ Government bonds
- ▫ Cash
- ■ Inflation

Source: Ibbotson Associates.

Hypothetical value of $1 invested at year-end 1925.
Assumes reinvestment of income and no transaction costs or taxes.
Past performance no guarantee of future results.

TYPE OF INVESTMENT	ENDING WEALTH	AVERAGE RETURN
Small-Company Stocks	$5,520	12.7%
Large-Company Stocks	$1,828	11.0%
Government Bonds	$39	5.2%
Cash	$14	3.8%
Inflation	$9	3.1%

Investors holding shares in only one company can experience serious problems. Even in a strong market the individual stock can take a big hit. IBM shareholders got a rude awakening in 1992. After years as the ultimate blue chip stock—one that could always be counted on to rise in value, while paying healthy annual dividends—the company faltered, and the stock declined by almost half to approximately $50 per share. All-American giants like IBM often make up a disproportionate share of the portfolios of small investors; perhaps the shares were an inheritance from Grandpa, who dabbled just a bit in the market. Shareholders who couldn't wait out the IBM slump were left muttering to themselves about their overreliance on this industry titan.

Certainly there may be times when an emergency or large purchase will require you to cash out part of your portfolio; at these times it is important to be well diversified, so you don't have to sell holdings at a low ebb. Today, thanks to mutual funds, even investment neophytes can avoid the pitfall of relying too heavily on a single investment. (By the way, investors who resisted the urge to bail out of IBM completely have experienced the happier side of market volatility: after several years of recovery, IBM has more than doubled in value from the point at which it *began* its tumble.)

Bond Risks. Bonds don't fluctuate so wildly in value, but there are subtler risks to keep in mind. If you buy or sell bonds between their time of issue and their time of maturity, there is some principal risk. That is, the market value of the bond goes down when prevailing interest rates are higher than the bond's rate and vice versa (so that the new buyer will, overall, be earning the market rate of return at the time of purchase). If you hold the bond to maturity, this is not a concern. In addition, a bond is only as strong as the company or agency that issues it; junk bonds in particular carry a significant risk of missed interest payments or outright default.

Asset Allocation

The ancient adage "Never keep all your eggs in one basket" is a sacred principle for investors, and it means more than simply owning *many* stocks. All investors should spread their risk into *different kinds* of investments in order to protect against a disaster in any one market segment. History is replete with investment fads that turned sour. For example, many popular real estate limited partnerships went bankrupt in the 1980s, leaving investors holding the bag. In early 1980 gold was $800+ per ounce; in September 1998 it was down to less than $300 per ounce, never again having matched that high peak. Beyond such horror stories, diversification helps reduce the overall volatility of a portfolio. Small companies perform differently than large ones, bonds provide a cushion for stock volatility, and foreign investments often march to the beat of a different drummer, rising and falling at different times than the U.S. markets. So get yourself a bunch of baskets!

The latest catch phrase for diversification is "asset allocation." Our Asset Allocation Guidelines can help you build a portfolio that will suit your personal priorities and economic needs. Use these guidelines as a starting point; then fill in the blanks with funds or individual investments that are aligned to your personal values.

Ready . . . Before you begin your investment plan, be sure to have ready access to enough cash to cover *three to six months of living expenses.* For maximum social impact, these funds can be kept in a savings account at a community bank or credit union.

. . . *Set* . . . Take a moment to revisit Worksheet #2 at the end of Section 2, in which you determined which of the four spokes of the Natural Investing Wheel you wanted to put to use. It's now time to set aside whatever proportion of your portfolio you'd like to put to work in Community Investing. Many Natural Investors allocate 10 percent or more of their monies to community investments, including CDs at community banks or credit unions and loans to local, regional, or international community loan funds.

. . . *And go!* Take the proportion of your portfolio that you've chosen to allocate to Avoidance Screening and Affirmative Screening, and step into the heart of your asset allocation process.

The Beach Lover's Guide to Asset Allocation

THE KEY TO asset allocation is defining your level of risk tolerance. Here's an enticing allegory that makes this step easy to visualize:

Picture yourself at a beautiful sandy beach on a warm, sunny day. The surf is up. The gentle beach represents conservative bond investments. The lively surf represents volatile stock investments.

If you are the kind of person who is a **land lover,** staying secure on the boardwalk, then you are really not a risk-taker. Please do not become a stock investor. Keep all your money in insured bank accounts and CDs. You might perhaps consider buying a fixed annuity from a financially stable insurance company.

You **sunbathers** put on a bathing suit primarily to get a tan on the beach, maybe venturing to the water's edge (but no farther) to wet your toes. You are conservative, very-low-risk types. Your goal: preserve capital. You don't want the value of your investments to fall much, if at all, for any length of time. You're willing to take small risks to achieve steady income with a slightly higher return than that offered by bank CDs.

The slightly conservative, low-risk investor is the **wader.** You will wade out to where the water is just about knee deep and it's easy to run back to the shore. Your goal: primarily income. You want to have a steady return of interest to augment your other income. You can put up with small, short-term losses in return for a degree of longer-term growth.

Braver souls are **dunkers.** You go out into the surf about waist high and occasionally lower yourself into the water to cool off your whole body. You would be classified as a growth-and-income-oriented, medium-risk investor. Your goal is a balance between income and growth. You're willing to accept some stock losses over the next three to four years. A bond component stabilizes your portfolio.

The confident **swimmer** who feels comfortable in deep water is known as the growth-oriented, high-risk investor. Your goal: capital growth. You want your portfolio to increase in value, and you hope it will grow significantly. You're willing to sustain capital losses over the next five years; you can live with market volatility because you seek long-term gains.

Last is the **surfer,** way out in the sea, waiting to ride the big wave. You are an aggressive-growth, very-high-risk investor. Your goal: capital appreciation. You're looking for the highest possible growth and are willing to accept losses over the next ten years if there's a major market correction. Surfers accept—and even thrive on—market volatility.

Picture yourself on the shoreline of finance and try to determine where you fall on the spectrum. You may feel you are in between categories, in which case just pick the one that seems the closest fit. As you gain more experience with investing, you may become braver; you can easily shift a few holdings into a riskier category. Likewise, if a burst of early enthusiasm carries you too far out to sea, you can make your portfolio more conservative. And rest assured that in the following chapters, as we dive deeper into the details of mutual funds and other options, the various terms will be introduced and will start to make sense to you. With all this in mind, we offer a framework for your consideration.

The portfolios shown in the accompanying table are structured around types of mutual funds. You'll want to tailor a plan with a maximum of eight to ten different funds. Scattering your holdings into more than that dilutes the process and adds a level of research and follow-up that will probably not be worth the time it will require. See Chapter 10 for brief descriptions of each fund class. Investors who are making direct investments in stocks and bonds should classify each choice to coincide with related mutual fund content.

Our next worksheet will help you locate yourself in this beach scene. The chapters that follow will help you complete your asset allocation plan. Chapter 10 covers socially screened mutual funds and Chapter 11 includes choices for specialized fund categories (such as sector funds and government bonds). Chapter 12 will bring us beyond the world of mutual funds to look at individual stocks and bonds and many other types of investments.

The Beach Lover's Asset Allocation Chart

	SUNBATHER	WADER	DUNKER	SWIMMER	SURFER
Bond Range	70–90%	50–70%	40–60%	30–50%	0–30%
Stock Range	10–30%	30–50%	40–60%	50–70%	70–100%
SAMPLE MUTUAL FUND PORTFOLIO*					
Bond Funds					
Long-Term Government Agency/ Mortgage-Backed	40%	35%	30%	25%	10%
Short-Duration Bond	15%	5%	0%	0%	0%
Income	20%	15%	15%	15%	5%
Stock Funds					
Utilities	10%	15%	5%	0%	0%
Balanced	10%	15%	10%	0%	0%
Large Cap**	5%	10%	20%	25%	30%
Midcap	0%	5%	10%	10%	15%
Small Cap	0%	0%	5%	5%	10%
International/Global	0%	0%	5%	10%	15%
Aggressive Growth	0%	0%	0%	5%	10%
Sector	0%	0%	0%	5%	5%

Notes:

*   Individual securities may be substituted for mutual funds (see Chapter 12).

**   Equity-income funds may be used for this asset class.

Worksheet #6: Asset Allocation

This worksheet begins the process of selecting your portfolio. It's time to define your financial objectives and take a look at your overall financial situation.

1. What dreams, needs, and desires would you like to invest for?

    A. _____

    B. _____

    C. _____

2. For each of the goals, how much money do you wish to save and when will you need it?

    A. Amount _____ Time frame _____

    B. Amount _____ Time frame _____

    C. Amount _____ Time frame _____

3. Are you out of debt?   Yes _____   No _____
    (If not, you'll need to stop here and return when you can say "yes." See Chapter 13 for a discussion of issues regarding spending and work.)

4. Do you have three to six months' living expenses set aside? Yes _____   No _____

5. How much do you have to invest right now? $_____

6. How much can you invest on a monthly basis? $_____

7. What amount or percentage of your portfolio will be allocated to Community Investing? $_____ or _____%

8. What amount or percentage of your portfolio will be allocated to Affirmative Screening (prospecting)? $_____ or _____%

9. Using the beach analogy (see page 173), which investor type do you feel most aligned with? Note that if your goals in Question 2 are relatively short-term, you should edge toward the beach (be more conservative). In general, most advisers advocate having at least a five-year time horizon for stock investments due to their inherent volatility.

    _____ Land lover

    _____ Sunbather

    _____ Wader

    _____ Dunker

    _____ Swimmer

C h a p t e r **10** *T e n*

Socially Screened Mutual Funds

N OW THAT YOU'VE decided to put your money where your values are, the next step is to start finding the investments that will be both financially solid and in line with your personal issues scorecard. So . . . do you turn to the *Wall Street Journal*'s stock and bond listings and start researching to find the right investment? That's a choice, to be sure, but one that most people would quickly find overwhelming.

Luckily for most of us, there are squadrons of well-trained research staffs already on the job, identifying companies that pass both avoidance and affirmative screens, working with investment analysts to find the ones most likely to be successful investments in the near and far future. To partake of the services of these socially attuned financial professionals, all you need to do is buy into any of the screened mutual funds.

Mutual funds are the simplest point of entry for most new investors. They are popular because of their liquidity (their shares are easy to sell if you need cash), their diversity, and their relative safety. A mutual fund is a pooled investment. You, along with countless other investors, buy shares of the fund. With the money you all invest in the fund, the fund's managers, in turn, invest in a diversified portfolio. With one investment in a stock mutual fund, you are suddenly the proud owner of stock in dozens—and with some funds, hundreds—of different companies. You are freed from the arduous tasks of constantly monitoring both the stock price and the outlook for each company you own; the management team is handling those chores daily. You can also rest easy, knowing that all your eggs are never in too few baskets, so that big changes in one company's fortunes won't have a drastic affect on the value of your overall portfolio.

Of course, you *are* now relying heavily on the expertise and instincts of your fund's management team. Most mutual funds have had great years as well as years when the management team was missing the mark or their investment style was out of favor, leaving their fund lagging behind others in its class. The best way to deal with this reality is to keep watch on the relative success of the funds you choose (so you can wisely sell a fund if it seems to perform consistently below par) and to spread your money out among several funds (so you are not relying too heavily on any one management team).

The socially responsible mutual fund industry has grown significantly over the last five years. In 1993 there were twelve socially screened funds. By 1998 this number had grown to forty-seven. Later in this chapter, you will find comprehensive profiles of each of these funds' screens, performance, and other features.

In addition, over 140 funds have limited screens, such as shunning tobacco or focusing on a specific issue such as women's rights. These are covered in Chapter 10, along with over a hundred nonscreened funds that focus on a specific industry or social sector that is aligned with the values of many Natural Investors.

Within the broad category of mutual funds, you can find funds that will direct your money into many distinct types of investments, running the gamut from high-gain/high-risk stocks (aggressive growth funds) to relatively safe and solid bonds (bond and income funds), with plenty of ground in between. You can find funds that aim for a good balance of stocks and bonds, funds that focus on the international market, and funds with specific religious orientations.

As you'll see, you can accomplish most of your financial and social goals working within the universe of mutual funds. For fun or to respond to specific social desires, you may want to put some of your money into individual stocks, bonds, or community investments. But chances are that you will leave much of your portfolio—and your worries—in the hands of a well-chosen group of mutual funds.

How Safe Are Mutual Funds?

THE BOTTOM-LINE ANSWER to this important question is: it depends on the sort of fund you're talking about. Stock funds, nearly totally invested in the market, will go up or down in value along with the market. The principal of investment-grade bond funds is likely to change only slightly, in response to the smaller fluctuations in interest rates. Balanced funds offer a tempered ride on the stock market roller coaster by including both stocks and bonds in their portfolios.

As for the overall safety of the mutual fund industry, you can rest easy: mutual funds are highly regulated. After the stock market crash of 1929, the Securities and Exchange Commission (SEC) was established to protect investors by monitoring companies issuing stock. The National Association of Securities Dealers (NASD) requires investment professionals to prove that they are knowledgeable of the law, and they face penalties for acting fraudulently in their dealings with the public. Continuing intense surveillance by the SEC and NASD protects the investing public from being cheated and gives investors proper recourse if they are wronged.

Tax Efficiency

IT IS WONDERFUL to profit from mutual fund investments, but please make certain that you carefully look at the *style* of each fund as part of your selection process. You will pay annual capital gains on the holdings of your mutual funds. Some funds have very low turnover of holdings and therefore generate very low capital gains; others have high turnover, sometimes 100 percent or greater each year. These high-turnover stock funds may generate large capital gains that trigger additional income tax, effectively reducing your real total return. In addition, it's a good idea to be aware of the date on which a stock mutual fund declares capital gains (usually in December); buying into the fund just before that date can give you an excessive tax burden.

Mutual Funds on a Shoestring

THE TYPICAL MUTUAL fund requires an initial investment of $1,000 to $2,500. This may be difficult for the small investor. Fortunately there are ways to get into mutual funds with less money. Security Social Awareness fund has a $100 minimum, and Pax World funds have a $250 minimum. Many funds allow an even lower initial investment if you sign up for an automatic investment program from your bank or credit union. Under this arrangement, you automatically invest $50 or more each month by direct transfer to the fund. This is a real blessing. Continuous, automatic dollar-cost-averaging investing is one of the most effective and painless ways to invest for long-term growth. The Aquinas, Ariel, Eclipse, Green Century, MMA Praxis, Noah, Rightime Social Awareness, and Women's Equity funds will let you start with $50 or less, and many other funds set their initial investments at $250 or less (see the profiles at the end of this chapter for the minimum for each fund). Note as well that most mutual funds lower the minimum initial investment for Individual Retirement Accounts and other pension plans.

Mutual Fund Reports

MUTUAL FUNDS MUST report to their shareholders regularly. They publish quarterly, semiannual, and annual reports showing the financial condition of the fund and listing the investments in the portfolio. Faithfully read these reports, especially the portfolio listing. Become familiar with the operation of the fund by reading the prospectus, which details your costs, rights to switch within the family of funds, and other important information. In the past, prospectuses were hard to read because of the profusion of legalese, but the industry and the SEC are taking steps to make them more user-friendly.

The prospectus formally defines the social issues that are addressed by the fund. Once defined in the prospectus, these issues can be changed only by a vote of the shareholders (the fund will solicit you for your vote on all management changes). This chapter covers only funds that are formally screened by *prospectus;* funds that are screened by *policy* (which can be changed by the fund's management *without* shareholder approval) are covered in Chapter 11.

Natural Investing Mutual Fund Listings: Finding Funds That Match Your Values

NOW WE BEGIN focusing on finding specific mutual funds to consider buying. You'll be looking for funds that match both your values and your asset allocation needs. We will offer you a number of listings that should provide good starting points for your decision-making process.

Be aware that some of the social screens (most commonly, nuclear power and military weapons) can get a little fuzzy. For example, the

Domini Social Equity Fund will include a company if it earns less than 2 percent of its income from military weapons production.

There are encouraging signs that the mutual fund industry is responding to consumer interest in moving beyond simple avoidance screens and beginning to address the other three spokes of the Natural Investing Wheel. Several funds are seeking proactively positive investments; for example, the Calvert Social Managed Growth fund earmarks part of its assets for small, proactive companies. And a few mutual funds have become more active in the realms of Shareholder Activism and Community Investing. The Calvert, Citizens, Domini, MMA Praxis, and Pax World funds have tended to be in the forefront of this expansion of mutual fund concerns. Read their annual reports for indications of their commitment to broadening the social impact of your investments.

To make it easier to identify funds that share your social values, we've compiled a Mutual Fund Screen Matrix. It lists each of the forty-seven broadly screened mutual funds, noting which social issues are screened, along with whether each is engaged in Shareholder Activism, Community Investing, or both. This chart will be a ready reference as you build your portfolio.

Types of Mutual Funds

In the preceding chapter you were introduced to the risk-tolerance questions that should underlie your asset allocation choices. As you fill in your personal investment plan, you'll need to seek mutual funds or individual investments that match your own asset allocation needs. The next few pages will introduce you to the various fund types, along with a list of screened fund options for each type. Detailed information on each fund can be found in the profiles at the end of this chapter.

Money-Market Funds These serve as a "parking place" for money needed as cash reserves. Money-market funds invest in very-short-term "paper": notes, bills and bonds, issued by corporations, the U.S. Treasury, U.S. government agencies, and government at all levels. They are available in taxable and tax-free form. Most money-market funds are instantly liquid: when opening the account you can even request that a checkbook be printed for you. Typically you can write checks for $250 or more. Interest rates are higher than those paid by ordinary savings accounts, comparable to the interest you would receive for one-year bank certificates of deposit (and with money-market accounts there

Mutual Fund Screen Matrix

FUND NAME	ALCOHOL	FIRE-ARMS	GAMBLING	TOBACCO	ENVIRONMENT	EMPLOYMENT
AQUINAS						
Balanced				A	A	A&S
Equity Growth				A	A	A&S
Equity Income				A	A	A&S
Fixed Income				A	A	A&S
ARIEL						
Appreciation	A	A		A	A&S	A&S
Growth	A	A		A	A&S	A&S
BRIDGEWAY SOCIAL RESPONSIBILITY	A			A	A&S	A&S
CALVERT						
Capital Accumulation	A	A	A	A	A&S	A&S
New Vision	A	A	A	A	A	A
Social Balanced	A	A	A	A	A&S	A&S
Social Bond	A	A	A	A	A&S	A&S
Social Equity	A	A	A	A	A&S	A&S
Social Managed Index	A	A	A	A	A&S	A&S
World Values	A	A	A	A	A&S	A&S
CITIZENS TRUST						
Citizens Emer.Growth	A	A	A	A	A&S	A&S
Citizens Global	A	A	A	A	A&S	A&S
Citizens Income	A	A	A	A	A&S	A&S
Citizens Index	A	A	A	A	A&S	A&S
CONCERT SOCIAL AWARENESS				A	S	A&S
CRUELTY FREE VALUE						
DELAWARE SOCIAL AWARENESS	A	A	A	A	A	
DEVCAP SHARED RETURN	A	A	A	A	A&S	A&S
DOMINI SOCIAL EQUITY	A	A	A	A	A&S	A&S
DREYFUS THIRD CENTURY	A	A	A	A	A&S	A&S
KEY:	A = Avoid		S = Seek			

MILITARY WEAPONS	NUCLEAR POWER	PRODUCT QUALITY	ANIMAL RIGHTS	OPPRESSIVE REGIMES	COMMUNITY INVESTMENTS	SHAREHOLDER ACTIVISM
A		A		A		S
A		A		A		S
A		A		A		S
A		A		A		S
A	A	A&S			S	S
A	A	A&S			S	S
A	A	A&S	A	A	S	S
A	A	A&S		A	S	S
A	A	A&S		A	S	S
A	A	A&S	A	A	S	S
A	A	A&S	A	A	S	S
A	A	A&S	A	A	S	S
A	A	A&S	A	A		S
A	A	A&S	A	A	S	S
A	A	A	A	A	S	S
A	A	A	A		S	S
A	A	A	A		S	S
A	A	A	A		S	S
A	A	A		A		
		A&S				
A	A		A			
A	A	A&S	A		S	
A	A	A&S	A			S
A	A	A&S		A	S	S

(continued on following page)

Mutual Fund Screen Matrix (*continued*)

FUND NAME	ALCOHOL	FIRE-ARMS	GAMBLING	TOBACCO	ENVIRONMENT	EMPLOYMENT
ECLIPSE ULTRA SHORT	A		A	A		
FLEX FUND						
Total Return Utility	A	A	A	A	A&S	A&S
GREEN CENTURY						
Balanced	A	A	A	A	A&S	A&S
Equity	A	A	A	A	A&S	A&S
MEYERS PRIDE VALUE	A		A	A	A&S	
MMA PRAXIS						
Growth	A		A	A	A&S	A&S
Intermediate Income	A		A	A	A&S	A&S
International	A		A	A	A&S	A&S
NEUBERGER BERMAN SOCIALLY RESPONSIVE	A	A	A	A	A&S	A&S
NEW ALTERNATIVES	A	A	A	A	A&S	A&S
NOAH	A		A	A	A	
PARNASSUS						
California Tax-Free	A	A	A	A	A&S	A&S
Equity Income	A	A	A	A	A&S	A&S
Fixed Income	A	A	A	A	A&S	A&S
Fund	A	A	A	A	A&S	A&S
PAX WORLD						
Fund	A	A	A	A	A&S	A&S
Growth	A	A	A	A	A&S	A&S
RIGHTIME SOCIAL AWARENESS	A	A	A	A	A&S	A&S
SECURITY SOCIAL AWARENESS	A	A	A	A	A&S	A&S
TIMOTHY PLAN	A		A	A		A
USAA FIRST START	A		A	A		
VICTORY LAKEFRONT						A&S
WOMEN'S EQUITY	A	A	A	A	A	A&S

KEY: A = Avoid   S = Seek

MILITARY WEAPONS	NUCLEAR POWER	PRODUCT QUALITY	ANIMAL RIGHTS	OPPRESSIVE REGIMES	COMMUNITY INVESTMENTS	SHAREHOLDER ACTIVISM
A	A				S	
A	A	A&S	A			S
A	A	A&S		A	S	S
A	A	A&S		A	S	S
	A&S	A	A		S	
A	A	A&S		A	S	S
A	A	A&S		A	S	S
A	A	A&S		A	S	S
A	A	A&S		A	S	
A	A	A&S	A		S	S
					S	
A	A	A&S	A	A		
A	A	A&S	A	A	S	S
A	A	A&S	A	A	S	S
A	A	A&S	A	A	S	S
A	A	S		A	S	S
A	A	S		A	S	S
A	A	A&S		A		
A	A	A&S		A		S
A	A	A&S	A			S

are never any penalties for early withdrawals). Mutual fund money-market funds are not insured.

Screened fund choices:
- ➤ Aquinas Money Market
- ➤ Calvert Social Money Market
- ➤ Citizens Money Market
- ➤ Domini/South Shore Bank
- ➤ Pax World Money Market

Most community banks and credit unions also offer insured money market checking options

Bond Funds Bond mutual funds hold a portfolio of many bonds with different maturities. This strategy helps stabilize fund share prices. The funds typically pay out monthly dividends, which are very convenient for people needing a steady income from investments. In many cases, the high minimum purchase requirements for individual bonds make bond mutual funds more attractive, allowing small investors to own some bonds and larger investors to more easily be diversified.

Government. U.S. government agency– and mortgage-backed bonds.
Screened fund choice:
- ➤ Eclipse Ultra Short-Term

Tax-Free. Bonds that are free of federal, state, or local income taxes, or all three.
Screened fund choice:
- ➤ Parnassus California Tax-Exempt

Income. Funds holding a blend of government and corporate bonds.
Screened fund choices:
- ➤ Aquinas Fixed Income
- ➤ Calvert Social Bond
- ➤ Citizens Income
- ➤ MMA Praxis Intermediate Income
- ➤ Parnassus Fixed-Income

Stock Funds
Large-Cap. Primarily companies with large capitalization (greater than $6 billion), commonly called "blue-chip" companies. This is generally the least volatile of the stock categories.
Screened fund choices:
- ➤ Aquinas Equity Growth
- ➤ Bridgeway Social Responsibility
- ➤ Calvert Social Equity

- Calvert Social Managed Index
- Citizens Index
- Delaware Social Awareness
- DevCap Shared Return
- Domini Social Equity
- Dreyfus Third Century
- Green Century Equity
- MMA Praxis
- Neuberger Berman Socially Responsive
- Noah
- Pax World Growth
- Security Socially Responsive
- USAA First Start Growth
- Victory Lakefront
- Women's Equity

Midcap. Primarily companies with a capitalization of $2 billion to $6 billion. These represent the midrange sector of the stock market and are usually more volatile than growth stocks.

Screened fund choices:

- Ariel Appreciation
- Calvert Capital Accumulation
- Cruelty-Free Value
- Timothy Plan

Small-Cap. Primarily smaller companies, with capitalization of under $2 billion. Some of these are bound to become the large companies of the future. Potential growth is the key to their popularity. This category is subject to high risk because many small companies do not survive.

Screened fund choices:

- Ariel Growth
- Calvert New Vision

Aggressive Growth. Funds that take higher risks. These funds use market timing, buy out-of-favor stocks, invest in emerging markets, or employ other aggressive techniques. A fund in this group may contain only large-, mid-, or small-cap stocks or a blend of all three.

Screened fund choices:

- Citizens Emerging Growth
- Green Century Balanced
- Parnassus
- Rightime Social Awareness

Equity-Income. Funds with portfolios that focus on high-yielding stocks rather than capital appreciation.

Screened fund choices:
➤ Aquinas Equity Income
➤ Parnassus Equity Income

Utility. Funds making investments in regulated and nonregulated essential service industries, including electrical energy, telephone, and water utilities.

Screened fund choice:
➤ Flex Funds Total Return Utilities

Sector. These funds invest in equities issued by corporations in a specific industry group, such as real estate, technology, or financial services. The equities can be of all sizes: large-, mid-, or small-cap. These funds are vulnerable to larger swings as short-term investors and industry speculators often aggressively switch sectors. Sector funds are riskier than the broader diversified stock funds. We will cover many more unscreened sector funds in Chapter 11.

Screened fund choice:
➤ New Alternatives (environmental fund)

Balanced Funds Mutual funds that contain both stocks and bonds. These funds are usually invested 55 to 65 percent in stocks with the remainder of their holdings in bonds. This combination attracts more conservative investors, as the bonds in the portfolio tend to protect the investor in down markets. For a small investor, balanced funds may be the number one choice; they provide maximum diversification within a single investment.

Screened fund choices:
➤ Aquinas Balanced
➤ Calvert Social Balanced
➤ Concert Social Awareness
➤ Pax World

Global and International Funds

Global Stock. Funds that invest in stocks of companies based outside the United States and those headquartered in the United States that serve global markets.

Screened fund choice:
➤ Citizens Global

International Stock. Funds whose investments are limited to stocks of companies based outside the United States. The funds invest in companies of all sizes and select those listed on stock exchanges throughout the world that are liquid.

Screened fund choices:

➤ Calvert World Values International Equity

➤ MMA Praxis International

Mutual Fund Profiles

Now we're getting down to the real nitty-gritty. The rest of this chapter is composed of detailed profiles on each of the forty-seven mutual funds that were socially screened by prospectus at the time of this writing. Any fund in the SRI Mutual Fund Screen Matrix, Mutual Fund Honor Roll, or fund types listings that caught your eye deserves further scrutiny here.

Terms Used in Each Profile

➤ *NIS Social Rating*^{SM} *(♥ to ♥♥♥♥♥).* We have developed a system of analyzing the social screens used by each fund. The number of screens, importance of each screen, and application of each screen have been weighted and scored. The resultant scores are then arranged into five twentieth percentiles. The funds in the lowest percentile are awarded one heart; those in the highest percentile are awarded five hearts.

➤ *12b-1 fee.* Under SEC rule 12b-1, a fund is permitted to use some of its shareholders' money to pay for marketing expenses. These may include the setting up and staffing of toll-free telephone service and compensation to brokers to service existing accounts. Some funds do not take this fee; management uses its own money for marketing and does not compensate brokers for maintaining existing accounts. Other funds assess a fee, which is typically 0.25 percent. The 12b-1 fee may be as high as 1.0 percent.

➤ *Total operating expense.* The sum of the management fee, 12b-1 fee, and other SEC-allowed expenses. The total operating expense can range from approximately 0.25 percent to 2.5 percent. Normally bond funds have lower expenses and aggressive growth funds have higher expenses. The highest expenses are usually those for international and global funds because there are higher costs involved in operating overseas. When making choices, look for the lowest possible fees consistent with an acceptable total return for the fund.

Socially Screened Funds That Have Made the Honor Roll

NIS Social Rating^SM ♥♥♥♥♥

Calvert Managed Index
Calvert Social Balanced
Calvert Social Bond
Calvert Social Equity
Citizens Emerging Growth
Citizens Global Equity
Citizens Income

Citizens Index
DevCap Shared Return
Domini Social Equity
Green Century Equity
Parnassus Equity Income
Parnassus Fixed Income
Parnassus Fund

NIS Social Rating^SM ♥♥♥♥

Bridgeway Social Responsibility
Calvert Capital Accumulation
Calvert World Values
Dreyfus Third Century
Flex Total Return
Green Century Balanced
MMA Praxis Growth
MMA Praxis Intermediate
  Income

MMA Praxis International
Neuberger Berman Socially
  Responsive
New Alternatives
Parnassus Tax Exempt
Pax World
Pax World Growth
Rightime Social Awareness
Women's Equity

➤ *Beta.* A statistic that measures a fund's volatility against the Standard & Poor's 500 stock index. A beta close to 1.00 indicates that the fund tends to track the S&P's ups and downs fairly closely. If the beta is greater than 1.00, the fund is more volatile; if it is less than 1.00, the fund is less volatile.

➤ *Sharpe (ratio).* A measure of risk-adjusted fund volatility. The Sharpe ratio compares the return to the amount of risk taken by choosing the particular fund in the first place. If two funds have the same return the more volatile one will have a lower Sharpe ratio. All other things being equal, higher Sharpe ratios are more desirable.

Performance Rating*: Top Twentieth Percentile in Category for One-, Three-, and Five-Year Periods

Ariel Appreciation—1,3,5

Ariel Growth—1,3,5

Bridgeway Social Responsibility—1

Citizens Emerging Growth—1,3

Citizens Global Equity—1,3

Citizens Income—1,3

Citizens Index—1,3

Citizens International—1,3

Concert Social Awareness—1,3,5

Domini Social Equity—3,5

Dreyfus Third Century—3

Green Century Equity—1,3

MMA Praxis International—1

Pax World—1,3,5

Rightime Social Awareness—1,3,5

Women's Equity—1

Based on annualized total returns as of December 31, 1998, that put funds in the top twentieth percentile of their asset class as rated by Lipper for one-year, three-year or five-year periods.

➢ *Annualized total returns.* The actual measure of the performance of the fund. It compares the current NAV to the NAV from a base period. It reflects increased value from dividends, capital gains, and other income received. The resulting calculation is then expressed as a percentage. The numbers in the profiles are annualized percentages. They do not reflect sales charges.

➢ *Yield.* The interest rate the fund is earning. This is a simple calculation of dividends paid divided by the current NAV, multiplied by 100 to express the yield as a percentage.

➤ *Portfolio turnover.* The percentage rate at which the fund buys and sells portfolio holdings. The larger the number, the higher the turnover. High turnover also generates more capital gains tax distributions to shareholders.

➤ *Ticker symbol.* The shorthand NASD-assigned symbol used to identify each mutual fund. It is given in parentheses after the fund name.

➤ *Share type.* The total commissions and fees paid by the customer. No-load funds charge no commission. A, B, and C shares entail commissions and fees as follows: A-load funds charge when you buy, B-load funds charge when you sell (with decreasing rates the longer you hold the fund), and C-load funds charge an annual percentage.

Performance Benchmarks:
Annualized Total Return as of December 31, 1998

TYPE OF INVESTMENT	1-YEAR	3-YEAR	5-YEAR
S&P 500 with Dividends	28.72	28.28	24.09
DJIA with Dividends	18.13	23.83	22.35
LIPPER			
Capital Appreciation	19.96	17.28	16.13
Growth	22.86	22.65	19.03
Small-Cap	-0.22	13.13	13.04
International	12.69	10.01	7.65
Balanced	12.69	15.88	13.93
Emerging Markets	-26.83	-8.03	-10.01
Corporate A-Rated Bonds	5.61	6.40	6.19
GNMA	6.47	6.49	6.51

Screened Mutual Fund Profiles

Screened Mutual Fund Profiles

AQUINAS FUNDS
www.aquinasfunds.com
5310 Harvest Hill Road, Suite 248 Dallas, TX 75230 [800-423-6369]

AQUINAS BALANCED (AQBLX)

Asset Class: Balanced
NIS Social Rating℠: ♥ ♥
Share Type: No Load
Date of Inception: 1/4/94
Assets: $29.5 Million
Fund Managers: Team Managed
12b-1 Fee: 0.00%
Total Operating Expense: 1.45%
Minimum Investment:
Initial: $500/Subsequently: $250
Automatic Investments:
Initial: $50/Subsequently: $50
Beta: 0.87   **Sharpe:** 0.96
Percentage of Stocks: 57%
Percentage of Bonds: 38%

Percentage of Cash/equiv.: 5%
Average Bond Maturity: 11 years
Annualized Returns as of 12/31/98:
1998: 8.46%, 3-year: 14.46%,
5-year: N/A, Since Inception: 12.38%
Top Ten Holdings as of 9/30/98:
U. S. Treasury Note 6.25%, IBM, Coca
Cola Enterprises 7.0%, Duke Energy,
GTE, J.C. Penny 7.4%, WMX
Technologies 7.1%, Motorola 6.5%,
Household Finance 7.125%,
Grand Metro Investments 7.45%
Portfolio Turnover: 94%
Comments: Fund screens using
Catholic Bishops' social guidelines.

AQUINAS EQUITY GROWTH (AQEGX)

Asset Class: Midcap
NIS Social Rating℠: ♥ ♥
Share Type: No Load
Date of Inception: 1/4/94
Assets: $43.0 Million
Fund Manages:
John McStay (since 1/4/94)
12b-1 Fee: 0.00%
Total Operating Expense: 1.49%
Minimum Investment:
Initial: $500/Subsequently: $250
Automatic Investments:
Initial: $50/Subsequently: $50
Beta: 0.99   **Sharpe:** 0.96

Percentage of Stocks: 94.68%
Percentage of Cash/equiv.: 5.32%
Annualized Returns as of 12/31/98:
1998: 21.95%, 3-year: 24.60%,
5-year: N/A, Since Inception: 18.75%
Top Ten Holdings as of 9/30/98: Fiserv,
Paychex, Capital One Financial,
HealthCare Financial Partner,
FINOVA Group, Microsoft, Nova (GA),
Affiliated Computer Svcs A, Reliastar
Financial, SunGard Data Systems
Portfolio Turnover: 104%
Comments: Fund Screens using
Catholic Bishops' social guidelines

AQUINAS EQUITY INCOME (AQEIX)

Asset Class: Equity Income
NIS Social Rating℠: ♥ ♥
Share Type: No Load
Date of Inception: 1/4/94
Assets: $66.4 Million
Fund Managers: Team Managed
12b-1 Fee: 0.00%
Total Operating Expense: 1.37%
Minimum Investment:
Initial: $500/Subsequently: $250
Automatic Investments:
Initial: $50/Subsequently $50
Beta: 0.78   **Sharpe:** 0.81
Yield: 1.54%

Percentage of Stocks: 96.84%
Percentage of Cash/equiv.: 3.16%
Average Bond Maturity: 11 years
Annualized Returns as of 12/31/98:
1998: 5.50%, 3-year: 17.48%,
5 year: N/A, Since Inception: 16.45%
Top Ten Holdings as of 9/30/98:
IBM, Duke Energy, GTE, Union
Planters, Intel, Lockheed Martin,
RJR Nabisco Holdings, Texaco,
Supervalu, Electronic Data Systems
Portfolio Turnover: 42%
Comments: Fund screens using
Catholic Bishops' social guidelines.

AQUINAS FIXED INCOME (AQFIX)

Asset Class: Income
NIS Social Rating℠: ♥ ♥
Share Type: No Load
Date of Inception: 1/4/94
Assets: $39.2 Million
Fund Manager:
Ronald Sellers since 1/4/94
12b-1 Fee: 0.00%
Total Operating Expense: 0.99%
Minimum Investment:
Initial: $500/Subsequently: $250
Automatic Investments:
Initial: $50/Subsequently: $50
Beta: 0.05   **Sharpe:** 0.41
Yield: 5.26%
Percentage of Bonds: 88.50%

Percentage of Cash/equiv.: 11.50%
Average Bond Maturity: 4 years
Annualized Returns as of 12/31/98:
1998: 7.17%, 3-year: 6.13%,
5 year: N/A, Since Inception: 6.16%
Top Ten Holdings as of 9/30/98:
U.S. Treasury Note 6.25%, U.S.
Treasury Note 7%, U.S. Treasury Bond
8%, Associates North Amer 5.4%,
Amresco Hm Eq Ln 8.075%, Lehman
Brothers HldgXerox 5.875%, WMX
Technologies 6.65%, Motorola 6.5%,
Household Financial 7.125%
Portfolio Turnover: 102%
Comments: Fund screens using
Catholic Bishops' social guidelines.

ARIEL FUNDS
www.arielmutualfunds.com
307 North Michigan Avenue, Suite 500 Chicago, IL 60601 [800-292-7435]

ARIEL APPRECIATION (CAAPX)

Asset Class: Midcap
NIS Social Rating℠: ♥ ♥ ♥
Share Type: No Load
Date of Inception: 1/1/90
Assets: $236.0 Million

Fund Manager:
Eric McKissack since 1/1/90
12b-1 Fee: 0.25%
Total Operating Expense: 1.36%
Minimum Investment:

ARIEL APPRECIATION (CAAPX) *continued*

Initial: $1,000/Subsequently: $50
Automatic Investments:
Inital: $50/Subsequently: $50
Beta: 0.67   **Sharpe:** 1.38
Percentage of Stocks: 96.99%
Percentage of Cash/equiv.: 3.01%
Annualized Returns as of 12/31/98:
1998: 19.55%, 3-year: 26.72%,
5 year: 18.32%,
Since Inception: 12.39%

Top Ten Holdings as of 9/30/98:
First Brand, Allergan, Century
Telephone, Hasbro, Rouse, MBIA,
Specialty Equipment, Longs, Whitman
Northern Trust
Portfolio Turnover: 19%
Comments: A top-performing, low
turnover fund. Ariel foundation con-
tributes scholarships for disadvantaged
inner-city students to keep them in
school through college.

ARIEL GROWTH (ARGFX)

Asset Class: Small cap
NIS Social Rating℠: ♥ ♥ ♥
Share Type: No Load
Date of Inception: 9/29/86
Assets: $180.0 Million
Fund Managers: John W. Rogers, Jr.
since 9/29/96
12b-1 Fee: 0.25%
Total Operating Expense: 1.31%
Yield: 0.32%
Minimum Investment:
Initial: $1,000/Subsequently: $50
Automatic Investments:
Initial: $50/Subsequently: $50
Beta: 0.65   **Sharpe:** 1.12

Percentage of Stocks: 98%
Percentage of Cash/equiv.: 2%
Annualized Returns as of 12/31/98:
1998: 9.89%, 3-year: 22.71%,
5-year: 16.02%,
Since Inception: 10.09%
Top Ten Holdings as of 9/30/98:
First Brands, Specialty Equipment,
MBIA, Rouse Allergan, Hasbro, Central
Newspapers Cl A Interface Cl A,
Longs Drug, Ecolab
Portfolio Turnover: 20%
Comments: See Ariel Appreciation for
comments.

BRIDGEWAY SOCIAL RESPONSIBILITY PORTFOLIO (BRSRX)

www.bridgewayfund.com
5650 Kirby Drive Suite 141
Houston, TX 77005
800-661-3550
Asset Class: Large cap
NIS Social Rating℠: ♥ ♥ ♥ ♥
Share Type: No Load
Date of Inception: 8/5/94
Assets: $1.4 Million
Fund Managers:
John Montgomery, Jr. since 8/5/94
12b-1 Fee: 0.00%
Total Operating Expense: 1.50%
Minimum Investment:

Initial: $2,000/Subsequently: $500
Automatic Investments:
Initial: $2,000/Subsequently: $200
Beta: 0.94   **Sharpe:** 1.16
Percentage of Stocks: 91%
Percentage of Cash/equiv.: 9%
Annualized Returns as of 12/31/98:
1998: 37.80%, 3-year: 27.17%,
5-year: N/A, Since Inception: 25.06%
Top Ten Holdings as of 9/4/98:
The Gap, Timberland Co.,
Home Depot Inc., Microsoft Corp.,
Sofamor/Danek Group, Herman Miller,
Safeway Stores, Safeskin Schering

Plough Corp, Pfizer Inc.
Portfolio Turnover: 23%
Comments: Shareholders are surveyed annually to determine social screens of concern to them. These are reflected in portfolio.

CALVERT FUNDS

www.calvertgroup.com
4550 Montgomery Avenue Bethesda, MD 20814 [800-368-2748]

CALVERT CAPITAL ACCUMULATION (CCAFX)

Asset Class: Midcap
NIS Social Rating℠: ♥ ♥ ♥ ♥
Share Types: A,B,C
Date of Inception: 10/31/94
Assets: $84.4 million
Fund Managers:
Eddie Brown since 10/31/94
12b-1 Fee:
A SHARES: 0.35%
B SHARES: 1.00%
C SHARES: 1.00%
Total Operating Expense:
A SHARES: 1.91%
B SHARES: 3.36%
C SHARES: 3.11%
Minimum Investment:
Initial: $2,000/Subsequently: $250
Automatic Investments:
Initial: $100/Subsequently: $100
Beta: 1.04   **Sharpe:** 0.60
Percentage of Stocks: 96.90%

Percentage of Cash/equiv.: 3.10%
Annualized Returns as of 12/31/98:
1998: 29.35%, 3-year: 19.88%,
5-year: N/A, Since Inception: 23.04%
Load:
A SHARES—Front load: 4.75%
B SHARES—Rear load: 5%
declining to 0 after 6 years
C SHARES—1% if sold before one year
Top Ten Holdings as of 10/31/98:
Solectron Corp. Network Assocs. Inc.,
Paychex Inc., Alza Corp., Equifax Inc.,
Harley Davidson Inc., Sterling Comm.
Inc., T. Rowe Price & Assoc. Inc.,
Smith Int'l Inc., Franklin Res. Inc.
Portfolio Turnover: 114%
Comments: The social screens in this fund are less stringent than the Calvert social funds. The fund invests 1% of its assets in Calvert "high social impact" community investments.

CALVERT NEW VISION (CNVAX)

Asset Class: Small cap
NIS Social Rating℠: ♥ ♥ ♥
Share Types: A,B,C
Date of Inception: 2/1/97
Assets: $64.6million
Fund Managers:
James Awad since 6/30/97
12b-1 Fee:
A SHARES: 0.25%
B SHARES: 1.00%
C SHARES: 1.00%

Total Operating Expense:
A SHARES: 1.87%
B SHARES: 2.99%
C SHARES: 2.74%
Minimum Investment:
Initial: $2,000/Subsequently: $250
Automatic Investments:
Initial: $100/Subsequently: $100
Beta: 0.95   **Sharpe:** 0.42
Percentage of Stocks: 88.40%
Percentage of Bonds: 3.20%

CALVERT NEW VISION (CNVAX) *continued*

Percentage of Cash/equiv.: 8.40%
Average Bond Maturity: N/A
Annualized Returns as of 12/31/98:
1998: -9.43%, 3-year: N/A,
5-year: N/A, Since Inception: -5.03%
Load:
A SHARES—Front load: 4.75%
B SHARES—Rear load: 5% declining
   to 0 after 6 years
C SHARES—1% if sold before one year
Top Ten Holdings as of 10/31/98:

Danaher Corp., National Data Corp.,
Zebra Technologies Corp., Elan PLC,
Doral Financial Corp., Shared Medi
Cal System, New Horizons Worldwide
Inc., Houghton Mifflin Co., Comdisco
Inc., Mid Atlantic Realty Tr.
Portfolio Turnover: 196%
Comments: A small cap fund that
includes "high social impact" invest-
ments. Designed to match the perfor-
mance of the Russell 1000 Index.

CALVERT SOCIAL BALANCED (CSIFX)

Asset Class: Balanced
NIS Social Rating℠: ♥ ♥ ♥ ♥ ♥
Share Type: A,B,C
Date of Inception: 10/21/82
Assets: $688.0 Million
Fund Managers: Maceo Sloan since
7/4/95, Eddie Brown since 9/30/96,
Reno Martini since 1/1/95
12b-1 Fee:
A SHARES: 0.24%
B / C SHARES: 1.00%
Total Operating Expense:
A SHARES: 1.14%
B SHARES: 2.54%
C SHARES: 2.29%
Minimum Investment:
Initial: $1,000/Subsequently: $250
Automatic Investments:
Initial: $100/Subsequently: $100
Beta: 0.63   **Sharpe:** 0.90
Yield: 2%
Percentage of Stocks: 59.54%
Percentage of Bonds: 38.32%
Percentage of Cash/equiv.: 2.14%
Average Bond Maturity: 5-years
Annualized Returns as of 12/31/98:
1998: 17.49%, 3-year: 15.01%,

5-year: 12.81%,
Since Inception: 11.99%
Bond Holdings: 100% U.S.
Government Agency
Load:
A SHARES—Front load: 4.75%
B SHARES—Rear load: 5% declining to
   0 after 6 years.
C SHARES—Rear load:1% if sold
   before one year
Top Ten Holdings as of 10/31/98:
Merck & Co., Microsoft Corp.,
Johnson & Johnson, Home Depot Inc.
Inc., Cardinal Health Inc., Illinois Tool
Works, IBM, Gillette Co., EMC Corp.
Mass. Century Tel. Enterprises
Portfolio Turnover: 215%
Comments: Calvert has provided lead-
ership in mutual fund social screening.
Calvert Social Balanced Fund (formerly
Managed Growth) is rigorously
screened and was the first to make
community and "high social impact"
investments. This fund is a solid, con-
servative long-term investment
vehicle.

CALVERT SOCIAL BOND (CSIBX)

Asset Class: Income
NIS Social Rating℠: ♥ ♥ ♥ ♥ ♥
Share Type: A,B,C
Date of Inception: 8/24/87
Assets: $65.3 Million
Fund Managers:
Greg Habeeb since 3/1/97
12b-1 Fee:
A SHARES: 0.20%
B / C SHARES: 1.00%
Total Operating Expense:
A SHARES: 1.19%
B SHARES: 2.78%
C SHARES: 2.53%
Minimum Investment:
Initial: $1,000/Subsequently: $250
Automatic Investments:
Initial: $100/Subsequently: $100
Beta: 1.08   **Sharpe:** 0.61
Yield: 5.61
Percentage of Stocks: 2.20%
Percentage of Bonds: 96.20%
Percentage of Cash/equiv.: 1.60%
Average Bond Maturity: 9 years

Top Ten Holdings as of 11/10/98:
Zurich Capital, Chase Credit Card,
Bankone Corp., FNMA, FHLMC,
Onbank Capital Trust, Allmerica
Financial Corp., Greenpoint Capital
Trust, FNMA, Conseco Inc.
Annualized Returns as of 12/31/98:
1998: 6.13%, 3-year: 6.25%,
5-year: 5.92%, Since Inception: 8.57%
Load:
A SHARES—Front load: 3.75%
B SHARES—Rear load: 4% declining
   to 0 after 6 years
C SHARES—Rear load:1% if sold
   before one year
Bond Holdings:
U.S. Government Agencies: 45%
Municipals: 21%, Corporate: 34%
Portfolio Turnover: 319%
Comments: This income fund invests in
government agency and investment
grade corporate bonds. The fund
applies the same social screening as
the Balanced Fund.

CALVERT SOCIAL EQUITY (CSIEX)

Asset Class: Large cap
NIS Social Rating℠: ♥ ♥ ♥ ♥ ♥
Share Type: A,B,C
Date of Inception: 8/27/87
Assets: $141.0 Million
Fund Managers:
Daniel Boone III since 9/30/98
12b-1 Fee:
A SHARES: 0.23%
B / C SHARES: 1.00%
Total Operating Expense:
A SHARES: 1.21%
B SHARES: 2.56%
C SHARES: 2.31%
Minimum Investment:
Initial: $1,000/Subsequently: $250

Automatic Investments:
Initial: $100/Subsequently: $100
Beta: 0.96   **Sharpe:** 0.41
Percentage of Stocks: 97%
Percentage of Cash/equiv.: 3%
Load:
A SHARES—Front load: 3.75%
B SHARES—Rear load: 4%
declining to 0 after 6 years
C SHARES—Rear load:1% if sold
   before one year
Annualized Returns as of 12/31/98:
1998: 10.89%, 3-year: 17.14%,
5-year: 11.23%,
Since Inception: 9.32%
Top Ten Holdings as of 10/31/98:
Sun Microsystems Inc., Merck & Co.

CALVERT SOCIAL EQUITY (CSIEX) *continued*

Inc., Mylan Labs Inc., Schering Plough Corp., Cisco Systems Inc., Office Depot Inc., BankAmerica Corp., New Colgate, Palmolive Co., Dayton Hudson Corp., Autozone Inc.

Portfolio Turnover: 93% as of 7/31/98
Comments: This large-cap growth fund is screened to the same standards as the Social Balanced Fund.

CALVERT SOCIAL MANAGED INDEX

Asset Class: Large cap
NIS Social Rating℠: ♥ ♥ ♥ ♥ ♥
Share Type: A,B,C
Date of Inception: 4/15/98
Assets: $141.0 Million
Fund Manager:
Arlene Rockefeller since 4/15/98
12b-1 Fee:
A SHARES: 0.25%
B / C SHARES: 1.00%
Total Operating Expense:
A SHARES: 1.21%
B SHARES: 2.56%
C SHARES: 2.31%
Minimum Investment:
Initial: $5,000/Subsequently: $250
Automatic Investments:
Initial: $5,000/Subsequently: $50
Beta: 1.03   **Sharpe:** 0.44
Percentage of Stocks: 97.39%
Percentage of Cash/equiv.: 2.61%

Load:
A SHARES—Front load: 4.75%
B SHARES—Rear load: 5% declining
to 0 after 6 years
C SHARES—Rear load:1% if sold
before one year
Annualized Returns as of 12/31/98:
1998: N/A, 3-year: N/A, 5-year: N/A,
Since Inception: 10.07%
Top Ten Holdings as of 10/31/98:
US West Inc. New, Bell South Corp., Merck & Co., Inc., Johnson & Johnson, Federal Nat'l Mtge Assn., Intel Corp., Microsoft Corp., BankAmerica Corp. New, Ameritech Corp., American Int'l Group
Portfolio Turnover: 27%
Comments: A new large-cap index fund that is designed to meet or exceed the Russell 1000 Index.

CALVERT WORLD VALUES: INTERNATIONAL EQUITY (CWVGX)

Asset Class: International
NIS Social Rating℠: ♥ ♥ ♥ ♥
Share Type: A,B,C
Date of Inception: 6/26/92
Assets: $218.8 Million
Fund Managers: Sue Muller/Andrew Preston since 6/29/92
12b-1 Fee:
A SHARES: 0.25%
B / C SHARES: 1.00%
Total Operating Expense:
A SHARES: 1.91%
B SHARES: 3.16%
C SHARES: 2.91%

Minimum Investment:
Initial: $2000/Subsequently: $250
Automatic Investments:
Initial: $100/Subsequently: $100
Beta: 1.04   **Sharpe:** 0.39
Percentage of Stocks: 95.90%
Percentage of Bonds: 1.35%
Percentage of Cash/equiv.: 2.75%
Load:
A SHARES—Front load: 4.75%
B SHARES—Rear load: 5% declining
to 0 after 6 years
C SHARES—Rear load:1% if sold
before one year

Annualized Returns as of 12/31/98:
1998: 16.10%, 3-year: 11.45%,
5-year: 8.55%, Since Inception: 9.65%
Top Ten Holdings as of 10/31/98:
Zurich Allied AG, VNU N.V.,
Allianz AG, Pinault-Printemps Redo,
Unicredito Italian, Telecom Italia Mob,
Christiania Bank, Volkswagen AG,
ING Groep NV, Telecom Corp. of NZ
Portfolio Turnover: 58%
Comments: A rigorously screened
international fund. It invests 3% of its
assets in "high social impact" commu-
nity investments.

CITIZENS TRUST FUNDS
www.citizensfunds.com
One Harbour Place, Portsmouth, NH 03801 [800-223-7010]

CITIZENS TRUST EMERGING GROWTH (WAEGX)

Asset Class: Aggressive growth
NIS Social Rating℠: ♥ ♥ ♥ ♥ ♥
Share Type: No Load
Date of Inception: 2/8/94
Assets: $76.7 Million
Fund Manager:
Rick Little since 12/8/97
12b-1 Fee: 0.25%
Total Operating Expense: 2.01%
Minimum Investment:
$2,500/Subsequently: $50
Automatic Investments:
Initial: $250/Subsequently: $50
Beta: 1.10   **Sharpe:** 0.75
Percentage of Stocks: 95.84%

Percentage of Cash/equiv.: 4.16%
Annualized Returns as of 12/31/98:
1998: 42.71%, 3-year: 24.04%,
5-year: N/A, Since Inception: 24.16%
Top Ten Holdings as of 9/30/98:
McKesson Corp, EMC Corp.,
Sofamor/Danek Group Inc., Comerica
Inc., Ascend Communications, Mylan
Labs Inc., Veritas Software Corp.,
Compuware Corp., America Online
Inc., HNC Software Inc.
Portfolio Turnover: 245%
Comments: A top performing compre-
hensively screened aggressive growth
fund.

CITIZENS TRUST GLOBAL EQUITY (WAGEX)

Asset Class: Global
NIS Social Rating℠: ♥ ♥ ♥ ♥ ♥
Share Type: No Load
Date of Inception: 2/8/94
Assets: $47.9 Million
Fund Manager:
Lilia Clemente since 6/95
12b-1 Fee: 0.25%
Total Operating Expense: 2.10%
Minimum Investment:
$2,500/Subsequently: $50
Automatic Investments:
Initial: $250/Subsequently: $50
Beta: 0.94   **Sharpe:** 0.97

Percentage of Stocks: 84.40%
Percentage of Cash/equiv.: 15.60%
Annualized Returns as of 12/31/98:
1998: 32.26%, 3-year: 21.43%,
5-year: N/A, Since Inception: 15.05%
Top Ten Holdings as of 9/30/98:
Airtouch Communications, Nokia
Corp., Cisco Systems Inc., Home
Depot Inc. Inc., MCI Worldcom Inc.,
Orange, Superdiplo SA, Intel
Corp.,Telecom Italia SPA, Olivetti SPA.
Portfolio Turnover: 72.33%
Comments: A top performing compre-
hensively screened fund.

CITIZENS TRUST INCOME (WAIMX)

Asset Class: Income
NIS Social Rating℠: ♥ ♥ ♥ ♥ ♥
Share Type: No Load
Date of Inception: 6/1/92
Assets: $56.9 Million
Fund Manager:
Gail Seneca since 11/1/93
12b-1 Fee: 0.25
Total Operating Expense: 1.43
Minimum Investment:
Initial: $2,500/Subsequently: $50
Automatic Investments:
Initial: $250/Subsequently: $50
Beta: 0.83   **Sharpe:** 0.66
Yield: 5.39%
Percentage of Bonds: 99.50%
Percentage of Cash/equiv.: 0.50%
Average Bond Maturity: 9 years

Bond Holdings: 25% U.S. Government Agencies, 75% Corporate.
Annualized Returns as of 12/31/98:
1998: 5.70%, 3-year: 6.76%,
5-year: 6.61%, Since Inception: 7.39%
Top Ten Holdings as of 9/30/98:
Fannie Mae, J. Q. Hammons Hotels, Freddie Mac, U. S. Home Corp., Time Warner Inc., Abbey National P.L.C., Morgan Stanley Capital, Microsoft Corp., Universal Health Services Inc., Weingarten Rlty Invstmts
Portfolio Turnover: 80%
Comments: This fund invests in high quality government agency and corporate bonds. It is another of the top rated funds in the Citizen's fund family.

CITIZENS TRUST INDEX (WAIDX)

Asset Class: Global
NIS Social Rating℠: ♥ ♥ ♥ ♥ ♥
Share Type: No Load
Date of Inception: 3/3/95
Assets: $325.0 Million
Fund Manager:
Sophia Collier since 9/15/98
12b-1 Fee: 0.25%
Total Operating Expense: 1.59%
Minimum Investment:
Initial: $2,500/Subsequently: $50
Automatic Investments:
Initial: $250/Subsequently: $50
Beta: 1.10   **Sharpe:** 1.45
Percentage of Stocks: 98.98%
Percentage of Cash/equiv.: 1.02%

Annualized Returns as of 12/31/98:
1998: 42.75%, 3-year: 33.21%,
5-year: N/A, Since Inception: 32.76%
Top Ten Holdings as of 9/30/98:
Microsoft Corp, Intel Corp., Coca-Cola Corp., Cisco Systems Inc., Lucent Technologies, MCI Worldcom , Dell Computer, SBC Communications Inc., Schering Plough Corp., Bell Atlantic Corp.
Portfolio Turnover: 14%
Comments: This is a comprehensively screened index fund that invests in 300 companies. The index includes 200 stocks from the S&P 500 Index. It has outperformed the S&P 500 index since inception.

CONCERT SOCIAL AWARENESS (SSAIX)

www.smithbarney.com
Smith Barney Mutual Funds
388 Greenwich St
New York, NY, 10013,
800-451-2010
Asset Class: Balanced
NIS Social Rating℠: ♥ ♥ ♥
Share Type: A, B
Date of Inception: 11/6/92
Assets: $227.8 Million
Fund Managers: Robert Brady/Ellen
Cammer since 11/6/92
12b-1 Fee: A SHARES: 0.25%,
B SHARES 1.00%
Total Operating Expense:
A SHARES: 1.19%, B SHARES: 1.95%
Minimum Investment:
Initial: $1,000/Subsequently: $50
Automatic Investments:
Initial: $250/Subsequently: $25
Beta: 1.14   **Sharpe:** 1.22
Yield: 3.94%

Percentage of Stocks: 77.70%
Percentage of Bonds: 21.80%
Percentage of Cash/equiv.: 0.50%
Average Bond Maturity: 9 years
Top Ten Holdings as of 11/31/98:
U.S. Treasury Note, Schering-Plough
Corp, EMC, Cisco Systems Inc., U.S.
Treasury Bond, IBM, MCI/World Com,
Xerox, U.S. Treasury Note, Unilever
Load: A SHARES—Front load: 5%
B SHARES—Rear load: 5%
declining to 0 after 6 years
Bond Holdings: U.S. Treasuries: 46%
Corporate: 36%, Other 18%
Annualized Returns as of 12/31/98:
1998: 27.50%, 3-year: 20.30%,
5-year: 16.50%,
Since Inception: 16.66%
Portfolio Turnover: 75%
Comments: This fund is only available
to clients of Smith Barney Inc.

CRUELTY FREE VALUE

www.crueltyfree.com
8260 Greensboro Drive, Suite 250
McLean, VA 22102-3801,
800-892-9626
Asset Class: Small cap
NIS Social Rating℠: ♥
Share Type: No Load
Date of Inception: 4/28/97
Assets: $2.0 Million
Fund Manager:
William F. Coughlin since 4/28/97
12b-1 Fee: 0.25%
Total Operating Expense: 1.95%
Minimum Investment:
Initial: $1,000/Subsequently: $50
Automatic Investments:
Initial: $1,000/Subsequently: $50
Beta: 1.20   **Sharpe:** N/A
Percentage of Stocks: 82.20%

Percentage of Cash/equiv.: 17.80%
Annualized Returns as of 12/31/98:
1998: 5.20%, 3-year: N/A, 5-year: N/A,
Since Inception: 9.83%
Top Ten Holdings as of 10/31/98:
Young Broadcasting, Doral Financial
Corp., Borg-Warner Automotive,
Scientific Atlanta, United Bankshares,
Tommy Hilfiger Corp., RMI Titanium,
Fleetwood Enterprises, Airborne
Freight, Land America Financial Corp.
Portfolio Turnover: 40%
Comments: This fund focuses on ani-
mal rights issues. It will not invest in
companies using animal testing on
products, having inappropriate use of
animals as entertainment or harming
animals in any way.

DELAWARE SOCIAL AWARENESS (DEQAX)

www.delawarefunds.com
1818 Market Street
Philadelphia, PA 19103
800-362-3863
Asset Class: Large cap
NIS Social Rating℠: ♥ ♥
Share Type: A,B,C
Date of Inception: 2/24/97
Assets: $32.9 Million
Fund Manager:
T. Scott Whitman since 2/24/97
12b-1 Fee: A SHARES: 0.30%
B / C SHARES: 1.00%
Total Operating Expense: A SHARES:
1.50%, B SHARES: 2.20%, C SHARES:
2.20%
Minimum Investment:
Initial: $1,000/Subsequently: $100
Automatic Investments:
Initial: $250/Subsequently: $25
Beta: 1.03   **Sharpe:** 1.85
Percentage of Stocks: 96.10%

Percentage of Cash/equiv.: 3.90%
Load:
A SHARES—Front load: 4.75%.
B SHARES—Rear load: 4% declining to
0 after 6 years.
C SHARES—Rear load:1% declining to
0 after 6 years.
Annualized Returns as of 12/31/98:
1998: 15.75%, 3-year: N/A,
5-year: N/A, Since Inception: 21.80%
Top Ten Holdings as of 10/31/98: Bell
South, Dell Computer, Microsoft Corp.,
AT & T, First Union Corp., EMC Corp.,
US West, Allegiance, Amgen Corp.,
Quaker Oats.
Portfolio Turnover: 29%
Comments: Fund was part of Variable
Annuity from 1988. Fund manager
took charge 1991. Fund was cloned on
2/24/97 to form this public version of
the fund. Uses KLD database to screen.

DEVCAP SHARED RETURN (DESRX)

www.devcap.org
207 East Buffalo St., Suite 400
Milwaukee, WI 53202
800-371-2655
Asset Class: Large cap
NIS Social Rating℠: ♥ ♥ ♥ ♥ ♥
Share Type: No Load
Date of Inception: 6/30/91
Assets: $6.9 Million
Fund Manager:
John R. O'Toole since 6/30/91
12b-1 Fee: 0.25%
Total Operating Expense: 1.75%
Minimum Investment:
Initial: $1,000/Subsequently: None
Automatic Investments:
Initial: $500/Subsequently: $25
Beta: 1.02   **Sharpe:** 1.10
Percentage of Stocks: 99.90%
Percentage of Cash/equiv.: 0.10%

Annualized Returns as of 12/31/98:
1998: 31.89%, 3-year: 28.67%,
5-year: 22.99%,
Since Inception: 18.18%
Top Ten Holdings as of 9/30/98:
Microsoft Corp., Merck & Co. Inc.,
Intel Corp., Coca-Cola Co., Wal-Mart
Stores Inc., AT&T, Johnson & Johnson,
Cisco Systems Inc., Proctor & Gamble
Co., Lucent Technology
Portfolio Turnover: 5%
Comments: Owned and operated by a
consortium of non-profit organizations.
Invests in the stocks listed in the
Domini 400 Social Index. Investors can
contribute their returns to non-profit
organizations working to improve the
welfare of under-privileged persons in
developing nations.

DOMINI SOCIAL EQUITY (DSEFX)

www.domini.com
P.O. Box 959
New York, NY 10159-0959
1-800-762-6814
Asset Class: Large cap
NIS Social Rating℠: ♥ ♥ ♥ ♥ ♥
Share Type: No Load
Date of Inception: 6/30/91
Assets: $717 Million
Fund Manager:
John O'Toole since 6/3/91
12b-1 Fee: 0.20%
Total Operating Expense: 0.98%
Minimum Investment:
Initial: $1,000/Subsequently: None
Automatic Investments:
Initial: $500/Subsequently: $50
Beta: 1.05   **Sharpe:** 1.28
Percentage of Stocks: 99.40%
Percentage of Cash/equiv.: 0.60%

Annualized Returns as of 12/31/98:
1998: 32.99%, 3-year: 29.86%,
5-year: 24.19%,
Since Inception: 19.47%
Top Ten Holdings as of 9/30/98:
Microsoft Corp., Merck & Co. Inc.,
Intel Corp., Coca-Cola Co., Wal-Mart
Stores Inc., AT&T, Johnson & Johnson,
Cisco Systems Inc., Proctor & Gamble
Co., Lucent Technology
Portfolio Turnover: 50%
Comments: The fund invests in the
stocks listed in the Domini 400 Social
Index (DSI). The DSI was developed by
Kinder, Lydenberg and Domini (KLD) in
1990 to stand as a socially screened
alternative to the S&P 500. The DSI has
outperformed the S&P 500 since its
inception.

DREYFUS THIRD CENTURY (DRTHX)

www.dreyfus.com
200 Park Avenue
New York, NY 10166
800-242-8671
Asset Class: Large cap
NIS Social Rating℠: ♥ ♥ ♥ ♥
Share Type: No Load
Date of Inception:
3/31/72
Assets: $841.3 Million
Fund Manager:
Paul Hilton since 8/31/98
12b-1 Fee: 0.00%
Total Operating Expense: 1.03%
Minimum Investment:
Initial: $2,500/Subsequently: $100
Automatic Investments:
Initial: $100/Subsequently: $100
Beta: 1.09   **Sharpe:** 1.18

Yield: 0.15
Percentage of Stocks: 99.43%
Percentage of Cash/equiv.: 0.57%
Annualized Returns as of 12/31/98:
1998: 30.20%, 3-year: 27.93%,
5-year: 21.35%,
Since Inception: 13.64%
Top Ten Holdings as of 9/30/98:
Home Depot Inc. Inc., Merck & Co
Inc, Bristol-Myers Squibb Inc.,
American International, Clorox,
Hershey Foods, Wal-Mart, Fannie Mae,
Safeway, Allstate Corp.
Portfolio Turnover: 70%
Comments: One of the oldest socially
screened funds. Invests in stocks that
do business in a manner that con-
tributes to the enhancement of the
quality of life in America.

ECLIPSE ULTRA SHORT TERM (ECUIX)

www.eclipsefund.com
144 East 30th St.
New York, NY 10016
800-872-2710
Asset Class: Income
NIS Social Rating℠: ♥ ♥
Share Type: No Load
Date of Inception: 12/27/94
Assets: $8.5 Million
Fund Managers: Sabella/McCain since 12/27/94
12b-1 Fee: 0.00
Total Operating Expense: 0.00
Minimum Investment:
Initial: $1,000/Subsequently: None
Automatic Investments:
Initial: No Minimum /Subsequently: $50

Beta: 0.15   **Sharpe:** 1.84
Yield: 6.58%
Percentage of Bonds: 98.35%
Percentage of Cash/equiv.: 1.65%
Average Bond Maturity: 1 year
Bond Holdings: 19.65% U.S. Government; 80.25% Corporate.
Annualized Returns as of 12/31/98:
1998: 6.26%, 3-year: 5.99%,
5-year: N/A, Since Inception: 6.38%
Portfolio Turnover: 43%
Comments: This fund is designed as a low-risk, high quality alternative to money markets. Investments include insured securities issued by community development banks.

FLEX TOTAL RETURN UTILITIES (FLRUX)

www.flexfunds.com
6000 Memorial Drive
Dublin, OH 43017
800-494-3539
Asset Class: Utility
NIS Social Rating℠: ♥ ♥ ♥ ♥
Share Type: No Load
Date of Inception: 6/24/95
Assets: $10.0 Million
Fund Manager:
Lowell Miller since 6/24/95
12b-1 Fee: 0.25%
Total Operating Expense: 1.80%
Minimum Investment:
Initial: $2500/Subsequently: $500
Automatic Investments:
Initial: $2,500/Subsequently: $100
Beta: 0.84   **Sharpe:** 0.78
Percentage of Stocks: 90.20%

Percentage of Cash/equiv.: 9.80%
Annualized Returns as of 12/31/98:
1998: 8.77%, 3-year: 16.60%,
5-year: N/A, Since Inception: 18.58%
Top Ten Holdings as of10/31/98:
MarketSpan Corp., SBC Communications, Quest Communications, Frontier Corp., Kinder Morgan Energy Partners, Williams Cos. Inc., Consolidated Natural Gas Co., Enron Corp., Quastar Corp., MCW Corp.
Portfolio Turnover: 41%
Comments: Fund is diversified across essential service areas: telephone, electric, water, and natural gas. Fund seeks companies involved with energy production from renewable and alternative resources.

GREEN CENTURY FUNDS
www.greencentury.com
29 Temple Place, Suite 200, Boston, MA 02111 [800-934-7336]

GREEN CENTURY BALANCED (GCBLX)

Asset Class: Balanced
NIS Social Rating℠: ♥ ♥ ♥ ♥
Share Type: No Load
Date of Inception: 3/18/92
Assets: $15.0 Million
Fund Manager:
Jackson W. Robinson since 9/11/95
12b-1 Fee: 0.25%
Total Operating Expense: 2.50%
Minimum Investment:
Initial: $2000/Subsequently: $50
Automatic Investments:
Initial: No Minimum /
Subsequently: $100
Beta: 1.35   **Sharpe:** 0.24
Percentage of Stocks: 65%
Percentage of Bonds: 30%
Percentage of Cash/equiv.: 5%
Average Bond Maturity: 7 years

Bond Holdings: 100% Corporate
Annualized Returns as of 12/31/98:
1998: -10.10%, 3-year: 10.14%,
5-year: 8.68%, Since Inception: 6.98%
Top Ten Holdings as of 11/4/98:
American Power Conversion, CBS,
Data Dimensions, KTI, OrbitalSciences,
PSS World Medical, Sepracor, Rexall
Sundown, Elan ADR, Stillwater Mining
Portfolio Turnover: 109%
Comments: Invests in companies that
offer solutions to environmental prob-
lems. Seeks companies that practice
waste minimization, prevent pollution,
and use natural resources efficiently.
An aggressive balanced fund. Stocks in
the portfolio are small cap; bonds are
below investment grade.

GREEN CENTURY EQUITY (GCEQX)

Asset Class: Large cap
NIS Social Rating℠: ♥ ♥ ♥ ♥ ♥
Share Type: No Load
Date of Inception: 9/11/95
Assets: $16.0 Million
Fund Manager:
Steve Lydenberg since 9/11/95
12b-1 Fee: 0.00%
Total Operating Expense: 1.50%
Minimum Investment:
Initial: $2000/Subsequently: $50
Automatic Investments:
Initial:No Minimum /
Subsequently: $100
Beta: 1.04   **Sharpe:** 1.36
Percentage of Stocks: 99.40%
Percentage of Cash/equiv.: 0.60%

Annualized Returns as of 12/31/98:
1998: 32.32%, 3-year: 29.75%,
5-year: 22.78, Since Inception: 29.08%
Top Ten Holdings as of 9/30/98:
Microsoft, Merck, Intel, Coca-Cola,
Wal-Mart, AT&T, Johnson & Johnson,
Cisco Systems, Proctor & Gamble,
Lucent Technology.
Portfolio Turnover: 5%
Comments: An index fund invested in
the stocks listed in the Domini 400
Social Index. Green Century Capital
Management is owned by a partnership
comprised of not-for-profit environ-
mental advocacy organizations. All
profits from management fees are dis-
tributed to organizations that preserve
and protect the environment..

MEYERS PRIDE VALUE (MYPVX)

www.pridefund.com
8901 Wilshire Blvd.
Beverly Hills, CA 90211
800-410-3337
Asset Class: Large cap
NIS Social Rating℠: ♥ ♥
Share Type: No Load
Date of Inception: 3/25/96
Assets: $3.0 Million
Fund Manager:
Shelly Meyers since 3/25/96
12b-1 Fee: 0.25%
Total Operating Expense: 2.25%
Minimum Investment:
Initial: $1,000/Subsequently: $100
Automatic Investments:
Initial: $250/Subsequently: $50

Beta: 1.13   **Sharpe:** 0.33
Percentage of Stocks: 95%
Percentage of Cash/equiv.: 5%
Annualized Returns as of 12/31/98:
1998: 13.61%, 3-year: N/A,
5-year: N/A, Since Inception: 17.06%
Top Ten Holdings as of 9/30/98:
Agouron Pharmaceuticals, General
Instrument, Atlantic Richfield, Whole
Foods Market Inc., Seagate Technology,
Amgen Inc., Advanced Micro Devices,
AT&T Corp., Homestake Mining Co.,
Sun Micro Systems.
Portfolio Turnover: 38%
Comments: Invests in companies that
have progressive policies towards gays
and lesbians.

MMA PRAXIS FUNDS
www.mmapraxis.com
3435 Stelzer Road, Suite 1000, Columbus, OH 43219 [800-977-2947]

MMA PRAXIS GROWTH (MMPGX)

Asset Class: Large cap
NIS Social Rating℠: ♥ ♥ ♥ ♥
Share Type: B
Date of Inception: 1/4/94
Assets: $115.3 Million
Fund Manager:
Keith Yoder since 1/4/94
12b-1 Fee: 0.43%
Total Operating Expense: 1.75%
Minimum Investment:
Initial: $500/ Subsequently: $50
Automatic Investments:
Initial: $50/Subsequently: $50
Beta: 0.91   **Sharpe:** 0.69
Percentage of Stocks: 94.90%
Percentage of Cash/equiv.: 5.10%
Rear Loadad 4% declining to zero after
5-years

Annualized Returns as of 12/31/98:
1998: 5.96%, 3-year: 16.33%,
5-year: N/A, Since Inception: 16.22%
Top Ten Holdings as of 9/30/98:
Allstate, Sigma Aldrich, Hewlett
Packard, Xerox Corp., United States
Filter Corp., Sysco Systems, Central
Newspapers, St. Jude Medical Center,
Fannie Mae, Boston Scientific Corp.
Portfolio Turnover: 28%
Comments: Investments based on
Mennonite religious beliefs. Actively
seeks to promote human well-being,
peace, and justice through investment
decisions.

MMA PRAXIS INTERMEDIATE INCOME (MMPIX)

Asset Class: Income
NIS Social Rating℠: ♥ ♥ ♥ ♥
Share Type: B
Date of Inception: 1/4/94
Assets: $40.2 Million
Fund Manager:
Delmar King since 1/4/94
12b-1 Fee: 0.05%
Total Operating Expense: 1.10%
Minimum Investment:
Initial: $500/Subsequently: $50
Automatic Investments:
Initial: $50/Subsequently: $50
Beta: 0.97   **Sharpe:** 0.32
Yield: 5.32%
Percentage of Bonds: 96.80%
Percentage of Cash/equiv.: 3.20%
Average Bond Maturity: 8 years
Bond Quality: AAA: 49.10%,
AA: 4.70% A: 30.30%, BBB: 15.90%
Below: 0.00%, Non-rated: 0.00%,
Bond Holdings: 48% U.S. Government
Agencies 52% Corporate
Rear Load: 4% declining to zero after
5-years
Annualized Returns as of 12/31/98:
1998: 7.29%, 3-year: 5.65%,
5-year: N/A, Since Inception: 5.96%
Top Ten Holdings as of 11/11/98:
FNMA 6.58s01, PSI Energy 6 1/2s05,
FHLB 5.89s08, Masco 7 1/8s13,
Weyerhaeuser 6.95s19, FNMA 380177
6.24s08, FNMA 251729 6.5s18,
GNMA ARM 6s23, FNMA 5 5/8s28,
FNMA 251787 6 1/2s18
Portfolio Turnover: 30%
Comments: See MMA Praxis Growth
Fund.

MMA PRAXIS INTERNATIONAL (MMPNX)

Asset Class: International
NIS Social Rating℠: ♥ ♥ ♥ ♥
Share Type: B
Date of Inception: 4/1/97
Assets: $21.7 Million
Fund Manager: Martina Oechsle-
Vasconcelles since 4/1/97
12b-1 Fee: 0.25%
Total Operating Expense: 2.00%
Minimum Investment:
Initial: $500/Subsequently: $50
Automatic Investments:
Initial: $50/Subsequently: $50
Beta: 0.81   **Sharpe:** 0.52
Percentage of Stocks: 95.40%
Percentage of Cash/equiv.: 4.60%
Load: Rear load 4% declining to zero
after 5-years
Annualized Returns as of 12/31/98:
1998: 23.98%, 3-year: N/A,
5-year: N/A, Since Inception: 13.20%
Top Ten Holdings as of 9/30/98:
Railtrack Group, Vodafone Group,
Somerfield, Suez-Lyonnaise De Eaux,
Glaxo Wellcome, Renault, VNU N.V.,
Telecom Italia, Nestle, ASDA Group
Portfolio Turnover: 28%
Comments: A top performing interna-
tional fund. Investments based on
Mennonite religious beliefs.

NEUBERGER BERMAN SOCIALLY RESPONSIVE (NBSRX)

www.nbfunds.com
605 Third Avenue, 2nd Floor
New York, NY 10158-0180
800-877-9700
Asset Class: Large cap
NIS Social Rating℠: ♥ ♥ ♥ ♥
Share Type: No Load
Date of Inception: 3/16/94
Assets: $100.3 Million
Fund Manager: Janet Prindle since

NEUBERGER BERMAN SOCIALLY RESPONSIVE (NBSRX) *continued*

3/16/94
12b-1 Fee: 0.00%
Total Operating Expense: 1.43%
Minimum Investment:
Initial: $1,000/Subsequently: $100
Automatic Investments:
Initial: $1,000/Subsequently: $100
Beta: 1.04   **Sharpe:** 0.76
Percentage of Stocks: 95.50%
Percentage of Cash/equiv.: 4.50%
Annualized Returns as of 12/31/98:

1998: 15.01%, 3-year: 19.20%,
5-year: N/A, Since Inception: 18.70%
Top Ten Holdings as of 9/30/98:
City Group, Warner-Lambert, Unisis, C.
R. Bard, Fannie Mae, MCI WorldCom
Inc., Well Point Health Network, Key
Span Industries, Valassis
Communications Inc., Wal-Mart Stores
Portfolio Turnover: 47%
Comments: A well-screened, long-term
growth fund.

NEW ALTERNATIVES (NALFX)

150 Broadhollow Road
Melville, NY 11747
800-423-8383
Asset Class: Sector
NIS Social Rating^{SM}**:** ♥ ♥ ♥ ♥
Share Type: A
Date of Inception: 9/3/82
Assets: $32.0 Million
Fund Managers: Maurice & David
Schoenwald since 9/3/82
12b-1 Fee: 0.00%
Total Operating Expense: 1.16%
Minimum Investment:
Initial: $2,500/Subsequently: $250
Automatic Investments:
Initial: $2,500/Subsequently: $50
Beta: 0.70   **Sharpe:** -0.02
Percentage of Stocks: 92.50%
Percentage of Cash/equiv.: 7.50%

Front Load: 4.75%
Annualized Returns as of 12/31/98:
1998: -10.01%, 3-year: 4.09%,
5-year: 5.39%, Since Inception: 9.92%
Top Ten Holdings as of 10/31/98:
U.S. Filter Corp., Enron Corp., Williams
Companies, Whole Foods Market Inc.,
Wild Oats Markets Inc., Norfolk
Southern Corp., KN Energy Inc., United
Natural Gas, National Fuel Gas,
Burlington Resources Inc.
Portfolio Turnover: 54%
Comments: Fund invests in companies
beneficial to the environment, such as
recycling, co-generation, geothermal
power, solar power, fuel cells, hydro-
electric power, natural gas, efficient
electric devices, clean air, and clean
water.

NOAH (NOAHX)

www.noahfund.com
975 Delchester Road, P.O. Box 727
Edgemont, PA 19028-0727
800-794-6624
Asset Class: Large cap
NIS Social Rating^{SM}**:** ♥
Share Type: No Load
Date of Inception: 5/17/96
Assets: $2.5 Million
Fund Managers: John Geewax/Bruce

Terker since 5/17/96
12b-1 Fee: 0.25%
Total Operating Expense: 1.42%
Minimum Investment:
Initial: $1,000/Subsequently: None
Automatic Investments:
Initial: No Minimum /Subsequently:
$50
Beta: 1.26   **Sharpe:** 0.99
Percentage of Stocks: 95.60%

Percentage of Cash/equiv.: 4.40%
Annualized Returns as of 12/31/98:
1998: 51.33%, 3-year: N/A,
5-year: N/A, Since Inception: 44.78%
Top Ten Holdings as of 10/26/98:
Pfizer, Cisco Systems, Microsoft,
Shering Plough, Intel, General Re,
Wal-Mart Stores, Abbot Labs,
America Online, Lucent Technology
Portfolio Turnover: 88%
Comments: A conservative Christian
fund. Management donates 10% of its
fees to the poor and needy.

PARNASSUS FUNDS

www.parnassus.com

One Market-Steuart Tower #1600, San Francisco, CA 94105 [800-999-3505]

PARNASSUS CALIFORNIA TAX-FREE (PRCLX)

Asset Class: Tax-free income
NIS Social Rating℠: ♥ ♥ ♥ ♥
Share Type: No Load
Date of Inception: 9/1/92
Assets: $7.4 Million
Fund Manager: Jerome Dodson since
9/1/92
12b-1 Fee: 0.00%
Total Operating Expense: 0.67%
Minimum Investment:
Initial: $2000/Subsequently: $50
Automatic Investments:
Initial: $500/Subsequently: $50
Beta: 1.09   **Sharpe:** 0.57
Yield: 4.30
Percentage of Bonds: 91.60%
Percentage of Cash/equiv.: 8.40%
Current Yield: 3.98%
Average Bond Maturity: 7 years
Loads: Rear Load 4% declining to zero
after 5-years
Annualized Returns as of 12/31/98:
1998: 6.12%, 3-year: 6.56,
5-year: 6.18%, Since Inception: 7.18%
Top Ten Holdings as of 11/10/98: L. A.
City Parks 5.5%, Folsom School
District 5.65%, Oakland G. O. 5.5%,
Pasadena Community Development
6.0%, L. A. Community
Redevelopment 5.0%, Murrieta Valley
School District 5.5%, L. A. Metro
Transit 5.0%, CA Education-CA Tech
6.0%, Belmont Redevelopment 6.4%,
Pomona Public Financing Authority
6.0%
Portfolio Turnover: 10%
Comments: Invests in California tax-
free bonds that have a positive social
and environmental impact. This
includes financing schools, libraries,
mass transit, pollution control and
energy conservation projects. Avoids
bonds with negative social and environmental impact.

PARNASSUS EQUITY INCOME (PRBLX)

Asset Class: Equity income
NIS Social Rating℠: ♥ ♥ ♥ ♥ ♥
Share Type: No Load
Date of Inception: 9/1/92
Assets: $38.9 Million
Fund Manager: Jerome Dodson since
9/1/92
12b-1 Fee: 0.00%
Total Operating Expense: 1.05%
Minimum Investment:
Initial: $2,000/Subsequently: $50
Automatic Investments::
Initial: $500/Subsequently: $50
Beta: 1.12   **Sharpe:** 0.55

PARNASSUS EQUITY INCOME (PRBLX) *continued*

Yield: 2.38%
Percentage of Stocks: 93.50%
Percentage of Cash/equiv.: 6.50%
Annualized Returns as of 12/31/98:
1998: 11.05%, 3-year: 12.53%, 5-year:
12.09%, Since Inception: 13.55%
Top Ten Holdings as of 11/10/98: L. A.
City Parks 5.5%, Folsom School
District 5.65%, Oakland G. O. 5.5%,
Pasadena Community Development
6.0%, L. A. Community
Redevelopment 5.0%, Murrieta Valley
School District 5.5%,

L. A. Metro Transit 5.0%, CA
Education-CA Tech 6.0%, Belmont
Redevelopment 6.4%, Pomona Public
Financing Authority 6.0%
Portfolio Turnover: 34%
Comments: On April 1, 1998 this fund
was created by converting the
Balanced portfolio to the Equity
Income Fund. It is comprehensively
screened with a diversified portfolio.
Up to 5% of the portfolio value may be
invested in pro-active community loan
development funds.

PARNASSUS FIXED INCOME (PRFIX)

Asset Class: Tax-free income
NIS Social Rating℠: ♥ ♥ ♥ ♥ ♥
Share Type: No Load
Date of Inception: 9/1/92
Assets: $10.3 Million
Fund Manager:
Jerome Dodson since 9/1/92
12b-1 Fee: 0.00%
Total Operating Expense: 0.82%
Minimum Investment:
Initial: $2,000/Subsequently: $50
Automatic Investments:
Initial: $500/Subsequently: $50
Beta: 1.21   **Sharpe:** 0.54
Yield: 4.76%
Percentage of Bonds: 46.40%
Percentage of Cash/equiv.: 53.60%
Current Yield: 4.54%
Average Bond Maturity: 3.6 years

Bond Holdings: 79.80% Government
Agencies, 20.20% Corporate
Annualized Returns as of 12/31/98:
1998: 6.97%, 3-year: 7.15%,
5-year: 6.89, Since Inception: 7.82%
Top Ten Holdings as of 11/10/98:
FNMA 6.77%, Gap 6.9%, FHLMC
6.51%, Sears 7.0%, FNMA 6.14%,
BankBoston 6.375%, FNMA 7.35%,
Polaroid 7.25%, Reebok 6.75%, FNMA
6.72%
Portfolio Turnover: 17%
Comments: A comprehensively
screened fund. Invests in government
agency bonds to support affordable
housing. Fund may invest up to 5% of
the portfolio in pro-active community
development loan funds.

PARNASSUS FUND (PARNX)

Asset Class: Aggressive Growth
NIS Social Rating℠: ♥ ♥ ♥ ♥ ♥
Share Type: A
Date of Inception: 5/2/85
Assets: $210.0 Million
Fund Manager:
Jerome Dodson since 5/2/85
12b-1 Fee: 0.00%

Total Operating Expense: 1.11%
Minimum Investment:
Initial: $2,000/Subsequently: $50
Automatic Investments:
Initial: $500/Subsequently: $50
Beta: 1.43   **Sharpe:** 0.28
Percentage of Stocks: 100%
Front load: 3.50%

Annualized Returns as of 12/31/98:
1998: 1.40%, 3-year: 13.62%, 5-year: 10.58%, Since Inception: 13.01%
Top Ten Holdings as of 9/30/98:
Intel Corp., Compaq Computer Corp., Western Digital Corp., Advanced Micro Devices, Electro Scientific Industries, Applied Materials Inc., Oxford Health Plans Inc., Hewlett-Packard Co., Cognex Corp., Building Materials Holding Corp.
Portfolio Turnover: 69%
Comments: A volatile "contrarian" fund that invests in stocks selling at depressed prices. Fund is comprehensively screened and may invest up to 5% of it assets in community development loan funds.

PAX WORLD FUNDS
www.paxfund.com
225 State Street, Portsmouth, NH 03801   [800-767-1729]

PAX WORLD (PAXWX)

Asset Class: Balanced
NIS Social Rating℠: ♥ ♥ ♥ ♥
Share Type: No Load
Date of Inception: 8/10/71
Assets: $730 Million
Fund Managers:
C. Brown/R. Colin since 4/15/98
12b-1 Fee: 0.13%
Total Operating Expense: 0.91%
Minimum Investment:
Initial: $250/Subsequently: $50
Automatic Investments:
Initial: $250/Subsequently: $50
Beta: 0.78   **Sharpe:** 1.61
Yield: 2.29%
Percentage of Stocks: 58.20%
Percentage of Bonds: 29.60%
Percentage of Cash/equiv.: 12.20%
Average Bond Maturity: 2 years
Bond Holdings: 100% U.S. Government Agencies

Annualized Returns as of 12/31/98:
1998: 24.62%, 3-year: 19.75%, 5-year: 17.92%,
Since Inception: 10.53%
Top Ten Holdings as of 9/30/98:
AirTouch Communications; Amgen, Inc.; Southern NE Telecom Corp.; Bay States Gas; Gap, Inc.; Peoples Energy; Enron Corp.; Pitney, Bowes, Inc.; Merck & Co., Inc.; MarketSpan Corp.
Portfolio Turnover: 14%
Comments: The oldest socially screened fund. It has consistently made returns higher than the average balanced fund. Shareholders have opportunity to have capital gains and dividends invested in Pax World Service Foundation which support peace projects and provides capital for sustainable development in third world countries.

PAX WORLD GROWTH (PXWGX)

Asset Class: Midcap
NIS Social Rating℠: ♥ ♥ ♥ ♥
Share Type: A
Date of Inception: 6/11/97
Assets: $9.7 Million
Fund Manager:

Robert P. Colin since 6/11/97
12b-1 Fee: 0.35%
Total Operating Expense: 1.49%
Minimum Investment:
Initial: $250/Subsequently: $50
Automatic Investments:

PAX WORLD GROWTH (PXWGX) *continued*

Initial: $250/Subsequently: $50
Beta: N/A   **Sharpe:** N/A
Percentage of Stocks: 83.05%
Percentage of Cash/equiv.: 16.95%
Front load: 2.50%
Annualized Returns as of 12/31/98:
1998: 15.22%, 3-year: N/A,
5-year: N/A, Since Inception: 7.14%
Top Ten Holdings as of 10/30/98:
EEX Corp., Host Marriott, R B Falcon
Corp., Airborne Freight, Pharmacia &
Upjohn, Inc., Sunrise Assisted Living
Inc., Netscape Comm. Corp., General
Instrument Corp., Baker Hughes Inc.,
Nextel Communications
Portfolio Turnover: 50%
Comments: A low-load fund that
invests in companies which provide
life-supportive goods and services.
Selects companies with sound environ-
mental policies and fair employment
practices.

RIGHTIME SOCIAL AWARENESS (RTAWX)

The Forest Pavilion,
218 Glenside Avenue
Wyncote, PA 19095
800-242-1421
Asset Class: Aggressive Growth
NIS Social Rating℠: ♥ ♥ ♥ ♥
Share Type: A
Date of Inception: 3/1/90
Assets: $15.0 Million
Fund Manager:
Dennis Houser since 3/1/90
12b-1 Fee: 0.50%
Total Operating Expense: 2.35%
Minimum Investment:
Initial: $1,000/Subsequently: $25
Automatic Investments:
Initial: $25 /Subsequently: $25
Beta: 0.39   **Sharpe:** 1.20

Percentage of Stocks: 100%
Front load: 4.75%
Annualized Returns as of 12/31/98:
1998: 36.34%, 3-year: 18.98%,
5-year: 17.11%,
Since Inception: 12.32%
Top Ten Holdings as of 10/31/98:
Merck, Fannie Mae, Home Depot Inc.,
Ameritech, Cisco Systems, Pepsico,
American Express, Freddie Mac, Bank
One, BankAmerica
Portfolio Turnover: 108%
Comments: Fund uses "market timing"
techniques. It attempts to outperform
the S&P 500 in rising markets and
makes defensive investments in declin-
ing markets. The Domini 400 Social
Index is used to screen investments.

SECURITY SOCIAL AWARENESS (SWAAX)

www.securitybenefit.com
700 SW Harrison Street
Topeka, KS 66636-0001
800-888-2461
Asset Class: Large cap
NIS Social Rating℠: ♥ ♥ ♥
Share Type: A,B
Date of Inception: 11/4/96
Assets: $8.2 Million
Fund Manager:
Cindy Shields since 11/4/96

12b-1 Fee:
A SHARES: 0.00%,
B SHARES:1.00%
Total Operating Expense:
A SHARES: 0.00%,
B SHARES: 1.00%
Minimum Investment:
Initial: $100/Subsequently: $100
Automatic Investments:
Initial: $100/Subsequently: $20
Beta: 0.94   **Sharpe:** N/A

Percentage of Stocks: 92.17%
Percentage of Cash/equiv.: 7.83%
Load:
A SHARES—Front load: 5.75%
B SHARES—Rear load: 5% declining
    to 0 after 5-years
Annualized Returns as of 12/31/98:
1998: 30.39%, 3-year: N/A,
5-year: N/A, Since Inception: 24.20%
Top Ten Holdings as of 9/30/98:

Microsoft, Intel, IBM, Merck & Co.,
Schering-Plough, Johnson & Johnson,
Coca Cola, AT&T, Cisco Systems, BMC
Software
Portfolio Turnover: 30%
Comments: A very solid growth fund. A
part of Security Benefit Life Insurance
Co., which is listed in the Best 100
Companies to Work for in America.

TIMOTHY PLAN (TPLNX)

www.timothyplan.com
1304 West Fairbanks Ave.
WinterPark, FL 32789
800-846-7526
Asset Class: Midcap
NIS Social Rating℠: ♥
Share Type: A, B
Date of Inception: 3/21/94
Assets: $13.4 Million
Fund Manager:
James Awad since 3/21/94
12b-1 Fee: A SHARES: 0.25%,
B SHARES: 1.00%
Total Operating Expense: A SHARES:
1.60%, B SHARES 2.35%
Minimum Investment:
Initial: $1,000/Subsequently: None
Automatic Investments:
Initial: $100/Subsequently: $100

Beta: 0.91   **Sharpe:** 0.29
Percentage of Stocks: 93.83%
Percentage of Bonds: 1.69%
Percentage of Cash/equiv.: 4.48%
Portfolio Turnover: 93%
Load:
A SHARES—Front load: 5.50%
B SHARES—Rear load: 5% declining
    to 0 after 5-years
Annualized Returns as of 12/31/98:
1998: -11.10%, 3-year: 6.67%,
5-year: N/A, Since Inception: 7.64%
Top Ten Holdings as of of 8/31/98:
Wiley & Sons – A, Damaher, Eltron,
Doral, Comdisco Inc., Elan, Gaylord
Entertainment, Investor's Financial, J.
M. Smucker Class B, New Horizon
Comments: A conservative Christian
fund.

USAA FIRST START GROWTH (USFGX)

9800 Fredericksburg Road
San Antonio, TX 78288
800-531-0553
Asset Class: Large cap
NIS Social Rating℠: ♥
Share Type: No Load
Date of Inception: 8/1/97
Assets: $46.7 Million
Fund Manager: Tom Honeycutt since
8/1/97
12b-1 Fee: 0.00%
Total Operating Expense: 1.42%

Minimum Investment:
Initial: $300/Subsequently: None
Automatic Investments:
Initial: $250/Subsequently: $20
Beta: N/A   **Sharpe:** N/A
Percentage of Stocks: 95%
Percentage of Cash/equiv.: 5%
Annualized Returns as of 12/31/98:
1998: 40.46%, 3-year: N/A,
5-year: N/A, Since Inception: 40.46%
Top Ten Holdings as of 9/30/98:
Hershey Foods, Proctor & Gamble,

USAA FIRST START GROWTH (USFGX) *continued*

Clear Channel Communications, General Electric, Newell Co, Johnson & Johnson, Microsoft, Dell Computer, Mattell, Lear Corp,
Portfolio Turnover: 52%

Comments: Invests in companies that provide goods and services familiar to young people. Designed to teach and stimulate interest in long-term investing.

VICTORY LAKEFRONT FUND (VLCIX)

P. O. Box 8527
Boston, MA 02266-8527
800-423-0898
Asset Class: Large cap
NIS Social Rating℠: ♥
Share Type: A
Date of Inception: 3/3/97
Assets: $1.0 Million
Fund Manager:
Nathaniel E. Carter since 3/3/97
12b-1 Fee: 0.00%
Total Operating Expense: 0.50%
Minimum Investment:
Initial: $500/Subsequently: $25
Automatic Investments:
Initial: $500/Subsequently: $25
Beta: N/A   **Sharpe:** N/A
Yield: 3.57

Percentage of Stocks: 96.30%
Percentage of Cash/equiv.: 2.70%
Front Load: 5.75%
Annualized Returns as of 12/31/98:
1998: 13.03%,
3-year: N/A, 5-year: N/A,
Since Inception: 16.95%
Top Ten Holdings as of 9/30/98:
Schering-Plough, Intel, IBM, Pharmacia & Upjohn, Bristol Myers Squibb, Texas Instruments, KMart, Chase Manhattan, Williams Cos., Sun Microsystems
Portfolio Turnover: 19%
Comments: Fund focuses on investing in companies with a commitment to diversity with respect to women and minorities.

WOMEN'S EQUITY (FEMMX)

www.womens-equity.com
625 Market Street, 16th Floor
San Francisco, CA 94105,
800-385-7003
Asset Class: Large cap
NIS Social Rating℠: ♥ ♥ ♥ ♥
Share Type: No Load
Date of Inception: 10/1/93
Assets: $7.4 Million
Fund Managers: Hydie Soumeria/ Bill Apfel since 7/1/98
12b-1 Fee: 0.25%
Total Operating Expense: 1.50%
Minimum Investment:
Initial: $1,000/Subsequently: $100
Automatic Investments:
Initial: $50/Subsequently: $50
Beta: 1.08   **Sharpe:** 0.98

Percentage of Stocks: 98.10%
Percentage of Cash/equiv.: 1.90%
Front Load: 5.75%
Annualized Returns as of 12/31/98:
1998: 28.77%, 3-year: 23.63%,
5-year: 17.46%, Since Inception: 16.66%
Top Ten Holdings as of 11/1/98:
Microsoft Corp., Medtronic Inc., Lucent Technologies Inc., Schering-Plough Corp., Merck & Co. Inc., Cisco Systems, Johnson & Johnson, Leggett & Platt, Norwest, SBC Communications,
Portfolio Turnover: 27%
Comments: Fund invests in companies that have policies and practices promoting women's social and economic equality.

Chapter 11 *Eleven*

Special-Interest Funds

ALTHOUGH MOST OF the attention in socially oriented investing has gone toward the actively screened funds highlighted in the previous chapter, there are plenty of other opportunities to invest with your values. This chapter presents funds that are not designed as socially screened funds but that may, by their very nature, be a fit for some Natural Investors. We focus here on investing in specific social or industrial sectors that could appeal to your sense of justice or simply your personal interests. Whether you want to be involved in government-backed mortgages, support farm or school loans, or would like to invest in an industry in which members of your family work, these funds may be for you.

Do not imagine that you should include most—or even any—of these sorts of funds in your portfolio. We offer them as suggestions from which to draw if you wish to make more specific choices than are available among the screened mutual funds presented in the previous chapter. These funds are especially helpful in fine-tuning the values element of your portfolio and for adding flexibility when developing your portfolio using the asset allocation process.

Bond Funds

ALTHOUGH MANY SCREENED bond funds (also known as income funds) provide good exposure for Natural Investors, if you want to be involved in specific types of bonds, you'll need to look to unscreened funds. Here we summarize several kinds of bond funds that are often of interest.

Mortgage-Backed Bond Funds

This is the largest and most popular government agency bond category among Natural Investors. These funds hold bonds issued by Fannie Mae (FNMA), the Federal Home Loan Mortgage Corporation, and the Government National Mortgage Association (GNMA or Ginnie Mae), which support various government mortgage guarantee programs. They are often owned by investors who wish to be involved in expanding homeownership and affordable housing opportunities. To be called a mortgage-backed bond fund, the fund must have at least 65 percent so invested. The remaining portfolio can contain other income investments, including U.S. Treasuries. The funds listed below contain less than 5 percent U.S. Treasury and other income investments:

➤ **American Century Benham GNMA** (800-345-2021)
➤ **Cardinal Government Obligation** (800-282-9446)
➤ **Dreyfus Premier GNMA** (800-373-9387)
➤ **Fidelity GNMA** (800-544-8888)
➤ **Franklin U.S. Government Securities** (800-342-5236)
➤ **Kemper U.S. Mortgage** (800-621-1048)
➤ **Lexington GNMA Income** (800-526-0056)
➤ **Safeco GNMA** (800-426-6730)
➤ **Smith Breeden Intermediate Duration U.S. Government** (800-221-3138)
➤ **Target Mortgage Backed Securities** (800-442-8748)
➤ **Vanguard GNMA** (800-662-7447)
➤ **Victory U.S. Government Mortgage** (800-539-3863)

Adjustable-Rate Mortgage Funds

Many homeowners have adjustable-rate mortgages on their property. The interest rates of adjustable-rate mortgages, as the name implies, are adjusted periodically as prevailing interest rates change. This results in a more stable share price for bonds invested in these types of mortgages. Adjustable-rate funds pay dividends that are lower than those of the standard mortgage funds listed earlier, but they are appealing because their share values are steadier. The government agencies listed previously support these mortgages. They are worth considering, especially if income is needed but one may need to sell the holding in less than five years. The following adjustable-rate funds hold less than 5 percent U.S. Treasuries:

➤ **Countrywide** (800-543-0407)
➤ **First American** (800-637-2548)

Federal Tax-Free Bond Funds

Many mutual funds hold a portfolio of bonds issued by state and local governments from around the nation. These bonds support housing, education, and other vital state and local government functions. Many Natural Investors will consider these bonds to be socially responsible, as they are used to fund state and local projects. But be aware that some of the bonds may not be to your liking; a tax-free bond fund may hold some bonds in its portfolio for projects (for example, those financing prison construction or nuclear power plants) that are not on your list of favorite issues.

The dividends paid by the funds are federally tax free. If the fund holds any bonds issued by the state in which you reside, you are exempt from paying state taxes on interest from those specific bonds.

See Appendix E, page 333, for a list of these funds.

State Municipal Bond Funds

There may be an advantage for your bond investments to be double tax free, that is, free of federal and state income taxes. Many mutual fund families offer a fund that invests only in bonds issued by communities or the state government in a single state; taxpayers residing in that state might seek these out both for the tax advantages and to target investments closer to home. As with the federal tax-free funds, these funds are often considered socially responsible since the bonds support education, mass transit, and other needed local services.

See Appendix E, page 333, for a list of unscreened state and municipal bond funds.

Special-Emphasis Funds

NATURAL INVESTORS HAVE many opportunities to really hone in on specific social issues as part of their portfolios, even while investing only in mutual funds. There are now many specialized funds offered by the mutual fund industry. Rather than using broad screens as do the funds described in the previous chapter, these funds employ more specific screens, usually as a matter of policy rather than prospectus. The Social Investment Forum lists 155 funds with some sort of social screen. We have selected those that may be of specific interest to our readers. Note that the funds marked with an star (*) have a full profile at the end of Chapter 10.

African Economy
Calvert New Africa Fund (800-368-2748). This fund was established in 1995 to provide needed investment capital to South Africa after the fall of apartheid; it now invests in the entire continent of Africa.

Alternative Energy
New Alternatives Fund (800-423-8383). This fund invests proactively in companies with innovative technologies for producing or conserving energy, as well as providing solutions to environmental problems.

Animal Rights
Cruelty-Free Value Fund (800-892-9626). This fund is dedicated to help end the suffering and abuse of animals and the extinction of hundreds of species annually.
IPS Millennium (800-524-1676). By written policy, this fund takes a strong activist position on animal rights. It will either avoid investments in companies with questionable records on animal-rights issues or else own stock in companies in order to take strong shareholder actions with regard to such issues. These issues include animal experimentation and testing, and the use of animals in circuses and events on which people bet. The fund will not invest in companies that are environmentally destructive or those in the tobacco, poultry, and fertilizer industries.

Gay Rights
Meyers Pride Value Fund (800-410-3337). This fund identifies companies that provide benefits to gay partners, advertise in gay publications, and show support for gays and lesbians in other ways.

Minority Ownership
DEM Fund (800-831-3175). This is a small-cap fund that invests in companies owned or controlled by African Americans, Asian Americans, Hispanics, and women.

Organized Labor

MFS Union Standard Equity Fund (800-225-2606). This is an index fund that specifically invests in companies that meet labor sensitivity criteria of interest to organized labor. MFS worked with American Capital Strategies Ltd. to develop a Labor Sensitivity Index (LSI) of approximately 550 companies, which make up the fund's portfolio. The LSI considers such labor-sensitive issues as whether a company has labor agreements; how much of its workforce is unionized; its history of strikes, lockouts, and labor boycotts; and foreign ownership.

Religious Funds

Sponsors of mutual funds are finding a large number of investors who wish to see their religious convictions reflected in their investment portfolios. With each continuing success, more keep coming to market. Religious funds screen out companies that violate the tenets of individual faiths and buy stocks that support their teachings.

CATHOLIC

Aquinas Funds (800-423-6369). A family of four funds: Balanced, Growth, Equity-Income, and Fixed Income.
Catholic Values (888-974-4486). A mid-cap fund.

CHRISTIAN SCIENCE

American Trust Allegiance (800-788-7285). A growth fund.

CONSERVATIVE CHRISTIAN

Noah Fund (800-794-6624). A large-cap fund.
Timothy Plan (800-846-7526). A pair of funds, investing in common stocks and convertible securities.

ISLAMIC

Amana Funds (800-728-8762). A pair of funds: Fixed Income and Growth.

LUTHERAN

Lutheran Brotherhood (800-328-4552). A family of six funds—the Lutheran Brotherhood Fund, 100 Leading Companies, Income, Municipal Bond, Opportunity Growth, and World Growth—that screen for alcohol-, tobacco-, and gambling-related investments.

MENNONITE

MMA Praxis (800-977-2947). A group of three funds: Growth, Intermediate Income, and International Stock.

Tobacco, Alcohol, and Gambling

Investors concerned about these issues can utilize virtually all the funds profiled in Chapter 10. In addition, the Pioneer, American Mutual, and Washington Mutual Investors families of funds have screened for these issues as a matter of policy for many years. Within the past two years, thanks to broad public support, many other fund families have chosen to apply these screens.

Here is a list of the funds with the specific issues for which they screen:

- ➤ *AARP* (800-322-2282). All thirteen funds screened for tobacco and alcohol.
- ➤ *AHA* (800-332-2111). Four funds screened for tobacco.
- ➤ *American Funds* (800-421-4120). *American Mutual* and *Washington Mutual Investors* exclude alcohol and tobacco.
- ➤ *Baron* (800-992-2766). Three funds exclude tobacco.
- ➤ *Bridgeway* (800-661-3550). Four funds screened for tobacco. In addition, the *★Social Responsibility Portfolio* fund is fully screened by prospectus (see Chapter 10).
- ➤ *Common Sense* (800-544-5445). Twelve funds that will not invest in a company deriving more than 25 percent of its income from the manufacture of alcohol or tobacco.
- ➤ *Pioneer* (800-225-6292). All thirty-nine funds in the family screen out alcohol and tobacco. *Pioneer Fund,* the original fund in the family, has screened for these issues since 1928.
- ➤ *Straton Growth* (800-634-5726). Screened for tobacco.
- ➤ *Thornburg* (800-847-0200). Six income funds and a value fund screen out tobacco.

Women's Economic and Social Issues

★Women's Equity Fund (800-385-7003). A growth fund that focuses on investing in companies that are proactive with respect to women's social and economic equality.

Workplace Diversity

★Victory Lakefront Fund (800-892-8383). This fund selects companies that have demonstrated positive policies for employment diversification with respect to minorities and women.

Young Investors

Two fund families have identified a need for a mutual fund designed for young people and adults wanting to invest in Uniform Gifts to Minors accounts to fund college educations. The funds invest in companies such as Hershey, PepsiCo, Walt Disney, and others that appeal to kids. They do not invest in companies engaged in the manufacture or sale of tobacco, alcohol, and similar products. They educate children and adults in the art of investing. Some parents may consider these sorts of companies to be at the heart of the commercial beast and therefore find this sort of fund contrary to their sense of social responsibility. For those whose kids have a positive connection with these companies, though, such funds have both financial and educational appeal.

USAA First Start Growth Fund (800-531-0533). Screened for alcohol, tobacco, and gambling.

Stein Roe Young Investor (800-338-2550). Screened for alcohol, tobacco, and gambling.

Sector Funds

SECTOR IS THE financial world term for a specific industry or geographic region; for example, investors often talk about the high tech sector, the real estate sector, or the Asian sector. At various times certain sectors outperform others. For either personal or financial reasons, many investors like to have a greater concentration in a particular sector than is possible in a general fund or by individual stock purchase. The stocks in a particular group may be appealing because the companies are manufacturers of a socially useful product or provide a socially needed service. Perhaps you or members of your family work in a particular industry. Or you may just enjoy working with computers and want to have some of your money reflect this interest.

These same companies might have terrible employment records, be the cause of environmental problems, or face other issues that would cause them to be avoided by a socially screened fund. However, if you are not troubled by the particular shortcomings of your sector of interest, it may be a Natural Investment for you.

Then again, you may choose to play in the sector realm simply to try to boost the overall value of your portfolio. Your social screen may be simply to avoid a few industries in which you do not want to be involved, rather than to seek out ones you support.

Sector funds are inherently more volatile than diversified stock mutual funds. In addition, sector funds are not required to invest exclusively in the sector. They can invest 20 to 25 percent of their portfolios in other securities. For example, a telephone and communications fund may also have a tobacco company holding. The Fidelity Select funds have the most narrowly defined sectors and the fewest unassociated stocks in their portfolios. With the foregoing in mind we offer the following sectors for your consideration.

Environment

Environmental issues are among the most common social screens; many investors would like to invest in companies that help improve the environment. Unfortunately stocks in this sector have suffered a prolonged period of underperformance, which has caused several environmental sector funds to go out of business. Of those remaining, it is disturbing to report that, with one notable exception, some of the stocks in their portfolios are in fact not environmentally clean. The stocks of waste management companies often fall into this category. Several of these companies have been found guilty of causing environmental contamination and fined by the Environmental Protection Agency. Other industries in this sector include pollution control, recycling, and other similar services and products. New Alternatives, with its special emphasis on renewable energy, is the only socially screened fund in this sector. The major funds are the following:

➤ Fidelity Select (800-544-8888)
➤ Invesco (800-525-8085)
➤ *New Alternatives (800-423-8383)

Natural Resources and Utilities

Most socially responsible investors have an aversion to owning stocks in all segments of the natural resources and utilities sectors. They usually shun companies that are primarily involved in petroleum products because of the pollution caused by the processing and burning of these substances. They also shun nuclear power companies. Most natural resources sector funds contain a wide array of stocks, in industries based on coal, steel, forest products, and chemicals, that are usually screened out of socially responsible portfolios. We advocate investing in natural gas and water utilities if you want to participate in this sector. The following sector funds meet these criteria:

➤ Fidelity Select Natural Gas (800-544-8888)
➤ *Flex Total Return Utilities (800-325-3539)
➤ Rushmore American Gas Index (800-621-7874)

Financial Services

The financial services sector is the glue of our economic system. The stocks in this sector include banks, savings and loan associations, insurance companies, and securities brokerage firms. Although some Natural Investors may find themselves holding their noses as they walk past this sector, you may have personal or financial reasons to embrace these funds. In the period July 1993 through July 1998 the sector posted returns above those of the market in general. However, in August and September 1998 it took a big hit—proving once again that sector funds are more volatile than the general market. We suggest that you check out the following fund families:

➤ Century Shares (800-321-1928)
➤ Davis (800-279-0279)
➤ Fidelity (800-544-8888)
➤ GT Global (800-824-1580)
➤ Invesco (800-525-8085)
➤ John Hancock (800-225-5291)
➤ Paine Webber (800-647-1568)
➤ Pilgrim American (800-334-3444)
➤ SIFE (800-332-5580)

Health and Biotechnology

The health and biotechnology sector includes companies involved in the manufacture of medical equipment and supplies, the making of pharmaceuticals, the operation of health care facilities, and applied research and development of new products related to health care. Returns were very rewarding financially from July 1993 through July 1998. Whether or not this high rate of return, fueled as it is by spiraling costs to consumers, is socially responsible is a matter of personal opinion. Those uncomfortable with the role of health maintenance organizations in our health care system may also want to step carefully in this sector. Here are the leading players in this sector:

➤ Dean Witter (800-869-3863)
➤ Eaton Vance Marathon (800-225-6265)
➤ Fidelity (800-544-8888)
➤ First American (800-637-2548)
➤ Franklin (800-342-5236)
➤ GT Global (800-824-1580)
➤ Invesco (800-525-8085)
➤ John Hancock (800-225-5291)
➤ Merrill Lynch (609-282-2800)
➤ Putnam (800-225-1581)
➤ T. Rowe Price (800-638-5660)
➤ Vanguard (800-662-7447)

The Internet

Internet stocks have captured the imagination of many investors—especially Net-savvy investors doing their own on-line trading—who want to get in on the ground floor of this rapidly growing industry. Prices for many Internet stocks have skyrocketed. For example, bookseller Amazon.com traded at a low of $9 per share in 1998. As of January 15, 1999, it was at $139 after reaching a high of $199. However, the company has yet to turn a profit. The risks of owning these kinds of stocks are tremendous; many companies will not survive. If you do decide to take a shot at investing in Internet companies, do so with only a small portion of your portfolio. Several mutual funds are now focusing on the Internet. Check out the following:

➤ Munder NetNet (800-239-3334)
➤ The Internet Fund (888-386-3999)
➤ WWW Internet (888-999-8331)

Real Estate

The real estate sector stirs up much controversy in socially responsible investment circles. Certainly everyone agrees that people must have shelter! However, many are concerned that development projects such as shopping malls, apartment complexes, storage units, and office towers do not use the Earth's resources in an environmentally sane and sustainable way. If you are in this camp, you may not feel comfortable with these sector funds. But if you want to invest in real estate, then you might want to check out the following funds:

➤ Alliance (800-227-4618)
➤ CGM Realty (800-345-4048)
➤ Cohen and Steers (800-437-9912)
➤ Columbia (800-547-1707)
➤ Crabbe Hudson (800-541-7827)
➤ Delaware (800-231-8002)
➤ Evergreen (800-807-2940)
➤ Excelsior (800-446-1012)
➤ Fidelity (800-544-8888)
➤ First American (800-637-2548)
➤ Flag Investors (800-645-3923)
➤ Franklin (800-342-5236)
➤ GrandView (800-525-3863)
➤ Heitman (800-435-1405)
➤ Invesco (800-525-8085)
➤ Morgan Stanley (800-282-4404)
➤ Munder (800-239-3334)
➤ Phoenix (800-243-4361)
➤ Pioneer (800-225-6292)
➤ Seneca (800-990-9331)
➤ United Services (800-873-8637)
➤ Van Kampen American Capital (800-421-5666)
➤ Vanguard (800-662-7447)

Technology

The technology sector has been the most dynamic and dominant force in modern times. Everyone is always seeking the next Microsoft or Intel, and new companies are constantly emerging. This sector includes companies involved with computers, communications, video, electronics, office and factory automation, and robotics. Many technology companies are also social innovators, with enlightened management practices aimed at promoting creativity and worker retention. However, there are also real questions about both the environmental and the social costs of high technology. Although these companies generally don't spew clouds of exhaust into the air, many high-tech manufacturing processes do use large amounts of local water and may emit pollutants. Working conditions are sometimes far from ideal, especially if manufacturing takes place overseas. And you may have doubts about the social value of video games, television, or computers in general. If so, steer clear of this sector.

But if you have a personal interest in the leading edge of technological development, you may find some of these funds attractive. Stocks in high-tech companies are extremely volatile and can be risky because of rapid product obsolescence and intensely competitive markets. For those capable of investing in stocks that are subject to massive gyrations, we suggest checking out the following companies' technology sector funds:

- Alliance (800-247-4154)
- Dean Witter (800-869-3863)
- Eaton Vance (800-225-6365)
- Excelsior (800-446-1012)
- Fidelity (800-544-8888)
- First American (800-637-2548)
- Flag Investors (800-645-3923)
- Franklin (800-342-5236)
- Gabelli (800-422-3554)
- GT Global (800-824-1580)
- Invesco (800-525-8085)
- Ivy (800-456-5111)
- John Hancock (800-225-5291)
- Kemper (800-621-1048)
- Merrill Lynch (609-282-2800)
- Montgomery (800-572-3863)
- PBHG (800-809-8008)
- PIMCO (800-426-0107)
- Robertson Stephenson (800-766-3863)
- Seligman (800-221-7844)
- Steadman (800-424-8570)
- T. Rowe Price (800-638-5660)
- United (800-236-2000)

Putting It All Together

WHEW! THE LAST couple of chapters have surely deepened your appreciation for the range of choices available to Natural Investors. We doubt that anyone is feeling that they don't have enough options to consider! Nevertheless we're going to continue broadening the scope in the following chapter, to include investment options other than mutual funds. If you want to include individual stocks or bonds, real estate investment trusts, annuities, or other nonfund choices in your portfolio, please return to this final worksheet after reading the next chapter.

However, knowing that many readers will be focusing most, if not all, of their investing on mutual funds (perhaps with some small-company prospecting thrown in for good measure), we've chosen to place this worksheet here. It's time to really get down to the nitty-gritty, identifying mutual funds that will allow you to move forward with your personal investment plan.

In the next chapter we leave the comfort of mutual funds to brave the world of individual investments. Get ready for a crash course that is sure to raise your financial IQ and enable you to dazzle your friends when talk turns to money!

Worksheet #7: Choosing Specific Investments

Please refer once again to Worksheets #3 and #4, which you completed at the end of Section 2. There you identified Avoidance Screening and Affirmative Screening issues that you'd like to consider. Look also at Worksheet #6, which you completed at the end of Chapter 9, in which you identified your own place on the risk/reward spectrum and set aside funds for Community Investing and Affirmative Screening.

Now we ask you to take out a separate piece of paper (this will take more than a few inches of space!) and begin making lists of potential investments.

1. Look at Worksheet #6, the Asset Allocation Worksheet. Based on your answers to the last question, look at the Beach Lover's Asset Allocation Chart on page 175 and list the types of mutual funds or individual investments you will be including in your portfolio, with a general sense of what proportion of your funds you'd like in each type:

BONDS

    Long-term government agency   _____

    Short-duration bond   _____

    Income   _____

STOCKS

    Utilities   _____

Balanced	_____
Large cap	_____
Midcap	_____
Small cap	_____
International	_____
Aggressive growth	_____

2. Now turn to Worksheet #3 to orient yourself to the screening issues most important to you. List all the issues for which you want to screen.
3. Next look back to Chapter 10 to begin identifying candidate mutual funds. The Mutual Fund Screen Matrix on pages 182–185 offers a brief look at each fund's key issue screens, while the more detailed profiles at the end of the chapter offer further grist for the mill. List all funds that can meet the needs you specified in the preceding question, noting the type of fund for each. Contact each fund and order their prospectus and annual report; make sure to read them before investing.
4. For sector and utility funds, as well as government bond programs in areas of special interest (such as student or farm loans or low-income housing), flip through Chapter 11 and list any that appeal to you.
5. If there are specific industries or companies with which you have a personal connection or interest, list them here, noting whether each is likely to be pursued through stocks or bonds, and to which asset allocation category it is likely to apply. You will use this list to supplement mutual fund choices as you make your final purchasing decisions.
6. If you are including any of the nonfund options covered in Chapter 12, list which categories you want to consider, leaving space for filling in a number of possibilities for each (list possibilities from the book or from your research in periodicals and other sources of information).
7. Now go down through your asset allocation list (Question 1) and begin making specific choices for each category. Begin by listing the investments you wish to pursue, then go back and fill in the amount you want to invest in each.
8. By golly, you've done it! Give yourself three cheers . . . and then sleep on it. Review your decisions another day, then contact your financial adviser, the mutual funds, or your discount or on-line brokerage, and go for it!

Chapter Twelve

Stocks, Bonds, and Beyond: The Natural Investing Universe

LTHOUGH MOST INVESTORS find that mutual funds offer an appealing combination of diversification and ease, there are good reasons for you to become familiar with the full range of available investment options.

The first and foremost reason is that your portfolio is likely to include mutual funds that focus on different types of holdings. A basic understanding of the various components will help you to really know what you're getting into. In addition, mutual funds can subject investors to additional capital gains taxes if they are unusually active in their buying and selling over the course of the year. (It is for this reason that many more sophisticated investors prefer to build their own diversified portfolios, in order to control their tax effects, to better customize them, or both.)

Beyond that, Natural Investors may also want to put part of their money into specific holdings, either for the pure excitement of it or to achieve greater diversification. Many small investors enjoy devoting a moderate amount of time to researching the common stock offerings of particular companies; others rely on their financial advisers to make recommendations based on their research. Either way, you may be surprised to find that you are more interested in (and connected to) the 5 to 10 percent of your portfolio that's in stocks you chose than the bulk of your investments in mutual funds.

Finally, even the most rigorously screened mutual funds fall short of the social goals of some investors. If this describes you, then you've come to the right place. You may wish to seek out the stock of a few companies in which you really believe, and blend those holdings with carefully chosen bonds and community investments. This way you can create a portfolio more closely tailored to your social interests than would be possible with mutual funds.

Ready? OK! Fasten your seat belts and prepare for a whirlwind tour of the universe of investment options available to the savvy Natural Investor.

Checking Accounts, Savings Accounts, and Certificates of Deposit

THE COMMUNITY BANKS and credit unions discussed in Chapter 7 provide the highest form of socially responsible banking. Another good alternative for meeting community needs is to do business with a locally owned bank within your community. If there are no local community banking options, you may need to consider a commercial bank (though banking at a distance can also be an option). If you must use a commercial bank, check out their Community Reinvestment Act record. All banks are required to allocate a portion of their loans to meet the needs of the communities they serve. Some are better than others in the area of loans to small businesses, minorities, and others who ordinarily would not pass rigid credit requirements. CANICCOR: An Interfaith Council on Corporate Accountability, which is affiliated with the Interfaith Council on Corporate Responsibility, monitors and reports on social responsibility issues in the banking industry.

CANICCOR
P.O. Box 426829
San Francisco, CA 94142
(415) 885-5102

Stocks

THE PICTURES YOU'VE seen of the stock traders on the floor of the New York Stock Exchange—with people shouting and madly waving their

Under the Buttonwood Tree

IN 1790 THERE were only two types of securities to trade: Revolutionary War bonds that the newly formed American government was selling to pay off an $80 million war debt, and shares of stock in the first national bank, called the Bank of the United States.

Those advocating the "greening of Wall Street" may be heartened to learn that the great New York Stock Exchange had its humble beginnings underneath a buttonwood tree (a type known today as the sycamore) located at what is now 68 Wall Street. The 1792 "Buttonwood Agreement" formalized this meeting place to facilitate stock and bond trading.[1]

arms, writing notes, and making frantic phone calls—are, remarkably, the actual core of the process of stock trading (although, by contrast, Nasdaq is silent and computerized). Those frenzied folks are employees of brokerage firms that have paid big bucks to have a "seat" on the exchange. If you use a full-service brokerage firm you pay a commission, which can typically be up to 2 percent of the total transaction amount. Lower trading costs are available through discount brokers that do not provide investment advice. In addition, many investors who are comfortable working on their own now place trades electronically at very low cost via the Internet.

Which Stocks Are Socially Responsible?

Do you want to do your own social screening of individual companies? If so, be prepared to devote a substantial amount of time and resources to this task. You will need to gather information on a company's full line of products and services, employment policies, product safety history, environmental record, military involvement, and other issues of interest. As a small investor, it is unlikely that you will be able to discuss these issues with upper management; it takes the clout of a mutual fund manager or major investor to gain this sort of access. Companies vary greatly in their responsiveness to requests for social disclosure; many investor relations departments are reluctant to provide full information to the public. Annual reports, although helpful, give limited information. Reports from various independent watchdog organizations and the media must also be consulted.

One good place to start your search is with the lists of companies in Appendix B, which features hundreds of companies listed on the major screened stock indexes as well as lists of companies linked with the various screening issues discussed in Chapters 5 and 6. Newsletters such as *Franklin Research's Insight* provide continuing updates and ideas for those interested in buying and selling socially screened stocks. We've also included in Appendix E contact information for some of the major watchdog organizations that can help you monitor corporate activity.

In addition, there are professional services—including Kinder, Lydenberg, Domini & Co. (KLD), the Investor Responsibility Research Center (IRRC), and the Council on Economic Priorities—that maintain information on thousands of corporations and can cross-reference the social issues associated with these companies. These are subscription services that are used primarily by socially responsible investment (SRI) professionals, but they are also available to individual investors. KLD offers SOCRATES, a computerized database that catalogs hundreds of companies; the IRRC has recently introduced a similar service to serve the professional community.

Preferred Stock

Preferred stocks are a special class of stocks issued by corporations, banks, insurance companies, utilities, financial institutions, and real estate investment firms. In practice, owning preferred stock is much like owning bonds; they pay a fixed interest rate of return (usually a bit better than that of bonds) and tend not to fluctuate in price very dramatically. Preferred stocks are very-low-risk investments if you choose those of investment grade: those rated BBB or higher by Standard and Poor's. As with bonds, you may get more or less than the purchase price when selling because of market interest rate fluctuations. Preferred stocks are subject to call, that is, redemption by the company at a fixed price after a given date.

SRI Application. We have identified twenty-six socially screened companies that offer preferred stock. These companies are noted in our master list of screened companies in Appendix B.

Corporate Bonds

Corporations issues bonds in order to raise funds for capital improvements and expansion. Yields on corporate bonds can be higher than those on comparable government bonds.

SRI Application. Many socially screened companies issue bonds. Check the portfolios of socially screened income funds, or see our company lists in Appendix B for a starting point.

In 1997 a University of Denver study reported that investors in bonds issued by the companies represented in the Domini 400 Social Index would achieve the same return as investors in the bonds of non-screened companies, when yields were compared on a risk-adjusted basis.[2] Once again, as with stock performance, we find that *there is no penalty for investing with your values.* Natural Investors can comfortably consider bonds from socially screened companies when performing their portfolio asset allocations.

U.S. Government Bonds

The U.S. Treasury issues bonds to finance those costs of running the government that cannot be covered through taxes. Treasuries can be purchased directly through the Federal Reserve without charge; a small transaction charge will be levied if they are bought through a bank or brokerage firm. There is a very active secondary market for buying and selling Treasuries prior to maturity through brokerage accounts.

U.S. Government Agency Bonds

U.S. Government agency bonds typically yield 1.5 percent more than Treasuries. As we mentioned in Chapter 9, many Natural Investors prefer to buy government agency bonds rather than Treasuries for intermediate- and long-term investments. Several government agencies (private corporations chartered by Congress to raise funds for specific purposes) issue bonds worthy of consideration. These agencies include:

> *The Federal Farm Credit Bank (FFCB).* Investments are channeled to rural America through a system of approximately 240 Farm Credit lending institutions commonly known as Federal Land Banks or Production Credit and Agricultural Credit associations.

> *The Federal Home Loan Bank (FHLB).* The FHLB is the largest supplier of home mortgage credit in the United States. Federal Home Loan Banks are privately capitalized, cooperative, government-sponsored enterprises.

> *The Federal Home Loan Mortgage Corporation (FHLMC or Freddie Mac).* The FHLMC issues bonds called Freddie Macs, which finance home loans and commercial loans for low-income and senior housing.

> *Fannie Mae (FNMA).* Fannie Mae (formerly known as the Federal National Mortgage Association) is a public company mandated by the U.S. government to provide liquidity to the mortgage market. It buys mortgages from lenders and packages them for resale as bondlike securities. Fannie Mae's backing allows lenders to offer mortgages for low-income and senior housing to people who would otherwise not be considered.

> *The Government National Mortgage Association (GNMA or Ginnie Mae).* The GNMA issues mortgage-backed bonds commonly known as Ginnie Maes. The bonds are issued specifically to fund large blocks of mortgages held by individuals who qualify for Federal Housing Authority and Veterans Administration reduced-interest-rate mortgages.

> *Student Loan Marketing Association (SLMA or Sallie Mae).* Sallie Mae specializes in funding education, working with banks that make low-cost student loans. The agency purchases loans from lenders in order to replenish their funds so that more student loans can be made. Sallie Mae funds approximately 40 percent of all insured student loans.

SRI Application. U.S. government agency bonds provide a safe, low-risk return that is higher than the returns from a bank certificate of deposit or a U.S. Treasury bond. It is reassuring to know that money loaned to a government agency will only be used for affordable housing, student loans, and other defined, useful purposes. These bonds deserve to be considered for every diversified portfolio that can handle the fully taxable status of such investments. High-tax-bracket investors should consider tax-free municipal bonds, which are discussed in the next section.

Municipal Bonds

Municipal bonds are inherently natural choices because they support state and local infrastructure. Many are earmarked for socially useful community needs, such as schools, pollution control, mass transit, and other voter-approved projects. For many specific bonds, there will undoubtedly be some values-driven investors who are eager to support the project and others who find it unconnected to their interests. Prison bonds and bonds to build stadiums may fall into this category. Those with a broader sense of community values may consider buying general revenue bonds, which are not linked to a specific project.

As previously discussed, the $5,000 minimum purchase requirement for bonds may make it necessary for small investors to participate through mutual funds. Unit investment trusts are another alternative; these carry a limited number of selected bond issues in their portfolios. You may find one that is congruent with your social values. They are discussed later in this chapter.

Limited Partnerships

A LIMITED PARTNERSHIP (LP) is an organization made up of a general partner, who manages a particular project, and limited partners, who are investors in that project with no active involvement and no liability beyond the amounts of their investments. The most common LPs are those formed to engage in real estate development or management, equipment leasing, oil and gas exploration, and low-income housing development. Others may be organized to produce movies or conduct certain research and development projects.

LPs got a very bad name in the early 1980s, when they were involved with aggressive tax-avoidance investment programs that often placed less emphasis on basic investment worthiness, and ultimately left investors holding an empty bag. Congress has since passed laws outlawing the worst LP abuses. However, the LP format is still viable, and there are partnerships with high social value that can provide very good returns; some partnerships (for example, many of those engaged in natural gas exploration) can serve as excellent sources of tax-advantaged income for the Natural Investor.

Cost. Partnership units are usually sold in denominations of $1,000, with a minimum purchase of five units. Investors also must meet certain *suitability requirements* (that is, have sufficient assets and income) because of the risks involved in this type of investment. Investments are normally sold through brokers, who receive an 8 percent commission. This relatively high sales cost should be factored in as you figure the real return on any partnership.

Risks. Among the risks inherent in LP investments are the following:

➤ LPs are illiquid. Each invested partner must find a replacement investor when that partner wants out. This is not always an easy or quickly accomplished task.

➤ A natural gas exploration project could hit a dry hole, rendering the entire investment worthless.

➤ Programs and projects undertaken by LPs typically last anywhere from seven to fifteen years, with full payback to investors (if it occurs) often deferred until the end of the project.

➤ Additional federal, state, and local income tax forms must be completed by limited partners.

SRI Choices

Low-income housing tax credit programs. These are one of the excellent lower-risk types of LP with high social impact. The general partner raises money from investors and proposes a low-income housing project to the Department of Housing and Urban Development. In recent years, many such federally funded projects have been built far from the inner cities, serving low-income families and senior citizens in suburban and even rural communities. The investor is entitled to a dollar-for-dollar tax credit for ten years. Note that this is not a tax *deduction,* but a *credit* that directly reduces the investor's federal tax liability. Returns are typically 10 to 12 percent per year on average. By the end of the tenth year the project may have appreciated in value. If it is sold, the investor participates in the gain. If it is not sold, the property continues to be operated as low-income housing, and the investor is provided with passive tax deductions until the property is sold. Two sponsors of such LPs are:

➤ Boston Capital (800-886-2282)

➤ WNC & Associates (800-451-7070)

Natural gas exploration. There are very high expenses associated with oil and natural gas exploration, but there are also tax benefits for investors with high income and high net worth. The formation of LPs makes it much more convenient for less wealthy individuals to participate in these ventures. Natural gas is the cleanest-burning, least environmentally damaging fossil fuel currently available, making natural gas exploration LPs worthy of consideration by Natural Investors. But remember: these are high-risk investments. Two companies that sponsor LPs for natural gas exploration are:

➤ Atlas (800-845-5546)

➤ Petroleum Development Corporation (800-624-3821)

Annuities

ANNUITIES ARE INVESTMENTS made through insurance companies. One of their main attractions is their tax-deferred status.

The basic concept is that investors make small, systematic investments in order to accumulate a future nest egg from which to draw for retirement or some other special purpose. Annuities can also be purchased with a lump-sum premium payment. The insurance companies invest the premiums they collect mostly in bonds. Gains in the policy are tax deferred.

There are three types of annuities: fixed, index, and variable:

➤ *Fixed annuities.* Backed by bond purchases. Fixed annuities generate guaranteed cash flow for conservative investors.

➤ *Index annuities.* Designed to achieve enhanced returns by investing some of the insurance premium dollars in stock index futures. Their returns are guaranteed, although at a lower rate than those for fixed annuities, and they increase in a strong market.

➤ *Variable annuities.* Designed for investors wanting full market returns and willing to accept full market risk. These policies allow the investor to invest in selected mutual funds under the umbrella of the insurance policy. The investor assumes all the risk regarding the investments' worth when the time comes to cash out of the annuity.

Currently no fixed or index annuity polices are socially screened, but many variable annuity policies contain socially responsible options. Annuities are included in this chapter because of their popularity. In considering annuities, you may decide to stray from the strict path of socially screened investments in order to meet your personal financial needs.

The great advantage of annuities is the tax deferral. On the other side of the coin, the major disadvantage is that the insurance company tacks on extra loads and expenses for the privilege of going this route. These can amount to an extra 0.5 to 1.5 percent. The tax benefits must clearly overcome the extra loads within the policy to make an annuity a wise financial choice. On the other hand, small companies seeking to set up 401(k) plans may find that so-called *turnkey* programs from insurance companies are cheaper to set up than those available from pension administrators.

The Greening of America's Biggest Pension Plan

HIDDEN AMID THE arcana of tax-sheltered annuity pension plans is one of the great stories of individual members putting pressure on an institution and creating real change. At a few points in this book, we've said that members of a church, union, or community that owns investments can lobby these institutions to incorporate elements of Natural Investing into their investment management approach. That's just what happened among teachers who are served by the nation's largest pension plan, known as the Teachers Insurance and Annuity Association–College Retirement Equities Fund (TIAA-CREF).

In 1989, after five years of education and action by a small group of concerned teachers calling themselves Social Choice for Social Change, TIAA-CREF established the Social Choice Account, which does Avoidance Screening for a number of social issues. With over $3 billion in holdings, it is now the nation's largest socially screened fund. Almost a decade later, the same activist energy is at work again, with a new project called "The Campaign for a New TIAA-CREF." The goal this time is to "allow a small portion (5 to 10 percent) of Social Choice Account

Many insurance companies offer socially screened mutual funds in their variable annuity policies. These include:

- Acacia Mutual (301-280-1084): CRI (Calvert) Money Market, Balanced, International, Midcap, Small Cap
- Aegon (800-866-6007): CRI (Calvert) Money Market, Balanced, International, MidCap, Small Cap Growth; Dreyfus Third Century
- Aetna (800-525-4225): CRI (Calvert) Social Balanced
- American General Life (800-247-6584): AGS Social Awareness; Dreyfus Third Century
- American United Life (800-634-1629): CRI (Calvert) MidCap Growth
- Diversified Investment Advisers (914-697-8000): CRI (Calvert) Social Balanced
- The Guardian (800-221-3253): Dreyfus Third Century
- The Hartford (800-862-6668): CRI (Calvert) Social Balanced

funds to be devoted to companies and other institutions such as community development banks that are positive models of environmental and social responsibility," according to campaign organizer Neil Wollman.[3] Currently the fund uses only avoidance screens.

Teachers served by the pension fund have worked on their own time to carry on a lengthy dialogue with TIAA-CREF managers, who are surprisingly resistant to this modest proposal. They are now gearing up to repeat several elements of their successful strategy from the earlier battle: seeking media coverage, mobilizing members to write to management and generate support on their campuses, and, if necessary, encouraging members to move their pension funds into more proactive vehicles. The teachers behind this effort have consistently been on the leading edge of values-based investing; they are a real inspiration for those in all walks of life who want to make their institutions more responsive to members' concerns.

To learn more about the Campaign for a New TIAA-CREF, contact Neil Wollman at MC Box 135, Manchester College, North Manchester, IN 46962, or NJW@Manchester.edu.

- ➤ Lincoln Life (800-341-0441): CRI (Calvert) Social Balanced
- ➤ Lincoln National (800-443-8137): (Security) Social Awareness
- ➤ Metropolitan Life (800-553-4459): CRI (Calvert) Social Balanced
- ➤ Mutual of America (212-224-1960): CRI (Calvert) Social Balanced
- ➤ Nationwide Life (800-848-6331): Dreyfus Socially Responsible, Dreyfus Third Century
- ➤ New York Life (800-538-2019): CRI (Calvert) Social Balanced
- ➤ Peoples Benefit Life (800-688-5177): Dreyfus Third Century
- ➤ Protective Life (800-628-6390): CRI (Calvert) Social Balanced, Small Cap Growth
- ➤ Security Benefit Life (800-888-2461): Social Awareness
- ➤ TIAA-CREF (800-223-1200): TIAA-CREF Social Choice Account
- ➤ Travelers (800-842-0125): Dreyfus Third Century
- ➤ United Investors Life (800-999-0317): Dreyfus Third Century

Real Estate Investment Trusts

MOST PEOPLE DO not have the resources to own income-producing real estate directly. One easy way to be invested in real estate with very little investment capital while also being free of the everyday work of property management, rent collection, and the like is to buy shares in real estate investment trusts (REITs).

REITs are trusts formed to own specific real estate properties. They are financed by investors who buy shares in the trust in the form of stocks. The stocks are traded just like corporate stocks. Investors are assured that at least 95 percent of the trust's taxable income will be distributed to the shareholders. These investments can provide income and the possibility of gain, as real estate *tends* to increase in value over time. During the first six months of 1998, REITs paid dividends of 6 to 10 percent, whereas the total return for REITs from July 1993 through July 1998 was approximately 12 percent per year.

Risk. REITs are in the moderate-risk category; they are subject to the uncertainties of the stock and housing markets. REITs are also sensitive to interest rates; increasing market interest rates can lower real estate values, and thus your stock prices. The upside of buying real estate through a REIT stock is that you can sell at your whim, rather than at the whims of the real estate market.

SRI Application. REITs invest in apartments, shopping centers, manufactured homes, health care facilities, hotels, office buildings, self-storage facilities, private prison construction, and other commercial real estate. Investing in individual REITs enables you to target any of these sectors. Many Natural Investors may not be drawn to these types of developments; but if you are interested in real estate, consider this form of diversification as part of your overall investment strategy. As noted in Chapter 11, mutual funds are also available that invest in the full spectrum of REITs.

There are currently 213 REITs from which to choose. The National Association of Real Estate Trusts has a Web site that details all the REITs in their database by property type, size, and stock exchange listing. Their contact information is as follows:

National Association of Real Estate Investment Trusts
1129 20th Street NW, Suite 305
Washington, DC 20036

800-362-7348

www.nareit.com

Over the horizon, we can hope that the new Industrial Revolution described in Chapter 6 (and the rebuilding of community to be discussed in Chapter 13) lead to the creation of Green Development REITs; until then, we must be content with the current state of the real estate sector.

Unit Investment Trusts

UNIT INVESTMENT TRUSTS (UITs) are an important and often overlooked investment product. UITs are pools of stocks or bonds in fixed portfolios. The sponsor bundles up the investments into a uniquely identified trust and sells units of the trust to the public. The resultant trust has a finite life: it will be closed out at the end of the stated period, with the investment proceeds returned to its shareholders. The appeal of such a vehicle lies in having an unchanging, diversified portfolio with a stable rate of return. However, they are not as liquid as mutual funds. Some trusts have a minimum investment of $1,000, although for most it is $5,000. UITs are purchased through a broker, not directly from the sponsor. The commission, ranging from 2 to 5 percent, should be factored into your decision making.

UITs are especially important as sources of income. Bond trusts can make either monthly, quarterly, semiannual, or annual interest distributions. Bond trusts typically have five to seven different bonds in the portfolio. There are trusts that put together GNMA or other taxable government agency bonds, municipal bonds, and corporate bonds. Insured bonds are very popular investments for the conservative investor who is willing to give up a little return in exchange for a steady paycheck from the highest-quality bonds. Retirees are often attracted to this form of investment.

In recent years, trusts holding corporate stocks—from such sectors as technology, the Internet, and financial services—have increased in popularity. Portfolios of stock indexes, small-cap stocks, and diversified stocks are also in vogue. Stock UITs are long-term investments.

SRI Application. UITs holding municipal bonds support local government services that inherently satisfy the social criteria of most Natural Investors. Government agency bonds are also good choices, as previously discussed. Carefully review the portfolio of any UIT holding corporate bonds to ensure that they meet your criteria. The company lists in the Appendix will assist you in this effort. Stock trusts that are not socially screened may also pass muster after a careful review of the portfolio.

Occasionally a UIT of socially screened stocks is offered by one of the major brokerages. Merrill Lynch assembled a "Principled Values Portfolio" UIT, containing twenty-five stocks screened by KLD. Other sponsors are currently putting together socially screened stock trusts that will be available through brokerage firms.

Closed-End Funds

CLOSED-END FUNDS ARE another tool that Natural Investors can use to customize their portfolios. Closed-end funds are similar to unit investment trusts in that they contain a fixed portfolio of investments and offer a fixed number of shares to the public. However, shares of closed-end funds are traded like stocks on the stock market. Therefore, depending on market demand for the stock, the shares in closed-end funds may be purchased at either a discount or a premium from the net asset value of the underlying portfolio.

Closed-end funds are bought for either growth or income. Each fund holds stocks or bonds; there are no hybrid stock/bond combinations. There is no automatic reinvestment of dividends in new shares. However, some sponsors will allow you to buy shares in their open-end mutual funds automatically with dividends from their closed-end funds.

Savvy investors often buy closed-end funds when they are selling at a discount. This can add to the total return in stock funds and lead to higher yields in bond funds. Another consideration is the fact that investors in a closed-end fund avoid the annual capital gains distributions that are generated within an open-end fund. Closed-end funds generate capital gains only on paid-out dividends and when you sell your shares on the market.

Many of the types of investments discussed in this chapter and throughout the book are available as closed-end funds. Natural Investors may seek out closed-end funds in specific areas of interest to them: stock funds for specific sectors or countries, or bond funds holding such issues as mortgage-backed or tax-free bonds. Investors seeking to invest in a particular foreign country or geographical region will find good choices in closed-end funds; one example is the New South Africa Fund. A complete listing of closed-end funds appears in the *Standard & Poor's Stock Guide*, as well as in *Barron's* and once a week in the *Wall Street Journal*.

SRI Application. Principled Equity Market Fund (PEM; 508-831-1171) is a broadly socially screened closed-end index fund that contains stocks of approximately 250 companies. The fund was developed by F. L Putnam Investment Management Company at the request of one of its major institutional clients, a Catholic organization. Therefore it honors the church's stance on the abortion issue. The fund has outperformed the S&P 500 since its inception on November 30, 1996.

Venture Capital

VENTURE CAPITAL INVESTING is one of the most overlooked but important aspects for Natural Investors on the Affirmative Screening spoke of the Natural Investment Wheel. By investing in early-stage companies that address unmet social and environmental needs, investors can and do make a real difference.

Providing venture capital involves high-risk investing in small business ventures that are not yet publicly traded. People with ideas for new products and services seek capital to develop, expand, and market those ideas. Often they are women and members of minority groups who would otherwise have a very difficult time raising the necessary capital to convert their ideas into viable businesses.

Financial professionals rarely recommend venture capital start-ups to average investors; they involve too much work and risk. Any investment offered to the public by registered advisers must be carefully scrutinized in what is known as the "due diligence" process, and analyzing a young company is an especially tricky business. The lack of a proven track record is compounded by the perception that many companies creating solutions to social problems are "mission based," that is, passionate about their purpose but not serious or experienced enough with business management. It all adds up to a daunting situation for financial professionals seeking to encourage the flow of venture capital, as well as for investors seeking worthy start-ups to fund.

Susan Davis was one of several people who set out to find solutions to these problems. In 1990 she launched Capital Missions Company (CMC) with the goal of linking potential investors with those seeking capital to create the products and services needed to make a better world. CMC conceived and financed a network called the Investors' Circle (IC). IC brought together a group of individuals and venture capitalists who were dedicated to putting venture capital to work for socially responsible causes and issues. It has now grown to some 160 members, who have invested more than $44 million into companies of every conceivable type, including manufacturers of organic food and electric cars, developers of affordable housing, development banks, and women- and minority-led businesses.

Davis reports that "Private investors are challenged by doing due diligence on venture deals, yet they put up the majority of the high-risk money when companies first get started. The Investors' Circle allowed the private investors to collaborate with the venture capitalists for the good of the entrepreneurs and for their own higher return. In fact, a number of the Circle's private investors realized that investing in the social venture capital funds themselves was a less risky way for them to do venture capital investing."[4]

In 1993 the Community Development Venture Capital Alliance (CDVCA) was formed. CDVCA is an alliance of fifty-four members operating forty active venture capital funds. CDVCA members provide venture capital to inner cities, regional communities, and international projects. Their focus is on creating jobs by establishing private-sector companies in high-unemployment areas. Many of the member funds take money from individual investors; others limit their intake of money to institutional investors. CDVCA is an excellent resource for individual investors planning venture capital investments.

One other group that ecologically minded investors will want to contact is the Environmental Capital Network. This project of the Center for Environmental Policy, Economics, and Science facilitates investment in companies commercializing environmental technologies, products, and services.

The typical minimum venture capital investment is $25,000, making such investments suitable only for high-net-worth investors and those willing to take the risk of total investment loss. However, there are now socially screened mutual funds that are committing a small portion of their portfolios to social venture capital, thus making it possible for mutual fund investors to participate in this exciting field.

Wayne Silbey, founder of the Calvert Group, was the first to craft a mutual fund that offered the option of investing a portion of its assets in small start-ups. Calvert's Special Equities program is committed to pursuing especially promising approaches to meeting social goals. Approximately 1 percent of the assets of Calvert's Social Balanced and Social Equity funds and 3 percent of the assets of its World Values International Equity fund are currently invested in its Special Equities program and other private-placement investments. As of September 15, 1998, Special Equities had invested $8 million in thirty-one companies.

Risks and Rewards. Venture capital is truly a high-risk investment. One can achieve very high returns—but also often lose one's entire investment. Of the companies funded by venture capital investors, some 35 percent go into bankruptcy. Of course, others succeed and become very profitable, providing long-term returns to their investors. Individual investors can minimize their risks by investing in funds that are part of CDVCA. Aside from the possibility of financial rewards, the personal rewards from partaking in this market are significant—the satisfaction of financing companies that are returning high "social dividends."

Resources. Here is contact information for the venture capital organizations discussed in this section:

➤ Capital Missions Company
5080 Huron Breeze Drive
Au Gres, MI 48703
517-876-8766

➤ Investors' Circle
3220 Sacramento Street
San Francisco, CA 94115
415-929-4910

➤ Community Development Venture Capital Alliance
915 Broadway, Suite 1703
New York, NY 10010
212-475-8104

➤ Environmental Capital Network
416 Longshore Drive
Ann Arbor, MI 48104
734-996-8387

Well done! You have worked your way through some challenging material, seeking investments that can put both your head and your heart at ease. You have gained knowledge that can serve you for a lifetime, and taken an active role in transforming our economic system. Now let's move toward the grand finale, where we use the strategies of Natural Investing to solve some of our thorniest personal, societal, and planetary challenges.

Section Four

The Sustainability Revolution

Designing a Greenprint
for the Future

Chapter Thirteen

Curing Affluenza:
Investing in Ourselves

W E'VE COVERED A lot of ground on this journey, exploring the vast, varied landscape of Natural Investing. You have learned how to apply the four spokes of the Natural Investing Wheel to create your own values-based portfolio. This may be quite a departure from the ways in which you've handled investments in the past; it certainly represents a quantum leap for Wall Street. We could end the book here, leaving you with proven strategies that enable you to make money and make a difference.

Instead, we're going to stretch the boundaries a bit further—even go out on some professional limbs. Although linking values with capital is absolutely essential, we cannot pretend that merely investing our money in goodness will beget the healthy future we all desire. It will take more than "clean portfolios" to heal fully the split between our personal finances and our natural desire to make the world a better place. Outdated economic structures are in need of fresh insight, and deep-seated habits of action and thought hold us back from walking our talk. Though often hidden from daily awareness, these obstacles have the power to sabotage all our good intentions.

As we invest our money in ways that are consistent with our values, we must also look for ways to invest our time and energy in these same directions. We are fortunate that human creativity has produced a wellspring of ideas aimed at solving the challenges facing our civilization. This section explores some of the most promising approaches. They suggest actions—both personal and social—that we can take to help create a healthier world. Like pieces of a puzzle, the four spokes of the Natural Investing Wheel, combined with the elements presented in these closing chapters, form a picture of a global economy that nurtures our highest values.

It Starts with Each of Us

HERE, NEAR THE end of our explorations of bringing values back into economics, we are ready to grapple with what may be the most challenging set of questions: the personal ones. This chapter looks at the non-investment side of money: how we spend it, earn it, and give it away. Emerging trends like voluntary abundance, spirit at work, and responsible wealth provide pathways for including values in these all-important decisions. We also look at ways that we can work in our communities to create stronger, more self-reliant local economies.

It's hard to say if the issues addressed here are the culmination or the starting point of Natural Investing. This chapter shifts our focus toward a conscious examination of our own actions. The small, incremental changes we make at home become the building blocks of the next economy. Society takes form through the deeds of each individual—everything we do *does* have an impact. This sampling of personal and community initiatives hints at the infinite array of methods that people are using to make their lives more meaningful and purposeful.

Voluntary Abundance:
From Consumer to Creator

> *Af-flu-en-za. n.* 1. The bloated, sluggish, and unfulfilled feeling that results from efforts to keep up with the Joneses. 2. An epidemic of stress, overwork, waste, and indebtedness caused by dogged pursuit of the American Dream.[1]

"Oh Lord, won't you buy me a Mercedes Benz? My friends all drive Porsches; I must make amends!" wails Janis Joplin in the famous 1960s hippie anthem, poking fun at our insatiable consumerism. Today a much broader cross section of Americans are looking at their cluttered houses and stress-filled lives and asking, why?

In the aptly titled PBS special *Affluenza,* pollster Richard Harwood reports "a universal feeling in this nation that we have become too materialistic, too greedy, too selfish, and too self-absorbed."[2] Our material prosperity goes far beyond the wildest imaginings of our ancestors: exotic fruits adorn our winter feasts while mechanical servants wash our dishes; the world's wittiest jesters entertain us at the snap of our remotes. Despite all this, few seem truly content. Maybe the Beatles got it right all those years ago when they sang "Money can't buy me love."

Voluntary abundance is our term for a more peaceful lifestyle that brings material and personal pursuits back into balance. It is known today as the "simplicity" movement, or "downsizing." We prefer to emphasize "abundance" because cutting back on consumption actually results in nonmaterial riches: greater energy; more time for family, friends, and personal reflection; more meaningful work; a healthier planet; and the chance to contribute to one's community. Would you be willing to give up some of your possessions and earnings if you could get all that? Most Americans say yes.

How did our material aspirations get so out of balance? In the bestseller *Your Money or Your Life,* Vicki Robin and the late Joe Dominguez address one of our culture's dirty little secrets: the ways in which business, government, and advertising have indoctrinated us as "consumers." Remember when we were called "citizens"?

Consumerism was deliberately foisted on Americans who, in the early twentieth century, were demanding time off to enjoy their newfound prosperity. Industrialists knew that growth would slow down if they couldn't make people desire the newest, biggest goodies. We were told that the goal in life was not to be happy and fulfilled, but to increase our "standard of living." "New wants will make way endlessly for newer wants," gloated a 1929 Herbert Hoover committee report. In the postwar era, Victor Lebow, a U.S. retailing analyst, proclaimed:

> Our enormously productive economy . . . demands that we make consumption our way of life, that we convert the buying and use of goods into rituals, that we seek our spiritual satisfaction, our ego satisfaction, in consumption. . . . We need things consumed, worn out, replaced, and discarded at an ever-increasing rate.[3]

For better or worse, Lebow's injunction has succeeded beyond measure. Today, by the time a person reaches age twenty, he or she will have seen one million advertisements. The message: fulfillment of our non-material needs—like love, self-esteem, and respect—can be bought at the mall.

Given the overwhelming social support for staying on the treadmill, how have so many managed to escape? For some, frustration with the "rat race" finally reaches a breaking point. "We are living in a time when if you can balance three spinning plates on three sticks, you are rewarded with a fourth. And then a fifth," says author Stephan Rechtshaffen.[4] People of all income levels are chronically stressed. Long hours on the job, long commutes, microwave suppers, kids on their own . . . the daily grind just wears people out. Both personal and family health suffer from what economist Juliet Schor calls "time poverty."[5]

Others come to voluntary abundance through a "green" doorway. All of the stuff we consume originally came from nature. Americans are taking raw materials from the Earth at rates far beyond what can be sustained: since 1950 Americans have consumed more resources than all of humanity before us. In two years, our waste would fill a convoy of garbage trucks stretching to the moon![6] Television now reaches around the globe, enticing even remote villagers to join us in this consumption craze. How many planets will we need to provide enough resources for all six billion of us to live the American Dream?

Finally, many people have come to voluntary abundance quite *involuntarily*! In *Trends 2000*, Gerald Celente points out that corporate downsizing has forced millions to adopt new strategies. "The upside of downsizing," he says, "is that people were forced into freedom. Millions of people found ways to take control of their lives and do what they had always wanted to do."[7] Many started their own businesses; others took lower-paying jobs that were more to their liking. People started asking questions: What's really important in my life? How much do I really need or want in order to do the things that matter to me? Once unshackled from the corporate ladder, many victims of downsizing began to see their layoffs as blessings in disguise.

Whether you're a frazzled corporate executive wanting to open up some space in your life, a wannabe back-to-the-land garlic farmer, or a dazed blue-collar worker whose "lifetime" job was just shipped off to Singapore, voluntary abundance offers useful guidance and support. The simplicity movement has become its own industry, with newsletters, books, and Web sites. (Appendix E can get you started.)

Why We Keep Our Lives So Hectic

ONE THING I'VE learned about maintaining a complicated life is that it's one of the best ways we have to avoid looking at some of the larger questions. It may not apply to everyone, but I believe it explains a lot about why we've been moving so fast. The prospect of getting reacquainted with ourselves can be daunting.

As long as we convince ourselves that we're too busy and our work is so vital and we can't afford to slow down, then we don't have to look at our own lives and the personal issues that are so difficult to address: a marriage that isn't working, a career that isn't satisfying, children we're out of touch with, friendships we've outgrown, the creativity we've been afraid to explore, our deepest fears of childhood traumas that have been holding us back from leading truly fulfilled lives.

An amazing thing happens when we slow down. We start to get flashes of inspiration. We reach a new level of understanding and wisdom. In a quiet moment we can get an intuitive insight that can change our entire life and the lives of the people around us in incredibly positive ways. And those changes can last a lifetime.

Living more simply will make it possible to create those quiet moments. Out of those quiet moments miracles happen. Be open to them.[8]

—ELAINE ST. JAMES

If you think that "simple" means hunting rabbits and wearing a loincloth, think again. Voluntary abundance is not a one-size-fits-all commitment. Downsizing often refers to professionals who make incremental adjustments. It can start with refusing to work overtime, or trading in the second car for a bicycle. In his landmark 1981 book *Voluntary Simplicity*, Duane Elgin interviewed a wise young woman who said, "Voluntary simplicity must evolve over a lifetime according to the needs of the individual . . . the person must grow and be open to new ideas—not jump on a bandwagon, but thoughtfully consider ideas and see how they relate to themselves."[9] With this in mind, these steps can help you make the transition from consumer to creator:

> *Check in.* The first step is to take a good look at your life. Take stock of your financial situation and of the ways your time is allocated. *Your Money or Your Life* starts by asking some penetrating questions, such as: Are you spending enough time with family and friends? Do you come home from your job full of life? Do you have time to participate in things you believe are worthwhile? Are you at peace with money? Your answers are important; they can point to areas in your life that need attention. While you're at it, don't forget to learn more about the ecological and social impacts of over-consumption.

> *Get out of debt.* Credit card debt, along with big-ticket financing of homes and cars, is a major force propelling the consumer spiral. Once you're in debt, you have far less flexibility to slow down or pause in your work life. This trap has snared everyone from the convenience store clerk to the high-powered attorney. A deliberate and patient process of lowering, then eliminating, debt will bring bountiful rewards.

> *Master your finances.* Here's where the fun really begins. *Your Money or Your Life* teaches a method for discovering how much of your life energy is exchanged to earn money. To the time you spend working, add the hours spent commuting to, preparing for, and decompressing from the job. From your pay, subtract the costs of wardrobe, eating out, child care, taxes, transportation, and stress-related health care. Your real hourly wage is probably at lot less than you thought. Knowing your real hourly wage provides a great incentive for cutting down on spending. Do you really want to trade a few days of your life for that fancy new coat? Keep track of every expense to find out exactly where the money goes. After a while, you'll be able to identify spending categories that you can cut back on without cramping your style too much.

> *Invest in yourself.* Consume! Buy! On Sale Now! It takes great willpower to discipline your spending; but Natural Investing can help. On page 179 we told you about one easy way to start saving: utilize the automatic investment feature offered by screened mutual

funds. Every month a certain amount (usually a minimum of $50) is transferred to the fund directly from your checking account. This is a great way to accumulate investment assets; it gets the money out of your account before you spend it, and you don't have to write the check yourself.

➤ *Create a new life.* There are many ways to simplify, from having a garage sale to planting a garden. What are your dreams? Are you doing work you love? Do you reap meaning and fulfillment, or just a paycheck? Voluntary abundance can give you more freedom; go ahead and start a new career. Or build up your nest egg (by spending less) until you are financially independent, able to live off your investments and spend your time as you choose.

These steps can help us create more fulfilling lives, but the stakes are much higher than simply reducing stress and producing happiness. America has taken the lead in promoting the consumer society; the eyes of the world are on us. It is incumbent upon us to pioneer satisfying life paths that do not endanger future generations. A big task, but at least we are not the first to walk this road:

> **"** *I went to the woods because I wished to live deliberately, to front only the essential facts of life, and see if I could not learn what it had to teach, and not, when I came to die, discover that I had not lived. I wanted to live deep and suck all the marrow of life.* **"**
>
> —HENRY DAVID THOREAU, *Walden*

Natural Shopping: Consuming with a Conscience

VOLUNTARY ABUNDANCE CAN help us get a grip on spending, preventing money from slipping out of our hands. But of course we still need to buy things. So the next step is to use the principles of Natural Investing when we shop. This means bringing our values into the marketplace. Every dollar we spend is a vote that supports a chain of producers, distributors, and sellers. As with investing, the first step is awareness. Pay the baby-sitter and you know who is getting your money. But buy a shirt

at the mall and a legion of multinational corporations rides its tails. Natural Shopping encourages us to be conscious of who profits—and who
suffers—from our spending.

Consuming with a conscience can take many forms. Sometimes it
means redirecting purchases toward locally owned stores or products
made close to home. Green consumers seek products made in an earth-
friendly manner. There are also activist strategies for consumers. Some
organize or participate in boycotts of companies who commit especially egregious violations of social principles. Other customers use their
clout to press for changes through dialogue. For example, recycling has
been largely consumer driven: many grocery stores now recycle plastic
bags, and companies like Canon recycle used toner cartridges from
their photocopiers and laser printers.

Co-op America is one organization that natural shoppers should put
on their lists. Each year they publish the *National Green Pages*, a directory of "products and services for people and the planet." The *Green
Pages* (available in print and also on-line at www.greenpages.org) let
your fingers do the walking to more than 2,000 companies, listed by category, that have pledged to act responsibly toward consumers, employees, the community, and the environment. Its handy cross-reference
index lets you find green businesses located in your area.

Spirit at Work

NOW LET'S TURN to the most time-intensive portion of our financial
lives: making a living. For many Americans, the workplace is not a
happy place. We often compromise our principles in order to survive
on the job. Is it possible to bring our deepest values into the profit-
driven workplace of the twenty-first century? Or must we leave our
humanity at the door when we go to work? As we've seen throughout
this book, the inclusion of values once again opens up unforeseen possibilities. Bringing values into the workplace is a win/win/win proposition: employees are more fulfilled, companies perform better, and the
community and the environment benefit.

Over the past several years, two *s* words—*soul* and *spirituality*—
have crept into the business lexicon. Books with titles like *Leading
with Soul, Jesus CEO,* and *How Would Confucius Ask for a Raise?*
indicate that the concept of "spirit at work" is penetrating the corpo-

rate world from the inside out. Even many CEOs are joining the soul parade. For example, Tom Chappell wrote about his experiences as CEO of the natural products company Tom's of Maine in his best-seller *The Soul of a Business: Managing for Profit and the Common Good.* Chappell says, "It's about how to use the two sides of all of us, the spiritual and the practical, to achieve whatever business goals you set for yourself."

Tom's of Maine (sorry, investors: Tom's is privately held) has been profitable and scores high on the social responsibility scorecard. They treat their employees well (offering flex-time, four-day work weeks, and subsidized child care), give 10 percent of pretax profits to charities, and pay employees to perform four hours of community service monthly. Chappell notes that "if integrating a sense of common good into their business strategy can actually help companies increase profits, what excuse can they make for moving forward unconcerned about their communities, the environment, and the future?"[10]

Spirit at work is not limited to a few new-age zealots in corporate garb. Blue-chip stalwarts like Boeing and AT&T have brought poet David Whyte into training programs for their top executives. Whyte uses poetry to penetrate the walls that separate our working selves from our passionate, creative selves. At the staid World Bank, Richard Barrett launched the Spiritual Unfoldment Society, a weekly staff meeting that explores practical applications of spirituality. Barrett, now a corporate consultant, teaches businesses to focus on the soul in order to help employees "tap into their deepest levels of creativity and highest levels of productivity."[11]

Many in the business world remain lukewarm, or even hostile, to mentioning spirituality in the workplace. Indeed, industrial corporations have perfected the art of treating workers like machines, keeping them narrowly focused on tasks in the quest for higher productivity. Messy distractions like nurturing the soul challenge this model. Others realize the need to address deeper concerns at work but fear that calling them "spiritual" would imply allegiance to a particular faith or interference with the religious convictions of their employees.

In fact, spirit at work is merely the acknowledgment that people are more than bodies and brains, that our highest capacities as humans can be realized only if our hearts and souls are included. What does this look like in practice? Incredibly varied. For some it is simply

Sacred Hoops

HERE'S AN EXAMPLE of a business leader using spiritual wisdom to achieve unparalleled success in one of the world's most competitive businesses. Phil Jackson has coached the Chicago Bulls basketball team throughout their long dynasty. In his book *Sacred Hoops: Spiritual Lessons of a Hardwood Warrior,* Jackson writes that "creating a successful team—whether it's an NBA champion or a record-setting sales force—is essentially a spiritual act. It requires the individuals involved to surrender their self-interest for the greater good so that the whole adds up to more than the sum of its parts."

Basketball is an ideal arena within which to witness spirituality in action. "To excel," notes Jackson, "you need to act with a clear mind and be totally focused on what everyone on the court is doing." His success stems from empowering each player to connect with something larger than himself:

> Even in this highly competitive world, I've discovered that when you free players to use all their resources—mental, physical, and spiritual—an interesting shift in awareness occurs. When players practice what is known as mindfulness—simply paying attention to what's actually happening—not only do they play better and win more, they also become more attuned with each other. And the joy they experience working in harmony is a powerful motivating force that comes from deep within, not from some frenzied coach pacing along the sidelines, shouting obscenities into the air.[12]

acknowledging the importance of basic human qualities like honesty and integrity. For others it's about tapping into deep veins of creativity, vision, and joy. Methods range from company policies that balance work, personal, and community priorities, to ongoing dialogues or even, in Chappell's case, taking a break to go to divinity school.

Spirituality is not the answer, says Martin Rutte, coauthor of *Chicken Soup for the Soul at Work,* but rather the question. It encourages each of us to explore the depths of our being—our longings, fears, and dreams. Rutte identifies several benefits to this spiritual quest. First, we become more creative. Being more peaceful and energized promotes insights, such as ideas for new services or ways to use resources more efficiently. Second, communication at work becomes more genuine. People need safety to speak their truth, without fear of retribution. Rather than playing office politics, companies are finding that the best decisions are made when everyone is encouraged to offer their unvarnished observations. Finally, spirituality increases ethical behavior. An atmosphere of trust engenders teamwork among employees and managers. Work becomes an expression of their natural desires to live in integrity and be of service. This attitude ripples out to customers, the community, and society.[13]

Even if we're not CEOs empowered to shape corporate culture around our personal vision, there are many ways to bring more of our selves to our jobs. As just one example, take the down-and-dirty work of sales. Sharon Drew Morgen, author of *Selling with Integrity,* introduces a visionary sales paradigm based on the belief that buyers have their own answers. It is far different from adversarial sales methods of convincing or coercing, or even polite badgering. Rather, Morgen advocates creating relationships of respect, in an environment of trust, with service as the goal. From this foundation, sales will naturally follow.

Spirit at work has only recently gained mainstream attention. An outbreak of books, publications, organizations, and events are stitching together the players in this diverse movement. For example, Craig and Patricia Neal have launched the Heartland Institute, which fosters dialogue and training through their Inner Life of Business seminars. The Message Company of Santa Fe, New Mexico, produces the International Conference on Business and Consciousness in Mexico every fall, bringing together hundreds of participants and well-known speakers; other similar conferences are springing up throughout the United States. Journals like *The Inner Edge* explore topics for "enlightened business practice."

If your joy and creativity feel limited by the constraints of your workplace's ways of working, we invite you to look more deeply into spirit at work resources (see Appendix E). The fact that these prophets are also good for profits is helping to open the heart of corporate America. As Michael Stephen, Chairman of Aetna International, suggests, "Wisdom, vision, and generosity are some of the characteristics of a successful CEO for the next millennium."[14] This is very good news, not only for employees but also for the planet.

Sharing the Wealth

NO BOOK ON values and money would be complete without mentioning philanthropy. In the United States, giving is an established, prominent feature of our social landscape. Steel magnate Andrew Carnegie lived by his own adage: "The man who dies rich dies disgraced." Carnegie believed that the wealthy should dispose of their surplus wealth for the public good, preferably during their lifetimes. True to his word, he started giving away his fortune in his thirties; his legacy includes the establishment of thousands of public libraries.

Many people find that giving money away is one of life's most gratifying experiences. A 1997 *Newsweek* article told the story of Irene Scott, an 83-year-old woman who wanted to express her gratitude to her doctor, who had treated her during the past forty years even when she couldn't pay. For four years she chiseled small amounts out of her $850 monthly stipends until the day came that she could present the doctor with a $1,000 check for a scholarship fund that he had set up.

Today Americans are often praised for their generosity: in 1996 over $150 billion was donated to charitable causes, the vast majority of it by individuals.[15] It is comforting to know that our materialistic culture has such a giving heart. But a closer look reveals that those who are truly in need—low-income children, the elderly, and the poor in general—don't always share in this largess.

Nearly half the proceeds from the collection plate go to religious institutions (and some of this money does end up serving the poor). However, much of the remainder primarily serves the interests of the well-to-do, such as private universities and prep schools, museums, symphonies, think tanks, and private hospitals.[16] These are all worthwhile causes; yet it's important to note that less than 10 percent of the philanthropic pie goes to the needy.

Natural Investors approach philanthropy just like they do investing—considering both financial and social goals. Of course, when you give money away you don't have to worry about your financial returns. But there are still many financial factors to look at when making donations, especially tax and estate issues. Those with substantial assets will want to seek professional assistance in deciphering the latest laws. Creative tactics such as charitable trusts are useful for those with more substantial assets.

It is important to take time to get clear on your social priorities and develop your personal strategy. You may want to direct all your resources toward a single issue or you might wish to disperse your giving to various causes. You should also consider whether your objective is to alleviate immediate suffering or to address the underlying causes. Certainly there is always an acute need to heal the sick and feed the hungry. However, a growing movement of social-change philanthropists seeks to address the underlying structural flaws that are causing these problems. For example, a social-change approach to hunger in Africa may look at patterns of land ownership and the displacement of self-sufficient villages by export-oriented plantations.

Coming Home to Community

NOW THAT YOUR own financial house is in order, it's time to walk out the front door and peruse the neighborhood. What shape is your community in? Do people know their neighbors, and do they look out for one another? Is there a sense of pride and broad participation in community activities? Are locally based initiatives improving the quality of life? Have social and environmental concerns been adequately addressed? Are children, the elderly, and others with special needs well cared for?

Most of us would love to live in a place where we could answer each of these questions with an emphatic *yes!* Instead the fabric of community seems to be slowly unraveling. Many pundits focus on symptoms of breakdown, such as drug addiction, crime, poor schools, and turmoil in the family. But these problems can never be solved without a thriving local economy. Throughout *Investing with Your Values,* we've shown that you can use your money as a tool for constructive change. In the remainder of this chapter, we bring Natural Investing to our neighborhoods, where each one of us has a voice that can be heard. We've uncovered a number of exciting grass-roots initiatives that are helping

Responsible Wealth

OPEN ANY MAGAZINE aimed at the rich and you'll see ads for diamonds, resorts, and cars that cost more than a house. But amazingly a growing, vocal group of wealthy individuals is working to change the very system that made them rich. Called Responsible Wealth, these folks are at the leading edge of social change. "As people with wealth," says their first newsletter, "we feel a responsibility to speak out against the rules that have been written to benefit us and to speak in favor of policies that benefit the long-term common good of all."[17]

Responsible Wealth promotes a two-pronged strategy to narrow the gap between the upper strata and everyone else (in the United States the wealthiest 1 percent of the population now own almost 40 percent of our country's private wealth—more than the bottom 92 percent combined). First, they advocate "leveling-up" strategies that can help the poor, such as universal health care, stronger public education, a shorter workweek to create more jobs, and a minimum wage that is a true living wage. More surprising are their "leveling-down" strategies, such as instituting a wealth tax on private assets, higher income taxes on the wealthy, a maximum wage, taxing investments the same as earned income, and increasing inheritance taxes. How's that for a platform with punch?

Their biggest media splash so far was made in April 1998. Over 125 wealthy individuals took the "Responsible Wealth Tax Break Pledge," refusing to keep the windfall they had received from the 1997 federal tax act. (This law reduced capital gains taxes; 80 percent of the savings from this law benefit the top 5 percent of U.S. households.) "Tax changes should benefit the poor, not the rich, in order to have a more equitable society," said one member.[18] Over $1 million of tax breaks were pledged to charity, much of it earmarked to groups working for greater tax fairness.

communities regain control over their economic destiny. These examples are just the tip of a giant community-development iceberg—some of the many ways that our most precious resources, our time and energy, can be invested in local issues to yield the highest social return. (Appendix E lists resources that can help you find out about projects in your area, as well as provide support for starting your own local version of those projects.)

Sustainability Indicators

In 1990 a meeting was held in Seattle to explore ways to make the region more sustainable. A small working group created a new organization, Sustainable Seattle, whose goal was to "improve our region's long-term health and vitality—cultural, economic, environmental, and social." They developed a set of indicators that could measure progress being made toward sustainability.

Forty different yardsticks are measured by Sustainable Seattle's volunteers. Their 1998 report was mixed: it gave the city poor marks for traffic congestion and increased fuel consumption, showed that wild salmon runs had stabilized but at dangerously low levels, and found some bright spots, such as the fact that a high proportion of Seattle's youth do volunteer work.

Sustainable Seattle has become a model for communities around the world. These programs are a localized response to the need to supplement the gross domestic product with meaningful social and environmental data. As Hazel Henderson says, "Trying to run a complex society on a single indicator like the Gross Domestic Product [GDP] is literally like trying to fly a 747 with only one gauge on the instrument panel."[19] Sustainability indicators enable communities to navigate toward a better future, making midflight corrections when one of the gauges indicates trouble. In Chapter 14, we'll look at what people are doing to create alternatives to the GDP at national and global levels.

Community Self-Reliance

In order for communities to solve their pressing social and environmental concerns, it is essential to have a thriving local economy. Many inner-city neighborhoods and poor rural regions have been left behind by the parade of progress. How can these communities create strong, diverse economies? Must we pursue "growth strategies" that rely on chasing outside industry (and sacrifice local control)?

A growing number of communities are learning to bootstrap their way to prosperity. Alamosa, Colorado, is one town that made a turnaround in the 1990s, including a dramatic revitalization of its downtown, developing alternative crops such as quinoa (a high-protein grain that originated in the Andes) to strengthen local agriculture, the advent of fish farming using local hot-springs water, and the creation of a community recreation program. These and many more projects were spurred by Alamosa's participation in the Rocky Mountain Institute's Economic Renewal program.

The Economic Renewal process involves a series of town meetings that begins with helping citizens envision their "preferred future" and acknowledge shared values. Next, an inventory is taken to identify the community's problems and strengths. Usually the problem is not so much a lack of capital as the fact that capital rushes out of town. "Plugging the leaks" is one of the most important steps; this means finding out where capital is leaving the community and developing local solutions that keep the money circulating in town. For example, a recent study showed that three-quarters of the money spent at a McDonald's restaurant immediately disappears from the local economy.[20]

Identifying the leaks also helps pinpoint new business opportunities. The Economic Renewal process focuses on producing and marketing more goods and services locally. First, existing businesses are supported with capital and technical expertise. Then programs are established to encourage locals to start new businesses. Last, when appropriate, compatible businesses can be recruited from outside the community to fill in the gaps.

Bottom-up strategies like the Economic Renewal process can help create diversified, self-reliant communities. By building upon their natural and human capital, communities can assert more control over their future and are in a better position to prosper, regardless of changing economic conditions.

Community Corporations

Many sports fans have been rudely disillusioned when their home team suddenly abandons its loyal supporters, moving to a city with a shiny new, taxpayer-subsidized stadium. But residents of Green Bay, Wisconsin, have no fears that their beloved Packers will ever pull such a stunt. The reason: the residents own the team! Back in the Depression, when the team was in dire financial straits, members of the Green Bay

Association of Commerce went door to door, selling $25 shares in the team, which was organized as a nonprofit corporation. Today the Packers' mission is to "field a competitive team and maintain the team in Green Bay in perpetuity."[21]

The Packers are the surprising stars (who would have thought that football would offer a model for community empowerment!) of *Going Local,* Michael Shuman's comprehensive 1998 guide to creating self-reliant communities. One of the most innovative ideas in the book is a new structure called a community corporation. Unlike a conventional corporation, Shuman proposes that "only members of a community would be allowed to own voting shares of stock" in a community corporation. This could entail issuing two classes of shares (not unlike the standard practice of issuing common shares with voting rights and nonvoting preferred shares) to accommodate nonresident investors.

Community corporations are a provocative hybrid that could appeal to both community activists and hard-nosed capitalists. As corporations, they would be free to pursue profit and growth strategies. But with a residential restriction on voting shares, the corporations would always maintain allegiance to the communities that gave them birth, acting in the best interests of local people and the environment.

Cooperatives

Cooperatives are a more traditional ownership model for community-based enterprises. From rural electric, water, and farm-products companies to health food stores, cooperatives have a long, successful, and much-appreciated history worldwide. Mondragon, Spain, for example, is home to an affiliated network of 160 cooperatives, many of which are large industrial producers of everything from computer chips to refrigerators.

In a cooperative, the enterprise is owned by the customers, the employees, or both. Management of cooperatives is by committee; however, all employees, customers, and owners are welcome to contribute their ideas and input. This often leads cooperatives to adopt high standards of social and ecological caring. Fairness is a prime feature of cooperatives: prices, capital costs, and wages are managed in ways that are deemed equitable. By supporting cooperatives with your time and money, you can help build a stronger community.

Start Your Own Community Financial Institution

Go downtown in any big city and look up. Who's got the tallest building? Most likely it's a bank. Does this give you community activists any ideas about how to achieve greater control and power?

Back in Chapter 7 we looked at a whole range of community development financial institutions (CDFIs) and the important economic niche they fill. Natural Investors are well aware of the high social returns provided by CDFIs. Less well known is the fact that these sorts of institutions can be started by a determined group of volunteers, even if they don't have much money. The process of starting a bank may be over your head, but loan funds, credit unions, and targeted banking programs are worthwhile projects that help circulate capital within communities.

For inspiration let's look at how communities in New Mexico were able to launch three CDFIs during the 1990s:

> *The New Mexico Community Development Loan Fund.* In 1988 a diverse group of New Mexicans (including coauthor Hal Brill) started looking for ways to empower low-income citizens with capital and business expertise. Following the model developed by the Institute for Community Economics, the group decided to form a statewide revolving loan fund. With funding from the New Mexico Council of Churches, a director was hired. In 1990 the first loan was made—a $5,000 loan that helped an organic farm purchase a greenhouse. The fund has now loaned millions of dollars to residents, supporting small businesses and affordable housing around the state.

> *Community Connections dedicated banking fund.* In 1996 environmentally oriented community activists worked with one of the few locally owned banks, First National Bank of Santa Fe, to establish a dedicated deposit program. Modeled after Vermont National Bank's Socially Responsible Banking Fund (featured in Chapter 7), the Community Connections fund allows checking, savings, or certificate of deposit funds to be dedicated to community development loans. The advisory committee that makes loan decisions includes both bank officials and community activists.

> *Permaculture Credit Union.* The newest and most leading-edge initiative is just getting off the ground in 1999. Permaculture is a set of design principles based on careful study of nature's cyclic patterns, applied first to agriculture but extended over the past two decades to community development and economic systems. Members of the credit union must be members of a permaculture organization any-

where in the country; lending criteria include both financial solidity and consistency with permaculture principles.

Community Currencies: Make Your Own Money

What do the communities of Lyon, France; Fremantle, Australia; and Ithaca, New York, have in common? They all have established their own systems of local currency; currency activists say that you can too! (Don't worry, it's quite legal.)

Local currencies are not exactly new—in the United States an estimated 300 communities had their own script during the Great Depression.[22] Today there are dozens of systems in this country and hundreds operating worldwide. Many different approaches are being tried: some communities print unique (and beautiful) paper bills that are exchanged like cash, whereas paperless systems use a computer to keep track of transactions.

The chief motivation behind all these systems is the desire to strengthen local economies. Members of the system agree to trade among themselves; resources circulate within the community. Historically local currencies have also served as a safety net, allowing commerce to continue during times of economic crisis. But one of the biggest benefits is the way these currencies help build a stronger sense of community.

In Ithaca, a person can use Ithaca HOURS (each HOUR is worth $10) to dine at fine restaurants, hire a baby-sitter, buy firewood and groceries, or go to a movie. Ithaca HOURS is one of the most successful community currency projects in the nation; over $65,000 worth of the local script is circulating among thousands of community members, including 370 local businesses. Since all of this money stays in the local community, it is estimated that Ithaca HOURS has stimulated several millions of dollars' worth of trade. The group offers a starter kit to help other communities launch their own currencies. Keep an eye out for new systems that integrate modern communications technology with local sensibilities.

One Step at a Time

AS YOU CAN see, there are countless approaches to incorporating values into our financial lives. In some ways, it is easier to bring values into our investment portfolios than it is to shift our daily habits. We rarely take time to reflect on our spending patterns or question "the way it's always been" at work and in our local economies.

Yet once we begin even to consider issues such as those raised in this chapter, the pressures and manipulations of the economic world begin to have less force in our lives. Whether you carefully consider every expenditure or simply take note, over time, of how well served you are by your spending choices, you have broken the spell of consumerism. And whether you start a community loan fund or just begin to seek out more opportunities to trade skills with friends, you've strengthened the bonds of your community. Each small step leads to rewards that inspire larger steps. Looking back, you'll find that your personal finances have become more and more integrated with your deeper values.

Chapter **14** *urteen*

The Healing
of Wall Street

N ATURAL INVESTORS MAY be innovative and creative, but they
still operate within the framework of the global economic system. (In this book we've taken poetic license and used "Wall
Street" to describe the whole worldwide economic enchilada.) While
acknowledging the efficiencies of our market economy, a host of
critics—including economists, billionaires, politicians, and engaged citizens alike—believe there are serious structural problems with our
economy. Most alarmingly, a growing chorus targets Wall Street, including both the public and private sectors, as an engine of environmental
and social degradation.

For most of us, trying to comprehend—let alone change—the economic system is like trying to build a computer from scratch. Fortunately some very smart people have blazed a trail, pointing out key
leverage points that could lead to a "healing of Wall Street." This chapter surveys a few of the boldest ideas circulating among leading thinkers
and economic activists, ideas that we believe have the potential to catalyze constructive, large-scale change.

We fully realize that every prescription for righting the economy is
fraught with controversy; these brief treatments cannot delve into all
the subtleties and counterpoints. They are intended to inspire further
study and provoke broader discussion. Please see the resources listed in
Appendix E to follow up on any that pique your interest. As you become
familiar with these ideas, we encourage you to consider taking an active

role in the creation of a new Wall Street that promotes stronger communities and environmental responsibility.

The Topsy-Turvy World of Indicators

IN THE SACRED scriptures of economics, one principle is worshiped above all others: growth. The "growth is good" doctrine is enshrined in virtually every public policy decision. No reasonable person would dare question growth, because growth has become our very definition of prosperity and public well-being. But in recent years, a strange phenomenon has become apparent. The economy, by all measures, has been booming, but many ordinary Americans are anxious and gloomy. Either we are all a bunch of whiners or, just maybe, the economic indicators traditionally used to measure "progress" are missing the real story.

Four times a year, a time-honored ritual is reenacted: the release of the current gross domestic product (GDP) figures. Wall Street reacts with either despair or glee. GDP figures are used to formulate major economic policies around the world. But this magic number tells us only one thing: how much money has changed hands through the market economy. Certainly it is an amazing feat to measure such a complicated process for a country as complex as ours. But is more always better?

> What if the chief of your local police department announced that "activity" on the city streets had increased by 15 percent? People would not be impressed. They would demand specifics. Exactly *what* increased? Tree planting or burglaries? Volunteerism or muggings? Car wrecks or neighborly acts of kindness?[1]

The GDP is equally vague—it makes no distinction between quality and quantity. An *Atlantic Monthly* article points out that under the GDP, the nation's economic hero is a terminal cancer patient who is going through a costly divorce, the happiest event is an earthquake or a hurricane, and the most desirable habitat is a multibillion-dollar Superfund site. Disasters like these would indeed add to the GDP, because they all cause money to change hands.[2] Sold some bombers to a cruel dictator? Pop the champagne, the GDP's going up! GDP makes no distinctions; both social and environmental values are considered irrelevant.

Here's just one example of GDP illogic at work: when a parent stays home to nurture and educate a child, the "economy" suffers. But send that parent to work, ship the kid off to day care, and bingo, two pluses for the GDP. No wonder Pat Buchanan thunders, "Conservatives who worship at the altar of an endlessly rising GDP should tell us: What is it they any longer wish to conserve?"[3] Family values can be undermined by the market itself. Television has replaced storytelling. Malls become our town squares. GDP goes up, but the role of families and communities declines.

Environmental responsibility is clearly compromised by GDP-mania. Why should some poor developing country leave a forest standing (worth zero on the balance sheet) when it can clear-cut, sell the logs at fire-sale prices, and be rewarded with a short-term blip on its World Bank report card? Pollution is a blessing: making toxins, cleaning them up, and paying the medical bills for the resulting mass illnesses all show up as positives.

This understanding puts a startling new twist on economic news: "The U.S. economy may not be growing at all, and may have ceased growing nearly 25 years ago," says Paul Hawken. Although the GDP has grown 2.5 percent per year since 1973, "there is little evidence of improved lives, better infrastructure, higher real wages, more leisure and family time, and greater economic security."[4] In fact, a 1996 Johns Hopkins University study showed that workers' real, spendable wages are no higher than they were thirty years ago.[5]

No business could run itself using this system. Depleting a fishery or an oilfield should show up as a loss of capital, not an economic windfall. Can we in fact create new indicators that actually tell us how we're doing? That let us know whether our lives or our economy is improving or deteriorating? Many economists just throw up their hands, saying that these things can't be measured.

You may notice that this struggle is similar to that faced by the early Natural Investors; the response then was to join with social researchers to measure the ethical conduct of corporations. A similar can-do attitude might be applied to this new set of "too-big" questions. It *is* hard to quantify Mom's home cooking or rain forest oxygen production. But does this mean they should be completely ignored? During the last decade, a flurry of new indicators have been created that provide more inclusive readings of our well-being.

Hazel Henderson has been leading the new-indicators charge for more than two decades. In *Building a Win-Win World,* she describes the Human Development Index (HDI), developed by the United

Nations Development Program. Launched in 1990, the HDI ranks 173 countries by factoring in both GDP and direct measurements of well-being, such as life expectancy and educational attainment.[6] Henderson's own Country Futures Indicators (CFI) were launched in 1996 as the Calvert-Henderson Quality-of-Life Indicators, as a public education service of the Calvert Group. This system is designed to provide a method for people themselves to determine which values and goals they want to measure. In the United States, the nonprofit group Redefining Progress has developed the Genuine Progress Indicator (GPI) and is focusing national attention on the indicator question.

These are but a few of the pathbreaking initiatives taking place around the world. Will the HDI, CFI, or GPI eventually share the limelight with the GDP? It's becoming clear that we've gone astray, setting our sights on raising the GDP rather than improving our welfare. As Henderson says, "We measure what we treasure."[7] It is time for us to measure our highest goals, like improving the health of our environment and communities and living happier lives. New indicators that track "more than money" can help us measure these and move us toward the world we want to pass on to our children.

> **" We seem to have surrendered community excellence and community values in the mere accumulation of material things. The GNP counts air pollution and ambulances to clear our highways of carnage, the destruction of the redwoods, and the death of Lake Superior. It grows with the production of napalm and missiles with nuclear warheads. Yet the GNP does not allow for the health of our children, the quality of their education, or the joy of their play. It measures neither our wit nor our courage; neither our wisdom nor our learning; neither our compassion nor our devotion to our country; it measures everything, in short, except that which makes life worthwhile; and it can tell us everything about America—except whether we are proud to be Americans. "**
>
> —ROBERT F. KENNEDY

The Natural Tax Shift

PAYING TAXES IS another sacred cow in need of fresh ideas. The current tax system isn't all bad; it does collect revenues needed to run the government. But there are many ways in which governments could collect money. What do we choose to tax most heavily? Jobs, paychecks, and investment. This emphasis distorts our economy by encouraging employers to scrimp on labor. Today a growing worldwide movement is calling for a *tax shift*, targeting things we *don't* want—such as pollution, traffic, and resource depletion—while reducing taxes on income. These proposals are designed to be revenue neutral, earning just as much money as our existing taxes while simultaneously tackling problems like unemployment and environmental degradation.

Natural Taxes are a logical extension of Natural Investing. Here we bring our values to the tax system, using taxes to discourage the "bads" and support the "goods." A 1998 poll shows that 70 percent of U.S. voters want a system that allows them to keep more of what they earn. As with existing "sin" taxes on cigarettes, Americans support asking those who cause harm to others—by polluting or wasting nonrenewable resources—to reimburse society for the true costs of their actions.[8]

Leadership has come from abroad. Several Scandinavian countries have already sliced national income taxes and replaced the revenue with taxes on emissions of sulfur dioxide (which cause acid rain) and carbon dioxide, which add to the greenhouse effect. Former Eastern bloc countries tax hundreds of pollutants, toxic waste, and even noise. A tax on every bag of trash in the city of Victoria, British Columbia, resulted in a significant reduction in the volume of trash.[9] Here at home, hundreds of environmental taxes have been implemented at the state level. In Iowa, a fee is charged on fertilizers that contain nitrogen, a pollutant of surface water and groundwater.[10]

Although proposals for tax shifting are sometimes called "green taxes," support for them has come from across the political spectrum. Payroll taxes are a huge burden on both small and large companies; reducing them would cut the cost of labor. This in turn would benefit working Americans, who would see their wages and job prospects improve. Taxing pollution and resource depletion would create a market mechanism to support such cleaner alternatives as solar energy and reward companies that minimize waste. This in turn would reduce the need for burdensome regulations.

There are of course a myriad of issues still to be worked out— Natural Taxes are not a cure-all for society's ills. Opposition from those who would suffer, such as the coal and oil industries, is fierce. New taxes must be phased in over a long period to minimize disruption and allow business to invest in cleaner technologies. The issue of tax fairness also needs careful attention; special provisions are needed to assure that resource taxes don't penalize rural and low-income families (who spend a higher proportion of their income on energy). Nonetheless, national dialogue on tax shifting is an important priority, deserving equal billing with the flat tax and national sales tax ideas currently being floated.

Corporations on the Dole

OUR COUNTRY HAS a long history of helping those in need. The intention of welfare programs is to help people "fare well," a superb expression of human compassion. In recent years, however, political debate has raged around these programs. Welfare reform legislation has toughened up government assistance programs, demanding that recipients take more personal responsibility for paying their own way. But while "welfare mothers" must undergo intense scrutiny before getting help with food or medical needs, hidden government subsidies and tax breaks hand out billions of taxpayer dollars in "corporate welfare," dwarfing the amount given to our nation's poor.

Corporate welfare is yet another example of the abuses that can take place when our values become divorced from financial decisions. *Time* magazine, in a bold four-part series on corporate welfare in 1998, reported that the federal government shells out $125 billion a year to corporate coffers.[11] Subsidies from state and local governments, locked in a fierce battle to attract employers, are more difficult to tally but are also vast. Sometimes they take the form of cash gifts, as when federal funds were given to McDonalds so they could market Chicken McNuggets in Singapore and to Pillsbury for promoting the Dough Boy overseas. In other cases special tax breaks are given, like that received by Royal Caribbean Cruise Lines, who paid zero taxes on profits of $158 million from 1989 to 1992.[12]

Corporations also receive indirect subsidies through the virtual give-away of public resources. How would you like to be able to buy precious wilderness that contains gold or silver deposits for $5.00 an acre from the federal government? The 1872 Mining Law, which is still alive and kicking, has enabled mining companies to do just that, walking away with an estimated $243 billion of mineral reserves. Senator Dale Bumpers calls this loophole "the biggest scam in America today" and is sponsoring legislation to change the law.[13] One example: in Northern Nevada, the Goldstrike mine, with estimated gold reserves of $11 billion, was sold to a foreign mining company for $9,000!

This subsidy is only one of many that make the environment the first place to look for misguided subsidy programs. In *The Natural Wealth of Nations,* David Roodman calculates that Americans could get a tax cut of around $500 per person by eliminating environmentally harmful subsidies; worldwide he targets $650 billion of waste for the chopping block. For example, subsidies for the global fishing fleet—some $15 billion to $20 billion a year—have helped produce enough boats, hooks, and nets to catch twice the fish that are actually available, contributing to overfishing. "Voters should know that they're paying twice when they shouldn't be paying at all," Roodman says. "Our taxes are paying for the subsidies that are causing the fisheries to collapse. Then, we pay more for the very fish our taxes are paying to deplete."[14]

Here is another issue that cuts across old political divisions. Although both the president and Congress have pledged to reduce corporate welfare, little progress has been made, despite broad public support for change. Free-market advocates, notably the Cato Institute, denounce government programs that benefit specific companies or industries. Friends of the Earth has partnered with conservative taxpayer groups to promote the "Green Scissors Campaign." Since 1995 Green Scissors has helped save more than $20 billion by cutting environmentally harmful subsidies. Even some corporate CEOs are coming on board. In 1997 dozens of technology companies signed a "Declaration of Independence: End Corporate Welfare" petition to the Senate. They believe that high taxes are more damaging than the benefits received by government spending, and they have pledged to support cuts—even to their own companies.

The original motivations behind subsidies and tax loopholes were usually noble, such as protecting jobs or helping farmers. But the *Time* magazine series documented numerous corporate welfare programs that cost taxpayers from $1 million to $10 million for every single job created. Certainly some programs are worth keeping; the Worldwatch Institute has developed guidelines for evaluating the true costs and benefits of subsidies. The petition from the technology company CEOs proposed forming an independent commission, similar to the one that decided on military base closures, to make impartial recommendations on programs to be cut. Legislation to bring this about was introduced in the Senate in 1997. But mustering the political will to cut corporate welfare is the hardest part of all. Natural Investors concerned about how their taxes are invested will want to make sure their voices are heard.

More Keys to Wall Street

SO FAR WE'VE touched on three crusades—new indicators, tax shifting, and stopping corporate welfare—that are crucial elements of the campaign for a values-based Wall Street. We've crossed into dangerous seas, leaving the relatively serene confines of investing and negotiating the contentious storms of politics. Since we're already in hot water, we may as well round out this discussion with a few more leverage points that could help speed the healing of Wall Street.

The Global Dance. Globalization is here to stay; nobody is going to repeal the Internet or MTV. This reality demands that we become more attuned to global issues. We are still in the early years of living under global trade pacts like NAFTA and GATT. The jury is still out on how well they are working, but many believe these treaties have had deleterious economic effects on workers both in the United States and abroad. In addition critics charge that these sorts of treaties pose a threat to local and national sovereignty; this battle is currently being played out in the challenge to Massachusetts' Burma selective purchasing law (see page 148) by the European Union and global corporate interests.

Unbeknownst to most Americans, new treaties like the Multilateral Agreement on Investment (MAI) are on the drawing board that would liberalize global investment by facilitating the movement of capital across borders. A global coalition of citizen groups opposes this pact, arguing that it shifts power toward unaccountable institutions like the World Trade Organization and fails to protect cultural, environmental, and labor interests. In late 1998, France pulled out of negotiations for the MAI, effectively derailing the talks.[15] However, it is likely that these issues will continually resurface. Globalization issues such as these are of central importance and deserve widespread public debate.

A Race to the Bottom or Leveling Up? As corporations prowl the globe in search of cheap labor and lax standards, Americans are realizing that social, economic, and environmental issues can no longer be addressed only in our own country. In response, labor unions are beginning to organize internationally. Investors, as we learned earlier, are demanding that corporations act responsibly overseas. An international "living wage" campaign is one approach that aims toward a flexible "global minimum wage"; it asks companies to pay workers at least enough for them to live at a reasonable level. Environmental issues such as the disappearing ozone layer must also be addressed globally.

Playing Fair in the Global Casino. An estimated $2 trillion changes hands every day in the world's unregulated currency markets—a global tidal wave of speculative money that destabilizes national economies. The last few years have seen an unending roller coaster of global recessions and currency gyrations creating social chaos, huge losses, and collapses of banks and brokerages in such far-flung places as East Asia, Russia, and Brazil.

Hazel Henderson and others have called for the creation of a global version of the U.S. Securities and Exchange Commission to harmonize regulation of securities and currency markets.[16] Even billionaire investor George Soros—who has profited heavily by legally "raiding" foreign currencies—has called for new controls. One intriguing idea is the "Tobin Tax," named for Nobel Laureate James Tobin, who in 1975 proposed placing a very small tax (0.05 percent) on currency transactions in order to discourage unfettered speculation.

Corporate Charter Reform. Ever since the late 1800s, case law has eroded the original, socially oriented foundations of the corporate system. Many would like to revisit two crucial court rulings that, first, granted corporations the rights and freedoms of individuals and, later, mandated that corporations maximize shareholder return. Those who favor a new look at corporate charter provisions aim to create new mandates (or at least legally substantive openings) for holding management to broader social and environmental concerns. Among the suggestions are broadening the makeup of boards of directors to include other stakeholders and creating various sorts of community oversight or input. Meanwhile, as we saw on page 148, activists are using existing laws to petition for the revocation of the charters of corporations that are felt to be operating in ways that consistently violate ethical standards.

Government for Hire. Finally, no discussion of money and values can ignore the urgent need for comprehensive political and campaign finance reform. Polls show that Americans are very aware, and extremely dismayed, by the blatant influence of lobbyists and moneyed special interests over our government. Money in politics gives a disproportionate voice to those with power and wealth. Cleaning up the system may be the most important action of all, shifting power away from major contributors and back toward ordinary citizens.

The Evolution of Change

THE IDEAS AND proposals presented in this chapter are rational, commonsense responses to shortcomings in the ways in which money circulates through our society. Taken together, they indicate a widely shared belief that something is amiss in our economy, that we must come back into balance with our deepest convictions. Certainly these proposals are ambitious, and perhaps even unrealistic in the current social and political climate. Nonetheless, a process of reevaluation is under way. Over the next decade or so, the questions raised in this chapter will receive increasing attention.

We are witnessing the first, small steps in the direction of building a sustainable economy: many investors are beginning to incorporate values-based factors into their financial lives, some industry insiders are questioning underlying assumptions, and a few leading-edge theorists are brainstorming new approaches to our economic structures. There's no telling if or when any of these early steps will move into the mainstream. But we are certain that the shape of our future economy will be influenced by the discussion of these ideas, and others yet to come.

Our hope, and our expectation, is that the next economy will be formed around the themes we've sketched in this book: a reintegration of money and core human values, an emergence of ecologically sustainable and socially equitable business practices, and a new balance between corporate and individual needs.

One final piece of the puzzle is presented in the last chapter. There we dive deep into the ways in which we look at the world, uncovering the profound, ongoing shift in worldviews that is the motivating source of all of the initiatives in this book. Join us as we complete the circle, within which the many vantage points of Natural Investing are seen to be integrated.

Chapter Fifteen

The Natural Worldview: Money and Values in the Evolutionary Dance

FOR THIS FINAL chapter you can put away your checkbook— we've completed our tour of the wide-ranging world of Natural Investing. You are now fully conversant on values-inclusive investment options, lifestyle choices, and activist strategies. Go pour yourself a cup of tea and relax; it's time to reflect on the deeper meanings of the journey and explore the larger patterns of social evolution within which Natural Investing plays its role.

To begin with, we know that many of you probably picked up this book to learn how to "make money and make a difference." But although linking values with capital is vitally important, it is only part of a much bigger picture. If we truly want to address the root causes of our social and ecological dilemmas, we must also encourage a fundamental shift in our culture's underlying worldview. For it is our worldview—our guiding beliefs and understandings about the mysteries of life—that is the prime determinant of our behavior patterns.

What gives us hope during these times of deepening crisis are signs that this shift is now taking place. On the leading edges of science, and within the eternal flames of human compassion, a more connective worldview is emerging. We are realizing that our picture of the Earth as a *machine* with *parts* is not accurate; we are beginning to recognize that we are part of a *living planet* of *interconnected systems*. This Natural Worldview is exerting a profound influence on every aspect of our society.

> **We are at the very point in time when a 400-year-old age is dying and another is struggling to be born—a shifting of culture, science, society, and institutions enormously greater than the world has ever experienced. Ahead, the possibility of the regeneration of individuality, liberty, community, and ethics such as the world has never known, and a harmony with nature, with one another, and with the divine intelligence such as the world has never dreamed.**
>
> —DEE HOCK, founder of Visa[1]

The emergence of, and resistance to, Natural Investing are only recent episodes in the unfolding play that Hock describes so eloquently. When you choose to integrate your values with your money, you are taking a role in this shift toward a Natural Worldview. Natural Investing recognizes and cares for the living, interconnected systems from which our monetary world emerges: biological and cultural systems rich in diversity. In turn, we find that the Natural Worldview provides a more realistic view of our economy; it behaves much more like a living system than a machine. Both investors and business leaders are beginning to embrace the wisdom contained in the Natural Worldview. Where this will lead is still anybody's guess.

If there is one lesson to be learned from each of the preceding chapters, it is this: it is now both possible and desirable to include our values in every major financial decision. One might then ask, "Why has Natural Investing had such a hard time gaining credibility in the mainstream?" This is an important question—despite its commonsense approach and a mountain of evidence proving its merits, the fact remains that Natural Investing is still a minority voice in the world of Wall Street. Even many died-in-the-wool Cultural Creatives are initially skeptical.

We believe that an outdated "mechanical worldview" has prevented Natural Investing from achieving critical mass and becoming business as usual in the mainstream. Natural Investing flies in the face of a long-dominant paradigm that warns us: "Don't mix money and values—you'll harm yourself and your ethical meddling will only mess up the efficient functioning of the marketplace and harm society!" But this wall between money and values is not carved in stone; our belief that values will disrupt the efficient machine of economics has arisen out of the pervasive mechanical worldview. As we're about to see, this wall was built on a very shaky foundation.

Roots of the Mechanical Worldview

IT'S OFTEN HARD to imagine the subtle forces at play in our distant past that created what has come to be regarded as The Truth. And since history is written by the victors, it's often hard to even remember the counterforces that have always been in play alongside whatever view is currently, if fleetingly, dominant.

We might trace the origins of our modern mechanical worldview to ancient Greece, where newly discovered principles of mathematics enthralled philosophers such as Pythagoras and Plato. They put forth the idea that the cosmos, and all of nature, were created with geometrical perfection, and furthermore that their ultimate truth could only be known through the abstraction of reason. This contrasted sharply with the ancient belief (still dominant in many cultures) in an organic cosmos in which all was alive, and the view that direct experience was the route to deepest knowledge.

It was of course in the seventeenth century—in the time of Descartes, Newton, and Galileo—that discoveries in physics and astronomy solidified belief in "the world as machine." Built upon the most complex mathematics of its time, the scientific method in essence co-opted the ancient path of direct, sensory experience. Science declared that only passive observation, narrowly focused on quantifiable data, provided a legitimate window on the world's workings. As enthusiasm surged for knowledge gleaned from the fruits of science, the old belief in participation in and relationship with the physical world was cast aside.

Fueled by Newtonian science, the machine metaphor dominated our view of the world and reigned over the whole of society to an extent few of us fully realize. It declared that the universe and everything in it, whether physical or biological (even people!), could best be understood as a clocklike mechanism. Everything was imagined to be composed of separate parts acting upon one another through precise, linear laws of cause and effect. Social sciences like economics and psychology emulated physics, creating mechanical models for their theories of human behavior.

In the early years of the scientific revolution, great advances were made in machine technology (as might be expected, with our imaginations fired by images of the world as a machine). Agriculture and manufacturing efficiencies grew in consort, freeing masses of the human population from their historic ties to the land and fueling the growth of cities. But, as we've seen throughout this book, our technological miracles have not come without a price.

The incredible power and fruits of the idea that the world, and the cosmos, is a machine and that God is the master watchmaker kept our doubts at bay for over two centuries. Eventually, though, cracks in this worldview began to appear. Early in this century, stunning breakthroughs revealed a vast uncertainty underlying the clockworks of science. Albert Einstein and other scientists proved that atoms are not solid building blocks but rather a baffling convergence of fields, forces, and fleetingly physical particles. And, as the social and ecological side effects of industrialization spread around the world, we were forced to notice problems that had previously been localized around the cities. It has become clear that mechanical models are woefully inadequate for describing reality, or for solving humanity's social, environmental, and economic dilemmas.

The Incredible Disappearing Invisible Hand

IN THE SEVENTEENTH century, while Isaac Newton was using scientific methodology to advance the study of physical phenomena, his friend Sir William Petty was using this same methodology to formulate the first theories of modern economics.[2] Today economics is still relying on assumptions that stemmed from its wholehearted acceptance of the mechanical worldview. Let's take a look at some rather peculiar notions that have resulted from this "rational" approach.

First, economics reduces everything to a number—its monetary value—in order to fit things into its theoretical models. Vast, vitally important aspects of life are considered to be "outside" the market. If something is hard to quantify it becomes an "externality," to be excluded from the equations and practices of economic policy. Our discussion of the gross domestic product (GDP) in the last chapter showed how this works in practice: the unpaid work of householders and volunteers in the community is an externality; likewise, pollution that threatens the capacity of the Earth to support life is an externality. Neither is considered relevant to economic planning.

The economic view of an individual is similarly limited. To fit us into marketplace theories, economics invented an abstraction called *Homo economicus.* Here we have individualism taken to the extreme: *Homo economicus*'s only goal in life is to acquire as much as possible, as efficiently as possible. Indeed our insatiable wants are modeled as having no point at which we have "enough"; there is no way for the underlying equations to include such a concept. Certainly we do have parts of our personality that crave more and more stuff, but building entire economic systems on this narrow view of humanity is proving to be a dangerous shortcoming.

Finally, one of the central tenets of the mechanical view of the economy is the notion of the "invisible hand" that guides free markets. First posited by Adam Smith in 1776, this idea has become the guiding principle proffered by advocates of laissez-faire capitalism. The belief is that if each member of the economy simply pursues his or her own self-interest, then the invisible hand of the market will assure that the best and most efficient result for the economy and society as a whole will result.

This is a prime example of the sort of outdated thinking and out-of-context rationalizations that are at the root of many of today's economic quandaries. Smith was writing about small-scale, largely local economies; his idea has been extrapolated into first national and now global arenas, on scales unimaginable in his time.

In fact, Smith was a moral philosopher; his writings speak of ethics, not mechanical functionings of the market. Smith envisioned a world populated by persons steeped with strong morals, who understood that enlightened self-interest includes notions of social equity. Smith's invisible hand was actually the hand of a deeper wisdom operating through individuals and societies.[3] His faith in this invisible hand was predicated on economies operating at personal scales, unhampered by government or corporate manipulation. In his time, when economies operated primarily on a local scale, such a view was idealistic, yet within reach. In our times, what is needed is a return of the *real* invisible hand that has been missing from our economic system, the one that brings along values.

However we interpret Smith's intent, neither his moral compass nor a mechanistic wisdom of the market is assuring that individual actions are creating the greatest public good. Indeed, it's clear that the interconnected webs of our modern economy create effects that run counter to the public good. Perhaps the key insight in a Natural Worldview is that the "public" being considered is ever-expanding. Thanks to the pursuit of private good by a coffee conglomerate, Americans have access to affordable, high-quality coffee; although this may be "good" for our society, at the same time it undermines the subsistence farming of Costa Rican communities and diminishes the biodiversity of the rain forest ecosystem.

The machine view of life served a crucial purpose during the past several centuries. It offered a way to break the unimaginably intricate webs of life into simplified pictures that we could begin to understand. It made possible the social and technological advances that have brought us to the point where we now stand—with satellites, global exchanges of knowledge, and computer processing power that are beginning to reveal the subtler connections and patterns underlying life itself. Now it is time to let go of our simplified machine models and embrace a new chapter in our story of coming to know our home planet. Freed from the bounds of mechanistic views, we can begin to expand our imaginations and conceptions.

The Natural Worldview

OUR ECONOMY, PEOPLE, and the universe-at-large have all stubbornly refused to fit into the machine box. As this antiquated worldview loses its grip, Western culture finds itself searching for fresh perspectives that provide a more accurate representation of reality and serve as a better template for designing social institutions.

Today, cross-disciplinary scientists are developing an exciting new picture of the world. This new view offers some much-needed handles that might help us to reorient ourselves toward more balanced and connected models of our economy. Labeled variously as complexity, chaos, self-organization, or living systems theory, this worldview understands that life is *not* a giant machine. Rather than model our view of the world on our most rigid and unchanging creations, this new view is modeled

The Economy of the Body

 ELISABET SAHTOURIS, BIOLOGIST and coauthor of *Biology Revisioned,* offers a striking analogy that highlights the limited thinking inherent in a mechanical view and the deeper wisdom contained in the principles of living systems:

> Consider world economics and imagine it as the economics of a living entity such as your body. Think what would happen in your body if the raw material blood cells in your bones and organs were mined as "resources" by the "northern industrial" lung and heart organs, transported to their production and distribution centers where blood is purified and oxygen added to make it a useful product. Imagine it is then announced that blood (and its rich stew of nutrients) will be distributed from the heart center to those organs that can afford the price posted that day. What is not bought is chucked out as surplus or stored until the market demand rises. How long could your body survive that system?
>
> Obviously, metaphors have their limits and I do not for a moment suggest we slavishly emulate body models. But bodies beat unrealistic mechanical metaphors of perfect societies running like well-oiled machines. They are something we all have in common regardless of our worldviews, our political or spiritual persuasions, and they do exemplify the main features and principles of all healthy living systems.[4]

on what we see in the world's creation of itself. In biology, physics, and even economics, studies have revealed organizing principles vastly more powerful, and vastly more mysterious, than cogs in a machine.

Of course there is nothing really new about these breakthroughs. Throughout all these centuries, and into the present time, native cultures and many Westerners have maintained a more natural view of the world. Based on direct human perception and experience, native economies are founded on their long and deep current of connection with nature's dynamics. Their worldview has served as the foundation for a wide variety of successful social systems and richly satisfying personal lives. Indeed, the "new" Natural Worldview is, in many ways, simply a modern integration of traditional native wisdom.

So what do we find when we look beyond the mechanistic worldview and rediscover the simple truths within the unfathomable complexity of nature? Probably the most striking feature is the awesome web of *interconnections* revealed by the Natural Worldview. We are learning that the exchanges taking place between and among life's pieces are far subtler, and far more powerful, than the simplified pictures painted by the world-as-machine mindset.

Whereas the mechanistic view fostered the belief that life's advances were achieved primarily through competition, we are now finding that although competition weeds out the field, it is *cooperation* that sparks most, if not all, new advances. Microbiologist Lynn Margulis has revealed that symbiosis among microbes is what forged the great evolutionary leap from single-celled life to plant and animal cells. Within our own complex animal cells are remnants of at least three different bacterial creatures; their mutual partnership enabled them to survive environmental challenges and create the "next step" in evolution.

A related insight of the Natural Worldview is that life is not made up of rigid, distinct hierarchies; rather, life expresses itself in *nested communities* (cells within organisms within communities within ecosystems within planets). These nested systems are structured so that each level supports not only itself but also its component subsystems and the systems of which it is a part. Your body maintains its own integrity by sustaining its organs and cells, and by maintaining a healthy relationship to its social and biological communities. Like a hologram, every part contains the whole; all things (and beings) are connected.

Most of all, living systems are alive! Unlike machines, life is continuously *self-organizing,* creating greater levels of complexity to support more diversity. "The universe is a living, creative, experimenting experience of discovering what's possible at all levels of scale, from microbe to cosmos," note Margaret Wheatley and Myron Kellner-Rogers in *A Simpler Way.*[5] This impulse for *diversity* provides the widest possible genetic pool, assuring survival under changing conditions.

The principles of nature have guided the successful evolution of life on Earth for over four billion years. The Natural Worldview is proving relevant to every field of human endeavor, as scientists continue to glean new insights from their study of living systems. Just as social architects of the seventeenth century both found liberation and achieved unimagined advances by building their society on the matrix of their early, simple understanding of life, so too might we create unimagined opportunities by modeling our systems on the best knowledge of our time.

The Natural Economy

WE'RE NOW READY to sketch the outlines of what an economy based on this Natural Worldview would look like. The best way to do this would be to compare it to the economy as it exists today. So, with a nod to David Letterman, we present . . .

The Top 10 Advantages of a Natural Economy:

MECHANICAL ECONOMY	NATURAL ECONOMY
10 Growth of GDP as society's goal. Throughput of economic activity given precedence, regardless of consequences.	**10** Social and environmental well-being as society's goal. New indicators, at both national and local levels, monitor progress toward sustainability.
9 Moneyed interests and corporations hold disproportionate political power and receive favorable tax breaks, subsidies, and trade pacts.	**9** People, communities, and nature come first. Policies, taxes, and subsidies favor socially and environmentally desirable activities.
8 Competitive behavior dominates. "Survival of the fittest" mentality allows extreme wealth to concentrate in the hands of fewer and fewer victors.	**8** Balance of cooperation and competition. Wealth circulates fairly throughout the system; all people have at least minimum levels of housing, food, health care, education, and opportunity.
7 Globalization led by absentee owners and multinational corporations.	**7** Localization emphasizing community-based production for local markets.
6 Socially oblivious investing. Investors focus on quarterly profits with little or no regard for social and environmental costs.	**6** Natural Investing. Investors favor activities with potential for long-term social, environmental, and financial benefits.

MECHANICAL ECONOMY	NATURAL ECONOMY
5 McWorld monoculture. Fast-food outlets and MTV conquer the world. Loss of cultural and biological diversity.	**5** Cultural diversity. Preservation and celebration of cultural and biological diversity.
4 People as consumers. Maximizes "standard of living" through buying more stuff. Encourages debt. Increases personal, family, and social stress.	**4** People as citizens. Quality of life is highest goal, emphasizing cultural, creative, intellectual, and spiritual growth. Voluntary abundance.
3 Workers as machines. Use of cheapest possible human labor under minimal working conditions.	**3** Right livelihood. Healthy integration of body, soul, and work.
2 Destruction of nature. Treats environment as mines and dumps; we take what we want from the Earth and create waste. Nature's life support capabilities threatened.	**2** Economy as subset of nature. Emphasis on long-term sustainability to maintain health of ecosystems.

#1   And, the number 1 advantage of a *natural economy* over a *mechanical economy*: values and money are reunited!

Changing the worldview of our economic system is the fundamental task of our lifetimes; the mechanistic model will not let go easily. But the mechanical foundation of modern economics has become the wall that separates values and money. "The avoidance of social issues in current economic theory is closely related to the striking inability of economists to adopt an ecological perspective," says Fritjof Capra in *The Turning Point*.[6] The achievements of the current system must not blind us to its limitations. As Herman Daly, former World Bank economist, points out, "With each passing year, the positive accomplishments of the economy have become less evident and the destructive consequences larger. There is a growing sense that it is time for a change."[7]

Natural Is Practical

AS WE INTEGRATE the Natural Worldview into economics, we will not throw the baby out with the bath water. Moving toward a Natural Economy does not mean abandoning marketplace efficiencies or material progress. Rather we must focus on some deeper priorities and use the best available tools—including science and technology—to achieve our goals.

It is worth noting that, like the mechanistic view, the Natural World-view is being built upon the most advanced mathematics of our time, nonlinear math. The power of computers is allowing us to move beyond the vastly simplified equations of linear mathematics. For the first time, more integrative models can be developed, which can incorporate more variables, including constantly changing factors. Not surprisingly, these models are far superior both at duplicating observed behaviors in nature and society and at exploring the possible forces at work inside actions far too complex to model in simple mechanistic ways.

The potential to gain better predictive skills has not been lost on investors. Over $200 billion is spent annually on research aimed at pre-dicting the future. Most of this money is wasted—Wall Street is littered with stock forecasts gone awry. Mainstream economics does not do a very good job of predicting or even explaining why markets bubble and burst. Despite our best attempts, high-priced analysts equipped with phalanxes of computers cannot predict the direction of interest rates tomorrow, let alone a year from now.

Wall Street's hapless prognosticators are hindered by their reliance on the mechanical worldview. *Barron's,* in a review of William Sher-den's book *The Fortune Sellers,* states that "the future defies prediction because consumers don't behave according to rational equations built on the assumption that money is their sole motivating force." Sherden points to many other factors—such as "power, prestige, fame, influence, conformity, hope, love, and affiliation"—that influence human behavior. He goes on to say that national economies are "complex organic sys-tems" that are in a continual state of change. "What happens today influences what happens tomorrow, which in turn influences what hap-pens the next day. The future isn't found, it's invented."[8]

Investors are already showing keen interest in early research aimed at explaining and predicting market behavior using complexity theory. At the Santa Fe Institute, where Ph.D.s from around the world come to share in a rare cross-disciplinary creative synergy, researchers are seek-ing to understand the dynamics of the stock market by using the new sciences of complex systems and nonlinear math.

Business, too, is reaching out to the Natural Worldview for a new organizational model. Ken Baskin, author of *Corporate DNA: Learn-ing from Life,* points to 3M as a company that credits its organic orga-nizational structure for catalyzing numerous innovations, including their well-known Post-It Notes. Rather than keeping each division separate, 3M relies on semipermeable boundaries and pathways of communication that give employees the big picture and encourage collaboration.[9]

The Evolutionary Dance

SO HOW DO we go about transitioning to an economy that reflects and fits within a Natural Worldview? This is no simple task; it's not something on which we can vote, and there's no "adopt-a-worldview" organization to which we can give our money. This sort of change must come from within, one person at a time. The important work we've covered in this book was pioneered by countless people who acted on their desire to make a difference. By following their trail, our personal and corporate actions can become part of a vast, conscious, but not entirely predictable (it's a self-organizing complex system!) move toward a sustainable future.

The Natural Worldview teaches us that we are not isolated from each other. Every time we take a step toward integrating our values and our money, we change the collective direction of humanity. As our society aligns its policies and structures with those we see in life, our social evolution will be empowered by the underlying processes that brought about the miracle of our very existence. In the big picture (the one beyond the next quarter or a five-year planning cycle), we believe that the whole-systems view, the Natural Worldview, is profoundly correct: the interconnections among related systems *do* matter, *do* affect the long-term stability of our culture and its economy.

Throughout *Investing with Your Values*, we've identified practical steps that can further the creation of a Natural Economy. Now you know the deeper reasoning behind our choice of the term *Natural Investing!* We know that the tasks ahead involve hard work, dedication, and clear thinking; *natural* does not imply *easy* when most of society is still operating from a mechanical mindset. But each of the pieces explored in this book can contribute, in a concrete way, to the gradual shift that is taking place.

So now we've come full circle. The Natural Worldview reminds us to consider the larger context with which we seem to have lost touch. What is the spark that burns at the heart of a Natural Economy? It is those same natural desires we identified in the introduction: the desire to make a difference and improve life on Earth, and the desire to walk our talk, to live consistently with our values. These universally felt desires underlie the daily, personal choices made by the Natural Investor.

> **"** *In spite of everything I still believe that people are really good at heart. I simply can't build up my hopes on a foundation consisting of confusion, misery, and death. I see the world gradually being turned into a wilderness; I hear the ever-approaching thunder, which will destroy us, too; I can feel the sufferings of millions, and yet, if I look up into the heavens, I think that it will all come right, that this cruelty too will end, and that peace and tranquility will return again.* **"**
>
> —ANNE FRANK, *Diary of a Young Girl*

Like Anne, we reconfirm our deep trust in the common decency and caring of people, and in what will result from the diverse expressions of these basic desires. What we are calling for is an economic populism—each person acting from their own sense of purpose and integrity. We envision the return of basic human values to the core place they deserve to hold in our social and economic systems. From our hearts, minds, and souls, we will bring forth unimaginably creative expressions of humanity in harmony with the eternal ways of life.

Appendixes

Appendix A: Resources

Key Organizations and Publications

Business Ethics
PO Box 8439, Minneapolis, MN 55408
612-879-0699, email Bizethics@aol.com
Bimonthly magazine that promotes ethical business practices.

Business for Social Responsibility
609 Mission Street, Second Floor, San Francisco, CA 94105
415-537-0888, www.bsr.org
Membership organization that helps companies be commercially successful in ways that demonstrate respect for ethical values, communities, people, and the environment.

Capital Missions
5080 Huron Breeze Drive, Au Gres, MI 48703
517-876-8766, e-mail: corkcmc@aol.com
Sponsors annual Making a Profit While Making a Difference conference; promotes social venture capital and business leadership networks.

CERES—The Coalition for Environmentally Responsible Economies
711 Atlantic Avenue, Boston, MA 02111
617-451-0927, www.ceres.org
Facilitates corporate reporting on environmental performance through the CERES Principles and the Global Reporting Initiative.

Co-op America
1612 K Street NW, #600, Washington, DC 20006
202-872-5307, www.coopamerica.org, www.greenpages.org
A membership organization that publishes the *National Green Pages* and the *Financial Planning Handbook*. Provides research and information on socially responsible investing, corporate responsibility, green business, and more.

Council on Economic Priorities (CEP)
30 Irving Place, New York, NY 10003
212-420-1133, www.cepnyc.org
Performs corporate social research and issues publications.

Franklin Research and Development
711 Atlantic Avenue, Boston, MA 02111
617-423-6655, www.frdc.com
Publishes *Investing for a Better World* and *Franklin Research's Insight*, monthly newsletters with information on socially responsible investing, stocks, community investing, and shareholder activism.

The GreenMoney Journal & Online Guide
West 608 Glass Avenue, Spokane, WA 99205
509-328-1741, www.greenmoney.com
Published since 1992, a quarterly newsletter with information on socially responsible investing, community investing, sustainable business, and green consumer resources.

Interfaith Center on Corporate Responsibility (ICCR)
475 Riverside Drive, #566, New York, NY 10115
212-870-2295
A coalition of 275 religious organizations that is a leader in shareholder activism. Publishes the newsletter *The Corporate Examiner.*

Investor Responsibility Research Center (IRRC)
1350 Connecticut Avenue NW, #700, Washington, DC 20036
202-833-0700, www.irrc.org
Performs research, analysis, and portfolio screening on companies worldwide.

Kinder, Lydenberg, Domini & Co. (KLD)
530 Atlantic Avenue, 7th Floor, Boston, MA 02210
617-426-5270, www.kld.com
Maintains the Domini 400 Social Index and publishes SOCRATES, a social research database.

Natural Investment Services (NIS)
PO Box 747, Paonia, CO 81428
970-527-6550,
   www.naturalinvesting.com
Provides financial consulting for individual investors and institutions. Maintains the NIS Social Rating^{SM}, which evaluates the social characteristics of socially screened mutual funds.

Social Investment Forum
1612 K Street NW, #650, Washington, DC 20006
202-872-5319, www.socialinvest.org
A trade organization for socially responsible investing professionals, primary clearinghouse, and activism catalyst. With Co-op America, publishes the

Financial Planning Handbook for Responsible Investors and the *Social Investment Forum Directory.*

Social Investment Organization (Canada)
366 Adelaide Street East, Suite 443, Toronto, Ontario M5A 3X9, Canada
416-360-6047, www.web.net/~SIO
Canadian trade organization for socially responsible investing professionals.

Social Venture Network
PO Box 29903, San Francisco, CA 94129
415-561-6501, www.svn.org
A progressive business network that offers support for companies that value social justice, community, cooperation, diversity, education, sustainability, and innovation.

Other Natural Investing Web Sites

Good Money Online
   www.goodmoney.com
First Affirmative Financial Network
   www.firstaffirmative.com
Investing with Your Values
   www.naturalinvesting.com
Social Funds   www.socialfunds.com
SRI in the Rockies Conference
   www.sriconf.com
SRI Links
   http://directory.mozilla.org/Business/Investing/Socially_Responsible
Students for Responsible Business
   www.srbnet.org

Books on Natural Investing and Related Topics

Banker to the Poor: Micro-Lending and the Battle Against World Poverty, Mohammad Yunus (Public Affairs, 1999)

Beyond the Bottom Line, Joel Makower (Simon & Schuster, 1994)

Cannibals with Forks: The Triple Bottom Line of the 21st Century Business, John Elkington (New Society, 1998)

Corporate Citizenship: Successful Strategies for Responsible Companies, Malcolm Mcintosh, Deborah Leipziger, Keith Jones, and Gill Coleman (Financial Times/Pitman Publishing, 1998)

The Corporate Report Card: Rating 250 American Corporations for the Socially Responsible Investor, the Council on Economic Priorities (Dutton, 1998)

Everybody's Business, Milton Moskowitz, Michael Katz, and Robert Levering (Doubleday/Currency, 1990)

Invested in the Common Good, Susan Meeker-Lowry (New Society, 1995)

Investing for Good, Peter Kinder, Steven Lydenberg, and Amy Domini (HarperBusiness, 1993)

Investing From the Heart, Jack Brill and Alan Reder (Crown, 1992)

Jews, Money & Social Responsibility: A "Torah of Money," Lawrence Bush (Shefa Fund, 1993)

Loosing the Bonds: The United States and South Africa in the Apartheid Years, Robert Massie (Doubleday, 1998)

The Mindful Money Guide: Creating Harmony with Values & Finances, Marshall Glickman (Wellspring/ Ballantine, 1999)

Mission-Based Investing: Extending the Reach of the Foundations, Endowments and NGOs, Steven Lydenberg and Peter Kinder (KLD, 1998)

Money and the Meaning of Life, Jacob Needleman (Doubleday/Currency, 1991)

The Post-Corporate World: Life after Capitalism, David Korten (Berrett-Koehler, 1999)

The Seven Stages of Money Maturity, George Kinder (Delacourte, 1999)

75 Best Business Practices for Socially Responsible Companies, Alan Reder (Tarcher/Putnam, 1995)

The Tao of Money: Six Simple Principles for Achieving Financial Harmony, Ivan Hoffman (Prima, 1994)

The Thoughtful Christian's Guide to Investing, Gary Moore (Zondervan, 1990)

Whole Life Economics, Barbara Brandt (New Society, 1995)

Appendix B:
Listings of Socially
Screened Companies

This appendix includes:
- ➤ Companies in the Citizens Index and Domini 400 Social Index
- ➤ Companies in the Good Money Industrial Average
- ➤ Companies in Natural Products Industry indices
- ➤ Clean utilities
- ➤ Companies appearing in various "Best Companies" lists relevant to Natural Investors
- ➤ Companies involved in sustainability sectors covered in Chapter 6

Companies Appearing in the Citizens Index and Domini 400 Social Index as of October 31, 1998

Key: Plain text = Citizens and Domini; *italics* = *Citizens;* <u>underline</u> = <u>Domini;</u> ° = preferred stock available.

Sources: Compiled by the authors using the following: Citizens Index Fund portfolio, supplied by Citizens Funds, Portsmouth, NH; used with permission. Domini 400 Social Index, copyright 1998 Kinder, Lydenberg, Domini & Co.; used with permission.

3Com Corp.
Accustaff, Inc.
AC Nielsen Corp.
<u>Acuson Corp.</u>
<u>Adaptec, Inc.</u>
ADC Telecommunication
Adobe Systems, Inc.
Advanced Micro Devices, Inc.
AES Corp.
°<u>Aetna, Inc.</u>
<u>AGL Resources, Inc.</u>
Ahmanson (H. F.) & Co.

Air Products & Chemicals, Inc.
<u>Airborne Freight Corp.</u>
Airtouch Communications
<u>Alaska Air Group, Inc.</u>
<u>Alberto-Culver Co.</u>
<u>Albertson's, Inc.</u>
<u>Allergan, Inc.</u>
Alltel Corp.
Altera Corp.
°<u>Aluminum Co. of America</u>
Alza Corp.

America Online, Inc.
American Express Co.
°American General Corp.
American Greetings Corp.
<u>American International Group, Inc.</u>
American Power Conversion
<u>American Stores Cos.</u>
American Water Works, Inc.
Ameritech
Amgen

303

Amoco Corp.
AMP, Inc.
AMR Corp.
Anadarko Petroleum
   Corp.
Analog Devices, Inc.
Angelica Corp.
AON Corp.
Apache Corp.
Apogee Enterprises, Inc.
Apple Computer, Inc.
Applied Materials, Inc.
Armstrong World
Ascend Communication
AT&T Corp.
Atlantic Richfield Co.
Ault, Inc.
Autodesk, Inc.
Automatic Data Process-
   ing, Inc.
Avery Dennison Corp.
Avnet, Inc.
Avon Products, Inc.
Baldor Electric Co.
Banc One Corp.
Bandag Inc.
Bank New York, Inc.
°BankAmerica Corp.
°BankBoston Corp.
°Bankers Trust New York
   Corp.
Banta Corp.
Barnes & Noble, Inc.
Bassett Furniture
   Industries
Battle Mountain Gold Co.
BB&T Corp.
Becton Dickinson and Co.
Belden, Inc.
Bell Atlantic Corp.
BellSouth Corp.
Bemis Co., Inc.
Ben & Jerry's Homemade,
   Inc.

Bergen Brunswig Corp.
Best Foods
Betz Laboratories
Biogen N V
Biomet, Inc.
Black & Decker Corp.
Block (H & R), Inc.
BMC Industries, Inc.
Bob Evans Farms, Inc.
Boston Scientific Corp.
Brady (W. H.) Co.
Broderbund Software,
   Inc.
Brown Group, Inc.
Brunos, Inc.
C-Cube Microsystems
Cabot Corp.
CalEnergy Co., Inc.
Calgon Carbon Corp.
Callaway Golf Co.
Campbell Soup Co.
Caraustar Industries, Inc.
Case Corp.
Celestial Seasonings
°*Cendant Corp.*
Centex Corp.
Ceridian Corp.
Champion Enterprises,
   Inc.
Charming Shoppes, Inc.
Chiron Corp.
Choice Hotels Inter-
   national I
Chubb Corp.
Church & Dwight Co.,
   Inc.
Cigna Corp.
Cincinnati Financial
   Corp.
Cincinnati Milacron, Inc.
Cintas Corp.
Circuit City Stores, Inc.
Cisco Systems, Inc.
Citizens Utilities Co.

Claire's Stores, Inc.
CLARCOR, Inc.
Cleco Corp.
Clorox Co.
Coca-Cola Co.
Coleman, Inc. New.
°Colgate-Palmolive Co.
Comcast Corp.
Comerica, Inc.
Compaq Computer
   Corp.
Computer Associates
   International, Inc.
Connecticut Energy
   Corp.
Consolidated Freight-
   ways Corp.
Consolidated Natural
   Gas Co.
Consolidated Papers, Inc.
Cooper Industries, Inc.
Cooper Tire and
   Rubber Co.
Costco Cos., Inc.
Countrywide Cr Inds.
CPI Corp.
Cross (A. T.) Co.
Crown Cork & Seal Co.,
   Inc.
Cummins Engine Co., Inc.
CVS Corp.
Cyanotech Corp.
Cymer, Inc.
Cyprus Amax Minerals Co.
Dana Corp.
Darden Restaurants I
Dayton Hudson Corp.
De Luxe Check Printers
Deere & Co.
Dell Computer Corp.
Delta Air Lines, Inc.
Deluxe Corp.
DeVry, Inc.
Dialogic Corp.

Dillard Department
   Stores, Inc.
Dime Bancorp
Dionex Corp.
Disney (Walt) Co.
Dollar General Corp.
Donnelley (R. R.) & Sons
   Co.
Dow Jones & Co.
Dun & Bradstreet Cos.
Dura Pharmaceuticals
Eastern Enterprises
Echo Bay Mines Ltd.
Edwards (A. G.), Inc.
Egghead, Inc.
El Paso Energy Corp.
EMC Corp.
Emerson Electric Co.
Energen Corp.
Enesco Group, Inc.
Engelhard Corp.
°Enron Corp.
Equifax, Inc.
Equitable Resources, Inc.
Fannie Mae
Fastenal Co.
FDX Holding Corp.
Fedders Corp.
°Federal Home Loan
   Mortgage Corp.
Federal-Mogul Corp.
Federated Dept. Store
Fifth Third Bancorp
°First Chicago NBD
   Corp.
First Data Corp.
FirstFed Financial Corp.
Fleetwood Enterprises,
   Inc.
Fleming Cos., Inc.
Footstar, Inc.
Forest Laboratories, Inc.
Fort James Corp.
Freddie Mac

Frontier Corp.
Fuller (H. B.) Co.
Gap, Inc. (The)
Gardenburger, Inc.
Gateway 2000, Inc.
GATX Corp.
General Mills, Inc.
General Re Corp.
General Semiconductor
General Signal Corp.
Genuine Parts Co.
Gerber Scientific, Inc.
Giant Food, Inc.
Gibson Greetings, Inc.
Gillette Co.
Golden West Financial
Graco, Inc.
Grainger (W. W.), Inc.
Granite Construction
   Inc.
Great Atlantic & Pacific
   Tea Co., Inc.
Guidant Corp.
Gymboree Corp.
Handleman Co.
Hannaford Bros. Co.
Harcourt General
Harland (John H.) Co.
Harley Davidson, Inc.
Harman International
   Industries, Inc.
Hartford Steam Boiler
   Inspection and
   Insurance
Hartmarx Corp.
Hasbro, Inc.
HBO & Co.
Healthsouth Corp.
Heinz (H. J.) Co.
Helmerich & Payne, Inc.
Herman Miller, Inc.
Hershey Foods Corp.
Hewlett-Packard Co.
Hilfiger (Tommy) Corp.

Hillenbrand Industries,
   Inc.
Home Depot, Inc.
HON Industries, Inc.
°Household Inter-
   national, Inc.
Hubbell, Inc.
Huffy Corp.
Humana Health Plans,
   Inc.
Hunt Manufacturing Co.
Huntington Bancshare
Hutchinson Technology
Idaho Power Co.
Idex Corp.
Idexx Labs Corp.
Ikon Office Solutions
Illinois Tool Works, Inc.
IMCO Recycling, Inc.
IMS Health
Inland Steel Industries,
   Inc.
Inprise Corp.
Intel Corp.
Interface, Inc.
Invacare Corp.
Ionics, Inc.
Isco, Inc.
Jefferson-Pilot Corp.
Johnson & Johnson
Jostens, Inc.
Kaufman & Broad Home
   Corp.
Kellogg Co.
Kelly Services, Inc.
Keycorp
Kimberly-Clark Corp.
King World Productions,
   Inc.
KLA-Tencor Corp.
Kmart Corp.
Kohls Corp.
Kroger Co.
Lands' End, Inc.

Lawson Products, Inc.
Lee Enterprises, Inc.
Leggett & Platt
LG&E Energy Corp.
Lillian Vernon Corp.
Limited, Inc. (The)
°Lincoln National Corp.
Liz Claiborne, Inc.
Longs Drug Stores Corp.
Lowe's Cos., Inc.
LSI Logic Corp.
Luby's Cafeterias, Inc.
Lucent Technologies, Inc.
°Mallinckrodt, Inc.
Manor Care, Inc.
Marketspan Corp.
Marquette Medical Systems, Inc.
Marriott International, Inc.
Marsh & McLennan Cos., Inc.
Marshall & Ilsley Co.
Masco Corp.
Mattel, Inc.
May Department Stores Co.
Maytag Corp.
MBIA, Inc.
°MBNA Corp.
McDonald's Corp.
McGraw-Hill Cos.
MCI Communications Corp.
°MCN Corp.
Mead Corp.
Media General, Inc.
MediaOne Group, Inc.
Medtronic, Inc.
Mellon Bank Corp.
Mercantile Bancorp
Merck & Co., Inc.
Meredith Corp.
Merix Corp.

°Merrill Lynch & Co., Inc.
MGIC Investment Corp.
Micron Technology, Inc.
Microsoft Corp.
Milacron, Inc.
Miller Herman, Inc.
Millipore Corp.
Modine Manufacturing Co.
Modis Professional Services
Molex, Inc.
Moore Corp.
°Morgan (J. P.) & Co. Inc.
Morton International, Inc.
Mylan Laboratories, Inc.
Nalco Chemical Co.
National City Corp.
National Semiconductor Corp.
National Service Industries, Inc.
Nature's Sunshine Products, Inc.
Networks Associates, Inc.
New Century Energies, Inc.
New England Business Service, Inc.
New York Times Co.
Newell Co.
Nextel Communication
NICOR, Inc.
Nielsen Media Research
Nordson Corp.
Nordstrom, Inc.
°Norfolk Southern Corp.
Northern Trust Corp.
Northwest Natural Gas Co.
Northwestern Corp.
Norwest Corp.

Novell, Inc.
Nucor Corp.
Odwalla, Inc.
Oklahoma Gas and Electric Co.
Omnicom Group, Inc.
Oneida Ltd.
Oneok, Inc.
Oneworld Systems, Inc.
Oryx Energy Co.
Oshkosh B'Gosh
Owens & Minor, Inc.
Oxford Health Plans, Inc.
Parametric Technology
Patterson Dental Co.
Penney (J. C.) Co., Inc.
Pennzoil Co.
Peoples Energy Corp.
Peoplesoft, Inc.
Pep Boys—Manny, Moe & Jack
PepsiCo, Inc.
Perkin-Elmer Corp.
Philadelphia Suburban Co.
Phillips–Van Heusen Corp.
Pitney Bowes, Inc.
PNC Bank Corp.
Polaroid Corp.
°Potomac Electric Power Co.
Praxair, Inc.
Procter & Gamble Co.
Progressive Corp. Ohio
Providian Corp.
Pulte Corp.
QRS Corp.
Quaker Oats Co.
Qualcomm, Inc.
Quarterdeck Corp.
Ralston Purina Co.
Reebok International Ltd.
Regions Financial Corp.
°ReliaStar Financial Corp.
Rite Aid Corp.

Roadway Express, Inc.
°Rouse Co.
Rowan Cos., Inc.
Rubbermaid, Inc.
Ruby Tuesday, Inc.
Russell Corp.
Ryan's Family Steakhouse, Inc.
Ryder System, Inc.
SAFECO Corp.
Santa Fe Energy Resources, Inc.
SBC Communications, Inc.
Schering-Plough Corp.
Scholastic Corp.
Schwab (Charles) Corp.
Scientific-Atlanta, Inc.
Sealed Air Corp.
Sears, Roebuck and Co.
Service Corp. International
Shared Medical Systems Corp.
Shaw Industries, Inc.
Sherwin-Williams Co.
Sigma-Aldrich Corp.
Silicon Graphics, Inc.
Skyline Corp.
Skytel Communication
Slm Hldg. Corp.
Smith (A. O.) Corp.
Smucker (J. M.) Co.
Snap-On, Inc.
Sofamor/Danek Group
Solectron Corp.
Sonat, Inc.
Sonoco Products Co.
Southern New England Telecommunications Corp.
Southwest Airlines Co.
Spartan Motors, Inc.
Springs Industries, Inc.

Sprint Corp.
SPX Corp.
St. Jude Medical, Inc.
St. Paul Cos., Inc.
Standard Products Co.
Standard Register Co.
Stanley Works
Staples, Inc.
Starbucks Corp.
State Street Corp.
Stratus Computer, Inc.
Stride Rite Corp.
Stryker Corp.
Student Loan Marketing Association
Sun Co., Inc.
Sun Healthcare Group
Sun Microsystems, Inc.
Sunamerica
Sunrise Medical, Inc.
SunTrust Banks, Inc.
SUPERVALU, Inc.
Sybase, Inc.
Synovus Financial Corp.
Sysco Corp.
Tandy Corp.
TCBY Enterprises, Inc.
Tecumseh Products Co.
Tektronix, Inc.
Tele-Communications, Inc.
Telephone and Data Systems, Inc.
Tellabs, Inc.
Tennant Co.
Texas Instruments, Inc.
Thomas & Betts Corp.
Thomas Industries, Inc.
Timberland Co. (The)
°*Time Warner, Inc.*
Times Mirror Co.
Timken Co.
TJ International, Inc.
TJX Cos., Inc.

Tootsie Roll Industries, Inc.
Torchmark Corp.
Toro Co.
Toys R Us, Inc.
°Transamerica Corp.
°Travelers Group, Inc.
Trigon Healthcare, Inc.
Tupperware Corp.
UAL Corp.
Union Pacific Resources Group, Inc.
Unisource Worldwide
United American Healthcare Corp.
Universal Health Service
UNUM Corp.
US West
V. F. Corp.
Value Line, Inc.
Venator Group, Inc.
Vermont Financial Services Corp.
Viacom, Inc.
°*Viad Corp.*
Vincam Group, Inc. (The)
VLSI Technology
Wachovia Corp.
Wal-Mart Stores, Inc.
Walgreen Co.
Warnaco Group, Inc.
Washington Gas Light Co.
Washington Mutual, Inc.
Washington Post Co.
Watson Pharmaceutica
Watts Industries
Wellman, Inc.
Wellpoint Health Net
Wells Fargo & Co.
Wendy's International, Inc.
Wesco Financial Corp.
Western Atlas, Inc.
Westvaco Corp.
Whirlpool Corp.

Whitman Corp.
Whole Foods Market, Inc.
Williams Cos.
Worthington Foods, Inc.

Worthington Industries,
    Inc.
Wrigley (Wm.) Jr. Co.
Xerox Corp.

Xilinx, Inc.
Yankee Energy Systems,
    Inc.
Yellow Corp.

Good Money Industrial Average Companies

Source: Good Money, Inc., Box 502, Dover, NH 03821, www.goodmoney.com.

Ametek
Amoco
Avon Products
Callaway Golf
Consolidated Papers
Cross (A. T.)
Cummins Engines
Dayton Hudson
Fannie Mae

First Virginia Banks
Herman Miller
Hershey Foods
Home Depot
Johnson & Johnson
Maytag
McDonald's
Merck & Co.
Microsoft

Nordstrom
Pitney Bowes
Procter & Gamble Co.
The Rouse Co.
US West Communi-
    cations
Washington Post
Worthington Industries

Natural Business Indexes

Some of the companies listed below focused only a minor portion of their overall business on natural products.

Key: 1 = Healthy Living Index, maintained by Adams, Harkness & Hill. Source: *Healthy Living Newsletter* (617-371-3900) (December 1998). 2 = Natural Business Composite Index, maintained by NationsBanc Montgomery Securities LLC. Source: *Natural Business Newsletter* (303-442-8983) (January 1999). 3 = Natural Food and Health Stock Index.

Source: Natural Food Merchandiser (303-939-8440) (February 1999).

BOTANICALS AND DIETARY SUPPLEMENTS

4Health Inc. (2, 3)
AMBI, Inc. (1, 2, 3)
Bionurtrics, Inc. (1, 2)
Carrington Laboratories
    (2)
Chai-Na-Ta Corp. (2, 3)
Chattem Inc. (2, 3)
Cyanotech (2, 3)
Futurebiotics (2, 3)

General Nutrition Co. (3)
Gumtech International
    Inc. (2)
HealthRite (2)
Imperial Ginseng (2)
IVC Industries (Interna-
    tional Vitamin) (1, 2, 3)
Martek Biosciences (2, 3)
Natrol Inc. (1, 2, 3)
Naturade (2)
Natural Alternatives Intl.
    (1, 2, 3)

Natural Health Trends (2)
NBTY Inc. (1, 2, 3)
NSA International (2)
Nutraceutical Interna-
    tional (1, 2, 3)
PacificHealth Labs Inc. (2)
Paracelsian (2)
PDK Labs Inc. (2)
Perrigo (2)
PharmaPrint (1, 2, 3)
Pure World (2, 3)
Quigley Corp. (2, 3)

Rexall Sundown (1, 2, 3)
Scottsdale Scientific Inc.
(2)
Shaman Pharmaceuticals
(2)
Superior Supplements (2)
Twinlab Corp. (1, 2, 3)
Weider Nutrition Inter-
national (1, 2, 3)
Whitewing Labs (2)
Zila Incorporated (2)

FOOD AND BEVERAGE

Ben & Jerry's Homemade
(2, 3)
Balance Bar (1, 2)
Celestial Seasonings
(1, 2, 3)
Delicious Brands Inter-
national (2)
Fresh Juice Co., Inc. (2, 3)
Galaxy Foods (2)
Gardenburger (1, 2, 3)
HJ Heinz (Earth's Best)
(2, 3)
Hain Food Group (1, 2, 3)
Hansen Natural Corp.
(2, 3)
Hauser (1, 3)
Horizon Organic (2, 3)
J. M. Smuckers (2, 3)
Lifeway (2)

Monterey Pasta Co. (2)
Odwalla (1, 2, 3)
Opta Food Ingredients
(1, 2, 3)
Organic Food Products (2)
Perrigo (2)
Tofutti Brands (2)
Vermont Pure Holdings
(2, 3)
Vitafort International (2)
Worthington Foods
(1, 2, 3)

CONSUMER PRODUCTS

Healthy Planet Products
(2)
Real Goods (2, 3)
Seventh Generation (2)

PERSONAL CARE PRODUCTS

CNS, Inc. (Breathe
Right) (2)
RMED International,
Inc. (Tushies) (2)
Senetek PLC (2)

NATURAL PRODUCT DIRECT
NETWORK MARKETING

Amway Asia Pacific Ltd.
(3)

Herbalife International
Inc. (1, 2, 3)
Nature's Sunshine Prod-
ucts (1, 2, 3)
Nu Skin Enterprises
(1, 2, 3)
Nutrition for Life Inter-
national, Inc. (1, 2)
Reliv International Inc.
(1, 2)
Usana Inc. (1, 2, 3)

RETAIL AND DISTRIBUTION

Amcon Distributing
(2)
Archer-Daniels-Midland
Co. (3)
Body Shop International
(2)
Garden Botanika (1, 2)
Garden Fresh Restau-
rants (1)
General Nutrition Cen-
ters (1, 2, 3)
United Natural Foods
(1, 2, 3)
Whole Foods Market
(1, 2, 3)
Wild Oats Markets
(1, 2, 3)

Clean Utilities

Source: Compiled by the authors, December 1998.

NATURAL GAS: UTILITIES
AND DISTRIBUTORS

AGL Resources
Aquila Gas Pipeline
Atmos Energy

Bay State Gas
BC Gas Berkshire Gas
Cascade Natural Gas
Chesapeake Utility
CMS Energy
Coastal

Colonial Gas
Connecticut Energy
Columbia Energy
Consolidated Natural Gas
Consumers Gas Group
CTG Resources

Delta Natural Gas
Eastern Enterprises
El Paso Energy
Enbridge
Energen
Energy West
Energynorth
Energysouth
Enron
Equitable Resources
Fall River Gas
Indiana Energy
Keyspan Energy
KN Energy
Laclede Gas
MCN Energy
MDU Resources
    Group
National Fuel Gas
Natural Fuel Gas
NC Natural Gas
Nicor
NJ Resources
Northwest Natural Gas
NUI
New Jersey Resources

North Carolina Natural
    Gas
Northern Border Partners
Northwest Natural Gas
Oneok
Pennsylvania Enterprises
Peoples Energy
Piedmont Natural Gas
Providence Energy
Public Service of NC
Roanoke Gas
Seagull Energy
SEMCO Energy
Sempra Energy
Sonat
South Jersey Industries
Southern Union
Southwest Gas
Southwestern Energy
TransCanada Pipelines
UGI
Valley Resources
Virginia Gas
Washington Gas & Light
Westcoast Energy
Western Gas Resources

WICOR
Williams Cos.
Yankee Energy Systems

WATER UTILITY
COMPANIES

American States Water
American Water Works
Aquarion
Artesian Resources
Birmingham Utilities
California Water Service
Connecticut Water
    Service
Consumers Water
Dominguez Services
E'Town
Middlesex Water
Pennichuck
Philadelphia Suburban
SJW Corp.
Southwest Water
United Water Resources
Western Water
York Water

Best Companies Lists

COUNCIL ON ECONOMIC PRIORITIES HONOR ROLL

CEP looks at eight separate categories: environment, community, charitable contributions, minority advancement, women advancement, workplace issues, family benefits, and public disclosure. They assign points for each category and then convert to a college grade system (4.0 being the highest score). The top 40 companies make their Honor Roll. Data are from research performed in 1997.

Adolph Coors Co.
Anheuser-Busch
Applied Materials
Avon Products, Inc.
BankAmerica Corp.
BankBoston Corp.
Baxter International

Ben & Jerry's Home-
    made, Inc.
Bristol-Myers Squibb
    Co.
Chevron Corp.
Citicorp
Coca-Cola Co.

Colgate-Palmolive
Corning, Inc.
Deluxe Corp.
Dole Food Co.
Gannett, Inc.
Healthy Planet Products,
    Inc.

Herman Miller, Inc.
Hewlett-Packard Co.
International Business
    Machines
Johnson & Johnson
Kellogg Co.
Keyspan

McGraw-Hill Cos.
Merck & Co., Inc.
Pacificare Health Sys-
    tems, Inc.
PepsiCo, Inc.
Pfizer, Inc.
Piper Jaffray Cos., Inc.

Polaroid Corp.
Seventh Generation, Inc.
Starbucks Corp.
Sun Co.
Tennant Co.
UNUM Corp.
Xerox Corp.

THE 100 BEST COMPANIES FOR WORKING MOTHERS

Source: O. Wilbur in *Working Mother,* October 1998. Reprinted with the permission of MacDonald Communications Corp. Copyright 1998 by MacDonald Communications Corp.

Acacia Life Insurance Co.
Aetna, Inc.
Allstate Insurance Co.
American Express Co.
American Home Prod-
    ucts Corp.
Amoco Corp.
AT&T Corp.
Autodesk, Inc.
Bankers Trust Corp.
Bausch & Lomb
Bayfront Medical Center,
    Inc.
The Benjamin Group,
    Inc.
Beth Israel Deaconess
    Medical Center
BP Exploration (Alaska),
    Inc.
Bristol-Myers Squibb Co.
Bureau of National
    Affairs, Inc.
Calvert Group
Chase Manhattan Bank
Chrysler Corp.
Cigna Corp.
Cinergy Corp.
Citicorp/Citibank
Commercial Financial
    Services, Inc.

Coopers & Lybrand
    LLP
Corning, Inc.
Dayton Hudson Corp.
Deloitte & Touche
Donaldson, Lufkin &
    Jenrette, Inc.
Dupont Co.
Dupont Pharmaceuticals
    Co.
Eastman Kodak Co.
Ernst & Young LLP
Fannie Mae
Federal Express Corp.
First Chicago NBD Corp.
First Tennessee Bank
First Union Corp.
Gannett Co., Inc.
General Mills, Inc.
Glaxo Wellcome, Inc.
GTE Corp.
Hallmark Cards, Inc.
Hewlett-Packard Co.
Hill, Holliday, Connors,
    Cosmopulos
Hoffman–La Roche, Inc.
IBM
Imation
JFK Medical Center
Johnson & Johnson

S. C. Johnson & Son, Inc.
KPMG Peat Marwick
    LLP
Life Technologies, Inc.
Eli Lilly & Co.
Lincoln Financial Group
Lotus Development
Lucent Technologies,
    Inc.
Marriott International
MassMutual
Mattel, Inc.
MBNA America Bank,
    N.A.
Mentor Graphics Corp.
Merck & Co., Inc.
Merrill Lynch & Co.,
    Inc.
Millipore Corp.
J. P. Morgan
NationsBank
Neuville Industries, Inc.
Northern Trust Corp.
Patagonia, Inc.
Pfizer, Inc.
Phoenix Home Life
    Mutual Insurance
Price Waterhouse LLP
Principal Financial
    Group

Procter & Gamble Co.
Prudential
Rex Healthcare, Inc.
Ridgeview, Inc.
Rockwell
Salt River Project
Sara Lee Corp.
SAS Institute, Inc.
Seattle Times Co.
Security Benefit Group
Sequent Computer Systems, Inc.

SNET (Southern New England Telecommunications)
St. Luke's Hospital of Kansas City
St. Paul Cos.
Stride Rite Corp.
Texas Instruments, Inc.
Tom's of Maine, Inc.
TRW, Inc.
Turner Broadcasting System, Inc.

Union Pacific Resources Group, Inc.
Universal Studios, Inc.
UNUM Life Insurance Co. of America
UPMC Health System
USAA (United Services Automobile Association)
Vanguard Group
Warner-Lambert Co.
Xerox Corp.

Sustainability Sector Companies

These companies are chosen for their participation in their respective industries. They are not necessarily screened for other social or environmental issues.

Source: Compiled by the authors.

SOLAR

Astropower (APWR)
Energy Conversion Devices (ENER)
Golden Genesis (GGGO)
Real Goods (RGTC)
Spire (SPIR)

BIOREMEDIATION

U.S. Microbics (BUGS)

FUEL CELLS AND HYDROGEN POWER

Ballard Power Systems (BLDPF)
Energy Research Corp. (ERC)

ENERGY CONSERVATION

Advanced Lighting (ADLT)
Southwall Technologies (SWTX)

CLEAN TRANSPORTATION

BAT International (BAAT)
Cannondale (BIKE)
Electric Fuel (EFCX)
GT Bicycles (GTBX)
IMPCO Technologies (IMCO)
Unique Mobility (UQM)
Zap Power Systems (ZAPP)

TREE-SAVERS

Kafus Environmental (KS)
TJ International (TJCO)

RECYCLING AND ENVIRONMENTAL CLEANUP

Appliance Recycling (ARCI)
Commodore Applied Technologies (CXI)
Green Oasis (GRNO)
Hi-Rise (HIRI)
IMCO Recycling (IMR)
N-Viro International (NVIC)
Recycling Industries (RECY)
Rich Coast (KRHC)
Safety-Kleen (SK)
Waste Recovery (WRII)
Wellman (WLM)

Appendix C:
Avoidance Screening Lists

Some Publicly Traded Alcoholic Beverage Companies

Source: Compiled by the authors.

Adolph Coors
American Craft
  Brewing
Anheuser-Busch
Beringer Wine Estates
Big Rock Brewery Ltd.
Boston Beer
Brown-Forman
Canandaigua Brands
Capital Beverage
Central European
  Distributors
Chalone Wine

Companhia Cervecerias
  Unidas
Corby Distillers
Diageo PLC
Fredrick Brewing
Geerlings & Wade
Golden State Vintners
Heineken NV
Independence Brewing
Kirin Brewery
Lion Brewery
LVMH Moët Hennessey
  LV

Minnesota Brewing
Molson Cos.
R. H. Phillips
Pyramid Breweries
Quilmes Industrial SA
Redhook Ale Brewery
Ricard Pernod
Robert Mondavi
Seagram Co. Ltd.
Todhunter International
Unibroue

Environmental Pollution: Companies Operating Facilities Releasing Highest Amounts of Toxic Chemicals into the Environment

Source: 1996 Toxic Release Inventory data from the Environmental Protection Agency, compiled by the Environmental Defense Fund.

ADM
Allied-Signal
American Chrome &
  Chemicals
Amoco Petroleum
  Products
Anchor Continental
Angus Chemical
Arco Chemical
Armco
Asarco
BASF

Bayer
BHP Copper Metals
BP Chemicals
Cabot
CF Industries
Champion International
Chemetals
Chevron Products
Chino Mines
Climax Molybdenum
Coastal Chem
Courtaulds Fibers

Cyprus Miami Mining
Cytec Industries
Devro-Teepak
Doe Run
Dow Chemical
DSM Chemicals NA
Dupont
Eastman Chemical
Eastman Kodak
Elkem Metal
Engelhard
Exxon Co. USA

Federal Paper Board
FMC
Gencorp
Georgia-Pacific
GM Powertrain
    Defiance
Granite City Steel
Great Southern Paper
Hoechst-Celanese
    Chemical
Huntsman Petroleum
IBP
IMC-Agrico
IMC Nitrogen
Inland Container
International Paper

ISP Technologies
Kennecott Utah Copper
Kerr-McGee Chemical
Lenzig Fibers
Magnesium Corp. of
    America
Mead Coated Board
Mobil Chemical
Mobil Oil
Monsanto
John Morrell & Co.
Northwestern Steel & Wire
Occidental Chemical
PCS Phosphate
Pharmacia & Upjohn
Phelps Dodge Hildago

Royal Oak
    Entertainment
Rubicon
SCM Chemical Americas
Sterling Chemicals
Terra Nitrogen
Triad Chemical
Union Camp
Uniroyal Chemical
United States Steel
Unocal Agricultural
    Products
Vicksburg Chemical
Westvaco
Weyerhaeuser
Witco Corp.

Some Publicly Traded Companies in Gambling and Related Industries

Source: Compiled by the authors.

Acres Gaming   ·
Alliance Gaming
Alpha Hospitality
American Coin Mer-
    chandise
American Gaming &
    Entertainment
American Wagering
Ameristar Casino
Anchor Gaming
Argosy Gaming
AutoTote
Aztar
Black Hawk Gaming &
    Development
Boyd Gaming
Casino Data Systems
Century Casinos
Churchill Downs
Circus Circus
Colonial Downs
Colorado Casino Resorts
Dover Downs

Florida Gaming
Full House Resorts
GLC
Global Casinos
Grand Casinos
Harrahs Entertainment
Harveys Casino Resorts
Hilton Hotels
Hollywood Casino
Hollywood Park
International Game
    Technology
International Lottery/
    Totalizer
Isle of Capri Casinos
Jackpot Enterprises
Ladbroke Group
MGM Grand
Mikohn Gaming
Mirage Resorts
Penn National Gaming
Players International
Powerhouse Technology

Primadonna Resort
Radica Games
Rio Hotel & Casino
Riviera Holdings
Shuffle Master
Silicon Gaming
Station Casinos
Stuart Entertainment
Trump Hotel & Casino
Wells-Gardner
WMS Industries

U.S. Public Utilities Operating Nuclear Power Plants

Source: American Nuclear Society Publication *Nuclear News,* March 1998. Data are valid as of August 31, 1997.

Ameren Corp.
American Electric Power
Arizona Public Service Co.
Baltimore Gas & Electric Co.
Boston Edison Co.
Carolina Power & Light Co.
Commonwealth Edison Co.
Consolidated Edison Co.
Consumers Energy Co.
Detroit Edison Co.
Duke Power Co.
Duquesne Light Co.
Energy Operations, Inc.
FirstEnergy
Florida Power & Light Co.
Florida Power Corp.
GPU Nuclear Energy
IES Utilities, Inc.

Illinois Power Co.
Nebraska Public Power District
New York Power Authority
Niagara Mohawk Power Corp.
North Atlantic Energy Service Corp.
Northeast Utilities
Northern States Power Co.
Omaha Public Power District
Pacific Gas & Electric Co.
PECO Energy Co.
PP&L, Inc.
Public Service Electric & Gas Co.
Rochester Gas & Electric Corp.
South Carolina Electric & Gas Co.

South Texas Nuclear Operating Co.
Southern California Edison Co. and San Diego Gas & Electric Co.
Southern Nuclear Operating Co.
Tennessee Valley Authority
Texas Utilities Electric Co.
Toledo Edison Co.
Vermont Yankee Nuclear Power Corp.
Virginia Power
Washington Public Power Supply System
Wisconsin Electric Power Co.
Wisconsin Public Service Corp.
Wolf Creek Nuclear Operating Corp.

Repressive Regimes: Some Companies Invested in Burma

This list is not in any representative order, nor is it comprehensive. The IRRC publishes a more comprehensive quarterly list of companies in Burma.

Source: Investor Responsibility Research Center.

Daewoo Corp. (South Korea)
Indochina Goldfields, Inc. (Canada)
InterDigital Communications Corp. (United States)

Mitsubishi Corp. (Japan)
Mitsui & Co. Ltd. (Japan)
Nippon Oil (Japan)
Petroliam Nasional Bhd. (Petronas) (Malaysia)

Premier Oil PLC (United Kingdom)
Total SA (France)
Unocal Corp. (United States)

Total is the largest foreign investor in Burma, and Unocal is the largest U.S. investor there. Both companies, along with Nippon, Petronas, and Premier, hold interests in

Burma's key development project: a $1.2 billion offshore gas project venture led by Total.

Tobacco Companies

Source: Social Investment Forum, May 1998.

800-JR Cigar, Inc.
American Group Ltd.
BAT Industries
Brooke Group Ltd.
Caribbean Cigar Corp.
Consolidated Cigar Corp.
Dimon, Inc.
Dominican Cigar Corp.
Empresas La Moderna
   SA DE CV

Gallaher Group PLC
General Cigar Corp.
Holt's Cigar Holdings
Imperial Tobacco Group
   PLC
Loews Corp.
Oroamerica, Inc.
Philip Morris Cos., Inc.
Premium Cigars Interna-
   tional

RJR Nabisco Holdings
   Corp.
Schweitzer Maudiut
   International
Standard Commercial Corp.
Swedish Match
Swisher International
Tamboril Cigar Corp.
Universal Corp.
UST, Inc.

The 100 Largest Military Contractors

Data are for fiscal year 1997. Numbers in parentheses indicate rank order.

Source: Publication DIOR/PO1-97, U.S. Government Printing Office, Washington, DC 20402.

Aerospace Corp. (41)
Alleghey Teledyne, Inc.
   (91)
Alliant Techsystems, Inc.
   (30)
Allied Signal, Inc. (23)
American Automar, Inc.
   (81)
AT&T (67)
Atlantic Richfield Co.
   (51)
Avondale Industries, Inc.
   (19)
BDM International, Inc.
   (29)
Bechtel Group, Inc. (50)
Bell Atlantic Corp. (99)
Bergen Brunswig Corp.
   (98)

Boeing Co. (2)
Boeing Sikorsky
   Comanche Team (78)
Booz Allen & Hamilton,
   Inc. (34)
BTG, Inc. (92)
CBS Corp. (15)
Chevron Corp. (48)
Chrysler Corp. (75)
Clark Enterprises, Inc.
   (73)
Computer Sciences Corp.
   (17)
Draper, Charles Starks,
   Laboratories (74)
Dyncorp (25)
Electronic Data Systems
   Corp. (33)
Exxon Corp. (24)

Federal Express Corp.
   (45)
Federal Prison Indus-
   tries, Inc. (71)
Federal Republic of Ger-
   many (95)
FMC Corp. (37)
Foundation Health Sys-
   tems, Inc. (18)
Gencorp, Inc. (89)
General Dynamics Corp.
   (4)
General Electric Co., Inc.
   (8)
General Electric Co.
   PLC (53)
General Motors Corp. (6)
Government of Canada
   (68)

Government Technology
   Services (77)
GTE Corp. (12)
Gulfstream Aerospace
   Corp. (94)
Halliburton Co., Inc. (44)
Harris Corp. (63)
Hensel Phelps Construc-
   tion Co. (69)
Highmark, Inc. (59)
Honeywell, Inc. (72)
Humana, Inc. (20)
International Business
   Machines (79)
International Shipholding
   Corp. (97)
ITT Industries, Inc. (13)
The Johns Hopkins Uni-
   versity, Inc. (76)
Johnson Controls, Inc.
   (47)
Kaman Corp. (90)
Kuwait Petroleum Corp.
   (86)
Litton Industries, Inc. (9)
Lockheed Martin Corp.
   (1)
Logicon, Inc. (35)
Longbow LLC (34)
Maersk, Inc. (61)
Mantech International
   Corp. (70)

Massachusetts Institute
   of Tech. (32)
MCI Communications
   Corp. (60)
McKesson Corp. (100)
Mitre Corp., The (40)
Motorola, Inc. (39)
Nassco Holdings, Inc. (46)
Newport News Ship-
   building, Inc. (16)
Nichols Research Corp.
   (52)
Northrop Grumman
   Corp. (3)
OHM Corp. (42)
Olin Corp. (82)
Oshkosh Truck Corp. (66)
Philip Morris Cos., Inc.
   (88)
Phillip Holzmann
   Aktiengesells (58)
Primex Technologies,
   Inc. (96)
Procter & Gamble Co. (56)
Raytheon Co., Inc. (5)
Renco Group, Inc. (38)
Rockwell International
   Corp. (28)
Rolls-Royce PLC (57)
Science Applications
   International Corp.
   (11)

Shell Oil Co. (43)
Soltek of San Diego (87)
Southwest Marine, Inc.
   (85)
Ssangyong (USA), Inc.
   (84)
Standard Missile Co.
   LLC (27)
Stewart & Stevenson Ser-
   vices (49)
Sverdrup Corp. (36)
Texas Instruments, Inc.
   (26)
Texas Instruments/Martin
   Marietta (62)
Textron, Inc. (10)
Thiokol Corp. (83)
Tracor, Inc. (22)
Triwest Healthcare
   Alliance (64)
TRW, Inc. (14)
Unisys Corp. (65)
United Defense, LP
   (21)
United States Depart-
   ment of Energy (31)
United Technologies
   Corp. (7)
Vanstar Corp. (80)
VSE Corp. (93)
Worldcorp., Inc. (55)

The Top 50 Nuclear Weapons Contractors

Data are for fiscal year 1997. Numbers in parentheses indicate rank order.

Source: Department of Defense data compiled by Eagle Eye Publishers.

Alliant Techsystems, Inc.
   (15)
Allied Signal, Inc. (16)
Bath Holding Corp.
   (8)

BDM Corp. (12)
Boeing Co. (2)
Colsa Corp. (26)
Computer Science/
   Raytheon (17)

Continental Maritime
   Industries (46)
Draper, Charles Stark,
   Laboratories (13)
Dynetics, Inc. (37)

Eaton Corp. (29)
Gencorp, Inc. (32)
General Dynamics Corp. (9)
General Electric Co. (7)
General Electric Co. PLC (48)
Thomas W. A. Hoffman (24)
Honeywell, Inc. (27)
ITT Corp. (36)
The Johns Hopkins University (45)
Johnson Controls (18)
K Systems, Inc. (34)
Litton Industries, Inc. (5)
Lockheed Martin Corp. (1)
Lucas Industries, Inc. (33)

Mevatec Corp. (38)
Motorola Corp. (30)
Nassco Holdings (50)
Newport News Shipbuilding, Inc. (10)
Nichols Research Corp. (22)
Northrop Grumman Corp. (3)
Ogden Corp. (47)
Olin Corp. (40)
Orbital Sciences Corp. (42)
Owen Corp. Systems Group (20)
Raytheon Co., Inc. (4)
Rolls Royce PLC (41)
Science Applications International Corp. (21)

Sequa Corp. (35)
Southwest Marine, Inc. (19)
Sparta, Inc. (43)
Teledyne, Inc. (23)
Texas Instruments, Inc. (39)
Textron, Inc. (44)
Thermo Electron Corp. (44)
Thiokol Corp. (31)
Tracor, Inc. (14)
TRW, Inc. (11)
United Technologies Corp. (6)
Wales-Weapon Systems Engineering (49)
Westinghouse Electric Corp. (28)

Some Publicly Traded Firearms and Ammunition Companies

Olin Industries (Winchester brand)

Sturn Ruger & Co. (Ruger brand)

Tompkins PLC (Smith & Wesson brand)

National Foreign Trade Council

As mentioned in Chapter 8, the National Foreign Trade Council (NFTC) brought suit against the state of Massachusetts in 1998, challenging the Massachusetts Burma Law. The companies listed here are on the board of directors of the NFTC, which has led the campaign to restrict local and state governments' right to enact selective purchasing laws.

Source: NFTC Web site (www.nftconline.org).

ABB
Allied Signal, Inc.
American Home Products Corp.
American International Underwriters
Amoco Corp.
ARCO
Arthur Andersen & Co.

AT&T International
Bank of America NT&SA
Bank of New York
Bankers Trust Co.
Bechtel Group, Inc.
Boeing Co.
Boise Cascade Corp.
Caltex Petroleum Corp.
Caterpillar, Inc.

Chase Manhattan Bank
Chevron USA, Inc.
Chrysler Corp.
Chubb Group of Insurance Cos.
Citibank NA
Colgate-Palmolive Co.
Dewey Ballantine
Digital Equipment Corp.

Dresser Industries., Inc.
E. I. du Pont de
    Nemours & Co.
Duracell International,
    Inc.
Eastman Kodak Co.
Ernst & Young
First National Bank of
    Chicago
General Electric Co.
General Motors Corp.
Gillette Co.
W. R. Grace & Co.
Halliburton Co.

IBM Corp.
Ingersoll-Rand Co.
ITT Corp.
Johnson & Johnson
Mars Inc.
McDermott Inc.
Mobil Oil Corp.
Monsanto Co.
National Foreign Trade
    Council
Oil Capital Ltd., Inc.
PepsiCo Foods & Bever-
    ages International
Pfizer International, Inc.

Price Waterhouse
Procter & Gamble Co.
Ridgewood Group Inter-
    national Ltd.
Rockwell International
    Corp.
Steptoe & Johnson
Texaco, Inc.
Towers Perrin
United Technologies
    Corp.
Warner-Lambert Co.
Westinghouse Electric
    Corp.

Appendix D:
Community Investing
Resources

Bank and Credit Union Associations

These organizations can help you find the community banks and credit unions in your area:

Coalition of Community Development Financial Institutions (CDFI)
924 Cherry Street, 2nd Floor, Philadelphia, PA 19107
215-923-5363, www.cdfi.org

National Federation of Community Development Credit Unions
120 Wall Street, 10th Floor, New York, NY 10005
212-809-1850, www.natfed.org

Some Community Banks and Credit Unions

Sources: Social Investment Forum Web site, *GreenMoney Journal.*

Albina Community Bank, Portland, OR, 800-814-6088, www.albinabank.com
Alternatives Federal Credit Union, Ithaca, NY, 607-273-4666, www.alternatives.org
Bank Boston/First Community Bank, Boston, MA, 617-434-5105, www.bank-boston.com
Community Bank of the Bay, Oakland CA, 800-632-3263
Community Capital Bank, Brooklyn, NY, 718-802-1212, www.cdfi.org/ccb.html
Elk Horn Bank, Arkadelphia, PA, 800-789-3428, www.ehbt.com
First National Bank of Santa Fe's Community Connection Banking Fund, Santa Fe, NM, 888-912-2265
Louisville Community Development Bank, Louisville, KY, 502-775-2510
NCB Savings Bank, Hillsboro, OH, 800-322-1251
Permaculture Credit Union, PO Box 3702, Pojoaque, NM 87501
Self-Help Credit Union, Durham, NC, 800-966-7353, www.self-help.org
Shorebank Pacific, Ilwaco, WA 888-326-2265, www.eco-bank.com
South Shore Bank of Chicago's Development Deposits, Chicago, IL, 800-669-7725, www.sbk.com

Vermont Development Credit Union, Burlington, VT, 802-865-3404, www.
vdcu.org
Vermont National Bank, Brattleboro, VT, 800-772-3863, www.vnb.com
Wainwright Bank and Trust, Boston, MA, 800-444-2265, www.wainwrightbank.com

Loan Fund and Community Development Resources

These organizations can help you find loan fund and community development
resources in your area:

Community Development Venture Capital Alliance
700 Lonsdale Building, Duluth, MN 55802
218-722-0861

Corporation for Enterprise Development
777 North Capitol Street NE, Suite 410, Washington, DC 20002
202-408-9788, www.cfed.org

National Community Capital Association (formerly the National Association
of Community Development Loan Funds)
924 Cherry Street, 2nd Floor, Philadelphia, PA 19107
215-923-4754, www.communitycapital.org

National Community Reinvestment Coalition
733 15th Street NW, #540, Washington, DC 20005
202-628-8866

National Congress for Community Economic Development
11 Dupont Circle, #325, Washington, DC 20036
202-234-5009

Woodstock Institute, 407 S. Dearborn, Suite 550, Chicago, IL 60605
312-427-8070, www.nonprofit.net/woodstock/

National Community Capital Association Members
Source: Membership list provided by the Association.

Alternatives Federal Credit Union, Ithaca, NY, 607-273-4611
Anawim Fund of the Midwest, Oak Park, IL, 708-848-2073
Boston Community Capital, Jamaica Plain, MA, 617-522-6768
Capital District Community Loan Fund, Albany, NY, 518-436-8586
Cascadia Revolving Fund, Seattle, WA, 206-447-9226
Chicago Community Loan Fund, Chicago, IL, 312-922-1350
Coastal Enterprise, Inc., Wiscasset, ME, 207-882-7552

Common Wealth Revolving Loan Fund, Youngstown, OH, 330-744-2667
Community First Fund, Lancaster, PA, 717-393-2351
Community Loan Fund of SW Pennsylvania, Pittsburgh, PA, 412-381-9965
Cooperative Fund of New England, Hartford, CT, 910-395-6008
Cornerstone-Homesource Regional Loan Fund, Cincinnati, OH, 513-985-0774
CSP of West Alabama's CDLF, Tuscaloosa, AL, 205-752-5429
Delaware Valley Community Reinvestment Fund, Philadelphia, PA, 215-925-1130
Enterprise Corporation of the Delta, Jackson, MS, 601-944-1100
Federation of Appalachian Housing Enterprise, Berea, KY, 606-986-2321
First State Community Loan Fund, Wilmington, DE, 302-652-6674
Greater New Haven Community Loan Fund, New Haven, CT, 203-789-8690
HEAD Community Loan Fund, Berea, KY, 606-986-3283
Housing Assistance Council, Washington, DC, 202-842-8600
Illinois Facilities Fund, Chicago, IL, 312-629-0060
Impact Seven, Inc., Alaena, WI, 715-357-3334
Institute for Community Economics, Springfield, MA, 413-746-8660
Lakota Fund, Kyle, SD, 605-455-2500
Leviticus 25:23 Alternative Fund, Yonkers, NY, 914-237-3306
Local Enterprise Assistance Fund, Boston, MA, 617-542-5363
Low Income Housing Fund, San Francisco, CA, 415-777-9804
MACED, Berea, KY, 606-986-2373
McAuley Institute, Silver Spring, MD, 301-588-8110
Mercy Loan Fund, Denver, CO, 303-830-3300
Montana Community Development Corp., Missoula, MT, 406-543-3550
Montreal Community Loan Association, Montreal, Quebec, 514-844-9882
Neighborhoods, Inc. of Battle Creek, Battle Creek, MI, 616-986-1113
New Hampshire Community Loan Fund, Concord, NH, 603-224-6669
New Jersey Community Loan Fund, Trenton, NJ, 609-989-7766
New Mexico Community Development Loan Fund, Albuquerque, NM,
    505-243-3196
Nonprofit Facilities Fund, New York, NY, 212-868-6710
Northcountry Cooperative Development Fund, Minneapolis, MN, 612-331-9103
Northeast Entrepreneur Fund, Virginia, MN, 218-749-4191
Northern California Community Loan Fund, San Francisco, CA, 415-392-8215
Northland Foundation, Duluth, MN, 218-723-4040
Ohio Community Development Finance Fund, Columbus, OH, 614-221-1114
Rural Community Assistance Corp., Sacramento, CA, 916-447-2854
Seedco, New York, NY, 212-473-0255
Self-Help Ventures Fund, Durham, NC, 919-956-4400
Unitarian Universalist Affordable Housing Corp., Washington, DC, 202-588-1010
Vermont Community Loan Fund, Montpelier, VT 05601, 802-223-1448
Washington Area Community Investment Fund, Washington, DC, 202-462-4727
Worcester Community Housing Resources, Worcester, MA, 508-799-6106

Other Community Development Loan Funds and Nonprofits

Source: Compiled by the authors, December 1998.

Accion New York, Brooklyn, NY, 718-599-5170
Adirondack Economic Development Corp., Saranac Lake, NY, 518-891-5523
California Organized Investment Network, 916-492-3525
Calvert Foundation's Community Investments, Bethesda, MD, 800-248-0337
Community Reinvestment Fund, Minneapolis, MN, 800-475-3050
Ecotrust, Portland, OR, 503-227-6225
Federation of Southern Cooperatives, Epes, AL, 205-652-9676
First Nations Development Institute, Fredericksburg, VA, 540-371-5615
Grassroots Economic Organizing Newsletter, New Haven, CT, 203-389-6194
Latino Economic Development Corp., Washington, DC, 202-588-5102
Manna, Inc., Washington, DC, 202-232-2844
Micro Industry Credit Rural Organization, Tucson, AZ, 520-622-3553
Partners for the Common Good Loan Fund, San Antonio, TX, 210-431-0616
Support Financial Services, Lafayette, CO, 303-499-8189
A Territory Resource, Seattle, WA, 206-624-4081
White Earth Land Recovery Project, White Earth, MN, 218-473-3110
Women's Initiative for Self-Employment, San Francisco, CA, 415-247-9473
Women's Opportunity Fund, Oak Brook, IL, 800-793-9455
Women's Self-Employment Project (Chicago Full Circle Fund), Chicago, IL, 312-606-8255
Working Capital, Cambridge, MA, 617-576-8620

International Community Development Financial Institutions

These organizations can help you find international community development financial institutions in your area:

Accion International and USA
120 Beacon Street, Somerville, MA 02143
617-492-4930, www.accion.org

Ecumenical Development Co-operative Society (EDCS)
1511 K Street NW, #1165, Washington, DC 20005
202-628-5067

Grameen Bank USA and Foundation
236 New York Avenue NW, #101, Washington, DC 20006
202-628-3560, www.citechco.net/grameen, www.grameenfoundation.org

Katalysis North/South Development Partnership
1331 North Commerce Street, Stockton, CA 95202
209-943-6165

Microcredit Summit Campaign
236 Massachusetts Avenue NE, #310, Washington, DC 20002
202-546-1900, www.microcreditsummit.org

Nicaraguan Community Development Loan Fund
c/o WCCN, PO Box 1534, Madison, WI 53701
608-257-7230, www.execpc.com/~wccn

One World /Community Development Resources
www.oneworld.org
The Self-Employed Women's Association (SEWA) (India)
www.soc.titech.ac.jp/icm/sewa.html

Shared Interest
80 Fifth Avenue, #803, New York, NY 10011
212-229-2709

The Virtual Library of Microcredit
www.soc.titech.ac.jp/icm/icm.html

Women's Development Network
4550 Massachusetts Avenue NW, Wesley Box 67, Washington, DC 20016
202-885-8778

Women's World Banking
8 West 40th Street, New York, NY 10016
212-768-8513

Other Community Investing Web Sites

Aspen Institute	www.aspeninst.org
Bank of America	www.bankamerica.com
Calvert Foundation	www.calvertgroup.com/foundation
Canadian Community Investing	www.web.net/~invest
Center for Enterprise Development	www.cfed.org
Coalition of CDFIs	www.cdfi.org
Cooperative Fund of New England	www.cooperativefund.org
Dubuque Bank & Trust	www.dubuquebank.com
Ecotrust	www.ecotrust.org
Enterprise Development	www.enterweb.org

Interaction	www.interaction.org
Microenterprise Innovation Project	www.mip.org
National Community Capital Bank	www.communitycapital.org
National Cooperative Bank	www.ncb.org
Results Education Fund	www.results.action.org
U.N. Development Project	www.undp.org
World Bank	www.worldbank.org
Wells Fargo	www.wellsfargo.com
West Coast Bankcorp	www.westcoastbankcorp.com
Social Investment Forum	www.socialinvest.org

Appendix E:
Chapter-by-Chapter
Resources

General Screening and Shareholder Activism Resources
(for Chapters 5, 6, and 8; see also Appendix A)

ORGANIZATIONS AND PUBLICATIONS

Corporate Watch
PO Box 29344, San Francisco, CA
   94129
415-561-6568, www.corpwatch.org
On-line magazine and resource center
   with tools for analyzing corporate
   activity.

Data Center
1904 Franklin Street, Suite 900, Oakland, CA 94612
510-835-4692, www.igc.org/datacenter
Provides information to activists working for progressive social change.

INFACT
256 Hanover Street, Boston, MA
   02113
617-742-4583, www.infact.org
A grass-roots corporate watchdog
   organization.

Multinational Monitor
PO Box 19405, Washington, DC 20036
202-387-8030, www.essential.org/
   monitor
Tracks corporate activity.

Right-to-Know Network
1742 Connecticut Avenue NW, Washington, DC 20009
202-234-8494, www.rtk.net
Provides access to numerous databases,
   text files, and conferences on the
   environment, housing, and sustainable development.

Avoidance Screening Resources
(for Chapter 5)

ALCOHOL

The Marin Institute
24 Belvedere Street, San Rafael, CA
   94901
415-456-5692, www.marininstitute.org

Mothers Against Drunk Driving
PO Box 541688, Dallas, TX 75354
972-744-6233, www.madd.org

National Clearinghouse for Alcohol and
   Drug Information
PO Box 2345, Rockville, MD
   20847
800-729-6686, www.health.org.

National Council on Alcohol and Drug
   Dependence
12 West 21st Street, New York, NY
   10010
212-206-6770, www.ncadd.org

ANIMAL RIGHTS

American Anti-Vivisection Society
801 Old York Road, #204, Jenkintown,
     PA 19046
215-887-0816, www.aavs.org

Americans for Medical Progress
421 King Street, Suite 401, Alexandria,
     VA 22314-3121
800-426-7872,
     www.amp@amprogress.org

Animal Rights Resource Site
www.envirolink.org/arrs

The Foundation for Biomedical
     Research
818 Connecticut Avenue NW, Suite 303,
     Washington, DC 20006
202-457-0654, www.fbresearch.org

Johns Hopkins Center for Alternatives
     to Animal Testing
111 Market Place, Suite 840, Baltimore,
     MD 21202-6709
410-223-1693, www.jhsph.edu/~altweb

People for the Ethical Treatment of
     Animals
501 Front Street, Norfolk, VA 23510
757-622-7382, www.peta-online.org

ENVIRONMENTAL POLLUTION AND
TOXIC PRODUCTS

Chemical Manufacturers Association,
     Responsible Care Initiative
1300 Wilson Boulevard, Arlington, VA
     22209
703-741-5000, www.cmahq.com

EnviroLink
www.envirolink.org

Environmental Defense Fund
257 Park Avenue South, New York, NY
     10010
800-684-3322, www.edf.org

Friends of the Earth
1025 Vermont Avenue NW, 3rd Floor,
     Washington, DC 20005
202-783-7400, www.foe.org

National Association of Physicians for
     the Environment
6410 Rockledge Drive, Suite 412,
     Bethesda, MD 20817
Fax: 301-530-8910, www.napenet.org

Natural Resources Defense Council
40 West 20th Street, New York, NY
     10011
212-727-2700, www.nrdc.org

Project Underground
www.moles.org

Rain Forest Action Network
221 Pine Street, Suite 500, San Fran-
     cisco, CA 94104
415-398-4404, www.ran.org

Sierra Club
85 Second Street, 2nd Floor, San Fran-
     cisco CA, 94105
415-977-5500, www.sierraclub.org

U.S. Environmental Protection Agency
401 M Street SW, Washington, DC
     20460
202-260-2090, www.epa.gov
Numerous programs of interest, includ-
     ing www.epa.gov/airsweb for air
     pollution data, www.epa.gov/iaq for
     information on indoor air quality,
     and the Superfund homepage at
     www.epa.gov/superfund.

EXECUTIVE PAY

Executive PayWatch
Web site operated by the AFL-CIO at
www.aflcio.org/paywatch

United for a Fair Economy
37 Temple Place, 5th Floor, Boston, MA
02111
617-423-2148, www.stw.org

GAMBLING

National Coalition Against Legalized
Gambling
110 Maryland Avenue NE, Washington,
DC 20002
800-664-2680. www.ncalg.org

North American Training Institute
A division of the Minnesota Council on
Compulsive Gambling
314 West Superior Street, Suite 702,
Duluth, MN 55802
218-722-1503, www.nati.org

GLOBAL WARMING

Intergovernmental Panel on Climate
Change
United Nations Environmental Program,
World Meteorological Organization
Building, 41 Avenue Giuseppe-
Motta, Case Postale No. 2300,
1211 Geneva 2, Switzerland
www.ipcc.ch

Sierra Club Global Warming Web site
www.toowarm.org

Union of Concerned Scientists
2 Brattle Square, Cambridge, MA
02238
617-547-5552, www.ucsusa.org

U.S. Global Change Research Program
PO Box 1000, Palisades, New York
10964
914-365-8930, www.gcrio.org/

Western Fuels Association Greening
Earth Society (the pro–fossil fuels
viewpoint)
430 Wilson Boulevard, Suite 805,
Arlington, VA, 22203
703-907-6168,
www.greeningearthsociety.org/

LABOR ISSUES

Coalition for Justice in the
Maquiladoras
3120 West Ashby, San Antonio, TX
78338
210-732-8957

Co-op America Sweatshop Web site
www.sweatshops.org

Global Exchange
2017 Mission Street, #303, San Francisco, CA 94110
415-255-7296, www.globalexchange.org

Human Rights Campaign
1101 14th Street NW, Washington, DC
20005
202-628-4160, www.hrc.org

International Labor Rights Fund
733 15th Street NW, Suite 920, Washington, DC 20005
202-347-4100, www.laborrights.org

Lambda Legal Defense and Education
Fund
120 Wall Street, #1500, New York, NY
10005
212-809-8585, www.lambdalegal.org

Leadership Conference on Civil Rights
1629 K St NW #1010, Washington, DC
    20006
202-466-3311, http://www.civilrights.org/

National Organization for Women
1000 16th Street NW #700, Washington
    DC 20036
202-331-0066, www.now.org

Sweatshop Watch
310 Eighth Street, Suite 309, Oakland,
    CA 94607
www.sweatshopwatch.org

NUCLEAR POWER

Citizens for Alternatives to Radioactive
    Dumping
144 Harvard SE, Albuquerque, NM
    87106
505-266-2663, www.unm.edu/~rekp/card

Greenpeace
1436 U Street NW, Washington, DC
    20009
202-462-1177,
    www.greenpeace.org/cnuk

Nuclear Energy Institute (nuclear
    industry)
1776 I Street NW, Suite 400, Washing-
    ton, DC 20006
202-739-8000, www.nei.org

Nuclear Information and Resource
    Service
1424 16th Street NW, #404, Washington,
    DC 20036
202-328-0002, www.nirs.org

Plutonium Free Future
PO Box 2589, Berkeley, CA 94702
510-540-7645, www.nonukes.org

U.S. Nuclear Regulatory Commission
2 White Flint North, 1545 Rockville
    Pike, Rockville, MD 20852
301-415-7000, www.nrc.gov

REPRESSIVE REGIMES

Amnesty International, 304 Pennsyl-
    vania Avenue SE, Washington, DC
    20003
202-544-0200, www.amnesty.org

Cultural Survival
96 Mount Auburn Street, Cambridge,
    MA 02138
617-441-5400, www.cs.org

Free Burma Coalition
PO Box 19405, Washington, DC 20036
202-777-6009, www.freeburma.org

Human Rights in China
350 Fifth Avenue, Suite 3309, New
    York, NY 10118
212-239-4495, www.hrichina.org

Human Rights Watch
350 Fifth Avenue, 34th Floor, New
    York, NY 10118
212-290-4700, www.hrw.org

Tibet Information Network
7a Southwood Hall, Muswell Hill Road,
    London N6 5UF, England
www.tibetinfo.net

U.S. State Department, Country
    Reports on Human Rights Practices
www.state.gov/www/global/human_rights

TOBACCO

"Tobacco's Changing Context: A Chal-
    lenge and Opportunity for Institu-

tional Investors," an in-depth report, is available free to download from the Social Investment Forum's Web site at www.socialinvest.org, or in hardcopy for $59 from SIF, 1612 K Street NW, Suite 650, Washington, DC 20006, 202-872-5319.

Action on Smoking and Health
2013 H Street NW, Washington, DC 20006
202-659-4310, www.ash.org

Centers for Disease Control, Tobacco Information and Prevention
1600 Clifton Road NE, Atlanta, GA 30333
404-639-3311, www.cdc.gov/tobacco

Foundation for a Smokefree America
PO Box 492028, Los Angeles, CA 90049
310-471-0303, www.tobaccofree.com

INFACT's Tobacco Industry Campaign
256 Hanover Street, Boston, MA 02113
617-742-4583, www.infact.org

National Center for Tobacco-Free Kids
1707 L Street NW, Suite 800, Washington, DC 20036
800-284-5437,
www.tobaccofreekids.org

WEAPONS AND THE MILITARY

Bulletin of the Atomic Scientists Educational Foundation for Nuclear Science
6042 South Kimbark Avenue, Chicago, IL 60637
773-702-2555, www.bullatomsci.org

Center for Defense Information
1779 Massachusetts Avenue NW, Washington, DC 20036
202-332-0600, www.cdi.org

Center for Economic Conversion
222 View Street, Mountain View, CA 94041
650-968-8798, www.conversion.org

Center to Prevent Handgun Violence
1225 I Street NW, Suite 1100, Washington, DC 20005
202-898-0792, www.cphv.org

International Campaign to Ban Landmines
www.icbl.org

National Rifle Association
11250 Waples Mill Road, Fairfax, VA 22030
800-NRA-3888, www.nra.org

Nuclear Weapons Cost Study Project
Brookings Institution, 1775 Massachusetts Avenue NW, Washington, DC 20036
202-797-6030, www.brook.edu/fp/projects/nucwcost/50.htm

U.S. Arms Control and Disarmament Agency
320 21st Street NW, Washington, DC 20451
800-581-2232, www.acda.gov/

Affirmative Screening Resources *(for Chapter 6; see also Appendix A)*

BOOKS

Driving EcoInnovation: A Break-through Discipline for Innovation and Sus-

tainability, Claude Fussler with Peter Jones (Financial Times/Pitman, 1997)

In Earth's Company: Business, Environment & the Challenge of Sustainability, Carl Frankel (New Society, 1998)

The Ecology of Commerce, Paul Hawken (HarperBusiness, 1993)

Mid-Course Correction: Toward a Sustainable Enterprise, Ray Anderson (Chelsea Green, 1998)

Natural Capitalism: The Worthy Employment of Resources, Paul Hawken, Amory Lovins, and Hunter Lovins (Little, Brown, 1999)

The Natural Step for Business: Wealth, Ecology and the Evolutionary Corporation, Brian Nattrass and Mary Altomare (New Society, 1999)

Restoring the Earth: Visionary Solutions from the Bioneers, Kenny Ausubel (H.J. Kramer, 1997)

The Socially Responsible Guide to Smart Investing, Samuel Case (Prima, 1996)

The Sustainable Business Challenge: A Briefing for Tomorrow's Business Leaders, Jan-Olaf Willums with the World Business Council on Sustainable Development (Greenleaf, 1998)

PERIODICALS

Environmental Building News, 802-257-7300, www.ebuild.com/

The Green Business Letter, 800-954-7336, www.greenbiz.com

Healthy Living Newsletter, 617-371-3900

Home Power Magazine, 800-707-6585, www.homepower.com

Hydrogen and Fuel Cell Letter, 914-876-5988, www.mhv.net/~hfcletter/

In Business: Creating Sustainable Enterprises and Communities, 610-967-4135, www.jgpress.com.

Natural Business: The Journal of Business and Financial News for the Natural Products Industry, 303-442-8983, www.naturalbiz.com. (They also sponsor the annual Natural Business Financial and Investment Conference.)

New Energy Report, 415-485-5825

Organic Business News, 407-628-1377

Permaculture Activist, 704-298-2812

Whole Earth, 415-256-2800

ORGANIZATIONS

The Natural Step
Box 29372, San Francisco, CA 94129
415-561-3344, www.naturalstep.org

Rocky Mountain Institute
1739 Snowmass Creek Road, Snowmass, CO 81654

970-927-3851, www.rmi.org

World Resources Institute
1709 New York Avenue NW, Washington, DC 20006
202-638-6300, www.wri.org

Worldwatch Institute
1776 Massachusetts Avenue NW, Washington, DC 20036
202-452-1999, www.worldwatch.org

WEB SITES

American Council for an Energy-Efficient Economy
www.aceee.org
Bioneers   www.bioneers.org
Center for Energy Efficiency and Renewable Technology
www.ceert.org
CoHousing Network
www.cohousing.org
Congress for the New Urbanism
www.cnu.org
Conscious Choice
www.consciouschoice
Excellence for Sustainable Development
www.sustainable.doe.gov
Fuel Cells 2000   www.fuelcells.org
Global Business Network
www.gbn.org
Global Ecovillage Network
www.gaia.org
Green Power   www.green-power.com
Hydrogen InfoNet
www.eren.doe.gov/hydrogen
National Renewable Energy Lab
www.nrelinfo.nrel.gov
Natural Investor
www.naturalinvestor.com
Partnership for a New Generation of Vehicles
www.epa.gov/oms/pngvhome.htm
Second Nature   www.2nature.org
Smart Wood Program, Rainforest

Alliance   www.smartwood.org
Solstice   www.solstice.crest.org
Sustainable Business
www.sustainablebusiness.com
Sustainable Business Network
www.envirolink.org/sbn
Sustainable Development Gateway
www.sdgateway.net
Sustainable Energy Stock Quotes
www.ecotopia.com/sestock
TRANET
www.nonviolence.org/tranet
Tree Savers New Uses Council
http//ag.arizona.edu/OALS/NUC/NUCHome.html
WBC for Sustainable Development
www.wbcsd.ch

Investment Primers
(for Chapter 9)

Big Decisions, Small Investor, Gordon K. Williamson (Adams Media, 1998)
Charles Schwab's Guide to Financial Independence, Charles R. Schwab (Crown, 1998)
The Complete Idiot's Guide to Making Money with Mutual Funds, 2d edition, Alan Lavine and Gail Liberman (Alpha, 1998)
Conquering Your Financial Stress, Bruce Eaton (Random House, 1998)
Co-op America's Financial Planning Handbook (Co-op America, 1998)
Feathering Your Nest: The Retirement Planner, Lisa Berger (Workman, 1993)
The First Book of Investing, Samuel Case (Prima, 1997)
Getting Started in Mutual Funds, Alan Lavine (John Wiley & Sons, 1994)
The Guide to Investing in Common Stocks, 2d edition, David Scott (Globe Pequot, 1995)

Inspired Philanthropy, Tracy Gary
    (Chardon, 1998)
Investing from Scratch: A Handbook for
    the Young Investor, James Lowell
    (Penguin, 1997)
The New Commonsense Guide to
    Mutual Funds, Mary Rowland
    (Bloomberg, 1998)
The Nine Steps to Financial Freedom,
    Suze Orman (Crown, 1997)
Straight Talk About Investing, John
    Slater (McGraw-Hill, 1995)
Tending Your Money Garden, Bob
    Dreizler (Rossonya, 1998)
The Wall Street Guide to Planning Your
    Financial Future, Kenneth M. Mor-
    ris, Alan M. Siegel, and Virginia B.
    Morris (Lighthouse, 1998)
You Earned It, Don't Lose It, Suze
    Orman (Newmarket, 1998)
Zenvesting: The Art of Abundance and
    Managing Money, Paul Sutherland
    (Financial Sourcebook, 1998)

Some Federal and State Tax-Free
Mutual Funds *(for Chapter 11)*

For more complete listings, see
www.bloomberg.com or
www.morningstar.net.

Source: Compiled by the authors
(December 1998).

Key: ° = Federal tax free; state abbre-
viations indicate availability of funds
whose dividends are exempt from both
state and federal taxes for residents of
those states.

°Alliance, 800-247-4154
AZ/FL/MA/MI/NJ/NY/OH/PA/VA
American Cent-Ben, 800-345-2021
AZ/FL
°BlackRock, 800-388-8734

NJ/OH/PA
°Calvert, 800-368-2748
MD/VA/VT
°Colonial, 800-426-3750
CT/FL/MA/MI/MN/NC/NY/OH
Crabbe Huson, 800-541-9732
OR
CrestFunds, 800-273-7827
MD/VA
Delaware-Voyageur, 800-373-9387
AZ/CO/FL/IA/ID/MN/MO/ND/NM/
    OR/UT/WA/WI
°Dreyfus, 800-866-0614
CT/FL/GA/MA/MD/MN/NC/NJ/NY/
    OH/PA/TX/VA
Dupree
KY/NC/TN
°Eaton Vance, 800-225-6265
AL/AR/AZ/CO/CT/FL/GA/HI/KS/KY/
    LA/MA/MD/MI/MN/MO/MS/
NC/NJ/NY/OH/OR/PA/RI/SC/TN/TX/
    VA/WV
°Evergreen, 800-343-2898
FL/GA/MA/MD/MO/NC/NJ/NY/PA/
    SC/VA
°Federated, 800-341-7400
MI/NY/OH/PA
°Fidelity Spartan, 800-544-888
AZ/CT/FL/MA/MD/MI/MN/NJ/NY/
    OH/PA
°First Invest M/S, 800-423-4026
AZ/CO/CT/FL/GA/MA/MD/MI/MN/
    MO/NC/NJ/NY/OH/OR/PA/VA
°Franklin, 800-342-5236
AL/AR/AZ/CO/CT/FL/GA/HI/IN/
    KY/LA/MA/MD/MI/MN/MO/
    NC/NJ/OH/OR/PA/PR/TN/TX/
    VA/WA
°IDS, 800-328-8300
MA/MI/MN/NY/OH
°Kemper, 800-621-1048
FL/MI/NY/NJ/OH/PA/TX
°Lord Abbett, 800-426-1130
CT/FL/GA/HI/MI/MN/MO/NJ/PA/TX/
    WA

°Merrill Lynch, 609-282-2800
AR/AZ/CO/CT/FL/MA/MD/MI/MN/
NC/NJ/NM/NY/OH/OR/PA/TX
°MFS, 800-637-2929
AL/AR/FL/GA/MA/MD/MS/NC/NY/
PA/SC/TN/VA/WV
°Mosaic, 888-670-3600
AZ/MD/MO/VA
°MSDW HI Municipal
°MSDW
AZ/FL/HI/MA/MN/NJ/OH/PA
°Munder, 800-239-3334
MI
°Nations, 800-321-7854
FL/GA/MD/NC/SC/TN/TX/VA
°Nuveen, 800-621-7227
AL/AZ/CO/CTFL/GA/KS/KY/LA/MA/
MD/MI/MO/NC/NJ/NM/NY/OH/
PA/SC/TN/VA/WI
°One Group, 800-480-4111
AZ/KY/LA/OH/WV
°Oppenheimer, 800-525-7048
FL/NJ/NY/PA
Parnassus, 800-999-3505
CA
°Prudential, 800-225-1852
FL/MA/MD/MI/NC/NJ/NY/OH/PA
°Putnam, 800-225-1581
AZ/FL/MA/MI/MN/NJ/NY/OH/PA
°Safeco, 800-426-6730
WA
°Scudder, 800-225-2470
MA/NY/OH/PA
°SEI, 800-342-5734
PA
°Seligman, 800-221-7844
CO/FL/GA/LA/MA/MD/MI/MN/MO/
NJ/NY/OH/OR/PA/SC
°Smith Barney, 800-451-2010
AZ/MA/FL/GA/NJ/NY/PA
°Stagecoach, 800-222-8222
AZ/OR
°STI Classic, 800-428-6970
FL/GA

°T. Rowe Price, 800-231-8432
FL/GA/MD/NJ/VA
°Thornburg, 800-847-0200
FL/NM/NY
°USAA, 800-531-8181
FL/TX/VA
°Van Kampen Am Cap, 800-421-5666
FL/PA
°Vanguard, 800-662-7447
FL/NJ/NY/OH/PA
Wachovia, 800-994-4414
GA/NC/SC/VA

Resources for Curing Affluenza
(for Chapter 13)

VOLUNTARY ABUNDANCE

Periodicals
The Simple Living Journal
4509 Interlake Avenue North, Box 149,
Seattle, WA 98103
206-464-4800, www.simpleliving.com

YES! A Journal of Positive Futures
PO Box 10818, Bainbridge Island, WA
98110
206-842-0216, www.futurenet.org

Organizations
Center for the New American Dream
6930 Carroll Avenue, Suite 900, Takoma
Park, MD 20912
301-891-3683, www.newdream.org.

Co-op America
1612 K Street NW, Suite 600, Washington, DC 20006
800-584-7336, www.coopamerica.org,
www.greenpages.org

New Road Map Foundation
PO Box 15981, Seattle, WA 98115
206-527-0437, www.slnet.com/cip/nrm

Northwest Earth Institute
921 SW Morrison, Suite 532, Portland,
OR 91205
503-227-2807, www.nwei.org

Seeds of Simplicity
PO Box 9955, Glendale, CA 91226
818-247-4332,
www.slnet.com/cip/seeds/

The Simple Living Network
www.slnet.com
Started in 1996 by Dave Wampler, the
site now has several thousand pages.
It provides tools for those who want
to learn about living a more conscious, simple, healthy, and earth-
friendly lifestyle.

Videos
Affluenza and *Escape from Affluenza,*
broadcast on PBS
www.pbs.org/affluenza
Available from Bullfrog Films,
800-543-3764,
www.bullfrogfilms.com.

Books
*Choose to Reuse: A Guide to Services,
Products and Programs,* Nikki and
David Goldbeck (CERES, 1995)

*The Circle of Simplicity: Return to the
Good Life,* Cecile Andrews (Harper-
Collins, 1997)

*Homemade Money: How to Save Energy
and Dollars in Your Home,* Richard
Heede and the Rocky Mountain
Institute (Brickhouse, 1995)

*Living the Simple Life: A Guide to
Scaling Down and Enjoying More,*
Elaine St. James (Hyperion, 1996)

*Mortgage-Free! Radical Strategies for
Home Ownership,* Rob Roy (Chelsea
Green, 1998)

*The Overspent American: Upscaling,
Downshifting and the New Consumer,* Juliet Schor (Basic Books,
1997)

*The Simple Living Guide: A Sourcebook
for Less Stressful, More Joyful Living,* Janet Luhrs (Broadway, 1997)

*Voluntary Simplicity: Toward a Way of
Life That Is Outwardly Simple,
Inwardly Rich,* Duane Elgin
(William Morrow, 1993)

*Your Money or Your Life: Transforming
Your Relationship with Money and
Achieving Financial Independence,*
Joe Dominguez and Vicki Robin
(Viking, 1992)

SPIRIT AT WORK

Periodicals
BusinesSpirit Journal
4 Camino Azul, Santa Fe, NM 87505
505-474-0998, www.bizspirit.com

The Inner Edge
101 Columbia, Suite 100, Aliso Viejo,
CA 92656
800-899-1712, www.inneredge.com

Spirit at Work
PO Box 420, Manalapan, NJ 07726
800-969-7176, www.spiritatwork.com

Organizations
The Heartland Institute
4243 Grimes Avenue South, Edina, MN
55416

612-925-5995,
www.heartlandinstitute.com

The World Business Academy
PO Box 191210, San Francisco, CA
94119
415-227-0106,
www.worldbusiness.org

Books

A wonderful bibliography of the
plethora of books on this topic,
updated regularly, can be seen at
www.spiritatwork.com/biblio.htm,
or ordered for $10 from Judi Neal,
Center for Spirit at Work, University
of New Haven, 300 Orange Avenue,
West Haven, CT 06513,
203-932-7372.

Events

International Conference on Business
and Consciousness
The Message Company, 505-474-0998,
www.bizspirit.com

International Symposium on Spirituality
and Business
617-965-9722,
www.ants.edu/spirit&bus

Web Sites

Richard Barrett and Associates
www.corptools.com
Business Enterprise Trust
www.betrust.org
Center for Visionary Leadership
www.visionarylead.org
Sharon Drew Morgen
www.newsalesparadigm.com
Robert Rabbin
www.robrabbin.com
Martin Rutte
www.martinrutte.com

SHARING THE WEALTH

More Than Money
A quarterly publication of The Impact
Project, 2244 Alder Street, Eugene,
OR 97405 800-255-4903,
www.efn.org/~impact

Resourceful Women
PO Box 29423, San Francisco, CA
94129
415-561-6520

Responsible Wealth, United for a Fair
Economy
27 Temple Place, Fifth Floor, Boston,
MA 02111
617-423-2148, www.stw.org/html/
responsible_wealth.html

COMMUNITY ECONOMICS

Organizations

Center for Living Democracy
289 Fox Farm Road, Brattleboro, VT
05301
802-254-1227

E. F. Schumacher Society
140 Jug End Road, Great Barrington,
MA 01230
413-528-4472,
www.schumachersociety.org

Institute for Local Self-Reliance
2425 18th Street NW, Washington, DC
20009
202-232-4108, www.ilsr.org

Rocky Mountain Institute/Economic
Renewal Program
1739 Old Snowmass Creek Road, Snowmass, CO 81654
970-927-3851, www.rmi.org

Sustainable America
42 Broadway, Suite 1740, New York, NY
    10004
212-269-9550, www.sanetwork.org

Books
Going Local: Creating Self-Reliant
    Communities in a Global Age,
    Michael Schuman (Free Press,
    1998). Includes a comprehensive
    resource section covering all aspects
    of community-based economics.

Reworking Success: New Communities
    at the Millennium, Robert Theobold
    (New Society, 1997)

Sustainability Indicators
Sustainable Seattle
Metrocenter YMCA, 909 4th Avenue,
    Seattle, WA 98104
206-382-5013, www.scn.org/sustainable
Web site on indicators by Maureen Hart
www.subjectmatters.com/indicators

Community Currency Resource
Ithaca HOURS
Box 6578, Ithaca, NY 14851
607-272-4330, www.lightlink.com
"A Hometown Money Starter Kit,"
    which is designed to help you start
    your own local money system, is
    available for $25.

Community Currency Web Sites
Community Information Resource
    Center
azstarnet.com/~circ/circhome.htm

Local Exchange Trading System
    www.gmlets.u-net.com

Time Dollar Institute
    www.cfg.com/timedollar

Transaction Net by Bernard Lietaer
    (information and comparisons of a
    wide selection of currency systems)
    www.transaction.net/money/

"Healing of Wall Street"
Resources (for Chapter 14)

Books
Beyond Growth: The Economics of Sus-
    tainable Development, Herman Daly
    (Beacon, 1996)

Building a Win-Win World: Life
    Beyond Global Economic Warfare,
    Hazel Henderson (Berrett-Koehler,
    1996)

The Natural Wealth of Nations: Har-
    nessing the Market for the Environ-
    ment, David Roodman (Norton,
    1998)

Organizations
The Center for Responsive Politics
1320 19th Street NW, Suite 620, Wash-
    ington, DC 20036
202-857-0044, www.crp.org

Friends of the Earth, Green Scissors
    Campaign
1025 Vermont Avenue NW, 3rd Floor,
    Washington, DC 20005
202-783-7400, www.foe.org/eco

Program on Corporations, Law, and
    Democracy
PO Box 806, Cambridge, MA 02141
508-487-3151

Redefining Progress
1 Kearny Street, 4th Floor, San Fran-
    cisco, CA 94108
415-781-1191, www.rprogress.org

Web Sites

Banneker Center, Economic Justice
and Tax Reform site
www.progress.org/banneker

Cato Institute   www.cato.org

Citizens for Tax Justice   www.ctj.org

Communications for a Sustainable
Future   csf.colorado.edu

Corporate Welfare Information Center
www.corporations.org/welfare

Hazel Henderson
www.hazelhenderson.com

People-Centered Democracy Forum
iisd1.iisd.ca/pcdf

Public Campaign
www.publicampaign.org

Share the Wealth   www.stw.org

Third World Network
www.twnside.org.sg

United Nations Human Development
Indicators
www.undp.org/hdro

Natural Worldview Resources
(for Chapter 15)

Organization

Institute of Noetic Sciences
475 Gate Five Road, Suite 300,
Sausalito, CA 94965
415-331-5650, www.noetic.org

Books

Awakening Earth: Exploring the Evolution of Human Culture and Con-
sciousness, Duane Elgin (William
Morrow, 1993)

Biology Revisioned, Willis W. Harman
and Elisabet Sahtouris (North
Atlantic, 1998)

*Conscious Evolution: Awakening the
Power of Our Social Potential,* Barbara Marx Hubbard (New World
Library, 1998)

Corporate DNA: Learning From Life,
Ken Baskin (Butterworth-Heineman, 1998)

*Global Mind Change: The Promise of
the 21st Century,* Willis Harman
(Berrett-Koehler, 1998)

A Simpler Way, Margaret Wheatley and
Myron Kellner-Rogers (Berrett-Koehler, 1996)

*The Turning Point: Science, Society, and
the Rising Culture,* Fritjof Capra
(Bantam, 1982)

Web Sites

Creation Spirituality
www.csnet.org

Duane Elgin, Awakening Earth
www.awakeningearth.org

Foundation for Conscious Evolution
www.cocreation.org

Foundation for Global Community
www.globalcommunity.org

Millennium Institute
www.igc.org/millennium/

Elisabet Sahtouris
www.ratical.org/lifeweb

Notes

Introduction

1 Soros, George. "The Capitalist Threat." *Atlantic Monthly,* February 1997, p. 45.

2 Elgin, Duane. From the booklet "Global Consciousness Change: Indicators of an Emerging Paradigm." San Anselmo, Calif.: Millennium Project, 1997, p. 3.

3 Kurtz, Lloyd. "No Effect, or No *Net* Effect? Studies on Socially Responsible Investing." *Journal of Investing* 6, no. 4 (1997): 37.

4 Yankelovich Partners, Inc. National survey of 800 mutual fund investors in October 1996. Cited in the booklet "Opening New Doors to an Untapped Market of Investors." Bethesda, Md.: Calvert Group, 1998.

5 Van Dyck, Thomas. Letter to the editor, *Mutual Funds Magazine,* November 1997, p. 15.

Chapter 1

1 Moskowitz, Milt, Michael Katz, and Robert Levering. *Everybody's Business: An Almanac.* New York: Harper and Row, 1980, p. 540.

2 Weatherford, Jack. *The History of Money.* New York: Three Rivers Press, 1997, p. 20.

3 Ibid., pp. 31–32, 43.

4 Ibid., pp. 41–42.

5 Ibid., p. 73.

6 Murningham, Marcy. "Corporations and Social Responsibility: A Historical Perspective," in *The Social Investment Almanac,* edited by Peter D. Kinder, Steven D. Lydenberg, and Amy L. Domini. New York: Henry Holt, 1992, p. 88.

7 Korten, David. *When Corporations Rule the World.* San Francisco: Berrett-Koehler, 1995, p. 55.

8 Murninghan, p. 90.

9 Grossman, Richard, and Frank Adams. *Taking Care of Business: Citizenship and the Charter of Incorporation.* Cambridge, Mass.: Red Sun Press, 1993, pp. 8, 9.

10 Ibid., p. 20.

11 Gilder, George. "The Soul of Silicon." *Forbes ASAP,* June 1, 1998, p. 116.

12 Korten, p. 59.

13 Kinder, Peter, and Amy Domini. "Social Screening: Paradigms Old and New." *Journal of Investing* 6, no. 4 (1997): 12.

14 Underwood, Paula. *Franklin Listens When I Speak.* San Anselmo, Calif.: A Tribe of Two Press, 1997, p. 115.

15 Moore, Gary D. *The Thoughtful Christian's Guide to Investing.* Grand Rapids, Mich.: Zondervan, 1990, p. 111.

16 Kinder, Peter, Steven Lydenberg, and Amy Domini. *Investing for Good.* New York: HarperCollins, 1994, pp. 92, 93, 96, 97.

17 Massie, Robert Kinloch. *Loosing the Bonds: The United States and South Africa in the Apartheid Years.* New York: Doubleday, 1998, p. 696.

18 Interview with the authors, October 1994.

Chapter 2

1 Naisbitt, John, and Patricia Aburdene. *Megatrends 2000: Ten New Directions for the 1990's.* New York: William Morrow, 1990, p. 335.

2 Elgin, Duane. From the booklet "Global Consciousness Change: Indicators of an Emerging Paradigm." San Anselmo, Calif.: Millennium Project, 1997, p. 4.

3 Peterson, Peter G. "Will America Grow Up Before It Grows Old?" *Atlantic Monthly,* May 1996, p. 60.

4 Elgin, p. 4.

5 Ray, Paul H. *The Integral Culture Survey: A Study of the Emergence of Transformational Values in America.* Sausalito, Calif.: Institute of Noetic Sciences, 1996.

6 Korten, David. "The Money World versus the Living World." *Common Future,* Autumn 1995, p. 29.

7 Hightower, Jim. "Chomp!" *Utne Reader,* March 1998, pp. 57–58.

8 Anderson, Ray. "Eco-Odyssey of a CEO." Speech presented at the Third International Conference on Spirituality in Business, Puerto Vallarta, Mexico, November 1997.

9 Elgin, pp. 9–11.

Chapter 3

1 Kinder, Peter, and Amy Domini. *Ethical Investing.* Reading, Mass.: Addison-Wesley, 1984, p. xi.

2 Interview with the authors, October 1994.

3 Lowry, Ritchie. *Good Money.* New York: W. W. Norton, 1991, p. 54.

4 Report compiled by Jon Hale, Morningstar, November 4, 1998; the data source is Morningstar Principia Pro.

5 Ibid.

6 Verschoor, Curtis. "Internal Control: A Weapon in the War Against Fraud." *Director's Monthly* (National Association of Corporate Directors, Washington, D.C.), February 1999, p. 7.

7 "Research Finds Green Business Practices Boost Profits." From the Social Investment Forum Web site: www.socialinvest.org/newsmosk.htm.

8 "News on Spirituality, Community Building." *The Inner Edge,* August 1998, p. 21.

9 "Feel Good Mutual Funds Haven't Yet Found Favor." *Wall Street Journal,* February 12, 1998, p. C1.

10 Elgin, Duane. *Awakening Earth—Exploring the Evolution of Human Culture and Consciousness.* New York: William Morrow, 1993, p. 265.

11 Williamson, Marianne. *The Healing of America.* New York: Simon & Schuster, 1997, pp. 104–5.

12 Russell, Peter. "Introducing An IONS Fellow." *Connections* (Institute of Noetic Sciences), January 1999, p. 9.

Chapter 4

1 "Feel Good Mutual Funds Haven't Yet Found Favor." *Wall Street Journal,* February 12, 1998, p. C1.

Chapter 5

1 National Institute on Alcohol Abuse and Alcoholism (NIAAA). Eighth Special Report to the U.S. Congress on Alcohol and Health (1993), pp. 165–76. From www.niaaa.nih.gov.

2 McGinnis, J., and W. Foege. "Actual Causes of Death in the United States." *Journal of the American Medical Association* 270, no. 18 (1993): 2208.

3 NIAAA, p. xi.

4 National Highway Traffic Safety Administration. *Traffic Safety Facts* (1996). From www.nhtsa.dot.gov.

5 NIAAA, p. xi.

6 NIAAA. Sixth Special Report to the U.S. Congress on Alcohol and Health (1987), p. 3. From www.niaaa.nih.gov.

7 NIAAA. *Alcohol Alert,* no. 9 (July 1990): 1.

8 Orlans, Barbara F. "Data on Animal Experimentation in the United States: What They Do and Do Not Show." *Perspectives in Biology and Medicine* (1994).

9 People for the Ethical Treatment of Animals. "Animal Experimentation: Sadistic Scandal." PETA Fact Sheet (May 15, 1997). From www.peta-online.org.

10 The Humane Farming Association. "The Truth about Factory Farming." From www.hfa.org/factory.

11 Ibid.

12 From the Greening Earth Society's Web site: www.greeningearthsociety.org.

13 Hawken, Paul. *The Ecology of Commerce: A Declaration of Sustainability.* New York: HarperCollins, 1993, pp. 21–22.

14 Brown, Lester, et al. *State of the World 1996.* New York: W. W. Norton, 1996.

15 Chandler, David L. "One for the Books: Record Heat and Extreme Weather." *Boston Globe,* December 28, 1998.

16 Soloman, Andy. "Antarctic Ice Melt May Come In Next Generation." Reuters, January 27, 1999.

17 Cutter Information Corporation. *Global Environmental Change Report* 9, no. 19 (1997). From www.cutter.com/envibusi.

18 Environmental Defense Fund. "Toxic Chemicals." From www.edf.org, 1997.

19 Environmental Working Group. "One Million Kids a Day Exposed to Unsafe Levels of Toxic Pesticides in Fruit, Vegetables, and Baby Food." From www.esg.org.
20 From the Environmental Working Group's "All You Can Eat" Web site: www.foodnews.org.
21 "Hormone Disruption Basics." From the Web site for the book *Our Stolen Future*, by Theo Colborn, Dianne Dumanoski, and John Peterson Myers. New York: Dutton/Penguin, 1996: www.osf-facts.org.
22 Environmental Working Group. "In the Drink." From www.esg.org.
23 Environmental Working Group. "Particulate Air Pollution, Human Mortality, Pollution Sources, and the Case for Tougher Clean Air Standards." From www.esg.org.
24 Environmental Protection Agency, citing a 1984 World Health Organization report.
25 Rain Forest Action Network. "Deforestation Rates in Tropical Forests and Their Climatic Implications." From www.ran.org/info_center/factsheets.
26 Quammen, David. "Planet of Weeds: Tallying the Losses of Earth's Animals and Plants." *Harper's Magazine*, October 1998, p. 61.
27 Senate, Senator Paul Simon on "The Explosive Growth of Gambling in the United States," 104th Congress, 2d sess., *Congressional Record* (July 31, 1995). From www.ncalg.org/pages/the_expl.htm.
28 From a mailing by the Public Concern Foundation, publishers of the *Washington Spectator*, from www.newslet.com.
29 Seifert, Amy. "Place Your Bets." Term Project Report, December 5, 1996, Journalism/Public Relations 525, Public Opinion (Dr. M. Mark Miller, Professor), University of Tennessee, Knoxville. From www.churchstreetumc.org/betscore.html.
30 Grey, Rev. Thomas, National Coalition Against Legalized Gambling. "The Facts." From www.ncalg.org.
31 Ison, Chris. "Dead Broke: How Gamblers Are Killing Themselves, Bankrupting Their Families and Costing Minnesota Millions." *Star Tribune* (St. Paul, Minn.), December 3, 1995, p. 1A.
32 Kindt, John Warren. "The Economic Impacts of Legalized Gambling Activities." *Drake Law Review* 43, 51–95.
33 Ison, p. 1A.
34 "Good For Business." The Federal Glass Ceiling Commission, Fact-Finding Report. Washington, D.C.: U.S. Department of Labor, March 1995, p. 7.
35 National Organization for Women, Equal Rights Amendment Campaign. From www.now.org.
36 Equal Employment and Opportunity Commission.
37 National Labor Committee. Synopsis of the video *Mickey Mouse Goes to Haiti: Walt Disney and the Science of Exploitation*. From www.nlc.org.
38 United Paperworkers International Union. "Two faces of Mattel." From their Web site: www.upiu.org/mattel2faces.html.
39 National Labor Committee. "Jobs with Justice." From www.nlcnet.org.
40 "Maquilas/Export Processing Zones." Adapted from a Maquila Solidarity Network pamphlet, June 1995. From www.web.net/~msn.
41 Committee for Nuclear Responsibility. "Selected Interviews with Dr. John Gof-

man." From www.ratical.org/radiation/cnr/jwgiviews.

42 Statement to the Unocal Annual Shareholders Meeting by the Central Executive Committee, Monland Restoration Council, June 3, 1996.

43 Ibid.

44 "Amnesty International: China." From www.amnesty.org/ailib/inteam/china/report/cctoc.

45 Ibid.

46 Reaney, Patricia. "HIV, Tobacco Are Biggest Killers Worldwide." Reuters, September 7, 1998.

47 "Medical Care Expenditures Attributable to Cigarette Smoking—United States, 1993." *Morbidity and Mortality Weekly Report,* July 8, 1994. From www.cdc.gov/tobacco.

48 INFACT Tobacco Campaign. "The Human Toll of Tobacco." From www.infact.org.

49 "Tobacco, Alcohol Worse Than Crack During Pregnancy." *The Spokesman-Review* (Spokane, Wash.), November 15, 1998. From www.spokane.net.

50 "Counseling Can Be Key to Quitting Smoking." CNN, January 1, 1999. From www.cnn.org.

51 "Documents from Cigarette Makers Show They Tested Methods to Enhance Nicotine." *New York Times,* March 1, 1998, p. 25.

52 "Tobacco Marketing to Kids" fact sheet. National Center for Tobacco-Free Kids, 1997. From www.tobaccofreekids.org.

53 Negin, Elliot. "Indefensible Defense Reporting." *The Nation,* July 20, 1998, p. 10.

54 Center for Defense Information. *A Code of Conduct for Weapons Sales.* Television program broadcast on May 22, 1994.

55 "Project Censored's Top Ten Censored Stories of 1997." From http://censored.sonoma.edu/projectcensored.

56 Kellermann, Arthur L. "Gun Ownership as a Risk Factor for Homicide in the Home." *New England Journal of Medicine* 329, no. 15 (1993).

57 National Center for Health Statistics, April 21, 1994.

58 Handgun Control, Inc. "America Still Leads Industrialized World in Handgun Homicide, Despite Gains Made Since Brady Law." Press release, March 30, 1998. From www.cphv.org.

59 National Center for Health Statistics, Department of Defense Almanac.

60 *Responsible Wealth Update* 12, no. 2 (1998), p. 3, citing a *Business Week* article.

61 Brill, Jack, and Alan Reder. *Investing From the Heart.* New York: Crown, 1993, pp. 28–29.

Chapter 6

1 Hawken, Paul. *The Ecology of Commerce: A Declaration of Sustainability.* New York: HarperCollins, 1993, p. 139.

2 Chan-Fishel, Michelle, and Manjke Tores. "Gambling with the Environment: How Governments and Big Investors Use Your Money to Plunder the Planet." *Friends of the Earth Magazine,* Spring 1998, p. 6.

3 Hawken, p. 17.

4 Interface Sustainability Report, p. 1. Atlanta: Interface Inc., 1998.

5 Case, Samuel. *The Socially Responsible Guide to Smart Investing.* Rocklin, Calif.: Prima, 1996, p. 40.

6 Greenpeace International. "Solar Not Oil." From www.greenpeace.org/~climate.

7 Case, p. 40.

8 Flavin, Christopher, and Molly O'Meara. "Solar Power Market Booms." *World Watch Magazine,* September 1998, p. 27.

9 Brown, Lester, Christopher Flavin, and Hal Kane. *Vital Signs 1996.* New York: W. W. Norton, 1996, p. 58.

10 Union of Concerned Scientists. "Renewable Energy Today and Tomorrow." From www.ucsusa.org.

11 "The World Turns to Wind Power." BBC Online Network, January 6, 1999. From news.bbc.co.uk.

12 "The 1995 Progress Report of the Secretary of Energy's Hydrogen Technical Advisory Panel." *The Green Hydrogen Report* 10.

13 Minnesotans for an Energy-Efficient Economy. "Minnesota Public Utilities Commission Votes 4–0 Ordering NSP to Build Additional 400MW of Wind Power." January 22, 1999. From www.me3.org.

14 Case, p. 136.

15 Worldwatch Institute. *State of the World 1998.* New York: W. W. Norton, p. 21.

16 Robert Shapiro, quoted in William McDonough and Michael Braungart. "The NEXT Industrial Revolution." *Atlantic Monthly,* October 1998, pp. 82–92.

17 Ibid.

18 Hawken, pp. 62–63.

19 Anderson, Ray. "Eco-Odyssey of a CEO." Speech presented at the Third International Conference on Spirituality in Business, Puerto Vallarta, Mexico, November 1997.

Chapter 7

1 Albina Community Bank, Portland, Oregon. *Possibilities* (newsletter), Spring/Summer 1997.

2 Interview with *GreenMoney Journal* editor Cliff Feigenbaum, Spring 1998.

3 Information provided in Grameen Foundation materials.

4 Carbona, Peter. "Here's a Business Plan to Fight Poverty." *Fast Company,* December 1997/January 1998, p. 60.

Chapter 8

1 Social Investment Forum Research Program. *1997 Report on Responsible Investing Trends in the United States.* Washington, D.C.: Social Investment Forum, p. 9.

2 Donlan, Thomas G. "Season for Suggestions." *Barron's,* June 9, 1997, p. 47.

3 Interfaith Center on Corporate Responsibility. *The Proxy Resolutions Book.* New York: ICCR, 1998, p. 27.

4 Investor Responsibility Research Center. *Investor's Tobacco Reporter* 2, no. 2 (1998): 83.

5 Interview with the authors, November 7, 1998.

6 Social Investment Forum. "Shareholder Rights Analysis: The Impact of Proposed SEC Rules on the Resubmission of Shareholder Resolutions." Washington, D.C.: Social Investment Forum Foundation and Co-op America Foundation.

7 Ibid.

8 Investor Responsibility Research Center. *Corporate Social Issues Reporter,* June/July 1998, p. 5.

9 "Take Your Investments Elsewhere, Please." An Interview with Burma Suukyi. *Business Week,* March 30, 1998. From archives at www.bwarchive.businessweek.com.

10 Billenness, Simon. "How Selective Purchasing Laws Work." *Franklin Research's Insight,* April 15, 1995, p. 5.

11 Billenness, Simon. "Bombshell Ruling in Burma Boycott Case." *Investing for a Better World,* November 1998, p. 7.

12 International Law Project for Human, Economic & Environmental Defense, National Lawyers Guild. "Environmental, Human Rights, Women's, and Pro-Democracy Groups Petition Attorney General of California to Revoke Unocal's Charter." Press release, September 10, 1998. From the Unocal Corporate Charter Revocation Action Center Web site: www.heed.net/revoke.html.

13 Sawyer, Herbert, ed. "The Sullivan Principles and Change in South Africa." In *Business in the Contemporary World.* New York: Wiley, 1988, p. 175.

14 Coalition for Justice in the Maquiladoras. "Maquiladora Standards of Conduct." *The CJM Newsletter,* 1992, p. 1.

15 Levi Strauss & Company. "Global Sourcing & Operating Guidelines."

16 Scott, Mary. "Can Consumers Change Corporations?" *Executive Female,* May/June 1996, p. 43.

17 Fabian, Teresa. "Social Accountability 8000 (SA8000)—The first auditable, global standard for ethical sourcing driven by CEPAA." Council on Economic Priorities, 1998.

18 Interfaith Center on Corporate Responsibility. *The Corporate Examiner* 26, no. 2 (1997).

19 CERES Annual Report, 1997.

20 Ibid.

21 "Survival and Security: Aaron Feuerstein's Malden Mills." In Dr. Mark S. Albion's *ML2: Making a Life, Making a Living* newsletter, no. 45, March 18, 1998. From www.you-company.com.

Chapter 9

1 Dreizler, Bob. *Tending Your Money Garden.* Sacramento, Calif.: Rossonya Books, 1998, p. 13.

Chapter 12

1 "NYSE, You, and the Investment World." From www.nyse.com.

2 D'Antonio, Louis, Tommi Johnsen, and R. Bruce Hutton. "Expanding Socially Screened Portfolios: An Attribution Analysis of Bond Performance." Daniels College of Business, University of Denver, 1997.

3 Social Investment Forum *Connections* newsletter, Fall 1998, p. 11.

4 Interview with the authors, January 1999.

Chapter 13

1 *Affluenza.* Television program broadcast on PBS, July 2, 1998. From www.pbs.org.

2 Ibid.

3 Dominguez, Joe, and Vicki Robin. *Your Money or Your Life.* New York: Penguin, 1992, p. 17.

4 Quoted in Dr. Mark S. Albion's *ML2: Making a Life, Making a Living* newsletter, no. 45, March 18, 1998. From www.you-company.com.

5 Quoted in Rublin, Lauren R. "Too, Too Much!" *Barron's,* March 9, 1998, p. 33.

6 *Affluenza.*

7 Celente, Gerald. *Trends 2000.* New York: Warner, 1997, p. 171.

8 St. James, Elaine. *Living the Simple Life: A Guide to Scaling Down and Enjoying More.* New York: Hyperion, 1996.

9 Elgin, Duane. *Voluntary Simplicity.* New York: William Morrow, 1981, p. 55.

10 Chappell, Tom. *The Soul of a Business: Managing for Profit and the Common Good.* New York: Bantam, 1993, p. ix.

11 From Richard Barrett's Web site: www.corptools.com.

12 Jackson, Phil, and Hugh Delehanty. *Sacred Hoops: Spiritual Lessons of a Hardwood Warrior.* New York: Hyperion, 1996, pp. 5–6.

13 From Martin Rutte's Web site: www.martinrutte.com.

14 Stephen, Michael. Speech presented at the 1998 International Conference on Business and Consciousness, Puerto Vallarta, Mexico, November.

15 "The Land of the Handout." *Newsweek,* September 29, 1997, p. 35.

16 Slepian, Anne, and Christopher Mogil. *Welcome to Philanthropy: Resources for Individuals and Families Exploring Social Change Giving.* San Diego: National Network of Grantmakers, p. 2.

17 *Responsible Wealth Update* 2, no. 2 (1998).

18 Ibid., p. 2.

19 Henderson, Hazel. *Paradigms of Progress.* Indianapolis: Knowledge Systems, 1991.

20 Shuman, Michael. *Going Local.* New York: Free Press, 1998, p. 107.

21 Ibid., p. 4.

22 Ibid., p. 133.

Chapter 14

1 Cobb, Clifford, Ted Halstead, and Jonathan Rowe. "If the GDP Is Up, Why Is America Down?" *Atlantic Monthly,* October 1995, p. 64.

2 Ibid., p. 65.

3 Ibid., p. 78.

4 Hawken, Paul. "Natural Capitalism." *Mother Jones,* March 1997, p. 46.

5 Cited in Gatto, John Taylor. "Universal Education." *Yes! A Journal of Positive Futures,* Winter 1998/99, p. 16.

6 Henderson, Hazel. *Building a Win-Win World: Life Beyond Global Economic Warfare.* San Francisco: Berrett-Koehler, 1996, pp. 225–26.

7 Interview with the authors, November 1998.

8 "Poll Finds U.S. Voters Favor Green Taxes." Friends of the Earth newsletter, June 17, 1998, p. 1.

9 Brown, Lester, Christopher Flavin, and Hal Kane. *Vital Signs 1996.* New York: W. W. Norton, 1996, p. 114.

10 *Citizen's Guide to Environmental Tax Shifting.* Washington, D.C.: Friends of the Earth, 1998, p. 31.

11 Barlett, Donald, and James Steele. "Corporate Welfare." *Time,* November 9, 1998, p.

12 Moore, Michael. *Downsize This!* New York: Random House, 1996, pp. 44–45.

13 Kelly, Marjorie. "Why Is Theft of Public Resources Legal?" *Business Ethics,* September 1998, p. 5.

14 Worldwatch Institute. Press release for *The Natural Wealth of Nations* by Dennis Roodman, 1998. From www.worldwatch.org.

15 "France Quits MAI Talks." *Yes! A Journal of Positive Futures,* Winter 1998/99, p. 8.

16 Henderson, Hazel. "Rules to Tame the Global Casino." InterPress Service, Rome, Italy, September 16, 1998.

Chapter 15

1 Cited in Hubbard, Barbara Marx. *Conscious Evolution: Awakening the Power of Our Social Potential.* Novato, Calif.: New World Library, 1998, frontispiece.

2 Capra, Fritjof. *The Turning Point: Science, Society, and the Rising Culture.* New York: Simon & Schuster, 1982, p. 197.

3 Correspondence with Peter D. Kinder, November 1998.

4 Sahtouris, Elisabet. "The Biology of Globalization," 1997. From her Web site: www.ratical.com/lifeweb/articles.

5 Wheatley, Margaret, and Myron Kellner-Rogers. *A Simpler Way.* San Francisco: Berrett-Koehler, p. 3.

6 Capra, p. 225.

7 Daly, Herman, and John Cobb. *For the Common Good.* Boston: Beacon Press, 1994, p. 6.

8 Liscio, John. "The Seer Syndrome." *Barron's,* March 2, 1998, p. 55.

9 Baskin, Ken. "Running a Business as a Complex Adaptive System." *The Inner Edge,* October 1998, p. 26.

Index

About Bloomberg

Bloomberg L.P., founded in 1981, is a global information services, news, and media company. Headquartered in New York, the company has nine sales offices, two data centers, and 80 news bureaus worldwide.

Bloomberg Financial Markets, serving customers in 100 countries around the world, holds a unique position within the financial services industry by providing an unparalleled combination of news, information, and analytic tools in a single package known as the BLOOMBERG® service. Corporations, banks, money management firms, financial exchanges, insurance companies, and many other entities and organizations rely on Bloomberg as their primary source of information.

BLOOMBERG NEWS℠, founded in 1990, offers worldwide coverage of economies, companies, industries, governments, financial markets, politics, and sports. The news service is the main content provider for Bloomberg's broadcast media, which include BLOOMBERG TELEVISION®— the 24-hour cable television network available in ten languages worldwide—and BLOOMBERG NEWS RADIO™—an international radio network anchored by flagship station BLOOMBERG NEWS RADIO AM 1130℠ in New York.

In addition to the BLOOMBERG PRESS® line of books, Bloomberg publishes BLOOMBERG® MAGAZINE, BLOOMBERG PERSONAL FINANCE™, and BLOOMBERG WEALTH MANAGER™.

To learn more about Bloomberg, call a sales representative at:

Frankfurt:	49-69-920-410
Hong Kong:	852-977-6000
London:	44-171-330-7500
New York:	1-212-318-2000
Princeton:	1-609-279-3000
San Francisco:	1-415-912-2960
São Paulo:	5511-3048-4500
Singapore:	65-438-8585
Sydney:	61-29-777-8686
Tokyo:	81-3-3201-8900

About the Authors

ALL THREE AUTHORS are dedicated financial activists who have had a long involvement with Socially Responsible Investing (SRI) and Natural Investing:

Hal Brill came to SRI in 1989 after a decade of work in the nonprofit sector. He started his career as a children's environmental educator, then participated in walks across the United States and Europe, and while living in Santa Fe, New Mexico, cofounded four community-based organizations addressing issues of low-income housing and economic development, youth education, and ecological living. A graduate of the University of California, Berkeley, Hal is a Registered Investment Advisory Representative. He lives in Paonia, Colorado, where he participates in community sustainability efforts and occasionally performs as the bass player in a local band, Tribal Revival.

Jack A. Brill left behind a thirty-year engineering career to enter SRI as a way to combine his passion for peace with investing. The last seventeen years he served as Director of Quality Assurance for the U.S. Navy's San Diego contracting office. Frustrated with daily moral compromises and excessive military buildup, he resigned that position in 1985. As coauthor of *Investing From the Heart* (Crown 1992), Jack has become one of the most recognized spokespersons for SRI. Since July 1993, he has been featured quarterly in an ongoing *New York Times* mutual fund study, recommending a portfolio of socially screened mutual funds. He is a Registered Investment Advisor and lives with his wife, Sandra, in San Diego, California.

Hal (son) and Jack (father) were among the first affiliates of First Affirmative Financial Network, the country's leading social investment firm, and are members of the Social Investment Forum. They are co-founders of Natural Investment Services, Inc., which provides investment services to individuals and institutions. They developed the NIS Social Rating(sm) to help investors evaluate socially screened mutual funds.

Cliff Feigenbaum is a leading voice in Socially Responsible Investing and Business. He is the founder and publisher of the *GreenMoney Journal,* a quarterly newsletter that has emerged as a leading clearinghouse for information on the SRI movement. More recently, he launched the GreenMoney Online Guide, one of the largest socially responsible investing and business Web sites. Cliff has contributed articles and information to numerous publications, and has appeared on many TV and radio programs. He has been nominated three times for the SRI in the Rockies conference's Socially Responsible Investing Service Award. He is an active member of the Social Investment Forum and Business for Social Responsibility. He is a graduate of Whitworth College and lives in Spokane, Washington.

Now that you know about
Natural Investing,

let's keep in touch.

(over)

_____
_____
_____
_____

Natural Investment Services, Inc.
P. O. Box 747
Paonia, CO 81428

We would greatly appreciate hearing your comments, suggestions, and personal stories about investing with your values.

Please visit our Web site at: www.NaturalInvesting.com
Here you will find supplemental information that couldn't fit in the book including articles, interviews, events, and links to hundreds of sites of interest to Natural Investors.

Cliff Feigenbaum may be reached at:
The GreenMoney Journal
608 West Glass Avenue, Spokane, WA 99205
cliff@NaturalInvesting.com

The GreenMoney Journal is the quarterly newsletter of Socially Responsible Investing and Business information. The publication was founded and is co-edited by Cliff Feigenbaum. A one-year subscription is $35; two years, $50.
To order call (800) 318-5725 or send check to address above.

Hal and Jack A. Brill may be reached at:
Natural Investment Services, Inc. (NIS)
P. O. Box 747, Paonia, CO 81428
Hal@NaturalInvesting.com
Jack@NaturalInvesting.com

NIS provides financial consulting for individual investors and institutions and maintains the NIS Social Rating℠, which evaluates the social characteristics of socially screened mutual funds.

If you'd like to be notified about our speaking schedules and workshops, audio tapes, revisions to *Investing With Your Values,* investment clubs, and other services and products for Natural Investors, please send an e-mail to info@NaturalInvesting.com, or use the attached reply card.

Investing With Your Values Information Card

Let's keep in touch. Please send me an occasional update.
In addition, I would like the following information:

___ I want my investments to make a difference. I'm interested in working with a financial adviser who specializes in Natural Investing. Send me a questionnaire and brochure from Natural Investment Services.

___ I am a concerned investor. Please send me Co-op America's socially responsible investing information, including a comprehensive directory of social investment products and services.

___ I am a financial professional. Please send information on the Social Investment Forum, a membership organization providing networking opportunities, research, and news.

Name _____

Address _____

_____

Phone _____

E-mail _____